# Colonial and Postcolonial Fiction

GARLAND REFERENCE LIBRARY OF THE HUMANITIES
VOLUME 1770

# COLONIAL AND POSTCOLONIAL FICTION

## AN ANTHOLOGY

*edited by*

ROBERT L. ROSS

GARLAND PUBLISHING, Inc.
A MEMBER OF THE TAYLOR & FRANCIS GROUP
NEW YORK & LONDON / 1999

Published in 1999 by
Garland Publishing Inc.
A Member of the Taylor & Francis Group
19 Union Square West
New York, NY 10003

10   9   8   7   6   5   4   3   2   1

Library of Congress Cataloging-in-Publication

Colonial and Postcolonial Fiction: An Anthology / edited by Robert L. Ross.
    p.cm. -- (Garland reference library of the humanities: vol. 1770)
    ISBN 0-8153-1431-0 (alk. paper)
    1. Commonwealth Fiction (English) 2. Great Britain--Colonies Fiction.
    3. Commonwealth Countries--Social Life and Customs Fiction. I. Ross,
    Robert L. II. Series
    PR9088.C65 1999                                          99-39139
    823.008'091712--dc21                                     CIP

Printed on acid-free, 250-year-life paper

Manufactured in the United States of America

031500-6600X8

# Contents

## THREE   Immigrant Encounters

## FOUR   Personal Encounters

# Introduction

> *I think that if all English literatures could be studied*
> *together, a shape would emerge which would truly*
> *reflect the new shape of the language in the world,*
> *and we could see that Eng. Lit. has never been in*
> *better shape, because the world language now also*
> *possesses a world literature, which is proliferating*
> *in every conceivable direction. . . . Perhaps "Com-*
> *monwealth literature" was invented to delay the day*
> *when we rough beasts actually slouch into Bethle-*
> *hem. In which case, it's time to admit that the center*
> *cannot hold.*
> —Salman Rushdie, *" 'Commonwealth Literature'*
> *Does Not Exist," from* Imaginary Homelands

When Salman Rushdie made these prophetic remarks in 1983, it most likely would have been necessary to defend a book such as this one. But what was long known as "Commonwealth Literature" has come into its own since then, has become respectable, even a bit fashionable. While the once accepted descriptive term is now considered too imperial and outdated, the problem of naming remains. What to call this impressive body of literature that turned up uninvited from the distant parts of the old British Empire? Of course, in the settler countries, writers and readers prefer "Australian literature" or "Canadian literature" or "New Zealand literature," and would rather their national literary treasures not be submerged into a collective pool of writing. Naming becomes more complicated in Africa where some countries have produced a body of English-language writing, but to call it "Kenyan literature" or "Nigerian literature," or whatever, would be imprecise considering that English is not the official language. The same holds true for India and Pakistan and the

Caribbean. So several all-encompassing names have been tried out and discarded. The Modern Language Association uses the awkward and demeaning term: "English Literature Other than British and American." Even though another title, "New Literatures in English," appears innocuous enough, it has been questioned by those who contend that the literature is not all that new. On the other hand, "International Literature in English" or "World Literatures Written in English" seem suitably vague, but these terms have been criticized because they do not exclude—or possibly do include—British and American writing. Perhaps someday soon when the "rough beasts actually slouch into Bethlehem" once and for all, the ordinary and sensible description of "literature in English," or even just plain "literature," will be used, thus settling the tiresome argument at last. For want of better names, this anthology employs the historical terminology, "colonial" and "postcolonial." That is, some of the selections were written during the "colonial period" when the empire was at its zenith; the rest were written in the "postcolonial period" after the dissolution of the empire following World War II.

In recent years a massive body of writing—called "Postcolonial Theory"—has emerged, separate from the literature and often having little to do with it. One major question that this project examines is whether English should be used for literary expression in countries where the foreign language was originally imposed onto the colonized by the colonizers, and could therefore be considered an instrument of continuing oppression. According to the African writer Ngugi wa Thiong'o, English in Africa is a "cultural bomb," which aids not only in the blotting out of traditional customs, language, and history but also functions in the service of neocolonialism. In opposition, other writers explain that publishing in English allows them to reach an international readership. As a result of this stand, they have been accused of pandering to an overseas audience at the expense of their own countries' cultural development.

Yet all of this circuitous quibbling seems hollow when a vast body of colonial/postcolonial English-language literature already exists, and more is being published daily. For example, the novel in English has never been healthier or more abundant in India, where some observers predicted its imminent death after independence in 1947. Many writers remind the linguistic worriers of the fate that English usage has met and continues to meet in faraway places. They explain that the language has been adapted, revised, colored, twisted, accented, disfigured, augmented, and reworked by its nonliterary and literary users around the world. This revision process holds true for those writers who live where English is not the dominant language— as in India and parts of Africa and the Caribbean, and for indigenous writers in the settler countries. The language undergoes another kind of configuration among those for whom English is a native tongue—as in Australia, Canada, New Zealand, and South Africa. The reader of this anthology will discover any number of variations, including dialect, unfamiliar slang, inventive syntax, and the insertion into the text without explanation of words and expressions taken from native languages. Following the practices of so-called standard English, or what was once known as the "Queen's English," is neither a priority nor a preference for these writers. They simply take a flexible instrument and play endless variations on it. Some observers have described this process as a retaliation against the leftover colonial language and a subversive act that will allow the expression of unfamiliar cultural experiences, the depiction of exotic settings, and the naming of indigenous flora and fauna.

To be honest, though, this anthology has no theoretical basis or biases, the kind of linguistic, political, cultural, gender, or territorial matters that occupy the postcolonial theorists. Its only aim is to present a collection of exemplary writing from the colonial and postcolonial period, some of what Matthew Arnold called "the best that has been thought and said." Of course, the major drawback of any anthology lies in its selective process, which could give rise to the accusation that the editor indulged in "canonization"—that is, determining what authors are most representative and whose work is most lasting. Over a period of time, pieces were chosen, a few set aside, new ones added, others deleted. When the table of contents finally stabilized, it did not reflect a newly discovered canon, only a sampling of the riches that are out there. Of course any anthology is no more than an hors d'oeuvre tray; a wide variety of main courses appear in the biocritical notes that precede each selection.

How to arrange work from such varied and scattered places, work taken from a century or so of writing: by country of origin? by date of publication? by an alphabetical listing of the writers? None of these customary practices appeared attractive. Gradually, maybe even miraculously, or perhaps logically, the selections themselves fell into place. For the individual stories told one ongoing story made up of a series of "encounters." First, the story records "colonial encounters," what Alan Paton in an introduction to B. Wongar's *The Track to Bralgu* supposed to be "the saddest theme . . . of all history." Its themes encompass personal isolation, exploitation, endurance, cruelty, and on occasion, heroism. The story then moves on to portray individuals caught up in a web of "postcolonial encounters," where dislocation and relocation intertwine, where hope and disillusionment converge, where violence erupts, and where the human spirit triumphs. And this larger story goes on to reveal a new drama about those from the former colonies who come to England and the United States. These "immigrant encounters" not only recount the pain of immigration—the condition of displacement, the disillusionment and disappointment, the shattered past and cast-off memories, but relate as well the joy and fulfillment. Finally, this extended story tells about "personal encounters," experiences that are rendered distinctive by place, whether it be South Africa or India or Australia, but at the same time are ordinary human occurrences without boundaries.

# PART 1
# Colonial Encounters

> *How could he speak honestly of the criminality of colonialism, the banditry of planters and trading empires, of the fools of men who strutted on the red carpets of tradition sustained by a bit of colored rag, centuries of acute class distinction and a belief in their own godhead? ...*
>
> *"You don't believe in the empire then? The value of the mother country?"*
>
> —Thea Astley, *Beachmasters*

# J. M. Coetzee

A novelist of notable originality, J. M. Coetzee has treated the dilemma of colonialism in allegorical form. Born in Cape Town, South Africa, 9 February 1940, he grew up in an Afrikaans family, his father a lawyer, his mother a teacher. He graduated from the University of Cape Town with two honors degrees, one in English, the other in mathematics. In England he worked as a systems programmer for IBM, then International Computers. After being transferred to the United States, Coetzee gave up his business career to attend the University of Texas at Austin, where he received a doctorate in English in 1969. He first taught at the State University of New York in Buffalo, then returned to South Africa in 1972 and joined the faculty of the University of Cape Town's English Department as a lecturer, and since 1984 he has served there as Professor of General Literature while carrying on his writing career.

Coetzee's first novel, *Dusklands*, was published in 1974, followed by *In the Heart of the Country* (1976), *Waiting for the Barbarians* (1980), *The Life and Times of Michael K* (1983), *Foe* (1986), *Age of Iron* (1990), and *The Master of Petersburg* (1994). He has also published criticism and essays, including *White Writing: On the Culture of Letters in South Africa* (1988) and *Giving Offense: Essays on Censorship* (1996). In 1997 an autobiographical account of his early years appeared, *Boyhood, Scenes from Provincial Life*. He has received numerous awards, including the Booker Prize and Prix Fémina Etranger for *The Life and Times of Michael K*.

As a South African writer during the era of apartheid, Coetzee did not ignore the national condition, but handled it in an oblique manner that transcended the borders of his troubled country. Even though his work has often been rightfully compared to that of Franz Kafka, Coetzee has developed a distinctive mode of symbolic and allegorical fiction. It is a fiction that examines the roots of brutality, injustice, oppression, and despotism, and at the same time explores how such forces affect the individual. Most often these forces lead to deterioration and destruction.

*Waiting for the Barbarians* is a brilliant allegory that delineates the evils of colonialism. The exact identity of the "barbarians" remains unclear. On the surface they are obviously the natives, but they could be the colonizers. The novel follows the decline of the Magistrate—an anonymous agent of an undesignated empire, who tries to protect the peaceful natives of his district. When an army marches into the frontier settlement to wipe out the nameless "barbarians," the aging Magistrate witnesses the horrors committed on behalf of the empire. Eventually he sides with the natives, realizing that they will outlast the colonizers. Once these imperial intruders have polluted and exploited the land until it is worthless and no longer able to feed them, they will leave; then the "barbarians" will wait patiently for the land to recover and reclaim it.

This excerpt from *Waiting for the Barbarians* shows the Magistrate, the one-time faithful servant of the empire, disgraced by his fraternization with the natives and thereby ostracized from his own people. Destined to wander like a displaced colonizer and beg for his keep, he represents the inevitable descent of empire.

# The Magistrate
from *Waiting for the Barbarians*

The barbarians come out at night. Before darkness falls the last goat must be brought in, the gates barred, a watch set in every lookout to call the hours. All night, it is said, the barbarians prowl about bent on murder and rapine. Children in their dreams see the shutters part and fierce barbarian faces leer through. "The barbarians are here!" the children scream, and cannot be comforted. Clothing disappears from washing-lines, food from larders, however tightly locked. The barbarians have dug a tunnel under the walls, people say; they come and go as they please, take what they like; no one is safe any longer. The farmers still till the fields, but they go out in bands, never singly. They work without heart: the barbarians are only waiting for the crops to be established, they say, before they flood the fields again.

Why doesn't the army stop the barbarians? people complain. Life on the frontier has become too hard. They talk of returning to the Old Country, but then remember that the roads are no longer safe because of the barbarians. Tea and sugar can no longer be bought over the counter as the shopkeepers hoard their stocks. Those who eat well eat behind closed doors, fearful of awaking their neighbor's envy.

Three weeks ago a little girl was raped. Her friends, playing in the irrigation ditches, did not miss her till she came back to them bleeding, speechless. For days she lay in her parents' home staring at the ceiling. Nothing would induce her to tell her story. When the lamp was put out she would begin to whimper. Her friends claim a barbarian did it. They saw him running away into the reeds. They recognized him as a barbarian by his ugliness. Now all children are forbidden to play outside the gates, and the farmers carry clubs and spears when they go to the fields.

The higher feeling runs against the barbarians, the tighter I huddle in my corner, hoping I will not be remembered.

It is a long time since the second expeditionary force rode out so bravely with its flags and trumpets and shining armor and prancing steeds to sweep the barbarians from the valley and teach them a lesson they and their children and grandchildren would never forget. Since then there have been no dispatches, no communiqués. The exhilaration of the times when there used to be daily military parades on the square, displays of horsemanship, exhibitions of musketry, has long since dissipated. Instead the air is full of anxious rumors. Some say that the entire thousand-mile frontier has erupted into conflict, that the northern barbarians have joined forces with the western barbarians, that the army of the Empire is too thinly stretched, that one of these days it will be forced to give up the defense of remote outposts like this one to concentrate its resources on the protection of the heartland. Others say that we receive no news of the war only because our soldiers have thrust deep into the enemy's territory and are too busy dealing out heavy blows to send dispatches. Soon, they say, when we least expect it, our men will come marching back weary but victorious, and we shall have peace in our time.

Among the small garrison that has been left behind there is more drunkenness than I have ever known before, more arrogance towards the townspeople. There have been incidents in which soldiers have gone into shops, taken what they wanted, and left without paying. Of what use is it for the shopkeeper to raise the alarm when the criminals and the civil guard are the same people? The shopkeepers complain to Mandel, who is in charge under the emergency powers while Joel is away with the army. Mandel makes promises but does not act. Why should he? All that matters to him is that he should remain popular with his men. Despite the parade of vigilance on the ramparts and the weekly sweep along the lakeshore (for lurking barbarians, though none has ever been caught), discipline is lax.

Meanwhile I, the old clown who lost his last vestige of authority the day he spent hanging from a tree in a woman's underclothes shouting for help, the filthy creature who for a week licked his food off the flagstones like a dog because he had lost the use of his hands, am no longer locked up. I sleep in a corner of the barracks yard; I creep around in my filthy smock; when a fist is raised against me I cower. I live like a starved beast at the back door, kept alive perhaps only as evidence of the animal that skulks within every barbarian-lover. I know I am not safe. Sometimes I can feel the weight of a resentful gaze resting upon me; I do not look up; I know that for some the attraction must be strong to clear the yard by putting a bullet through my skull from an upstairs window.

There has been a drift of refugees to the town, fisherfolk from the tiny settlements dotted along the river and the northern lakeshore, speaking a language no one understands, carrying their households on their backs, with their gaunt dogs and rickety children trailing behind them. People crowded around them when they first came. "Was it the barbarians who chased you out?" they asked, making fierce faces, stretching imaginary bows. No one asked about the imperial soldiery or the brushfires they set.

There was sympathy for these savages at first, and people brought them food and old clothing, until they began to put up their thatched shelters against the wall on the side of the square near the walnut trees, and their children grew bold enough to sneak into kitchens and steal, and one night a pack of their dogs broke into the sheepfold and tore out the throats of a dozen ewes. Feelings then turned against them. The soldiers took action, shooting their dogs on sight and, one morning when the men were still down at the lake, tearing down the entire row of shelters. For days the fisherfolk hid out in the reeds. Then one by one their little thatched huts began to reappear, this time outside the town under the north wall. Their huts were allowed to stand, but the sentries at the gave received orders to deny them entry. Now that rule has been relaxed, and they can be seen hawking strings of fish from door to door in the mornings. They have no experience of money, they are cheated outrageously, they will part with anything for a thimbleful of rum.

They are a bony, pigeon-chested people. Their women seem always to be pregnant; their children are stunted; in a few of the young girls there are traces of a fragile, liquid-eyed beauty; for the rest I see only ignorance, cunning, slovenliness. Yet what do they see in me, if they ever see me? A beast that stares out from behind a gate; the filthy underside of this beautiful oasis where they have found a precarious safety.

One day a shadow falls across me where I doze in the yard, a foot prods me, and I look up into Mandel's blue eyes.

"Are we feeding you well?" he says. "Are you growing fat again?"

I nod, sitting at his feet.

"Because we can't go on feeding you forever." There is a long pause while we examine each other. "When are you going to begin working for your keep?"

"I am a prisoner awaiting trial. Prisoners awaiting trial are not required to work for their keep. That is the law. They are maintained out of the public coffer."

"But you are not a prisoner. You are free to go as you please." He waits for me to take the ponderously offered bait. I say nothing. He goes on: "How can you be a prisoner when we have no record of you? Do you think we don't keep records? We have no record of you. So you must be a free man."

I rise and follow him across the yard to the gate. The guard hands him the key and he unlocks it. "You see? The gate is open."

I hesitate before I pass through. There is something I would like to know.

I look into Mandel's face, at the clear eyes, windows of his soul, at the mouth from which his spirit utters itself. "Have you a minute to spare?" I say. We stand in the gateway, with the guard in the background pretending not to hear. I say: "I am not a young man any more, and whatever future I had in this place is in ruins." I gesture around the square, at the dust that scuds before the hot late summer wind, bringer of blights and plagues. "Also I have already died one death, on that tree, only you decided to save me. So there is something I would like to know before I go. If it is not too late, with the barbarian at the gate." I feel the tiniest smile of mockery brush my lips, I cannot help it. I glance up at the empty sky. "Forgive me if the question seems impudent, but I would like to ask: How do you find it possible to eat afterwards, after you have been . . . working with people? That is a question I have always asked myself about executioners and other such people. Wait! Listen to me a moment longer, I am sincere, it has cost me a great deal to come out with this, since I am terrified of you, I need not tell you that, I am sure you are aware of it. Do you find it easy to take food afterwards? I have imagined that one would want to wash one's hands. But no ordinary washing would be enough, one would require priestly intervention, a ceremonial of cleansing, don't you think? Some kind of purging of one's soul too—that is how I have imagined it. Otherwise how would it be possible to return to everyday life—to sit down at table, for instance, and break bread with one's family or one's comrades?"

He turns away, but with a slow claw-like hand I manage to catch his arm. "No, listen!" I say. "Do not misunderstand me, I am not blaming you or accusing you, I am long past that. Remember, I too have devoted a life to the law, I know its processes, I know that the workings of justice are often obscure. I am only trying to understand. I am trying to understand the zone in which you live, I am trying to imagine how you breathe and eat and live from day to day. But I cannot! That is what troubles me! If I were he, I say to myself, my hands would feel so dirty that it would choke me—"

He wrenches himself free and hits me so hard in the chest that I gasp and stumble backwards. "You bastard!" he shouts. "You fucking old lunatic! Get out! Go and die somewhere!"

"When are you going to put me on trial?" I shout at his retreating back. He pays no heed.

There is nowhere to hide. And why should I? From dawn to dusk I am on view on the square, roaming around the stalls or sitting in the shade of the trees. And gradually as word gets around that the old Magistrate has taken his knocks and come through, people cease to fall silent or turn their backs when I come near. I discover that I am not without friends, particularly among women, who can barely conceal their eagerness to hear my side of the story. Roaming the streets, I pass the quartermaster's plump wife hanging out the washing. We greet. "And, how are you, sir?" she says. "We heard that you had such a hard time." Her eyes glitter, avid though cautious. "Won't you come in and have a cup of tea?" So we sit together at the kitchen table, and she sends the children to play outside, and while I drink tea and munch steadily at a plate of delicious oatmeal biscuits she bakes, she plays out the first moves in her roundabout game of question and answer: "You were gone so long, we wondered if you would ever be coming back . . . And then all the trouble you had! How things have changed! There was none of this commotion when you were in charge. All these strangers from the capital, upsetting things!" I take my cue, sigh: "Yes, they don't understand how we go about things in the provinces, do they. All this trouble over a girl . . ." I gobble another biscuit. A fool in love is laughed at but in the end always forgiven. "To me it was simply a matter of common sense to take her back to her family, but how could one make them understand that?" I ramble on; she listens to these half-truths, nodding, watching me like a hawk; we pretend that the voice she hears is not the voice of the man who swung from the tree shouting for mercy loud enough to waken the dead. ". . . Anyhow, let us hope it is all over. I still have pains"—I touch my shoulder—"one's body heals so slowly as one gets older . . ."

So I sing for my keep. And if I am still hungry in the evening, if I wait at the barracks gate for the whistle that calls the dogs and slip in quietly enough, I can usually wheedle out of the maids the leftovers from the soldiers' supper, a bowl of cold beans or the rich scrapings of the soup-pot or half a loaf of bread.

Or in the mornings I can saunter over to the inn and, leaning over the flap of the kitchen door, breathe in all the good smells, marjoram and yeast and crisp chopped onions and smoky mutton-fat. Mai the cook greases the bak-ing-pans: I watch her deft fingers dip into the pot of lard and coat the pan in three swift circles. I think of her pastries, the renowned ham and spinach and cheese pie she makes, and feel the saliva spurt in my mouth.

"So many people have left," she says, turning to the great ball of dough, "I can't even begin to tell you. A sizable party left only a few days ago. One of the girls from here—the little one with the long straight hair, you may re-member her—she was one of them, she left with her fellow." Her voice is flat as she imparts the information to me, and I am grateful for her considerate-ness. "Of course it makes sense," she continues, "if you want to leave you must leave now, it's a long road, dangerous too, and the nights are getting colder." She talks about the weather, about the past summer and signs of ap-proaching winter, as though where I had been, in my cell not three hundred paces from where we stand, I had been sealed off from hot and cold, dry and wet. To her, I realize, I disappeared and then reappeared, and in between was not part of the world.

I have been listening and nodding and dreaming while she talks. Now I speak. "You know," I say, "when I was in prison—in the barracks, not in the new prison, in a little room they locked me into—I was so hungry that I did not give a thought to women, only to food. I lived from one mealtime to the next. There was never enough for me. I bolted my food like a dog and wanted more. Also there was a great deal of pain, at different times: my hand, my arms, as well as this"—I touch the thickened nose, the ugly scar under my eye by which, I am beginning to learn, people are surreptitiously fascinated. "When I dreamed of a woman I dreamed of someone who would come in the night and take the pain away. A child's dream. What I did not know was how longing could store itself in the hollows of one's bones and then one day without warning flood out. What you said a moment ago, for instance—the girl you mentioned—I was very fond of her, I think you know that, though delicacy prevented you . . . When you said she was gone, I confess, it was as if something had struck me here, in the breast. A blow."

Her hands move deftly, pressing circles out of the sheet of dough with the rim of a bowl, catching up the scraps, rolling them together. She avoids my eyes.

"I went upstairs to her room last night, but the door was locked. I shrugged it off. She has a lot of friends, I never thought I was the only one . . . But what did I want? Somewhere to sleep, certainly; but more too. Why pretend? We all know, what old men seek is to recover their youth in the arms of young women." She pounds the dough, kneads it, rolls it out: a young woman herself with children of her own, living with an exacting mother: what appeal am I making to her as I ramble on about pain, loneliness? Bemused I listen to the discourse that emerges from me. "Let everything be said!" I told myself when I first faced up to my tormentors. "Why clamp your lips stupidly together? You have no secrets. Let them know they are working on flesh and blood! Declare your terror, scream when the pain comes! They thrive on stubborn silence: it confirms to them that every soul is a lock they must patiently pick. Bare yourself! Open your heart!" So I shouted and screamed and said whatever came into my head. Insidious rationale! For now what I hear when I loosen my tongue and let it sail free is the subtle whining of a beggar. "Do you know where I slept last night?" I hear myself saying. "Do you know that little lean-to at the back of the granary? . . ."

But above all it is food that I crave, and more intensely with every passing week. I want to be fat again. There is a hunger upon me day and night. I wake up with my stomach yawning, I cannot wait to be on my rounds, loitering at the barracks gate to sniff the bland watery aroma of oatmeal and wait for the burnt scrapings; cajoling children to throw me down mulberries from the trees; stretching over a garden fence to steal a peach or two; passing from door to door, a man down on his luck, the victim of an infatuation, but cured now, ready with a smile to take what is offered, a slice of bread and jam, a cup of tea, in the middle of the day perhaps a bowl of stew or a plate of onions and beans, and always fruit, apricots, peaches, pomegranates, the wealth of a bounteous summer. I eat like a beggar, gobbling down my food with such appetite, wiping my plate so clean that it does the heart good to see it. No wonder I am day by day creeping back into the good books of my countrymen.

And how I can flatter, how I can woo! More than once have I had a tasty snack prepared especially for me: a mutton chop fried with peppers and chives, or a slice of ham and tomato on bread with a wedge of goats' milk cheese. If I can carry water or firewood in return, I do so gladly, as a token, though I am not as strong as I used to be. And if for the time being I have exhausted my sources in the town—for I must be careful not to become a burden on my benefactors—I can always stroll down to the fisherfolk's camp and help them clean fish. I have learned a few words of their language, I am received without suspicion, they understand what it is to be a beggar, they share their food with me.

I want to be fat again, fatter than ever before. I want a belly that gurgles with contentment when I fold my palms over it, I want to feel my chin sink into the cushion of my throat and my breasts wobble as I walk. I want a life of simple satisfactions. I want (vain hope!) never to know hunger again.

# Bessie Head

Bessie Head has been credited with enlarging the scope of African fiction. Born on 6 July 1937 in Pietermaritzburg, South Africa, she was the child of a white mother, who came from a wealthy family, and a black stable hand. As a result of the pregnancy, Head's mother was placed in a mental hospital, where the child was born and named after her mother. Head grew up in a foster home until she entered an Anglican mission orphanage in 1950. There she completed schooling and earned a teachers' certificate. After teaching for two years, she began working as a journalist. In 1960 she married a newspaper reporter, Harold Head, and they had one son. Following her divorce, she left South Africa in 1964 on an exit permit, which prohibited reentry into the country, and settled in Serowe, Botswana. In 1979 she became a Botswanan citizen. She died in Serowe on 17 April 1986.

Head's best known novel, *A Question of Power* (1974), chronicles in fictional terms her mental breakdown in 1969, a condition from which she emerged a year later. *The Black Scholar* ranked the novel as the eighth of the fifteen "most influential books for the decade"; it was also short-listed for the Booker Prize, and is considered by most critics as her finest work. Her other novels include *When Rain Clouds Gather* (1969), *Maru* (1971), and *A Bewitched Crossroad: An African Saga* (1984). She published two volumes of short stories, *The Collector of Treasures and Other Botswana Village Tales* (1977) and *Tales of Tenderness and Power* (1989), and a social history, *Serowe: Village of the Rain Wind* (1981).

Head's first three novels are autobiographical in nature. In these books, the protagonists look inward as they face the psychological stress created by being disconnected from their outer worlds. The fictional quest evolves into a struggle to reconcile the interior and the exterior. Once Head had exorcised her own demons, ones engendered by the discovery of her mixed parentage, feelings of rejection, the constant awareness of racism, and the condition of women, she moved on in her writing to present a larger picture of Africa.

The final novel and short stories take place in Botswana and set out to make known the tribal history of its people, their contact with missionaries, the practice of witchcraft, and the difficulties women face in such a structured and traditional society. She was acutely aware of sexual discrimination and racism through her own experience, and passionate in her feelings about these wrongs. Yet she never identified herself wholly with either feminism or African nationalism. It has been noted that Head feared most of all the misuse of political power, and believed instead in the power of goodness and love.

"The Coming of the Christ-Child" represents Head's second period of writing, which took a broader view of Africa. Although told in the form of a short story, the selection is actually a tribute to Robert Sobukwe, written shortly after his death. Born in South Africa, Sobukwe (1924–1978) was the first president of the Pan-Africanist Congress, which he helped found as an alternative to the African National Congress with which he and others had become disillusioned. He spent several years in prison for his activities. Head considered Sobukwe the ideal leader, and once said that his "view of Pan Africanism gave me a comfortable black skin to live in and work with." This tale outlines in clear terms the tragedy of colonialism. Its ironic title is drawn from the Xhosa tradition of sitting quietly at midnight each Christmas Eve to await the coming of the Christ-Child.

# The Coming of the Christ-Child

He was born on a small mission station in the Eastern Cape and he came from a long line of mission-educated men; great-grandfathers, grandfathers and even his own father, had all been priests. Except for a brief period of public activity, the quietude and obscurity of the life was to cling around him all his days. Later, in the turmoil and tumult of his life in Johannesburg, where Christmas Eve was a drunken riot, he liked to tell friends of the way in which his parents had welcomed the coming of the Christ-Child each Christmas Eve.

"We would sit in silence with bowed heads; just silent like that for a half an hour before midnight. I still like the way the old people did it . . ."

One part of the history of South Africa was also the history of Christianity because it was only the missions that represented a continuous effort to strengthen black people in their struggle to survive and provided them with a tenuous link between past and future. The psychological battering the older generations underwent was so terrible as to reduce them to a state beyond the non-human. It could also be said that all the people unconsciously chose Christianity to maintain their compactness, their wholeness and humanity for they were assaulted on all sides as primitives who were two thousand years behind the white man in civilization. They were robbed of everything they possessed—their land and cattle—and when they lost everything, they brought to Christianity the same reverence they had once offered to tribe, custom and ancestral worship. The younger generations remembered the elders, Christianity created generations of holy people all over the land.

From *Tales of Tenderness and Power* by Bessie Head. Copyright © by The Estate of Bessie Head 1989. Used by permission of Heinemann Educational Publishers, a division of Reed Educational and Professional Publishing Ltd.; and by permission of John Johnson (Authors' Agent), London.

And so the foundations of a new order of life were laid by the missions and since the ministry was a tradition in his own family, its evolutionary pattern could be traced right from his great-grandfather's time when the lonely outpost mission church was also the first elementary school existing solely to teach the Bible. From Bible schools, children began to scratch on slates and receive a more general education, until a number of high schools and one University College, attached to missions, spread like a network throughout the land. He was a product of this evolutionary stream and by the time he was born his family enjoyed considerable prestige. They were affluent and lived in a comfortable house, the property of the church, which was surrounded by a large garden. Their life belonged to the community; their home life was the stormy center of all the tragedies that had fallen on the people, who, no matter which way they turned, were defaulters and criminals in their own land. Much is known about the fearful face of white supremacy; its greed and ruthless horrors. They fell upon the people like a leaden weight and they lay there, an agonizing burden to endure.

One day there was—but then there were so many such days—a major catastrophe for the church. The police entered during the hour of worship (it was a point with all the white races of the land that no part of a black man's life was sacred and inviolable) and arrested most of the men as poll tax defaulters. The issue at that time was how people, with an income of twenty shillings a year could pay a poll tax of twenty shillings a year. There was only such misery in the rural areas, grandly demarcated as the "native reserves." Land was almost non-existent and people thrust back into the reserves struggled to graze stock on small patches of the earth. The stock were worthless, scabby and diseased and almost unsaleable. Starving men with stock losses were driven into working on the mines and the Boer farms for wages just sufficient to cover their poll tax. When their labor was no longer needed in the mines they were endorsed back to the mythical rural areas. There was no such thing as the rural areas left—only hard patterns of greed of which all the people were victims. It was impressed on people that they were guilty of one supposed crime after another and in this way they were conditioned to offer themselves as a huge reservoir of cheap labor.

Thus it was that the grubby day to day detail of human misery unfolded before the young man's eyes. Often only five shillings stood between a man and his conviction as a defaulter of some kind and it was his father's habit to dip deep into his own pocket or the coffers of the church to aid one of his members. That day of the mass arrest of men in church was to linger vividly in the young man's mind. His father walked up and down for some time, wringing his hands in distress, his composure shaken to the core. Then he had attempted to compose himself and continue the disrupted service, but a cynical male voice in the congregation shouted:

"Answer this question, Father. How is it that when the white man came here, he had only the Bible and we the land. Today, he has the land and we the Bible," and a second disruption ensued from weeping women whose husbands were among those arrested.

From habit the old man dropped to his knees and buried his face in his hands. The remainder of his congregation filed out slowly with solemn faces. He knelt like that for some time, unaware that his son stood quietly near observing him with silent, grave eyes. He was a silent, pleasant young man, who often smiled. He liked reading most and could more often than not be found with his head buried in a book. Maybe his father was praying. If so, his son's words cut so sharply into the silence that the old man jerked back his head in surprise.

"There is no God, father," the young man said in his quiet way. "These things are done by men and it is men we should have dealings with. God is powerless to help us, should there even be such a thing."

"Do you get these ideas from books, my son?" his father asked, uncertainly. "I have not had the education you are having now because there was no University College in my days, so I have not traveled as far as you in loss of faith, even though I live in the trough of despair."

This difference in views hardly disrupted the harmonious relationship between father and son. Later, people were to revere an indefinable quality in the young politician, not realizing that he rose from the deep heart of the country, where in spite of all that was said, people were not the "humiliated, down-trodden blacks" but men like his father. Later, he was to display a courage unequaled by any black man in the land. The romance and legends of the earlier history still quivered in the air of the rural area where he was born. Nine land wars had the tribes fought against the British. Great kings like Hintsa had conducted the wars, and in spite of the grubbiness and despair of the present, the older generations still liked to dwell on the details of his death. Hintsa had been a phenomenon, a ruler so brilliant that on his death his brains had been removed from his head so that some part of him could remain above ground to be revered and worshipped. It was a tradition of courage that his people treasured.

On graduating from university he did not choose the ministry as his career. Instead, he had one of those rare and elegant positions as Professor of Bantu Languages at the University of the Witwatersrand in Johannesburg. He was as elegant and cultured as his job and ahead of him stretched years and years of comfort and security. The black townships surrounding the city of Johannesburg absorbed genius of all kinds in astounding combinations. The poor and humble and the rich and talented lived side by side. Brilliant black men, with no outlet for their talents for management and organization, were the managers and organizers of huge crime rings around the country with vast numbers of men in their employ. They flashed about the townships in flashy American cars of the latest design and sold their stolen goods at backdoor prices to the millions of poor, honest black laborers who served the city. Johannesburg was the pulsing heart of the land; everything of significance that happened in the country, first happened in Johannesburg. It was also the center of the big labor shuttle; the gold mines stretching along the Witwatersrand with their exhaustible resources needed thousands and thousands of black hands to haul those riches above ground. The city was complex, as international as the gold that flowed to all the banking houses of the world. It had also been the center of ruthless exploitation and major political protest and it seemed to have aged in cynicism and weariness ahead of the rest of the country. It was a war-weary and apathetic world that he entered in 1948. It was as though people said: "Ah, political protest? You name it, we've done it. What is it all for?" It took something new and fresh to stir the people out of their apathy and exhaustion.

Almost immediately he attracted a wide range of thinking men. Immediately, the details of his life attracted interest and he slipped into the general color of the environment. But he carried almost the totality of the country with him. It wasn't so much his reading habits—there were hundreds of men there acquainted with Karl Marx and the Chinese revolution; there were hundreds of men there who wore their intellectual brilliance as casually as they wore their clothes. It was the fillers he provided on parts of the country that were now myths in the minds of urban dwellers—the strange and desperate struggles waged by people in the rural areas.

"I've just been reading this book on some of the land struggles in China after the revolution," he'd say. "It was difficult for Mao Tse-Tung to get people to cultivate land because ancestor worship was practiced there. I've seen people do the same thing in the Transkei where I was born. There was hardly any land left to cultivate but people would rather die of starvation than plough on the land where their ancestors were buried . . ."

Almost nightly there was an eager traffic of friends through his home. He enjoyed the circle of friends that gathered round him. He enjoyed knocking out his ideas against the ideas of other men and it was almost as though he were talking an unintelligible language. His friends no longer knew of the sacred values of the tribes—that all people had ever once wanted was a field where they might plough their crops and settled home near the bones of their ancestors. Like the young men of his circle, he was a member of the Youth League of an organization that for forty-seven years had been solely representative of the interests of black people. They had brought people out on the streets on protests and demonstrations. People had been shot dead and imprisoned. A strange hypnotic dialogue pervaded the country. It was always subtly implied that black people were violent; yet it had become illegal in the year 1883 for black men to possess arms. They had little beyond sticks and stones with which to defend themselves. Violence was never a term applied to white men, but they had arms. Before these arms the people were cannon fodder. Who was violent?

Year after year, at convention after convention this kindly body of the people's representatives mouthed noble sentiments:

"Gentlemen, we ought to remember that our struggle is a non-violent one. Nothing will be gained by violence. It will only harden the hearts of our oppressors against us . . ."

In 1957 there were more dead black bodies to count. Gopane village, eighteen miles outside the small town of Zeerust in the Transvaal was up until that year a quiet and insignificant African village. A way of life had built up over the years—the older people clung to the traditional ways of ploughing their fields and sent their children to Johannesburg, either to work or to acquire an education. In 1957 a law was passed compelling black women to carry a "pass book." Forty years ago the same law had been successfully resisted by the women who had offered themselves for imprisonment rather than carry the document. The "pass book" had long been in existence for black men and was the source of excruciating suffering. If a man walked out of his home without his "pass book" he simply disappeared from society for a stretch of six months or so. Most men knew the story. They supplied a Boer farmer for six months with free labor to harvest his potatoes. A "boss-boy" stood over the "prisoners" with a whip. They dug out potatoes with such speed that the nails on their fingers were worn to the bone. The women were later to tell a similar tale but in that year, 1957, people still thought they could protest about laws imposed on them. Obscure Gopane village was the first area in the country where the "pass book" was issued to women. The women quietly accepted them, walked home, piled them in a huge heap and burnt them. Very soon the village was surrounded by the South African Police. They shot the women dead. From then onwards "pass books" were issued to all black women throughout the country without resistance.

Was it sheer terror at being faced with nameless horrors—who would shoot unarmed women dead? —or did the leaders of the people imagine they represented a respectable status quo? There they were at the very next convention, droning on again:

"Gentlemen," said speaker number one, an elderly, staid, complacent member of the community. "Gentlemen, in spite of the tragedy of the past year, we must not forget that our struggle is essentially a non-violent one . . ."

He was going on like that—after all the incident had passed into history and let's attend to matters at hand—when there was a sudden interruption of the sort that had not disrupted those decorous boring proceedings for years. Someone had stood up out of turn. Speaker number one looked down his nose in disdain. It was the young Professor of Bantu languages. He was only in the Youth League section and of no significance.

"Gentlemen!" and to everyone's amazement the young man's voice quivered with rage. "May I interrupt the speaker! I am heartily sick of the proceedings of this organization. Our women were recently killed in a violent way and the speaker still requests of us that we follow a non-violent policy . . ."

"What are you suggesting that we do?" asked speaker number one, alarmed. "Are you suggesting that we resort to violence against our oppressors?"

"I wish that the truth be told!" and the younger man banged his hand on the table in exasperation. "Our forefathers lived on this land long before the white man came here and forced a policy of dispossession on us. We are hardly human to them! They only view us as objects of cheap labor! Why is the word *violence* such a terrible taboo from *our* side! Why can't we state in turn that *they* mean nothing to us and that it is our intention to get them off our backs! How long is this going to go on? It will go on and on until we say: 'NO MORE!'" And he flung his arms wide in a gesture of desperation. "Gentlemen! I am sick of the equivocation and clever talk of this organization. If anyone agrees with me, would they please follow me," and he turned forthwith and left the convention hall.

Everything had happened so abruptly that there was a moment's pause of startled surprise. Then half the assembly stood up and walked out after the young man and so began a new short era in the history of political struggle in South Africa. His political career lasted barely a year. George Padmore's book *Pan Africanism or Communism* was the rage in Johannesburg at that time and he and his splinter group allied themselves with its sentiments.

In spite of the tragedies of the country, that year seemed to provide a humorous interlude to the leaders of the traditional people's movement. Their whole attention was distracted into ridiculing the efforts of their new rival; they failed to recognize a creative mind in their midst. The papers that were issued in a steady stream were the work of a creative artist and not that of a hardened self-seeking politician. The problems they outlined were always new and unexpected. They began slowly from the bottom, outlining basic problems.

> "We can make little progress if our people regard themselves as inferior. For three hundred years the whites have inculcated a feeling of inferiority in us. They only address us as 'boy' and 'girl,' yet we are men and women with children of our own and homes of our own. Our people would resent it if we called them 'kwedini' or 'mfana' or 'moshemane,' all of which mean 'boy.' Why then do they accept indignity, insult and humiliation from the white foreigner . . .?"

A counter paper was immediately issued by the people's traditional movement:

"We have some upstarts in our midst who have promised to lead the people to a new dawn but they are only soft gentlemen who want to be 'Sir-ed' and 'Madam-ed.' Who has led the people in mass demonstrations? Who is the true voice of the people . . .?"

They arranged for stones to be cast at him as he addressed public rallies and for general heckling and disruption of the proceedings. Yet during that single year he provided people with a wide range of political education such as the traditional people's movement had not been able to offer in all their long history. His papers touched on everything from foreign investment in the land which further secured the bonds of oppression, to some problems of the future which were phrased as questions:

"Can we make a planned economy work within the framework of a political democracy? It has not done so in any of the countries that practice it today . . . We cannot guarantee minority rights because we are fighting precisely that group-exclusiveness which those who plead for minority rights would like to perpetuate. Surely we have guaranteed the highest if we have guaranteed individual liberties . . .?"

The land could be peaceful for months, even years. There was a machinery at hand to crush the slightest protest. Men either fled its ravenous, insensitive brutal jaws, or, obsessed as a few men often are with making some final noble gesture or statement, they walked directly into the brutal jaws. It was always a fatal decision. No human nobility lit up the land. People were hungry for ideas, for a new direction, yet men of higher motivation were irresistibly drawn towards the machine. That machine was already gory with human blood and since it was only a machine it remained unmoved, unshaken, unbroken. Obsessed with clarifying a legality, he walked directly into the machine. The laws of the land were all illegal, he said. They were made exclusively by a white minority without consulting the black majority. It was a government of a white minority for a white minority; therefore the black majority was under no moral obligation to obey its laws. At his bidding thousands of black men throughout the land lay down their "pass books" outside the gates of the police stations.

He had a curious trial. White security police had attended all his public meetings and taken notes but there were no witnesses for the State except one illiterate black policeman. He gave a short halting statement that made people in the public gallery roar with laughter.

"I attended a political gathering addressed by this man. I heard him say: 'The pass book. That is our water-pipe to parliament.' "

There were sixty-nine dead bodies outside a Sharpeville police station. He was sentenced to three years imprisonment for sedition. Then a special

bill was passed to detain him in prison for life. He was released after nine
years but served with so many banning orders that he could barely communicate with his fellow-men. Then he became ill and died.

An equivalent blanket of silence fell upon the land. The crack-down on
all political opposition was so severe that hundreds quailed and fled before
the monstrous machine. It was the end of the long legend of non-violent
protest. But a miracle people had not expected was that from 1957 onwards
the white man was being systematically expelled from Africa, as a political
force, as a governing power. Only the southern lands lay in bondage. Since
people had been silenced on such a massive scale, the course and direction of
events was no longer theirs. It had slipped from their grasp some time ago
into the hands of the men who were training for revolution.

When all was said and done and revolutions had been fought and won,
perhaps only dreamers longed for a voice like that of the man who was as
beautiful as the coming of the Christ-Child.

# Chinua Achebe

Through the art of fiction, Chinua Achebe set out to record Nigeria's experience with colonialism, and to tell that story from an African viewpoint. Born in eastern Nigeria, 16 November 1930, Achebe was the son of a catechist for the Church Missionary Society. He received his early education in the society's village school, and at age fourteen enrolled in Government College at Unuahia. He was a member of the first class to attend the recently founded University College, Ibadan. After graduating in 1953, he taught briefly before beginning a twelve-year career as a producer for the Nigerian Broadcasting Corporation. In 1957 he traveled to London where he attended the British Broacasting Corporation Staff School. One of his teachers was the novelist and critic Gilbert Phelps, who recognized the distinctive character of Achebe's first novel, *Things Fall Apart*, and recommended it for publication. The book appeared in 1958, and since then has gained a place as a classic in world literature, having been translated into forty languages.

Three more novels, *No Longer at Ease* (1960), *Arrow of God* (1964), and *A Man of the People* (1966) followed. Just a few days after the publication of his fourth novel, the first military coup d'état in Nigeria took place, and Achebe resigned as director of external broadcasting. He returned to his birthplace, which became a part of Biafra when the eastern region declared independence from Nigeria in 1967. During the civil war that ensued, Achebe traveled abroad to seek help for the Biafran cause. Once the strife ended and Nigeria fell under one military dictatorship after another, Achebe left Africa to take up teaching positions in Canada and the United States, where he still lives. In 1987 he published *Anthills of the Savannah*, his first novel in nearly twenty years. He has also published poetry, commentary, and essays, as well as two collections of short stories, *The Sacrificial Egg and Other Stories* (1962) and *Girls at War and Other Stories* (1972).

In his essay "The Novelist as Teacher," Achebe advised his countrymen that a knowledge and appreciation of their own culture would assist them in nation building: "This theme—put quite simply—is that African people did not hear of culture for the first time from Europeans; that their societies were not mindless but frequently had a philosophy of great depth and value and beauty, that they had poetry and, above all, they had dignity. It is this dignity that African people all but lost during the colonial period, and it is this that they must now regain." His five novels form a continuing history of one segment of African people—and by extension the history of all of Africa.

"The Sacrificial Egg" reveals several aspects of colonialism: the one-sided trade developed by the Europeans, the overlay of European civilization among those Africans who are educated and city bred, and the importation of disease. In contrast, though, African tradition plays its part throughout the story.

# The Sacrificial Egg

Julius Obi sat gazing at his typewriter. The fat Chief Clerk, his boss, was snoring at his table. Outside, the gatekeeper in his green uniform was sleeping at his post. You couldn't blame him; no customer had passed through the gate for nearly a week. There was an empty basket on the giant weighing machine. A few palm-kernels lay desolately in the dust around the machine. Only the flies remained in strength.

Julius went to the window that overlooked the great market on the bank of the River Niger. This market, though still called Nkwo, had long spilled over into Eke, Oye, and Afo with the coming of civilization and the growth of the town into a big palm-oil port. In spite of this encroachment, however, it was still busiest on its original Nkwo day, because the deity who had presided over it from antiquity still cast her spell only on her own day—let men in their greed spill over themselves. It was said that she appeared in the form of an old woman in the center of the market just before cock-crow and waved her magic fan in the four directions of the earth—in front of her, behind her, to the right and to the left—to draw to the market men and women from distant places. And they came bringing the produce of their lands—palm-oil and kernels, kola nuts, cassava, mats, baskets and earthenware pots; and took home many-colored cloths, smoked fish, iron pots and plates. These were the forest peoples. The other half of the world who lived by the great rivers came down also—by canoe, bringing yams and fish. Sometimes it was a big canoe with a dozen or more people in it; sometimes it was a lone fisherman and his wife in a small vessel from the swift-flowing Anambara. They moored their canoe on the bank and sold their fish, after much haggling. The woman then walked up the steep banks of the river to the heart of the market to buy salt and oil and, if the sales had been very good, even a length of cloth. And for her children at home she bought bean cakes and mai-mai which the Igara women cooked. As evening approached, they took up their paddles again and paddled away, the water shimmering in the sunset and their canoe becoming smaller and smaller in the distance until it was just a dark crescent on the water's face and two dark bodies swaying forwards and backwards in it. Umuru then was the meeting place of the forest people who were called Igbo and the alien riverain folk whom the Igbo called Olu and beyond whom the world stretched in indefiniteness.

Julius Obi was not a native of Umuru. He had come like countless others from some bush village inland. Having passed his Standard Six in a mission school he had come to Umuru to work as a clerk in the offices of the all-powerful European trading company which bought palm kernels at its own price and sold cloth and metalware, also at its own price. The offices were situated beside the famous market so that in his first two or three weeks Julius had to learn to work within its huge enveloping hum. Sometimes when the Chief Clerk was away he walked to the window and looked down on the vast anthill activity. Most of these people were not there yesterday, he thought, and yet the market had been just as full. There must be many, many people in the world to be able to fill the market day after day like this. Of course they say not all who came to the great market were real people. Janet's mother, Ma, had said so.

"Some of the beautiful young women you see squeezing through the crowds are not people like you or me but mammy-wota who have their town in the depths of the river," she said. "You can always tell them, because they are beautiful with a beauty that is too perfect and too cold. You catch a glimpse of her with the tail of your eye, then you blink and look properly, but she has already vanished in the crowd."

Julius thought about these things as he now stood at the window looking down on the silent, empty market. Who would have believed that the great boisterous market could ever be quenched like this? But such was the strength of Kitikpa, the incarnate power of smallpox. Only he could drive away all those people and leave the market to the flies.

When Umuru was a little village, there was an age-grade who swept its market-square every Nkwo day. But progress had turned it into a busy, sprawling, crowded and dirty river port, a no-man's-land where strangers outnumbered by far the sons of the soil, who could do nothing about it except shake their heads at this gross perversion of their prayer. For indeed they had prayed—who will blame them—for their town to grow and prosper. And it had grown. But there is good growth and there is bad growth. The belly does not bulge out only with food and drink; it might be the abominable disease which would end by sending its sufferer out of the house even before he was fully dead.

The strangers who came to Umuru came for trade and money, not in search of duties to perform, for they had those in plenty back home in their village which was real home.

And as if this did not suffice, the young sons and daughters of Umuru soil, encouraged by schools and churches were behaving no better than the strangers. They neglected all their old tasks and kept only the revelries.

Such was the state of the town when Kitikpa came to see it and to demand the sacrifice the inhabitants owed the gods of the soil. He came in confident knowledge of the terror he held over the people. He was an evil deity, and boasted it. Lest he be offended those he killed were not killed but decorated, and no one dared weep for them. He put an end to the coming and going between neighbors and between villages. They said, "Kitikpa is in that village," and immediately it was cut off by its neighbors.

Julius was sad and worried because it was almost a week since he had seen Janet, the girl he was going to marry. Ma had explained to him very gently that he should no longer go to see them "until this thing is over, by the power of Jehovah." (Ma was a very devout Christian convert and one reason why she approved of Julius for her only daughter was that he sang in the choir of the CMS church.)

"You must keep to your rooms," she had said in hushed tones, for Kitikpa strictly forbade any noise or boisterousness. "You never know whom you might meet on the streets. That family has got it." She lowered her voice even more and pointed surreptitiously at the house across the road whose doorway was barred with a yellow palm frond. "He has decorated one of them already and the rest were moved away today in a big government lorry."

Janet walked a short way with Julius and stopped; so he stopped too. They seemed to have nothing to say to each other yet they lingered on. Then she said goodnight and he said goodnight. And they shook hands, which was very odd, as though parting for the night were something new and grave.

He did not go straight home, because he wanted desperately to cling, even alone, to this strange parting. Being educated he was not afraid of whom he might meet, so he went to the bank of the river and just walked up and down it. He must have been there a long time because he was still there when the wooden gong of the night-mask sounded. He immediately set out for home, half-walking and half-running, for night-masks were not a matter of superstition; they were real. They chose the night for their revelry because like the bat's their ugliness was great.

In his hurry he stepped on something that broke with a slight liquid explosion. He stopped and peeped down at the footpath. The moon was not up yet but there was a faint light in the sky which showed that it would not be long delayed. In this half-light he saw that he had stepped on an egg offered in sacrifice. Someone oppressed by misfortune had brought the offering to the crossroads in the dusk. And he had stepped on it. There were the usual young palm-fronds around it. But Julius saw it differently as a house where the terrible artist was at work. He wiped the sole of his foot on the sandy path and hurried away, carrying another vague worry in his mind. But hurrying was no use now; the fleet-footed mask was already abroad. Perhaps it was impelled to hurry by the threatening imminence of the moon. Its voice rose high and clear in the still night air like a flaming sword. It was yet a long way away, but Julius knew that distances vanished before it. So he made straight for the co-coyam farm beside the road and threw himself on his belly, in the shelter of the broad leaves. He had hardly done this when he heard the rattling staff of the spirit and a thundering stream of esoteric speech. He shook all over. The sounds came bearing down on him, almost pressing his face into the moist earth. And now he could hear the footsteps. It was as if twenty evil men were running together. Panic sweat broke all over him and he was nearly impelled to get up and run. Fortunately he kept a firm hold on himself . . . In no time at all the commotion in the air and on the earth—the thunder and torrential rain, the earthquake and flood—passed and disappeared in the distance on the other side of the road.

The next morning, at the office the Chief Clerk, a son of the soil spoke bitterly about last night's provocation of Kitikpa by the headstrong youngsters who had launched the noisy fleet-footed mask in defiance of their elders, who knew that Kitikpa would be enraged, and then . . .

The trouble was that the disobedient youths had never yet experienced the power of Kitikpa themselves; they had only heard of it. But soon they would learn.

As Julius stood at the window looking out on the emptied market he lived through the terror of that night again. It was barely a week ago but already it seemed like another life, separated from the present by a vast emptiness. This emptiness deepened with every passing day. On this side of it stood Julius, and on the other Ma and Janet whom the dread artist decorated.

# Witi Ihimaera

Witi Ihimaera said that his writing career was instigated in part by a commentator who lamented the absence of Maori novelists in New Zealand. Of mixed Maori and European descent, Witi Ihimaera was born in 1944 and grew up in rural New Zealand. Although he spent his early years in a Maori environment, his parents were Mormons and the language at home was English, not Maori. Along with many Maoris in the 1960s, he moved to an urban area, where he attended Victoria University in Wellington and completed a bachelor's degree in literature. He then worked as a journalist for several years. During the 1970s he started publishing short stories in New Zealand magazines, including English-language Maori publications, and received several regional awards for his work. Ihimaera's success as a storyteller led him into another career when New Zealand's prime minister, impressed by the young writer's work, offered him a position in the Ministry of Foreign Affairs. Starting his diplomatic career in 1976, he served in overseas postings to Australia and the United States, where he was New Zealand consul general in New York until 1989. Ihimaera now lives in Auckland, continues to write and edit, and lectures in English at Auckland University. He is also deeply involved in Maori cultural and political life.

In addition to his own work, one of his major accomplishments is the co-editing with D.S. Long of an inaugural anthology of Maori writing, *Into the World of Light* (1982). He also wrote *Maori*, which was published by the New Zealand government in 1975. This books provides background on Maori culture and history, and offers a forthright commentary on race relations in New Zealand. Ihimaera criticizes in particular what he calls the "one-way process" of integration that requires change only on the part of the Maoris.

Ihimaera's first collection of short stories, *Pounamu, Pounamu* (1972), and early novels, *Tangi* (1973) and *Whanau* (1974), depict Maori life in a rural area. They are striking in their naïveté and innocence, as they celebrate childhood, the extended family, pastoral pleasures, nature's beauty, and the inevitable progress toward maturity. This fiction avoids direct confrontation with the Pakeha (European) values, even though these values constantly threaten Maori culture.

The title of the 1977 short story collection, *The New Net Goes Fishing*, suggests that Ihimaera's work is moving into new waters. Here he takes up cultural erosion and dislocation among the Maoris who have relocated in urban areas. Another collection, *Dear Miss Mansfield* (1989), responds to the work of New Zealand's best-known writer, Katherine Mansfield, through replies to some of her stories and variations on others to show the Maori side of life in Aotearoa, the original name for New Zealand. A new novel, *Bulibasha, King of the Gypsies*, appeared in 1994, and once more focuses on the conflicts in Maori rural life.

This selection from *The Matriarch* (1986) serves as the pivotal scene in a highly confrontational novel, which examines all aspects of the Maori's long struggle for their rightful place in New Zealand society. Here the narrator attempts to re-create a childhood experience, which bordered on the supernatural, at a Maori feast, and to understand its long-lasting significance. The passage may also be read independently as a vivid picture of Maori tradition, which survived in spite of colonization.

# From *The Matriarch*

One of the head cook's men had asked, "How long now, before the food is cooked?" The head cook had said two and a half hours. Oh, how he had sweated during the mihimihi. Aue, how he had silently railed against the matriarch when her ope had arrived late and prolonged the welcoming ceremonials. Aeee, and he had been ready to throttle the photographer when he had asked to take a photograph of the gathering. And was that a telltale wisp of steam arising from the hangi already? Oh no. Oh yes. Oh no. Oh yes. Oh!

This had been his inner turmoil, but he had put a face of impassivity upon it. And his men admired his seeming imperturbability and his impeccable timing; immediately following the karanga to kai, he had turned to them and said, "Okay, boys. Out it comes."

They had been able to tell, as soon as they began uncovering the hangi, that the food was well and truly cooked. The omens were therefore to be praised with vigor and thanksgiving. And as they began to carry the wire baskets into the kitchen, and to carve up the meat, the head cook allowed himself the luxury of a surreptitious "whew."

("It was quite amazing," the journalist said. "There we all were, sniffing the air, hoping not to smell overcooked or smoked meat. And yet not one person dared to voice an opinion until one old man, bravely, averred, "Ah yes, the hangi is going to be good." With that pronouncement the whole crowd surged into the dining hall and into the place of the kai.

"Oh, it was so good to relax after the mihimihi and to feel the tensions between people beginning to disappear. You Maoris must know quite a bit about psychology! A feast, like the hakari, is a wonderful way to get people laughing and talking and forgetting any animosities they may have had. For instance, I happened to see your grandmother with the Prime Minister's private secretary: whatever differences they may have earlier had now seemed to have been settled. As luck would have it, I was actually able to take a table near to her. She was so superb.")

The child entered the dining hall with Hiraina and Manaaki, and he was instantly confronted with the cornucopia of the land. "Come on," Hiraina said to him. "Let's sit here."

There was a great hubbub of approval and admiration for the visual and very real feast which had been placed on the rows and rows of tables in the room. Under the inverted V of the roof, with its painted kowhaiwhai arms opening out to welcome the visitors, had been spread a remarkable array of kai. Plates of seafood, aerated drinks, cakes, biscuits, paraoa rewana, paraoa koroue, paraoa parai, fresh fruit, sweets, dried shark, eel, jelly, fermented corn spilled throughout the dining room in glorious disarray. Plates of bread, butter, cheese, jam, sugar, salt had been put on each table, with a cutlery setting and a breadplate for each guest. The young beauties of the local people waited gravely to serve their guests, excited by the admiration being voiced by the manuhiri. Indeed, as they had entered the dining room, some of the visitors had actually begun to waiata, and one old lady had been so overwhelmed that she had stood to karanga the festival appearance of the hall and of the hakari.

"This is all for you, e mokopuna," the matriarch said.

Although she was far away, across the other side of the room, the child heard the matriarch's voice whispering to him. The pearls in her hair shimmered and sent splinters of light through the hall.

Suddenly there came a sound of young girls singing. With an explosion of color, a long line of women, beautifully dressed in Maori costume, entered the hall. Each carried a kono of green flax, a plaited basket containing the hangi kai, the mutton, beef, chicken, pork, kumara, pumpkin, puha, and other greens which had just been prepared in the earth oven.

"Only for you, my dearest grandson." Her voice was honeyed and loving, intimate and full of pride, and there was a tinge of triumph flooding through it like a glorious cantilena, an arching sound of pure beauty soaring above the buzz of the assembly.

The women came skipping like songbirds through the hall, flirting and glorifying their guests, singing, "Haere mai e te manuhiri, haere mai." And the congress of the tribes roared with acclamation.

"Only for—" the matriarch's voice broke in pieces. And suddenly, it seemed to the child that he was borne in a maelstrom of anger beyond all imagination. Hiraina felt it too and cried out.

("I was watching your grandmother. She was glowing with such a strange light. She was smiling her madonna smile. But suddenly, she gripped the table and stood up. She was looking straight at you.")

"*Kia tupato,*" she said.

An old man had come to stand behind the child. He laid a kono before him. Then he smiled at him and lifted his right hand.

("Oh, her look was so deathly. You see, one of the elders of the paepae had come up to you. Apparently he knew full well what he was doing, yes indeed.")

"*Manaaki! Hiraina! Guard the child,*" she said.

The hubbub, the acclamation was all around the hall.

The old man smiled again. Mockingly, he saluted the matriarch with his right hand.

"*The child.*"

Then, slowly and with obscene deliberation, the old man began to lower his hand upon the child's head.

Because the male is tapu, his body is also sacred. An enemy or a woman could destroy the tapu, either wittingly or unwittingly, by a number of acts. For instance, if a woman stepped over a man her noa qualities could cancel out his sacredness; such an act, whether accidental or not, could only be rewarded by death. Again, in times of war, the victor could obtain the sacredness of his victim, thereby increasing his own tapu, by consuming his flesh. And, a final example, if the victor wished to ensure that all knew his triumph, he would sever the victim's head and place it on a stake so that nobody could doubt that the tapu of the victim was his.

Of all parts of the body the head is the most sacred. The Maori word for the head is "upoko" and veneration of it explains why modern Maoris have abhorred the continuing sale of Maori heads ("and what are we bid on this beautiful Maori head with its fabulous Maori moko? Ladies and gentlemen, do I hear £5,000?"). It also might serve to underline the grief that Maori people feel at the continuing retention in museums over the world of so-called "mummies," or bodies stolen from Maori burial grounds, for display in the ghoul-glass cases of the world.

All an enemy needed to do was to *touch the head* of the male against whom he wished ill. Just a touch was enough to take away the tapu (and I telephoned Te Ariki one day, saying, "Te Ariki, a Pakeha whom I don't know touched my head. I am sure he did not do so intentionally, Te Ariki, but I need your blessing, I need your blessing, my father.")

And when the new religions of the Pakeha came to Aotearoa they took away much more than the old religions of the Maori. They also took away the tapu of the male in baptism and in the conferring of priesthood, and so the Maori was made noa, without sacredness, all for the Pakeha God.

When my grandfather Ihaka wished to give me his blessing I saw the palms of his hands reaching out to enclose my skull. He had wanted to give me a gift, the mantle of Artemis and his own. But he could also have taken away my tapu. For the matriarch had warned me, "Kia tupato, mokopuna. Be careful. Do not trust your grandfather."

The reports are conflicting, so it is difficult to piece together what actually happened in the dining hall that day. You must remember that this all occurred in 1949 and that time has dimmed the reality and added to the legend that has grown around the incident itself. Even so, I have tried to divine the truth from the pattern, the facts from the flawed recollections. If I could but reconstruct the physical stage for the incident that might help to pinpoint the truth; alas, the dining hall no longer exists, having been burnt to the ground in 1953 when a kerosene lamp fell from a table and its flames caught upon curtains at an open window. Fanned by the wind, the flames roared through the hall and could not be stopped.

But this is the setting: imagine a long hall, medieval in appearance, with a timbered ceiling supported by massive kauri beams. The timbers have been roughly adzed and some bear rudimentary carvings in the shapes of manaia and other mythical creatures. Others have been painted in kowhaiwhai colors, but the smoke and soot of many feasts have discolored the panels. The whole ceiling area is vaulted with darkness, like another world. The sunlight never reaches there, nor the wind. Perhaps this is why the curtains of spider webs have reached such beautiful dimensions, like cathedrals spun with silver, delicate suspensions spun with air.

Beneath that timbered ceiling, far, far below, the people have gathered for the feast. The dining hall is lit by twenty single electric bulbs hanging from the apex of the ceiling. There are seven long tables running the length of the hall with one at each end running across.

The matriarch is seated at one of the end tables in the place reserved for the main guests to the hui. Although she is talking to the private secretary, her eyes are seeking out a small child where he sits with his uncle and aunt. *All this is just for you, e mokopuna, only for you.*

Suddenly, the kitchen doors open. Young women, bearing food in their hands, are singing as they distribute their kono to the guests. There is a roar of approval at the blaze of color and the burst of song, for it is not often now, in these days of the pakeha, that such pageantry is seen.

But quickly now! Look *there*. It is the elder of the paepae. He is like a dark presence moving amid the young men and women. It is he who precipitates the drama of the piece and the appearance of nga pungawerewere.

Oh, if only Uncle Manaaki was still living, for his testimony would have been impeccable. He was the epitome of truth, and his view on the event that happened in the hall would have been authoritative. But he has gone now, gone into Te Po, this uncle, brother to Te Ariki, whom we all loved and cherished.

*Manaaki, Hiraina, guard the child.* In his absence, let me try to reconstruct Uncle Manaaki's part in the drama. First, I don't think he was even aware of the presence of the elder of the paepae. Like the rest of the ope, he must have assumed that the danger was over, now that we had been welcomed on the marae. Second, while there is no doubt that he took his duties of guardianship seriously he had in fact relaxed his guard—but then we all had, even the matriarch. Not one of us could possibly have foreseen the intentions of the elder of the paepae. Third, it is obvious that he was distracted by the theatricals of the occasion. The women skipping like songbirds through the hall. The responsiveness of the guests as they roared with approval. In that melée, he would not have seen the elder suddenly take one of the plaited kono from one of the servers, make a quick authoritative gesture to her, and begin to push his way through the singing women toward me.

Only the matriarch saw it. Or perhaps she was warned of it by witnessing a sudden shuddering of the webbed cathedrals above the gathering. Her mind would have tried to divine the source of the danger. Then she would have seen him, the elder, bearing the kono in both hands, and a smile of triumph on his lips.

Uncle Manaaki was seated to my right. Aunt Hiraina was at my left. I doubt if either of them heard her voice alerting them. But certainly the instruction registered itself forcefully on those nearest the source of the delivery—those seated with the matriarch at her table. The private secretary recalls her sudden cry. ("We were chatting together and, in mid-sentence, I saw her eyes widen with turmoil, and she looked away from me, stood up and started to hunt through the crowd with her eyes. Then suddenly those words hurled like a thunderbolt through my head. But her lips never moved, that is the strangest aspect of all.") Others at the table have verified that the matriarch did call across the space of the hall. The call has been described variously as loud and vibrant, like a taxi message cutting across a radio program, frightening and supernatural, otherworldly and emphatic, lightning in the head. One of the witnesses can recall putting both hands to her ears to protect herself from this invasion into her brain. "I had this absurd notion" she said, "that someone was inside my head. It was an awful feeling, I can assure you."

The witnesses all agree that the voice was the matriarch's and that, coupled with her sudden rising from the table, it focused their attention on her. However, participants at other tables, when questioned, do not recollect hearing her voice at all. What is interesting, though, is that some of the testimony admits to a sudden impression of unease, of premonition, a shiver down the spine, a presence of darkness somewhere in those bright surroundings, a sense of tension. But the brilliance of the occasion seems to have obscured this presence to some degree and, certainly, by the time the young men had entered to perform action songs for their guests, the sensitivity to darkness had largely been dispelled. The men were handsome and virile as they moved towards the stage to perform some waiata. One of the performers recalls an older man, bearing a kono in both hands, whom he almost collided with on his way to the stage. "Hey, old one . . ." he laughed as he went to steady the kono. The old man glared at him, "Be on your way, boy."

The young performer joined the ranks on the stage. "We were all having fun there, just singing for the manuhiri," he told me. "Well, I happened to look up and, you know, I had this funny feeling. I seemed to see a dark haze floating down from the ceiling. It looked like dust."

I have tried to divine the truth from the pattern, the facts from the flawed recollections. It has been so difficult for, once the legend was established, the recollections began to align themselves with that rather than with the reality. But the outlines are clear: there is no doubt that the matriarch called to Uncle Manaaki and Hiraina, *guard the child* (and years later, I called in the same fashion to my daughter, Miranda, and she appeared beside me saying, "Yes, Daddy? You wanted me?"). It is also probable that Manaaki and Hiraina did not hear the warning, but the child did. He turned to look at the matriarch. She was standing there, and she looked so far away. And it seemed as if he was looking through her eyes, and he saw young men moving down the aisles between the tables, singing and dancing on their way to the stage. One of the young men almost collided with an old man, bearing a plaited basket of food in his hands. The old man's face became suffused with ugliness. But he recovered his bearing and, smiling, approached the child.

And now, we must deal with Hiraina's testimony. Dear, sweet, silly Hiraina, she was always one to tell stories and to make me laugh, and that is why I loved her and always will. But she had a penchant for making herself come out smelling like a rose, so her version of the incident is suspect to say the least. Well, Hiraina swears that she *did* hear the voice of Artemis and was aware of the danger all along. She says she tried to get Uncle Manaaki's attention, but that Uncle could not hear her in the hubbub. She says she saw the shadow of the elder from the paepae as he stood behind me and placed the kono on the table. She says that he gave a slight mocking bow both to me and to the matriarch. Then, slowly, and with obscene deliberation, the old man began to lower his hand upon the child's head. And that as he did so, there was stirring in the darkness of the vaulted ceiling and a cloud of fine black dust began to drift down into the hall.

("It was then," the journalist said, "that the matriarch began to chant.") Perhaps his version of the incident, as it appeared in the newspapers, is definitive.

("The sound was soft and guttural," the journalist told me. "It had the presence of death in it. The chant was not a long one, but it was quick, rather like an incantation. An invocation.")

Someone in the crowd screamed.

("She was looking up at the ceiling while she chanted," the journalist said. "I was wondering what she was doing. Then I noticed that dust was falling from the beams. And I saw what I had never seen before—the huge spider webs strung between the rafters.")

All eyes were looking up to the ceiling.

("The webs were beginning to sway and billow," the journalist said, "but there was no wind. Then suddenly, I could see small black shapes, hundreds of them, seething in the bellies of the webs.")

The matriarch stopped the chant.

She drew an unseen line between the webs and the place where the elder from the paepae was standing. His right hand was motionless, above the head of the child.

("By that time," the journalist said, "everybody was aware of the dust and was looking up at the ceiling. There was absolute silence. Stunning silence.")

The matriarch closed her eyes. She gave one, brief, nod.

The web cathedrals suddenly ripped open. As they did so they released hundreds of small black spiders, suspended from crystal threads and falling like a cloud upon the elder from the paepae.

# Katherine Mansfield

One of the most brilliant writers of short fiction in the English Language, Katherine Mansfield (originally Kathleen Mansfield Beauchamp) grew up in Wellington, New Zealand, where she was born into a wealthy family on 14 October 1888. Following the custom of the time, her father sent Mansfield and his three other daughters to a London finishing school in 1903. When they returned five years later, Mansfield found Wellington unbearable and eventually talked her father into allowing her to go back to England, with an allowance of one hundred pounds per year. She arrived in London shortly before her twentieth birthday. Although her life soon fell into disarray—a condition that continued and often worsened through the years, she published in 1911 her first collection of short stories, *In a German Pension*. In spite of recurrent illness and depression, personal problems, and financial difficulties, Mansfield managed to harness her creativity and published four more collections before her death in France from tuberculosis on 9 January 1923. Her husband, John Middleton Murry, edited additional volumes of stories as well as selections from her poetry, journals, and letters, which appeared posthumously. In recent years editions of more poems, letters, and dramatic sketches have been published.

But it is for the short story that Mansfield will be remembered. Some critics have noted that Mansfield experimented so endlessly that she failed to develop a distinctive style. That constant experimentation, though, lends the stories their singular character and constitutes the elusive style. No two are alike, even as recurrent themes emerge: family relationships; lack of communication in romantic relationships; class distinctions; loneliness and isolation; the victimization of women and the acceptance of their condition; and the weakness of men in spite of their effort to dominate. Mansfield manipulates plot and character in such original and striking ways that each story extends its meaning in diverse directions and insinuates thematic variations.

Much of Mansfield's fiction is set in various parts of Europe and reflects the disjointed life she led there for fifteen or so years. Still, the stories only border on the autobiographical, for Mansfield sifts experience and restates it in fictional terms that probe the human condition with uncanny accuracy. Mansfield never returned to New Zealand, but she drew material from her childhood years for some of her best stories, such as her most widely known work, "The Garden Party." Although the labor of memory, the New Zealand stories avoid sentimentality in their candid depiction of family relationships, social pretensions, and class distinctions. These stories may also present some of the clearest images of nineteenth-century colonial life as played out by a successful, business-oriented family. Imitating British ways in the remote colony, they considered themselves more closely tied to their spiritual home, England, than to their actual home. This theme surfaces in much of the early literature from the settler countries.

"The Woman at the Store" depicts colonial life at its worst. Of course the crudity and the isolation contrasted dramatically with Mansfield's privileged life in Wellington, but were not uncommon conditions in the colony. During a horseback trip through the volcanic area of New Zealand's North Island, Mansfield and her friends camped in a valley similar to the one described in the story and there met the original woman at the store. A few years later in Europe, Mansfield converted that memory into compelling fiction about colonial life and the way its harshness victimized women.

# The Woman at the Store

All that day the heat was terrible. The wind blew close to the ground; it rooted among the tussock grass, slithered along the road, so that the white pumice dust swirled in our faces, settled and sifted over us and was like a dry-skin itching for growth on our bodies. The horses stumbled along, coughing and chuffing. The pack horse was sick—with a big, open sore rubbed under the belly. Now and again she stopped short, threw back her head, looked at us as though she were going to cry, and whinnied. Hundreds of larks shrilled; the sky was slate color, and the sound of the larks reminded me of slate pencils scraping over its surface. There was nothing to be seen but wave after wave of tussock grass, patched with purple orchids and manuka bushes covered with thick spider webs.

Jo rode ahead. He wore a blue galatea shirt, corduroy trousers and riding boots. A white handkerchief, spotted with red—it looked as though his nose had been bleeding on it—was knotted round his throat. Wisps of white hair straggled from under his wideawake—his mustache and eyebrows were called white—he slouched in the saddle, grunting. Not once that day had he sung

"I don't care, for don't you see,
My wife's mother was in front of me!"

It was the first day we had been without it for a month, and now there seemed something uncanny in his silence. Jim rode beside me, white as a clown; his black eyes glittered, and he kept shooting out his tongue and moistening his lips. He was dressed in a Jaeger vest, and a pair of blue duck

From *Something Childish and Other Stories*, Constable and Co. Ltd., 1924. First published in *Rhythm*, Spring 1911.

trousers, fastened round the waist with a plaited leather belt. We had hardly spoken since dawn. At noon we had lunched off fly biscuits and apricots by the side of a swampy creek.

"My stomach feels like the crop of a hen," said Jo. "Now then, Jim, you're the bright boy of the party—where's this 'ere store you kep' on talking about? 'Oh, yes,' you says, 'I know a fine store, with a paddock for the horses and a creek runnin' through, owned by a friend of mine who'll give yer a bottle of whisky before 'e shakes hands with yer.' I'd like ter see that place— merely as a matter of curiosity—not that I'd ever doubt yer word—as yer know very well—but . . ."

Jim laughed. "Don't forget there's a woman too, Jo, with blue eyes and yellow hair, who'll promise you something else before she shakes hands with you. Put that in your pipe and smoke it."

"The heat's making you balmy," said Jo. But he dug his knees into the horse. We shambled on. I half fell asleep, and had a sort of uneasy dream that the horses were not moving forward at all—then that I was on a rocking- horse, and my old mother was scolding me for raising such a fearful dust from the drawing-room carpet. "You've entirely worn off the pattern of the carpet," I heard her saying, and she gave the reins a tug. I sniveled and woke to find Jim leaning over me, maliciously smiling.

"That was a case of all but," said he. "I just caught you. What's up? Been bye-bye?"

"No!" I raised my head. "Thank the Lord we're arriving somewhere."

We were on the brow of the hill, and below us there was a whare roofed with corrugated iron. It stood in a garden, rather far back from the road—a big paddock opposite, and a creek and a clump of young willow trees. A thin line of blue smoke stood up straight from the chimney of the whare; and as I looked a woman came out, followed by a child and a sheep dog—the woman carrying what appeared to me a black stick. She made gestures at us. The horses put on a final spurt, Jo took off his wideawake, shouted, threw out his chest, and began singing, "I don't care, for don't you see. . . ." The sun pushed through the pale clouds and shed a vivid light over the scene. It gleamed on the woman's yellow hair, over her flapping pinafore and the rifle she was car- rying. The child hid behind her, and the yellow dog, a mangy beast, scuttled back into the whare, his tail between his legs. We drew rein and dismounted.

"Hallo," screamed the woman. "I thought you was three 'awks. My kid comes runnin' in ter me. 'Mumma,' says she, 'there's three brown things comin' over the 'ill,' says she. An' I comes out smart, I can tell yer. 'They'll be 'awks,' I says to her. Oh, the 'awks about 'ere yer wouldn't believe."

The "kid" gave us the benefit of one eye from behind the woman's pinafore—then retired again.

"Where's your old man?" asked Jim.

The woman blinked rapidly, screwing up her face.

"Away shearin'. Bin away a month. I suppose yer not goin' to stop, are yer? There's a storm comin' up."

"You bet we are," said Jo. "So you're on your lonely, missus?"

She stood, pleating the frills of her pinafore, and glancing from one to the other of us, like a hungry bird. I smiled at the thought of how Jim had pulled Jo's leg about her. Certainly her eyes were blue, and what hair she had was yellow, but ugly. She was a figure of fun. Looking at her, you felt there was nothing but sticks and wires under that pinafore—her front teeth were knocked out, she had red pulpy hands, and she wore on her feet a pair of dirty Bluchers.

"I'll go and turn out the horses," said Jim. "Got any embrocation? Poi's rubbed herself to hell!"

"'Arf a mo!" The woman stood silent a moment, her nostrils expanding as she breathed. Then she shouted violently. "I'd rather you didn't stop. . . . You *can't,* and there's the end of it. I don't let out that paddock any more. You'll have to go on; I ain't got nothing!"

"Well, I'm blest!" said Jo, heavily. He pulled me aside. "Gone a bit off 'er dot," he whispered. "Too much alone, *you know,*" very significantly. "Turn the sympathetic tap on 'er, she'll come round all right."

But there was no need—she had come round by herself.

"Stop if yer like!" she muttered shrugging her shoulders. To me—"I'll give yer the embrocation if yer come along."

"Right-o, I'll take it down to them." We walked together up the garden path. It was planted on both sides with cabbages. They smelled like stale dishwater. Of flowers there were double poppies and sweet-williams. One little patch was divided off by pawa shells—presumably it belonged to the child—for she ran from her mother and began to grub in it with a broken clothes-peg. The yellow dog lay across the doorstep, biting fleas; the woman kicked him away.

"Gar-r, get away, you beast . . . the place ain't tidy. I 'aven't 'ad time ter fix things to-day—been ironing. Come right in."

It was a large room, the walls plastered with old pages of English periodicals. Queen Victoria's Jubilee appeared to be the most recent number. A table with an ironing board and wash tub on it, some wooden forms, a black horsehair sofa, and some broken cane chairs pushed against the walls. The mantelpiece above the stove was draped in pink paper, further ornamented with dried grasses and ferns and a colored print of Richard Seddon. There were four doors—one, judging from the smell, let into the "Store," one on to the "back yard," through a third I saw the bedroom. Flies buzzed in circles round the ceiling, and treacle papers and bundles of dried clover were pinned to the window curtains.

I was alone in the room; she had gone into the store for the embrocation. I heard her stamping about and muttering to herself: "I got some, now where did I put that bottle? . . . It's behind the pickles . . . no, it ain't." I cleared a place on the table and sat there, swinging my legs. Down in the paddock I could hear Jo singing and the sound of hammer strokes as Jim drove in the tent pegs. It was sunset. There is no twilight in our New Zealand days, but a curious half-hour when everything appears grotesque—it frightens—as though the savage spirit of the country walked abroad and sneered at what it saw. Sitting alone in the hideous room I grew afraid. The woman next door was a long time finding that stuff. What was she doing in there? Once I thought I heard her bang her hands down on the counter, and once she half moaned, turning it into a cough and clearing her throat. I wanted to shout "Buck up!" but I kept silent.

"Good Lord, what a life!" I thought. "Imagine being here day in, day out, with that rat of a child and a mangy dog. Imagine bothering about ironing. *Mad,* of course she's mad! Wonder how long she's been here—wonder if I could get her to talk."

At that moment she poked her head round the door.

"Wot was it yer wanted?" she asked.

"Embrocation."

"Oh, I forgot. I got it, it was in front of the pickle jars."

She handed me the bottle.

"My, you do look tired, you do! Shall I knock yer up a few scones for supper! There's some tongue in the store, too, and I'll cook yer a cabbage if you fancy it."

"Right-o." I smiled at her. "Come down to the paddock and bring the kid for tea."

She shook her head, pursing up her mouth.

"Oh no. I don't fancy it. I'll send the kid down with the things and a billy of milk. Shall I knock up a few extry scones to take with yer ter-morrow?"

"Thanks."

She came and stood by the door.

"How old is the kid?"

"Six—come next Christmas. I 'ad a bit of trouble with 'er one way an' another. I 'adn't any milk till a month after she was born and she sickened like a cow."

"She's not like you—takes after her father?" just as the woman had shouted her refusal at us before, she shouted at me then.

"No, she don't! She's the dead spit of me. Any fool could see that. Come on in now, Else, you stop messing in the dirt."

I met Jo climbing over the paddock fence.

"What's the old bitch got in the store?" he asked.

"Don't know—didn't look."

"Well, of all the fools. Jim's slanging you. What have you been doing all the time?"

"She couldn't find this stuff. Oh, my shakes, you are smart!"

Jo had washed, combed his wet hair in a line across his forehead, and buttoned a coat over his shirt. He grinned.

Jim snatched the embrocation from me. I went to the end of the paddock where the willows grew and bathed in the creek. The water was clear and soft as oil. Along the edges held by the grass and rushes, white foam tumbled and bubbled. I lay in the water and looked up at the trees that were still a moment, then quivered lightly, and again were still. The air smelt of rain. I forgot about the woman and the kid until I came back to the tent. Jim lay by the fire, watching the billy boil.

I asked where Jo was, and if the kid had brought our supper.

"Pooh," said Jim, rolling over and looking up at the sky. "Didn't you see how Jo had been titivating? He said to me before he went up to the whare, 'Dang it! she'll look better by night light—at any rate, my buck, she's female flesh!' "

"You had Jo about her looks—you had me, too."

"No—look here. I can't make it out. It's four years since I came past this way, and I stopped here two days. The husband was a pal of mine once, down the West Coast—a fine, big chap, with a voice on him like a trombone. She'd been barmaid down the Coast—as pretty as a wax doll. The coach used to come this way then once a fortnight, that was before they opened the railway up Napier way, and she had no end of a time! Told me once in a confidential moment that she knew one hundred and twenty-five different ways of kissing!"

"Oh, go on, Jim! She isn't the same woman!"

"Course she is. . . . I can't make it out. What I think is the old man's cleared out and left her: that's all my eye about shearing. Sweet life! The only people who come through now are Maoris and sundowners!"

Through the dark we saw the gleam of the kid's pinafore. She trailed over to us with a basket in her hand, the milk billy in the other. I unpacked the basket, the child standing by.

"Come over here," said Jim, snapping his fingers at her.

She went, the lamp from the inside of the tent cast a bright light over her. A mean, undersized brat, with whitish hair, and weak eyes. She stood, legs wide apart and her stomach protruding.

"What do you do all day?" asked Jim.

She scraped out one ear with her little finger, looked at the result and said, "Draw."

"Huh! What do you draw? Leave your ears alone!"

"Pictures."

"What on?"

"Bits of butter paper an' a pencil of my Mumma's."

"Boh! What a lot of words at one time!" Jim rolled his eyes at her. "Baa-lambs and moo-cows?"

"No, everything. I'll draw all of you when you're gone, and your horses and the tent, and that one"—she pointed to me—"with no clothes on in the creek. I looked at her where she couldn't see me from."

"Thanks very much. How ripping of you," said Jim. "Where's Dad?"

The kid pouted. "I won't tell you because I don't like yer face!" She started operations on the other ear.

"Here," I said. "Take the basket, get along home and tell the other man supper's ready."

"I don't want to."

"I'll give you a box on the ear if you don't," said Jim, savagely.

"Hie! I'll tell Mumma. I'll tell Mumma." The kid fled.

We ate until we were full, and had arrived at the smoke stage before Jo came back, very flushed and jaunty, a whisky bottle in his hand.

"'Ave a drink—you two!" he shouted, carrying off matters with a high hand. "'Ere, shove along the cups."

"One hundred and twenty-five different ways," I murmured to Jim.

"What's that? Oh! stow it!" said Jo. "Why 'ave you always got your knife into me? You gas like a kid at a Sunday School beano. She wants us to go up there to-night, and have a comfortable chat. I"—he waved his hand airily—"I got 'er round."

"Trust you for that," laughed Jim. "But did she tell you where the old man's got to?"

Jo looked up. "Shearing! You 'eard 'er, you fool!"


The woman had fixed up the room, even to a light bouquet of sweet-williams on the table. She and I sat one side of the table, Jo and Jim the other. An oil lamp was set between us, the whisky bottle and glasses, and a jug of water. The kid knelt against one of the forms, drawing on butter paper. I wondered, grimly, if she was attempting the creek episode. But Jo had been right about night time. The woman's hair was tumbled—two red spots burned in her cheeks—her eyes shone—and we knew that they were kissing feet under the table. She had changed the blue pinafore for a white calico dressing jacket and a black skirt—the kid was decorated to the extent of a blue sateen hair ribbon. In the stifling room, with the flies buzzing against the ceiling and dropping on to the table, we got slowly drunk.

"Now listen to me," shouted the woman, banging her fist on the table. "It's six years since I was married, and four miscarriages. I says to 'im, I says, what do you think I'm doin' up 'ere? If you was back at the coast, I'd 'ave you lynched for child murder. Over and over I tells 'im—you've broken my spirit and spoiled my looks, and wot for—that's wot I'm driving at." She clutched her head with her hands and stared round at us. Speaking rapidly, "Oh, some days—an' months of them—I 'ear them two words knockin' inside me all the time—'Wot for!' but sometimes I'll be cooking the spuds an' I lifts the lid off to give 'em a prong and I 'ears, quite sudden again, 'Wot for!' Oh! I don't mean only the spuds and the kid—I mean—I mean," she hiccoughed—"you know what I mean, Mr. Jo."

"I know," said Jo, scratching his head.

"Trouble with me is," she leaned across the table, "he left me too much alone. When the coach stopped coming, sometimes he'd go away days, some-times he'd go away weeks, and leave me ter look after the store. Back 'e'd come—pleased as Punch. 'Oh, 'allo,' 'e'd say. ''Ow are you gettin' on. Come and give us a kiss.' Sometimes I'd turn a bit nasty, and then 'e'd go off again, and if I took it all right, 'e'd wait till 'e could twist me round 'is finger, then 'e'd say, 'Well, so long, I'm off,' and do you think I could keep 'im?—not me!"

"Mumma," bleated the kid, "I made a picture of them on the 'ill an' you an' me, an' the dog down below."

"Shut your mouth!" said the woman.

A vivid flash of lightning played over the room—we heard the mutter of thunder.

"Good thing that's broke loose," said Jo. "I've 'ad it in me 'ead for three days."

"Where's your old man now?" asked Jim, slowly.

The woman blubbered and dropped her head on to the table. "Jim, 'e's gone shearin' and left me alone again," she wailed.

"'Ere, look out for the glasses," said Jo. "Cheer-o, 'ave another drop. No good cryin' over spilt 'usbands! You Jim, you blasted cuckoo!"

"Mr. Jo," said the woman, drying her eyes on her jacket frill, "you're a gent, an' if I was a secret woman, I'd place any confidence in your 'ands. I don't mind if I do 'ave a glass on that."

Every moment the lightning grew more vivid and the thunder sounded nearer. Jim and I were silent—the kid never moved from her bench. She poked her tongue out and blew on her paper as she drew.

"It's the loneliness," said the woman, addressing Jo—he made sheep's eyes at her—"and bein' shut up 'ere like a broody 'en." He reached his hand across the table and held hers, and though the position looked most uncom-fortable when they wanted to pass the water and whisky, their hands stuck to-gether as though glued. I pushed back my chair and went over to the kid, who immediately sat flat down on her artistic achievements and made a face at me.

"You're not to look," said she.

"Oh, come on, don't be nasty!" Jim came over to us, and we were just drunk enough to wheedle the kid into showing us. And those drawings of hers were extraordinary and repulsively vulgar. The creations of a lunatic with a lunatic's cleverness. There was no doubt about it, the kid's mind was diseased. While she showed them to us, she worked herself up into a mad excitement, laughing and trembling, and shooting out her arms.

"Mumma," she yelled. "Now I'm going to draw them what you told me I never was to—now I am."

The woman rushed from the table and beat the child's head with the flat of her hand,

"I'll smack you with yer clothes turned up if yer dare say that again," she bawled.

Jo was too drunk to notice, but Jim caught her by the arm. The kid did not utter a cry. She drifted over to the window and began picking flies from the treacle paper.

We returned to the table—Jim and I sitting one side, the woman and Jo, touching shoulders, the other. We listened to the thunder, saying stupidly, "That was a near one," "There it goes again," and Jo, at a heavy hit, "Now we're off," "Steady on the brake," until rain began to fall, sharp as cannon shot on the iron roof.

"You'd better doss here for the night," said the woman.

"That's right," assented Jo, evidently in the know about this move.

"Bring up yer things from the tent. You two can doss in the store along with the kid —she's used to sleep in there and won't mind you."

"Oh Mumma, I never did," interrupted the kid.

"Shut yer lies! An' Mr. Jo can 'ave this room."

It sounded a ridiculous arrangement, but it was useless to attempt to cross them, they were too far gone. While the woman sketched the plan of action, Jo sat, abnormally solemn and red, his eyes bulging, and pulling at his mustache.

"Give us a lantern," said Jim, "I'll go down to the paddock." We two went together. Rain whipped in our faces, the land was light as though a bush fire was raging. We behaved like two children let loose in the thick of an adventure, laughed and shouted to each other, and came back to the whare to find the kid already bedded in the counter of the store. The woman brought us a lamp. Jo took his bundle from Jim, the door was shut.

"Good-night all," shouted Jo.

Jim and I sat on two sacks of potatoes. For the life of us we could not stop laughing. Strings of onions and half-hams dangled from the ceiling—wherever we looked there were advertisements for "Camp Coffee" and tinned meats. We pointed at them, tried to read them aloud—overcome with laughter and hiccoughs. The kid in the counter stared at us. She threw off her blanket and scrambled to the floor, where she stood in her gray flannel nightgown, rubbing one leg against the other. We paid no attention to her.

"Wot are you laughing at?" she said, uneasily.

"You!" shouted Jim. "The red tribe of you, my child."

She flew into a rage and beat herself with her hands. "I won't be laughed at, you curs—you." He swooped down upon the child and swung her on to the counter.

"Go to sleep, Miss Smarty—or make a drawing—here's a pencil—you can use Mumma's account book."

Through the rain we heard Jo creak over the boarding of the next room—the sound of a door being opened—then shut to.

"It's the loneliness," whispered Jim.

"One hundred and twenty-five different ways—alas! my poor brother!"

The kid tore out a page and flung it at me.

"There you are," she said. "Now I done it ter spite Mumma for shutting me up 'ere with you two. I done the one she told me I never ought to. I done the one she told me she'd shoot me if I did. Don't care! Don't care!"

The kid had drawn the picture of the woman shooting at a man with a rook rifle and then digging a hole to bury him in.

She jumped off the counter and squirmed about on the floor biting her nails.

Jim and I sat till dawn with the drawing beside us. The rain ceased, the little kid fell asleep, breathing loudly. We got up, stole out of the whare, down into the paddock. White clouds floated over a pink sky—a chill wind blew; the air smelled of wet grass. Just as we swung into the saddle Jo came out of the whare—he motioned to us to ride on.

"I'll pick you up later," he shouted.

A bend in the road, and the whole place disappeared.

# Henry Lawson

One of Australia's cherished writers from the colonial era, Henry Lawson was born in the outback region of New South Wales in 1867. As a child, he grew up in poverty, received only a scattered education, suffered deafness from the age of nine, and endured the marital conflicts between his mother and father. In 1883 his parents separated, and his mother moved to Sydney where she involved herself in the women's movement and publishing. Lawson joined her and by 1887 he had started to publish poems and short stories.

Once he was established as a regular contributor to the *Bulletin*, Australia's venerable newspaper and literary journal, Lawson received funds to make a trip into the outback and there gathered material for his best stories. Several volumes of his bush tales appeared in quick succession and found a wide audience. Ironically, this literary spokesman for the arduous life in Australia's outback actually spent most of his days in Sydney. After marrying, he and his wife lived for periods in New Zealand and England. In 1902, his marriage failing, his inspiration sagging, and his appetite for alcohol increasing, Lawson started to disintegrate personally, and his best work lay behind him. Although he eventually received a state pension, he spent time during these years both in prison and in mental hospitals, and depended often on faithful friends for care and lodging, or wandered Sydney streets trying to cadge a drink. He died in 1922, and was given a state funeral. Today his picture appears on the Australian ten-dollar bill. Several biographies and authoritative editions of his work have been published in recent years.

In spite of Lawson's personal problems, his popularity with the Australian public never flagged—and still has not. He has been called "the poet of the people," who in his fiction and poetry articulated the true voice and sensibility of Australians. Today his prose is more widely read and appreciated than the poetry. While his fiction appears deceptively simple, almost documentary at times, he renders the bush world in genuine and unforgettable tones.

"The Drover's Wife" remains one of Australia's favorite short stories. Characteristic of Lawson's fiction, the account seems almost prosaic. The woman accepts her lot and faces every hardship the bush has to serve up— fire, drought, flood, isolation and loneliness, snakes, disreputable intruders, and countless other dangers. "Her surroundings are not favorable to the development of the 'womanly' or sentimental side of nature," the narrator says. Yet she overcomes these outward calamities and remains "womanly"—or simply human—within. And her son's promise at the end of the story lends resonance to the drover's wife's spiritual victory. In this story, as in all of his best work, Lawson celebrates the colonizers' life in the bush, never romanticizing it or ignoring the hardships. Instead he reveals both the trials and the personal triumphs.

# The Drover's Wife

The two-roomed house is built of round timber, slabs, and stringy-bark, and floored with split slabs. A big bark kitchen standing at one end is larger than the house itself, veranda included.

Bush all round—bush with no horizon, for the country is flat. No ranges in the distance. The bush consists of stunted, rotten native apple-trees. No undergrowth. Nothing to relieve the eye save the darker green of a few she-oaks which are sighing above the narrow, almost waterless creek. Nineteen miles to the nearest sign of civilization—a shanty on the main road.

The drover, an ex-squatter, is away with sheep. His wife and children are left here alone.

Four ragged, dried-up-looking children are playing about the house. Suddenly one of them yells: "Snake! Mother, here's a snake!"

The gaunt, sun-browned bushwoman dashes from the kitchen, snatches her baby from the ground, holds it on her left hip, and reaches for a stick.

"Where is it?"

"Here! gone into the wood-heap!" yells the eldest boy—a sharp-faced urchin of eleven. "Stop there, mother! I'll have him. Stand back! I'll have the beggar!"

"Tommy, come here, or you'll be bit. Come here at once when I tell you, you little wretch!"

The youngster comes reluctantly, carrying a stick bigger than himself. Then he yells, triumphantly:

"There it goes—under the house!" and darts away with club uplifted. At the same time the big, black, yellow-eyed dog-of-all-breeds, who has shown the wildest interest in the proceedings, breaks his chain and rushes after that snake. He is a moment late, however, and his nose reaches the crack in the

From *While the Billy Boils* by Henry Lawson, 1896.

slabs just as the end of its tail disappears. Almost at the same moment the boy's club comes down and skins the aforesaid nose. Alligator takes small notice of this, and proceeds to undermine the building; but he is subdued after a struggle and chained up. They cannot afford to lose him.

The drover's wife makes the children stand together near the dog-house while she watches for the snake. She gets two small dishes of milk and sets them down near the wall to tempt it to come out; but an hour goes by and it does not show itself.

It is near sunset, and a thunderstorm is coming. The children must be brought inside. She will not take them into the house, for she knows the snake is there, and may at any moment come up through a crack in the rough slab floor; so she carries several armfuls of firewood into the kitchen, and then takes the children there. The kitchen has no floor—or rather, an earthen one— called a "ground floor" in this part of the bush. There is a large, roughly-made table in the center of the place. She brings the children in, and makes them get on this table. They are two boys and two girls—mere babies. She gives them some supper, and then before it gets dark, she goes into the house, and snatches up some pillows and bedclothes—expecting to see or lay her hand on the snake any minute. She makes a bed on the kitchen table for the children, and sits down beside it to watch all night.

She has an eye on the corner, and a green sapling club laid in readiness on the dresser by her side; also her sewing basket and a copy of the *Young Ladies' Journal.* She has brought the dog into the room.

Tommy turns in, under protest, but says he'll lie awake all night and smash that blinded snake.

His mother asks him how many times she has told him not to swear.

He has his club with him under the bedclothes, and Jacky protests:

"Mummy! Tommy's skinnin' me alive wif his club. Make him take it out."

Tommy: "Shet up, you little ——! D'yer want to be bit with the snake?"

Jacky shuts up.

"If yer bit," says Tommy, after a pause, "you'll swell up, an' smell, an' turn red an' green an' blue all over till yer bust. Won't he, mother?"

"Now then, don't frighten the child. Go to sleep," she says.

The two younger children go to sleep, and now and then Jacky complains of being "skeezed." More room is made for him. Presently Tommy says: "Mother! listen to them (adjective) little possums. I'd like to screw their blanky necks."

And Jacky protests drowsily.

"But they don't hurt us, the little blanks!"

Mother: "There, I told you you'd teach Jacky to swear." But the remark makes her smile. Jacky goes to sleep.

Presently Tommy asks:

"Mother! Do you think they'll ever extricate the (adjective) kangaroo?"

"Lord! How am I to know, child? Go to sleep."

"Will you wake me if the snake comes out?"

"Yes. Go to sleep."

Near midnight. The children are all asleep and she sits there still, sewing and reading by turns. From time to time she glances round the floor and wall-plate, and, whenever she hears a noise, she reaches for the stick. The thunder-storm comes on, and the wind, rushing through the cracks in the slab wall, threatens to blow out her candle. She places it on a sheltered part of the dresser and fixes up a newspaper to protect it. At every flash of lightning, the cracks between the slabs gleam like polished silver. The thunder rolls, and the rain comes down in torrents.

Alligator lies at full length on the floor, with his eyes turned towards the partition. She knows by this that the snake is there. There are large cracks in that wall opening under the floor of the dwelling-house.

She is not a coward, but recent events have shaken her nerves. A little son of her brother-in-law was lately bitten by a snake, and died. Besides, she has not heard from her husband for six months, and is anxious about him.

He was a drover, and started squatting here when they were married. The drought of '18— ruined him. He had to sacrifice the remnant of his flock and go droving again. He intends to move his family into the nearest town when he comes back, and, in the meantime, his brother, who keeps a shanty on the main road, comes over about once a month with provisions. The wife has still a couple of cows, one horse, and a few sheep. The brother-in-law kills one of the latter occasionally, gives her what she needs of it, and takes the rest in return for other provisions,

She is used to being left alone. She once lived like this for eighteen months. As a girl she built the usual castles in the air; but all her girlish hopes and aspirations have long been dead. She finds all the excitement and recreation she needs in the *Young Ladies' Journal*, and Heaven help her! takes a pleasure in the fashion-plates.

Her husband is an Australian, and so is she. He is careless, but a good enough husband. If he had the means he would take her to the city and keep her there like a princess. They are used to being apart, or at least she is. "No use fretting," she says. He may forget sometimes that he is married; but if he has a good check when he comes back he will give most of it to her. When he had money he took her to the city several times—hired a railway sleeping compartment, and put up at the best hotels. He also bought her a buggy, but they had to sacrifice that along with the rest.

The last two children were born in the bush—one while her husband was bringing a drunken doctor, by force, to attend to her. She was alone on this occasion and very weak. She had been ill with a fever. She prayed to God to send her assistance. God sent Black Mary—the "whitest" gin in all the land.

Or, at least, God sent King Jimmy first, and he sent Black Mary. He put his black face round the door post, took in the situation at a glance, and said cheerfully: "All right, missus—I bring my old woman, she down alonga creek."

One of the children died while she was here alone. She rode nineteen miles for assistance, carrying the dead child.

It must be near one or two o'clock. The fire is burning low. Alligator lies with his head resting on his paws, and watches the wall. He is not a very beautiful dog, and the light shows numerous old wounds where the hair will not grow. He is afraid of nothing on the face of the earth or under it. He will tackle a bullock as readily as he will tackle a flea. He hates all other dogs—except kangaroo dogs—and has a marked dislike to friends or relations of the family. They seldom call, however. He sometimes makes friends with strangers. He hates snakes and has killed many, but he will be bitten some day and die; most snake-dogs end that way.

Now and then the bushwoman lays down her work and watches, and listens, and thinks. She thinks of things in her own life, for there is little else to think about.

The rain will make the grass grow, and this reminds her how she fought a bush-fire once while her husband was away. The grass was long, and very dry, and the fire threatened to burn her out. She put on an old pair of her husband's trousers and beat out the flames with a green bough, till great drops of sooty perspiration stood out on her forehead and ran in streaks down her blackened arms. The sight of his mother in trousers greatly amused Tommy, who worked like a little hero by her side, but the terrified baby howled lustily for his "mummy." The fire would have mastered her but for four excited bushmen who arrived in the nick of time. It was a mixed-up affair all round; when she went to take up the baby he screamed and struggled convulsively, thinking it was a "blackman," and Alligator, trusting more to the child's sense than his own instinct, charged furiously, and (being old and slightly deaf) did not in his excitement at first recognize his mistress's voice, but continued to hang on to the moleskins until choked off by Tommy with a saddle-strap. The dog's sorrow for his blunder, and his anxiety to let it be known that it was all a mistake, was as evident as his ragged tail and a twelve-inch grin could make it. It was a glorious time for the boys; a day to look back to, and talk about, and laugh over for many years.

She thinks how she fought a flood during her husband's absence. She stood for hours in the drenching downpour, and dug an overflow gutter to save the dam across the creek. But she could not save it. There are things that a bushwoman cannot do. Next morning the dam was broken, and her heart was nearly broken too, for she thought how her husband would feel when he came home and saw the result of years of labor swept away. She cried then.

She also fought the pleuro-pneumonia—dosed and bled the few remaining cattle, and wept again when her two best cows died.

Again, she fought a mad bullock that besieged the house for a day. She made bullets and fired at him through cracks in the slabs with an old shot-gun. He was dead in the morning. She skinned him and got seventeen-and-sixpence for the hide.

She also fights the crows and eagles that have designs on her chickens. Her plan of campaign is very original. The children cry "Crows, mother!" and she rushes out and aims a broomstick at the birds as though it were a gun, and says "Bung!" The crows leave in a hurry; they are cunning, but a woman's cunning is greater.

Occasionally a bushman in the horrors, or a villainous-looking sundowner, comes and nearly scares the life out of her. She generally tells the suspicious-looking stranger that her husband and two sons are at work below the dam, or over at the yard, for he always cunningly inquires for the boss.

Only last week a gallows-faced swagman—having satisfied himself that there were no men on the place—threw his swag down on the veranda, and demanded tucker. She gave him something to eat; then he expressed his intention of staying for the night. It was sundown then. She got a batten from the sofa, loosened the dog, and confronted the stranger, holding the batten in one hand and the dog's collar with the other. "Now you go!" she said. He looked at her and at the dog. said "All right, mum," in a cringing tone, and left. She was a determined-looking woman, and Alligator's yellow eyes glared unpleasantly—besides, the dog's chawing-up apparatus greatly resembled that of the reptile he was named after.

She has few pleasures to think of as she sits here alone by the fire, on guard against the snake. All days are much the same to her; but on Sunday afternoon she dresses herself, tidies the children, smartens up baby, and goes for a lonely walk along the bush-track, pushing an old perambulator in front of her. She does this every Sunday. She takes as much care to make herself and the children look smart as she would if she were going to do the block in the city. There is nothing to see, however. and not a soul to meet. You might walk for twenty miles along this track without being able to fix a point in your mind, unless you are a bushman. This is because of the everlasting, maddening sameness of the stunted trees—that monotony which makes a man long to break away and travel as far as trains can go, and sail as far as ship can sail—and further.

But this bushwoman is used to the loneliness of it. As a girl-wife she hated it, but now she would feel strange away from it.

She is glad when her husband returns, but she does not gush or make a fuss about it. She gets him something good to eat, and tidies up the children.

She seems contented with her lot. She loves her children, but has no time to show it. She seems harsh to them. Her surroundings are not favorable to the development of the "womanly" or sentimental side of nature.

It must be near morning now; but the clock is in the dwelling-house. Her candle is nearly done; she forgot that she was out of candles. Some more wood must be got to keep the fire up, and so she shuts the dog inside and hurries round to the wood-heap. The rain has cleared off. She seizes a stick, pulls it out and—crash! the whole pile collapses.

Yesterday she bargained with a stray blackfellow to bring her some wood, and while he was at work she went in search of a missing cow. She was absent an hour or so, and the native black made good use of his time. On her return she was so astonished to see a good heap of wood by the chimney, that she gave him an extra fig of tobacco, and praised him for not being lazy. He thanked her, and left with head erect and chest well out. He was the last of his tribe and a King; but he had built that wood-heap hollow.

She is hurt now, and tears spring to her eyes as she sits down again by the table. She takes up a handkerchief to wipe the tears away, but pokes her eyes with her bare fingers instead. The handkerchief is full of holes, and she finds that she has put her thumb through one, and her forefinger through another.

This makes her laugh, to the surprise of the dog. She has a keen, very keen, sense of the ridiculous, and some time or other she will amuse bushmen with the story.

She had been amused before like that. One day she sat down "to have a good cry," as she said—and the old cat rubbed against her dress and "cried too." Then she had to laugh.

It must be near daylight now. The room is very close and hot because of the fire. Alligator still watches the wall from time to time. Suddenly he becomes greatly interested; he draws himself a few inches nearer the partition, and a thrill runs through his body. The hair on the back of his neck begins to bristle, and the battle-light is in his yellow eyes. She knows what this means, and lays her hand on the stick. The lower end of one of the partition slabs has a large crack on both sides. An evil pair of small bright bead-like eyes glistens at one of these holes. The snake—a black one—comes slowly out, about a foot, and moves its head up and down. The dog lies still, and the woman sits as one fascinated. The snake comes out a foot further. She lifts her stick, and the reptile, as though suddenly aware of danger, sticks his head in through the crack on the other side of the slab, and hurries to get his tail round after him. Alligator springs. and his jaws come together with a snap. He misses, for his nose is large, and the snake's body close down in the angle formed by the slabs and the floor. He snaps again as the tail comes round. He has the snake now, and tugs it out eighteen inches. Thud, thud, comes the woman's club on the ground. Alligator pulls again. Thud, thud. Alligator gives another pull and he has the snake out—a black brute, five feet long. The head rises to dart about, but the dog has the enemy close to the neck. He is a big, heavy dog, but quick as a terrier. He shakes the snake as though he felt the original curse in common with mankind. The eldest boy wakes up, seizes his stick, and tries to get out of bed, but his mother forces him back with a grip of iron. Thud, thud—the snake's back is broken in several places. Thud. thud—its head is crushed, and Alligator's nose skinned again.

She lifts the mangled reptile on the point of her stick, carries it to the fire, and throws it in; then piles on the wood and watches the snake burn. The boy and dog watch too. She lays her hand on the dog's head, and all the fierce, angry light dies out of his yellow eyes. The younger children are quieted, and presently go to sleep. The dirty-legged boy stands for a moment in his shirt, watching the fire. Presently he looks up at her, sees the tears in her eyes, and, throwing his arms round her neck exclaims:

"Mother, I won't never go drovin'."

And she hugs him to her breast and kisses him; and they sit thus together while the sickly daylight breaks over the bush.

# Olive Schreiner

Olive Schreiner has earned a secure place as South Africa's first important novelist, and is acknowledged as well as one of the first colonial writers to gain international attention. The ninth of twelve children, Schreiner was born on 24 March 1855 in a remote area of the Cape Colony where her German-born father, along with his English wife, served as a missionary. When he lost his post for violation of trading regulations, the destitute family scattered. Shifting from one household of friends or relatives to another, Schreiner never received a formal education, but read widely in the works of such writers as Herbert Spenser, John Stuart Mill, Charles Darwin, Goethe, Ralph Waldo Emerson, and Thomas Carlyle. From 1876 to 1880 she worked as a governess on isolated farms. In 1881 she went to England, taking along her manuscript of *The Story of an African Farm*. After several rejections, the novel fortunately fell into the hands of a distinguished publisher's reader, George Meredith, and appeared in 1883 to immediate acclaim.

Six years later she returned to South Africa, no longer the daughter of a disgraced and impoverished missionary but a novelist of considerable reputation. She married a gentleman farmer and businessman, Samuel Cronwright, who took her maiden name to become Cronwright-Schreiner. After the death of their only child, whose body Schreiner reportedly carried with her for years in a white coffin, the marriage disintegrated, and they spent long periods apart. The years passed, marked in part by involvement in political and social causes, including feminism, socialism, and pacificism, as well as anti-sexism, anti-imperialism, and anti-racism—all of which she wrote about in her far-ranging nonfiction publications.

Given to depression and illness, asthma in particular, Schreiner worked for nearly forty years on what she hoped would be her greatest novel, *From Man to Man*. This sprawling and intriguing narrative traces the lives of two sisters, both of whom are considered prostitutes, one a wife, the other the real thing. Still unfinished at the time of her death on 10 December 1920, the book was edited by her husband and published in 1926, followed three years later by another novel, *Undine*. Cronwright-Schreiner also published a biography of his wife, *The Life of Olive Schreiner*, in 1924. Although *The Story of an African Farm* and Schreiner's other work were eclipsed over the years to some extent by emerging writers from South Africa, the rise of feminism, in part, revived her fiction—the first novel especially. Extensive critical work, biographies, and new editions of Schreiner's books have appeared recently.

Appropriately described by Richard Rive in his introduction to the 1975 Africana Library edition of the novel as a "remarkable achievement" in spite of "its obvious weaknesses, its clumsy construction, its special pleading, its faulty characterization," *The Story of an African Farm* does indeed overcome its flaws to emerge as a very modern novel far ahead of its time. The chapter "A Boer Wedding" first of all offers a precise account of the Boers, the name given to the descendants of the Dutch who settled in South Africa. Yet that is hardly Schreiner's sole intention, as she speaks through Lyndall to state her revolutionary views on religion and society, on the state of women in a remote colony—and elsewhere undoubtedly, and on the inherent right of individuals, male or female, to claim their identity and to fulfill their ambitions.

# A Boer Wedding
from *The Story of an African Farm*

"I didn't know before you were so fond of riding hard," said Gregory to his little betrothed.

They were cantering slowly on the road to Oom Muller's on the morning of the wedding.

"Do you call this riding hard?" asked Em in some astonishment.

"Of course I do! It's enough to break the horses' necks, and knock one up for the whole day besides," he added testily; then twisted his head to look at the buggy that came on behind. "I thought Waldo was such a mad driver; they are taking it easily enough today," said Gregory. "One would think the black stallions were lame."

"I suppose they want to keep out of our dust," said Em. "See, they stand still as soon as we do."

Perceiving this to be the case, Gregory rode on.

"It's all that horse of yours: she kicks up such a confounded dust, I can't stand it myself," he said.

Meanwhile the cart came on slowly enough.

"Take the reins," said Lyndall, "and make them walk. I want to rest and watch their hoofs today—not to be exhilarated; I am so tired."

She leaned back in her corner, and Waldo drove on slowly in the gray dawn light along the level road. They passed the very milk-bush behind which, so many years before, the old German had found the Kaffir woman. But their thoughts were not with him that morning: they were thoughts of the young, that run out to meet the future and labor in the present. At last he touched her arm.

"What is it?"

---

From *The Story of an African Farm* by Olive Schreiner. Originally published in 1883 by Chapman & Hall, London.

"I feared you had gone to sleep, and might be jolted out," he said; "you sat so quietly."

"No; do not talk to me; I am not asleep"; but after a time she said suddenly, "it must be a terrible thing to bring a human being into the world."

Waldo looked round; she sat drawn into the corner, her blue cloud wound tightly about her, and she still watched the horses' feet. Having no comment to offer on her somewhat unexpected remark, he merely touched up his horses.

"I have no conscience, none," she added; "but I would not like to bring a soul into this world. When it sinned and when it suffered something like a dead hand would fall on me,—'You did it, you, for your own pleasure you created this thing! See your work!' If it lived to be eighty it would always hang like a millstone round my neck, have the right to demand good from me, and curse me for its sorrow. A parent is only like to God: if his work turns out bad so much the worse for him; he dare not wash his hands of it. Time and years can never bring the day when you can say to your child, 'Soul, what have I to do with you?'"

Waldo said dreamily:

"It is a marvelous thing that one soul should have power to cause another."

She heard the words as she heard the beating of the horses' hoofs; her thoughts ran on in their own line.

"They say, 'God sends the little babies.' Of all the dastardly revolting lies men tell to suit themselves, I hate that most. I suppose my father said so when he knew he was dying of consumption, and my mother when she knew she had nothing to support me on, and they created me to feed like a dog from stranger hands. Men do not say God sends the books, or the newspaper articles, or the machines they make; and then sigh, and shrug their shoulders, and say they can't help it. Why do they say so about other things? Liars! 'God sends the little babies!'" She stuck her foot fretfully against the splashboard. "The small children say so earnestly. *They* touch the little stranger reverently who has just come from God's far country, and they peep about the room to see if not one white feather has dropped from the wing of the angel that brought him. On their lips the phrase means much; on all others it is a *deliberate lie*. Noticeable too," she said, dropping in an instant from the passionate into a low, mocking tone, "when people are married, though they should have sixty children, they throw the whole onus on God. When they are not, we hear nothing about God's having sent them. When there has been no legal contract between the parents, who sends the little children then? The Devil, perhaps!" she laughed her little silvery, mocking laugh. "Odd that some men should come from hell and some from heaven, and yet all look so much alike when they get here."

Waldo wondered at her. He had not the key to her thoughts, and did not see the string on which they were strung. She drew her cloud tighter about her.

"It must be very nice to believe in the Devil," she said; "I wish I did. If it would be of any use I would pray three hours night and morning on my bare knees, 'God, let me believe in Satan.' He is so useful to those people who do. They may be as selfish and as sensual as they please, and, between God's will and the Devil's action, always have some one to throw their sin on. But we, wretched unbelievers, we bear our own burdens; we must say, 'I myself did it, *I*. Not God, not Satan; I myself!' That is the sting that strikes deep. Waldo," she said gently, with a sudden and complete change of manner, "I like you so much, I love you." She rested her check softly against his shoulder. "When I am with you I never know that I am a woman and you are a man; I only know that we are both things that think. Other men when I am with them, whether I love them or not, they are mere bodies to me; but you are a spirit; I like you. Look," she said quickly, sinking back into her corner, "what a pretty pinkness there is on all the hill-tops! The sun will rise in a moment."

Waldo lifted his eyes to look round over the circle of golden hills; and the horses, as the first sunbeams touched them, shook their heads and champed their bright bits, till the brass settings in their harness glittered again.

It was eight o'clock when they neared the farm-house: a red-brick building, with kraals to the right and a small orchard to the left. Already there were signs of unusual life and bustle: one cart, a wagon, and a couple of saddles against the wall betokened the arrival of a few early guests, whose numbers would soon be largely increased. To a Dutch country wedding guests start up in numbers astonishing to one who has merely ridden through the plains of sparsely-inhabited karoo.

As the morning advances, riders on many shades of steeds appear from all directions, and add their saddles to the long rows against the walls, shake hands, drink coffee, and stand about outside in groups to watch the arriving carts and ox-wagons, as they are unburdened of their heavy freight of massive Tantes and comely daughters, followed by swarms of children of all sizes, dressed in all manner of print and moleskin, who are taken care of by Hottentot, Kaffir and half-caste nurses, whose many-shaded complexions, ranging from light yellow up to ebony black, add variety to the animated scene. Everywhere is excitement and bustle, which gradually increases as the time for the return of the wedding party approaches. Preparations for the feast are actively advancing in the kitchen; coffee is liberally handed round, and amid a profound sensation, and the firing of guns, the horsewagon draws up, and the wedding party alight. Bride and bridegroom, with their attendants, march solemnly to the marriage chamber, where bed and box are decked out in white, with ends of ribbon and artificial flowers, and where on a row of chairs the party solemnly seat themselves. After a time bridesmaid and best man rise, and conduct in with ceremony each individual guest, to wish success and to kiss bride and bridegroom. Then the feast is set on the table, and it is almost sunset before the dishes are cleared away, and the pleasure of the day begins. Everything is removed from the great front room, and the mud floor, well rubbed with bullock's blood, glistens like polished mahogany. The female portion of the assembly flock into the side-rooms to attire themselves for the evening; and re-issue clad in white muslin, and gay with bright ribbons and brass jewelry. The dancing begins as the first tallow candles are stuck up about the walls, the music coming from a couple of fiddlers in a corner of the room. Bride and bridegroom open the ball, and the floor is soon covered with whirling couples, and everyone's spirits rise. The bridal pair mingle freely in the throng, and here and there a musical man sings vigorously as he drags his partner through the Blue Water or John Speriwig; boys shout and applaud, and the enjoyment and confusion are intense, till eleven o'clock comes. By this time the children who swarm in the side-rooms are not to be kept quiet longer, even by hunches of bread and cake; there is a general howl and wail, that rises yet higher than the scraping of fiddles, and mothers rush from their partners to knock small heads together, and cuff little nursemaids, and force the wailers down into unoccupied corners of beds, under tables, and behind boxes. In half an hour every variety of childish snore is heard on all sides, and it has become perilous to raise or set down a foot in any of the side-rooms lest a small head or hand should be crushed. Now, too, the busy feet have broken the solid coating of the floor, and a cloud of fine dust arises, that makes a yellow halo round the candles, and sets asthmatic people coughing, and grows denser, till to recognize any one on the opposite side of the room becomes impossible, and a partner's face is seen through a yellow mist.

At twelve o'clock the bride is led to the marriage-chamber and undressed; the lights are blown out, and the bridegroom is brought to the door by the best man, who gives him the key; then the door is shut and locked, and the revels rise higher than ever. There is no thought of sleep till morning, and no unoccupied spot where sleep may be found.

It was at this stage of the proceedings on the night of Tant' Sannie's wedding that Lyndall sat near the doorway in one of the side-rooms, to watch the dancers as they appeared and disappeared in the yellow cloud of dust. Gregory sat moodily in a corner of the large dancing-room. His little betrothed touched his arm.

"I wish you would go and ask Lyndall to dance with you," she said; "she must be so tired; she has sat still the whole evening."

"I have asked her three times," replied her lover shortly. "I'm not going to be her dog, and creep to her feet, just to give her the pleasure of kicking me—not for you, Em, nor for anybody else."

"Oh, I didn't know you had asked her, Greg," said his little betrothed humbly; and she went away to pour out coffee.

Nevertheless, some time after, Gregory found he had shifted so far round the room as to be close to the door where Lyndall sat. After standing for some time he inquired whether he might not bring her a cup of coffee. She declined: but still he stood on (why should he not stand there as well as anywhere else?), and then he stepped into the bedroom.

"May I not bring you a stove, Miss Lyndall, to put your feet on?"

"Thank you."

He sought for one, and put it under her feet.

"There is a draught from that broken window; shall I stuff something in the pane?"

"No; we want air."

Gregory looked round, but, nothing else suggesting itself, he sat down on a box on the opposite side of the door. Lyndall sat before him, her chin resting in her hand; her eyes, steel-gray by day but black by night, looked through the doorway into the next room. After a time he thought she had entirely forgotten his proximity, and he dared to inspect the little hands and neck as he never dared when he was in momentary dread of the eyes being turned upon him. She was dressed in black, which seemed to take her yet further from the white-clad, gewgawed women about her; and the little hands were white, and the diamond ring glittered. Where had she got that ring? He bent forward a little and tried to decipher the letters, but the candle-light was too faint. When he looked up her eyes were fixed on him. She was looking at him—not, Gregory felt, as she had ever looked at him before; not as though he were a stump or a stone that chance had thrown in her way. Tonight, whether it were critically, or kindly, or unkindly he could not tell, but she looked at him, at the man, Gregory Rose, with attention. A vague elation filled him. He clenched his fist tight to think of some good idea he might express to her; but of all those profound things he had pictured himself as saying to her, when he sat alone in the daub-and-wattle house, not one came. He said at last:

"These Boer dances are very low things;" and then, as soon as it had gone from him, he thought it was not a clever remark, and wished it back.

Before Lyndall replied, Em looked in at the door.

"Oh, come," she said; "they are going to have the cushion-dance. I do not want to kiss any of these fellows. Take me quickly."

She slipped her hand into Gregory's arm.

"It is so dusty, Em; do you care to dance any more?" he asked, without rising.

"Oh, I do not mind the dust, and the dancing rests me."

But he did not move.

"I feel tired; I do not think I shall dance again," he said.

Em withdrew her hand, and a young farmer came to the door and bore her off.

"I have often imagined," remarked Gregory—but Lyndall had risen.

"I am tired," she said. "I wonder where Waldo is; he must take me home. These people will not leave off till morning, I suppose; it is three already."

She made her way past the fiddlers, and a bench full of tired dancers, and passed out at the front door. On the "stoep" a group of men and boys were smoking, peeping in at the windows, and cracking coarse jokes. Waldo was certainly not among them, and she made her way to the carts and wagons drawn up at some distance from the homestead.

"Waldo," she said, peering into a large cart, "is that you? I am so dazed with the tallow candles, I can see nothing."

He had made himself a place between the two seats. She climbed up and sat on the sloping floor in front.

"I thought I should find you here," she said, drawing her skirt up about her shoulders. "You must take me home presently, but not now."

She leaned her head on the seat near to his, and they listened in silence to the fitful twanging of the fiddles as the night-wind bore it from the farm-house, and to the ceaseless thud of the dancers, and the peals of gross laughter. She stretched out her little hand to feel for his.

"It is so nice to lie here and hear that noise," she said. "I like to feel that strange life beating up against me. I like to realize forms of life utterly unlike mine." She drew a long breath. "When my own life feels small, and I am oppressed with it, I like to crush together, and see it in a picture, in an instant, a multitude of disconnected unlike phases of human life—medieval monk with his string of beads pacing the quiet orchard, and looking up from the grass at his feet to the heavy fruit-trees; little Malay boys playing naked on a shining sea-beach; a Hindoo philosopher alone under his banyan tree, thinking, thinking, thinking, so that in the thought of God he may lose himself; a troop of Bacchanalians dressed in white, with crowns of vine-leaves, dancing along the Roman streets; a martyr on the night of his death looking through the narrow window to the sky, and feeling that already he has the wings that shall bear him up" (she moved her hand dreamily over her face); "an epicurean discoursing at a Roman bath to a knot of his disciples on the nature of happiness; a Kaffir witch-doctor seeking for herbs by moonlight, while from the huts on the hillside come the sound of dogs barking, and the voices of women and children; a mother giving bread and milk to her children in little wooden basins and singing the evening song, I like to see it all; I feel it run through me—that life belongs to me; it makes my little life larger; it breaks down the narrow walls that shut me in."

She sighed, and drew a long breath.

"Have you made any plan?" she asked him presently.

"Yes," he said, the words coming in jets, with pauses between; "I will take the gray mare—I will travel first—I will see the world—then I will find work."

"What work?"

"I do not know."

She made a little impatient movement.

"That is no plan; travel—see the world—find work! If you go into the world aimless, without a definite object, dreaming—dreaming, you will be definitely defeated, bamboozled, knocked this way and that. In the end you will stand with your beautiful life all spent, and nothing to show. They talk of genius—it is nothing but this, that a man knows what he can do best, and does it, and nothing else. Waldo," she said, knitting her little fingers closer among his, "I wish I could help you; I wish I could make you see that you must decide what you will be and do. It does not matter what you choose—be a farmer, business-man, artist, what you will—but know your aim, and live for that one thing. We have only one life. The secret of success is concentration; wherever there has been a great life, or a great work, that has gone before. Taste everything a little, look at everything a little; but live for one thing. Anything is possible to a man who knows his end and moves straight for it, and for it alone. I will show you what I mean," she said, concisely; "words are gas till you condense them into pictures.

"Suppose a woman, young, friendless as I am, the weakest thing on God's earth. But she must make her way through life. What she would be she cannot be because she is a woman; so she looks carefully at herself and the world about her, to see where her path must be made. There is no one to help her; she must help herself. She looks. These things she has—a sweet voice, rich in subtle intonation; a fair, very fair face, with a power of concentrating in itself, and giving expression to, feelings that otherwise must have been dissipated in words; a rare power of entering into other lives unlike her own, and intuitively reading them aright. These qualities she has. How shall she use them? A poet, a writer, needs only the mental; what use has he for a beautiful body that registers clearly mental emotions? And the painter wants an eye for form and color, and the musician an ear for time and tune, and the mere drudge has no need for mental gifts. But there is one art in which all she has would be used, for which they are all necessary—the delicate, expressive body, the rich voice, the power of mental transposition. The actor, who absorbs and then reflects from himself other human lives, needs them all, but needs not much more. This is her end; but how to reach it? Before her are endless difficulties: seas must be crossed, poverty must be endured, loneliness, want. She must be content to wait long before she can even get her feet upon the path. If she has made blunders in the past, if she has weighted herself with a burden which she must bear to the end, she must but bear the burden bravely, and labor on. There is no use in wailing and repentance here: the next world is the place for that; this life is too short. By our errors we see deeper into life. They help us." She waited for a while. "If she does all this,—if she waits patiently, if she is never cast down, never despairs, never forgets her end, moves straight towards it, bending men and things most unlikely to her purpose—she must succeed at last. Men and things are plastic; they part to the right and left when one comes among them moving in a straight line to one end. I know it by my own little experience," she said. "Long years ago I resolved to be sent to school. It seemed a thing utterly out of my power; but I waited, I watched, I collected clothes, I wrote, took my place at the school; when all was ready I bore with my full force on the Boer-woman, and she sent me at last. It was a small thing; but life is made up of small things, as a body is built up of cells. What has been done in small things can be done in large. Shall be," she said softly.

Waldo listened. To him the words were no confession, no glimpse into the strong, proud, restless heart of the woman. They were general words with a general application. He looked up into the sparkling sky with dull eyes.

"Yes," he said; "but when we lie and think, and think, we see that there is nothing worth doing. The universe is so large, and man is so small—"

She shook her head quickly.

"But we must not think so far; it is madness, it is a disease. We know that no man's work is great, and stands for ever. Moses is dead, and the prophets, and the books that our grandmothers fed on the mold is eating. Your poet and painter and actor,—before the shouts that applaud them have died their names grow strange, they are milestones that the world has passed. Men have set their mark on mankind for ever, as they thought; but time has washed it out as it has washed out mountains and continents." She raised herself on her elbow. "And what, if we *could* help mankind, and leave the traces of our work upon it to the end? Mankind is only an ephemeral blossom on the tree of time; there were others before it opened; there will be others after it has fallen. Where was man in the time of the dicynodont, and when hoary monsters wallowed in the mud? Will he be found in the aeons that are to come? We are sparks, we are shadows, we are pollen, which the next wind will carry away. We are dying already; it is all a dream.

"I know that thought. When the fever of living is on us, when the desire to become, to know, to do, is driving us mad, we can use it as an anodyne, to still the fever and cool our beating pulses. But it is a poison, not a food. If we live on it it will turn our blood to ice; we might as well be dead. We must not, Waldo; I want your life to be beautiful, to end in something. You are nobler and stronger than I," she said; "and as much better as one of God's great angels is better than a sinning man. Your life must go for something."

"Yes, we will work," he said.

She moved closer to him and lay still, his black curls touching her smooth little head.

Doss, who had lain at his master's side, climbed over the bench, and curled himself up in her lap. She drew her skirt up over him, and the three sat motionless for a long time.

"Waldo," she said, suddenly, "they are laughing at us."

"Who?" he asked, starting up.

"They—the stars!" she said softly. "Do you not see? there is a little white, mocking finger pointing down at us from each one of them! We are talking of tomorrow, and tomorrow, and our hearts are so strong; we are not thinking of something that can touch us softly in the dark, and make us still for ever. They are laughing at us, Waldo."

Both sat looking upwards.

"Do you ever pray?" he asked her in a low voice.

"No."

"I never do; but I might when I look up there. I will tell you," he added, in a still lower voice, "where I could pray. If there were a wall of rock on the edge of a world, and one rock stretched out far, far into space, and I stood alone upon it, alone, with stars above me, and stars below me—I would not say anything; but the feeling would be prayer."

There was an end to their conversation after that, and Doss fell asleep on her knee. At last the night-wind grew very chilly,

"Ah," she said, shivering, and drawing the skirt about her shoulders, "I am cold. Span-in the horses, and call me when you are ready."

She slipped down and walked towards the house, Doss stiffly following her, not pleased at being roused. At the door she met Gregory.

"I have been looking for you everywhere; may I not drive you home?" he said.

"Waldo drives me," she replied, passing on; and it appeared to Gregory that she looked at him in the old way, without seeing him. But before she had reached the door an idea had occurred to her, for she turned.

"If you wish to drive me you may."

Gregory went to look for Em, whom he found pouring out coffee in the back room. He put his hand quickly on her shoulder.

"You must ride with Waldo; I am going to drive your cousin home."

"But I can't come just now, Greg; I promised Tant' Annie Muller to look after the things while she went to rest a little."

"Well, you can come presently, can't you? I didn't say you were to come now. I'm sick of this thing," said Gregory, turning sharply on his heel. "Why must I sit up the whole night because your step-mother chooses to get married?"

"Oh, it's all right, Greg, I only meant—"

But he did not hear her, and a man had come up to have his cup filled.

An hour after, Waldo came in to look for her, and found her still busy at the table.

"The horses are ready," he said; "but if you would like to have one dance more I will wait."

She shook her head wearily.

"No; I am quite ready. I want to go."

And soon they were on the sandy road the buggy had traveled an hour before. Their horses, with heads close together, nodding sleepily as they walked in the starlight, you might have counted the rise and fall of their feet in the sand; and Waldo in his saddle nodded drowsily also. Only Em was awake, and watched the starlit road with wide-open eyes. At last she spoke.

"I wonder if all people feel so old, so very old, when they get to be seventeen?"

"Not older than before," said Waldo, sleepily, pulling at his bridle.

Presently she said again:

"I wish I could have been a little child always. You are good then. You are never selfish; you like every one to have everything; but when you are grown-up there are some things you like to have all to yourself, you don't like any one else to have any of them."

"Yes," said Waldo, sleepily, and she did not speak again.

When they reached the farm-house all was dark, for Lyndall had retired as soon as they got home.

Waldo lifted Em from her saddle, and for a moment she leaned her head on his shoulder and clung to him.

"You are very tired," he said, as he walked with her to the door; "Let me go in and light a candle for you."

"No thank you; it is all right," she said. "Good night, Waldo, dear."

But when she went in she sat long alone in the dark.

# Alex La Guma

Alex La Guma traveled far in his life, from the colored (or mixed-race) community of Cape Town, South Africa, where he was born on 20 February 1925, to Havana, Cuba, where he died in 1985. That long journey was instigated by racial politics. The son of poor parents but ones who were politically involved, La Guma left school to work in a factory. There he soon helped to organize a strike to gain better working conditions, thus initiating his lifelong career as an activist. He joined the Communist Party in 1948, but when the party became illegal in South Africa two years later, La Guma continued to work toward equality as an active member in the South African Coloured Peoples Organization, which merged into the African National Congress (ANC) in 1955. That year La Guma and 155 others were tried for treason, but were acquitted five years later. Until his voluntary exit from South Africa in 1966, La Guma spent long periods under house arrest or in prison for his continued opposition to apartheid. After leaving South Africa, he participated in the exiled division of the ANC, and at the time of his death was the congress's representative in the Caribbean.

His literary career began in journalism when he started writing for the *New Age*. Most of his reports for this left-wing weekly focused on the social and economic conditions prevalent in Cape Town's colored community. Two years later he published his first short story. In 1962 his first novel, *A Walk in the Night*, appeared, later published in an edition along with several short stories. His other novels include *And a Threefold Cord* (1964), *The Stone Country* (1967), *In the Fog of the Seasons* (1972), and *Time of the Butcherbird* (1979).

In an interview La Guma said that during his entire life he had been involved "with the struggle of the oppressed people of South Africa for a better social, economic and cultural life, and for participation in a political life . . .

which promotes a non-racial, democratic society." He then explained that this "lifelong aim" dominated his fiction as well as his political action. Still, the short stories and novels remain free of propaganda and didacticism. La Guma's obsessive concern with equality is imbued in the atmosphere he captures so flawlessly, embedded in the narrative structure that determines the characters' behavior, and revealed through the dialogue that makes such unobtrusive use of dialect. Whether the characters fight to survive in the ramshackle, colored suburb of Cape Town—the setting for much of the fiction, or in a South African prison—the setting for *The Stone Country*, they possess a dynamism and authenticity, which consistently saves them from being counterfeit humans who merely spout a political ideology.

Such is the case with the deceptively simple "A Matter of Taste," where more is left unsaid than said. The narrator and Chinaboy obviously belong to the colored community, and Chinaboy, who has "kinky hair" and eyes that are "dark oriental ovals," apparently carries oriental as well as black and white blood. When the man with "the pale white face" approaches them, the three overcome race and join in a fellowship that is fueled through the dominant symbol of food. Their destitute condition contrasts starkly with those who actually eat the foods they can only imagine, that is, those who enjoy the basic needs determined by political, social, and economic forces—privileges that all men and women, black or white or colored, deserve. Typical of much of La Guma's work, the comic touch in "A Matter of Taste" masks the serious face of the thematic implications.

# A Matter of Taste

The sun hung well towards the west now so that the thin clouds above the ragged horizon were rimmed with bright yellow like the spilt yolk of an egg. Chinaboy stood up from having blown the fire under the round tin and said, "She ought to boil now." The tin stood precariously balanced on two half-bricks and a smooth stone. We had built the fire carefully in order to brew some coffee and now watched the water in the tin with the interest of women at a childbirth.

"There she is," Chinaboy said as the surface broke into bubbles. He waited for the water to boil up and then drew a small crushed packet from the side pocket of his shredded wind-breaker, untwisted its mouth and carefully tapped raw coffee into the tin.

He was a short man with gray-flecked kinky hair, and a wide, quiet, heavy face that had a look of patience about it, as if he had grown accustomed to doing things slowly and carefully and correctly. But his eyes were dark oriental ovals, restless as a pair of cockroaches.

"We'll let her draw a while," he advised. He put the packet away and produced an old rag from another pocket, wrapped it around a hand and gingerly lifted the tin from the fire, placing it carefully in the sand near the bricks.

We had just finished a job for the railways and were camped out a few yards from the embankment and some distance from the ruins of a onetime siding. The corrugated iron of the office still stood, gaping in places and covered with rust and cobwebs. Passers had fouled the roofless interior and the platform was crumbled in places and overgrown with weeds. The cement curbing still stood, but cracked and covered with the disintegration like a welcome notice to a ghost town. Chinaboy got out the scoured condensed-milk tins we used for cups and set them up. I sat on an old sleeper and waited for the ceremony of pouring the coffee to commence.

It didn't start right then because Chinaboy was crouching with his rag-wrapped hand poised over the can, about to pick it up, but he wasn't making a move. Just sitting like that and watching something beyond us.

The portjackson bush and wattle crackled and rustled behind me and the long shadow of a man fell across the small clearing. I looked back and up. He had come out of the plantation and was thin and short and had a pale white face covered with a fine golden stubble. Dirt lay in dark lines in the creases around his mouth and under his eyes and in his neck, and his hair was ragged and thick and uncut, falling back to his neck and around his temples. He wore an old pair of jeans, faded and dirty and turned up at the bottoms, and a torn leather coat.

He stood on the edge of the clearing, waiting hesitantly, glancing from me to Chinaboy, and then back at me. He ran the back of a grimy hand across his mouth.

Then he said hesitantly: "I smelled the coffee. Hope you don' min'."

"Well," Chinaboy said with that quiet careful smile of his. "Seeing you's here, I reckon I don' min' either." He smiled at me, "you think we can take in a table boarder, pal?"

"Reckon we can spare some of the turkey and green peas."

Chinaboy nodded at the stranger. "Sit, pally. We were just going to have supper."

The white boy grinned a little embarrassedly and came around the sleeper and shoved a rock over with a scarred boot and straddled it. He didn't say anything, but watched as Chinaboy set out another scoured milk-tin and lifted the can from the fire and poured the coffee into the cups.

"Help yourself, man. Isn't exactly the mayor's garden party." The boy took his cup carefully and blew at the steam. Chinaboy sipped noisily and said, "Should've had some bake bread. Nothing like a piece of bake bread with cawfee."

"Hot dogs," the white boy said.

"Huh."

"Hot dogs. Hot dogs go with coffee."

"Ooh ja. I heard," Chinaboy grinned. Then he asked: "You going somewhere, Whitey?"

"Cape Town. Maybe get a job on a ship an' make the States."

"Lots of people want to reach the States," I said.

Whitey drank some coffee and said: "Yes, I heard there's plenty of money and plenty to eat."

"Talking about eating," Chinaboy said: "I see a picture in a book, one time. 'Merican book. This picture was about food over there. A whole mess of fried chicken, mealies what they call corn—with mushrooms an' gravy, chips and new green peas. All done up in colors, too."

"Pass me the roast lamb," I said sarcastically.

"Man," Whitey said warming up to the discussion "Just let me get to something like that and I'll eat till I burst wide open."

Chinaboy swallowed some coffee: "Worked as a waiter one time when I was a youngster. In one of those big caffies. You should've seen what all them bastards ate. Just sitting there shoveling it down. Some French stuff too, patty grass or something like that."

I said: "Remember the time we went for drunk and got ten days? We ate mealies and beans till it came out of our ears!"

Chinaboy said, whimsically: "I'd like to sit down in a smart caffy one day and eat my way right out of a load of turkey, roast potatoes, beet-salad and angel's food trifle. With port and cigars at the end."

"Hell," said Whitey, "it's all a matter of taste. Some people like chicken and other's eat sheep's heads and beans!"

"A matter of taste," Chinaboy scowled. "Bull, it's a matter of money, pal. I worked six months in that caffy and I never heard nobody order sheep's head and beans!"

"You heard of the fellow who went into one of these big caffies?" Whitey asked, whirling the last of his coffee around in the tin cup. "He sits down at a table and takes out a packet of sandwiches and puts it down. Then he calls the waiter and orders a glass of water. When the waiter brings the water, this fellow says: 'Why ain't the band playing?'"

We chuckled over that and Chinaboy almost choked. He coughed and spluttered a little and then said, "Another John goes into a caffy and orders sausage and mash. When the waiter bring him the stuff he take a look and say: 'My dear man, you've brought me a cracked plate.' 'Hell,' says the waiter. 'That's no crack. That's the sausage.'"

After we had laughed over that one Chinaboy looked westward at the sky. The sun was almost down and the clouds hung like bloodstained rags along the horizon. There was a breeze stirring the wattle and portjackson, and far beyond the railway line.

A dog barked with high yapping sounds.

Chinaboy said: "There's a empty goods going through here around about seven. We'll help Whitey, here, onto it, so's he can get to Cape Town. Reckon there's still time for some more pork chops and onions." He grinned at Whitey. "Soon's we've had dessert we'll walk down the line a little. There's a bend where it's the best place to jump a train. We'll show you."

He waved elaborately towards me: "Serve the duck, John!"

I poured the last of the coffee into the tin cups. The fire had died to a small heap of embers, Whitey dug in the pocket of his leather coat and found a crumpled pack of cigarettes. There were just three left and he passed them round. We each took one and Chinaboy lifted the twig from the fire and we lighted up.

"Good cigar, this," he said, examining the glowing tip of the cigarette.

When the coffee and cigarettes were finished, the sun had gone down altogether, and all over the land was swept with dark shadows of a purple hue. The silhouetted tops of the wattle and portjackson looked like massed dragons.

We walked along the embankment in the evening, past the ruined siding, the shell of the station-house like a huge desecrated tombstone against the sky. Far off we heard the whistle of a train.

"This is the place," Chinaboy said to Whitey. "It's a long goods and when she takes the turn the engine driver won't see you, and neither the rooker in the guard's van. You got to jump when the engine's out of sight. She'll take the hill slow likely, so you'll have a good chance. Jus' you wait till I say when. Hell, that sound like pouring a drink!" His teeth flashed in the gloom as he grinned. Then Whitey stuck out a hand and Chinaboy shook it, and then I shook it.

"Thanks for supper, boys," Whitey said.

"Come again, anytime," I said, "we'll see we have a tablecloth." We waited in the portjackson growth at the side of the embankment while the goods train wheezed and puffed up the grade, its headlamp cutting a big yellow hole in the dark. We ducked back out of sight as the locomotive went by, hissing and rumbling. The tender followed, then a couple of boxcars, then some coal-cars and a flat-car, another box-car. The locomotive was out of sight.

"Here it is," Chinaboy said pushing the boy ahead. We stood near the train, hearing it click-clack past. "Take this coal box coming up," Chinaboy instructed. "She's low and empty. Don't miss the grip, now. She's slow. And good luck, pal!"

The coal-car came up and Whitey moved out, watching the iron grip on the far end of it. Then as it drew slowly level with him, he reached out, grabbed and hung on, then got a foothold, moving away from us slowly.

We watched him hanging there, reaching for the edge of the car and hauling himself up. Watching the train clicking away, we saw him straddling the edge of the truck, his hand raised in a salute. We raised our hands too.

"Why ain't the band playing? Hell!" Chinaboy said.

# Mulk Raj Anand

Mulk Raj Anand has been called the Zola or Balzac of India. Through his English-language fiction he has served as "the secretary of Indian life" over several decades. The son of a Punjabi soldier, Anand was born in Peshawar, India, 12 December 1905. Early on he rebelled against his father's subservience to the British masters and his mother's unquestioning acceptance of religious rituals and superstition. This resistance to colonialism and tradition figures prominently in his fiction, which has sometimes been called "propagandistic."

After graduating from the University of Punjab, he received a doctorate in 1929 from University College, London. He remained in Europe for several years, teaching in Geneva, studying at Cambridge, dabbling in Marxism, and fighting with the Republicans in the Spanish civil war. After returning to India, he participated in the independence movement and associated closely with Gandhi and his circle. As well as teaching at various Indian universities, Anand has played an important role in Indian cultural life as a journal editor, a publisher, an international representative, and former cultural adviser to India's prime minister. He has also assisted rural communities in opening schools, building roads, and improving sanitation. Married to a classical Indian dancer, Anand lives in Bombay. In addition to fiction, he has published art and literary criticism.

Although the author of some sixteen novels, numerous volumes of short stories, and books for children, he remains best known for his first two novels, *Untouchable* and *Coolie*. Rejected by nineteen British publishers, *Untouchable* was finally accepted, and appeared in 1935 with an introduction by E.M. Forster. *Coolie* followed a year later. Anand revised the two novels in the 1970s; translated into twenty-four languages, both books have sold innumerable copies worldwide and continue to be in print. Classic protest novels, they reveal the harsh conditions of Indian life under colonial rule, but do so in human terms, not in a didactic fashion. The books remain relevant, for the injustice Anand sees in Indian life did not disappear when the British went home. Throughout his writing career, which has extended into the 1980s, he has consistently championed the oppressed and condemned greed, intolerance, and inhumanity.

Although much of Anand's work has been eclipsed to some degree by the more sophisticated work of later Indian writers in English, he has earned a secure place in Indian literature. After all, he was one of the first Indians to write about India in English, and to gain an international reputation. Before Anand's books appeared, overseas readers generally learned about India through British writers' eyes.

While "The Gold Watch" makes a harsh statement against imperialism and the offhand treatment of its subjects, it does so gently through the experience of the ordinary clerk, Sharma. Anand also captures the stifling atmosphere of the office full of Indian functionaries who serve the marmalade company and in turn the empire—fearful of their jobs and fiercely competitive. The almost saintly Sharma and his ordered life at home contrast sharply with the artificial world created by the Sahibs.

# The Gold Watch

There was something about the smile of Mr. Acton, when he came over to Srijut Sudarshan Sharma's table, which betokened disaster. But as the Sahib had only said, "Mr. Sharma, I have brought something for you specially from London—you must come into my office on Monday and take it," the poor old despatch clerk could not surmise the real meaning of the General Manager's remark. The fact that Mr. Acton should come over to his table at all, fawn upon him and say what he had said was, of course, most flattering. For very rarely did the head of the firm condescend to move down the corridor where the Indian staff of the distribution department of the great Marmalade Empire of Henry King & Co. worked. But that smile on Mr. Acton's face!—specially as Mr. Acton was not known to smile too much, being a morose, old Sahib, hard working, conscientious and a slave driver, famous as a shrewd business-man, so devoted to the job of spreading the monopoly of King's Marmalade, and sundry other products, that his wife had left him after a three month's spell of marriage and never returned to India, though no one quite knew whether she was separated or divorced from him or merely preferred to stay away. So the fact that Acton Sahib should smile was enough to give Srijut Sharma cause for thought. But then Srijut Sharma was, in spite of his nobility of soul and fundamental innocence, experienced enough in his study of the vague, detached race of the white Sahibs by now and clearly noticed the slight awkward curl of the upper lip, behind which the determined, tobacco-stained long teeth showed for the briefest moment, a snarl suppressed by the deliberation which Acton Sahib had brought to the whole operation of coming over and pronouncing those kind words. And what could be the reason for his having been singled out, from among the twenty-five odd members of the distribution department? In the usual way, he, the despatch clerk, only received an occasional greeting, "Hello Sharma—how you getting on?" from the head of his own department, Mr. West; and twice or thrice a year he was called into the cubicle by West Sahib for a reprimand, because some letters or packets had gone astray; otherwise, he himself, being the incarnation of clock-work efficiency and well-versed in the routine of his job, there was no occasion for any break in the monotony of that anonymous, smooth working Empire, so far at least as he was concerned. To be sure, there was the continual gossip of the clerks and the accountants, the bickerings and jealousies of the people above him, for grades and promotions and pay, but Sharma, who had been employed twenty years ago as a special favor, was not even a matriculate, but had picked up the work somehow, and though unwanted and constantly reprimanded by West Sahib in the first few years, had been retained because of the general legend of saintliness which he had acquired. He had five more years of service to do, because then he would be fifty-five, and the family raising—the *grhst*, portion of his life in the fourfold scheme prescribed by religion—finished, he hoped to retire to his home town Jullunder, where his father still ran the confectioner's shop off the Mall Road.

"And what did Acton Sahib have to say to you, Mr. Sharma?" asked Miss Violet Dixon, the plain snub-nosed Anglo-Indian typist in her singsong voice.

Because he was an old family man of fifty, who had grayed prematurely, she considered herself safe enough with this "gentleman" and freely conversed with him, specially during the lunch hour, while she considered almost everyone else as having only one goal in life—to sleep with her.

"Han," he said, "he has brought something for me from England."

"There are such pretty things in U.K.," she said. "MY! I wish I could go there! My sister is there, you know. Married."

She had told Sharma all these things before. So he was not interested. Specially today, because all his thoughts were concentrated on the inner meaning of Mr. Acton's sudden visitation and the ambivalent smile.

"Well, half day today, I am off," said Violet and moved away with the peculiar snobbish agility of the Mem Sahib she affected to be.

Srijut Sharma stared at her blankly, though taking in her regular form into his subconscious with more than the old uncle's interest he had always pretended. It was only her snub nose, like that of Sarupnaka, the sister of the demon king Ravana, that stood in the way of her being married, he felt sure, for otherwise she had a tolerable figure. But he lowered his eyes as soon as the thought of Miss Dixon's body began to simmer in the cauldron of his inner life, because, as a good Hindu, every woman, apart from the wife, was to him a mother or a sister. And his obsession about the meaning of Acton Sahib's words returned with greater force now that he realized the vast space of time he would have to wait in suspense before knowing what the boss had brought for him and why.

He took up his faded sola topee, which was, apart from the bush shirt and trousers, one of the few concessions to modernity he had made throughout his life as a good Brahmin, got up from his chair, beckoned Dugdu sepoy from the verandah on his way out and asked.

"Has Acton Sahib gone, you know?"

"Abhi-Sahib in lift going down," Dugdu said.

Srijut Sharma made quickly for the stairs and, throwing all caution about slipping on the polished marble steps to the winds, hurried down. There were three floors below him and he began to sweat, both through fear of missing the Sahib and the heat of mid-April.

As he got to the ground floor, he saw Acton Sahib already going out of the door.

It was now or never.

Srijut Sharma rushed out. But he was conscious that quite a few employees of the firm would be coming out of the two lifts and he might be seen talking to the Sahib. And that was not done—outside the office. The Sahibs belonged to their private worlds, where no intrusion was tolerated, for they refused to listen to pleas of advancement through improper channels.

Mr. Acton's uniformed driver opened the door of the polished Buick and the Sahib sat down, spreading the shadow of grimness all around him.

Srijut Sharma hesitated, for the demeanor of the Goanese chauffeur was frightening.

By now the driver had smartly shut the back door of the car and was proceeding to his seat.

That was his only chance.

Taking off his hat, he rushed up to the window of the car, and rudely thrust his head into the presence of Mr. Acton.

Luckily for him, the Sahib did not brush him aside, but smiled a broader smile than that of a few minutes ago and said:

"You want to know, what I have brought for you—well, it is a gold watch with an inscription on it. See me Monday morning." The Sahib's initiative in anticipating his question threw Srijut Sharma further off his balance. The sweat poured down from his forehead, even as he mumbled: "Thank you, Sir, thank you."

"Chalo, driver!" Sahib ordered.

And the chauffeur turned and looked hard at Srijut Sharma.

The despatch clerk withdrew with a sheepish, abject smile on his face and stood, hat in left hand, the right hand raised to his forehead in the attitude of a military salute.

The motor car moved off.

Bur Srijut Sharma still stood, as though he had been struck dumb. He was neither happy nor sad at this moment. Only numbed by the sock of surprise. Why should he be singled out from the whole distribution department of Henry King & Co. for the privilege of the gift of a gold watch? He had done nothing brave that he could remember. "A gold watch, with an inscription on it!" He knew now—the intuitive truth rose inside him. The Sahib wanted him to retire.

He reeled a little, then adjusted himself and got on to the pavement, looking after the car, which had already turned the corner into Nicol Road.

He turned and began to walk towards Victoria Terminus station. From there he had to take his train to Thana, thirty miles out where he had resided for cheapness almost all the years he had been in Bombay. His steps were heavy, for he was reasonably sure now that he would get notice of retirement on Monday. He tried to think of some other possible reason why the Sahib may have decided to give him the gift of a gold watch with an inscription. There was no other explanation. His doom was sealed. What would he say to his wife? And his son had still not passed his matric. How would he support the family? The provident fund would not amount to very much, specially in these days of rising prices.

He felt a pull at his heart. He paused for breath and tried to calm himself. The blood pressure! Or was it merely wind? He must not get into a panic at any cost. He steadied his gait and walked along, muttering to himself, "Shanti! Shanti! Shanti!" as though the very incantation of the formula of peace would restore his calm and equanimity.

During the weekend, Srijut Sharma was able to conceal his panic and confusion behind the façade of an exaggerated bonhomie with the skill of an accomplished natural actor. On Saturday night he went with wife and son to see Professor Ram's circus, which was performing opposite the Portuguese Church; and he got up later than usual on Sunday morning; spent a little longer on his prayers, but seemed normal enough on the surface.

Only he ate very little of the gala meal of the rice-kichri put before him by his wife and seemed lost in thought for a few moments at a time. And his illiterate but shrewd wife noticed that there was something on his mind.

"You have not eaten at all today," she said, as he had left the tasty papadum and the mango pickle untouched. "Look at Hari! He has left nothing in his thali."

"Hoon," he answered abstractedly. And, then, realizing he might be found out for the worried, unhappy man he was, he tried to bluff her. "As a matter of fact, I was thinking of some happy news that the Sahib gave me yesterday. He said he brought a gold watch as a gift for me from Vilayat. . . ."

"Then Papaji, give me the silver watch, which you are using now," said Hari his young son impetuously. "I have no watch at all and I am always late everywhere."

"Not so impatient, son," counseled Hari's mother. "Let your father get the gold watch first and then he will surely give you his silver watch."

In the ordinary way, Srijut Sudarshan Sharma would have endorsed his wife's sentiments. But today he felt that on the face of it his son's demand was justified. How should Hari know that the silver watch and the gold watch and a gold ring would be all the jewelry he, the father, would have for security against hard days if the gold watch was, as he thought, only a token being offered by the firm to sugarcoat the bitter pill they would ask him to swallow— retirement five years before the appointed time. He hesitated, then lifted his head, smiled at his son and said:

"Acha, Kaka, you can have my silver watch."

"Can I have it, really, Papaji," the boy shouted, rushing away to fetch the watch from his father's pocket. "Give it to me now, today."

"Vay, son, you are so selfish," his mother exclaimed. For, with the peculiar sensitiveness of the woman, she had surmised from the manner in which her husband had hung his head down and then tried to smile as he lifted his face to his son, that the father of Hari was upset inside him, or at least not in his usual mood of accepting life evenly, accompanying this acceptance with the pious invocation—"Shanti! Shanti!"

Hari brought the silver watch, adjusted it to his left ear to see if it ticked, and, happy in the possession of it, capered a little.

Srijut Sharma did not say anything, but, pushing his thali away, got up to wash his hands.

The next day it happened as Srijut Sharma had anticipated.

He went in to see Mr. Acton as soon as the Sahib came in, for the suspense of the weekend had mounted to a crescendo by Monday morning and he had been trembling, pale, and completely unsure of himself. The General Manager called him in immediately after the peon Dugdu presented the little slip with the despatch clerk's name on it.

"Please, sit down," said Mr. Acton, lifting his gray-haired head from the papers before him. And then, pulling his keys from his trousers' pocket by the gold chain to which they were adjusted, he opened a drawer and fetched out what Sharma thought was a beautiful red case.

"Mr. Sharma, you have been a loyal friend of this firm for many years— and—you know, your loyalty has been your greatest asset here—because . . . er . . . Otherwise, we could have got someone with better qualifications to do your work. Now . . . we are thinking of increasing the efficiency of the business all round. And, well, we feel that you would also like, at your age, to retire to your native Punjab. . . . So, as a token of our appreciation for your loyalty to Henry King & Co. we are presenting you this gold watch." And he pushed the red case towards him.

Srijut Sharma began to speak, but though his mouth opened, he could not go on. "I am fifty years old," he wanted to say, "and I still have five years to go." His facial muscles seemed to contract, his eyes were dimmed with the fumes of frustration and bitterness, his forehead was covered with sweat. At least they might have made a little ceremony of the presentation. He could not even utter the words: "Thank you, Sir."

"Of course, you will also have your provident fund and one month's leave with pay before you retire."

Again, Srijut Sharma tried to voice his inner protest in words that would convey his meaning without seeming to be disloyal, for he did not want to obliterate the one concession the Sahib had made to the whole record of his service with the firm. It was just likely that Mr. Acton may remind him of his failings as a despatch clerk if he should so much as indicate that he was unamenable to the suggestion made by the Sahib on behalf of Henry King & Co.

"Look at the watch—it has an inscription on it which will please you," said Mr. Acton, to get over the embarrassment of the tension created by the despatch clerk's silence.

These words hypnotized Sharma and, stretching his hands across the large table, he reached out for the gift.

Mr. Acton noticed the unsureness of his hand and pushed it gently forward.

Srijut Sharma picked up the red box, but, in his eagerness to follow the Sahib's behest, dropped it, even as he had held it aloft and tried to open it.

The Sahib's face was livid as he picked up the box and hurriedly opened it. Then, lifting the watch from its socket, he wound it and held it to his ear. It was ticking. He turned it round and showed the inscription to the despatch clerk.

Srijut Sharma put both his hands out, more steadily this time, and took the gift in the manner in which a beggar receives alms. He brought the glistening object within the orbit of his eyes, but they were dimmed with tears and he could not read anything. He tried to smile, however, and, then, with a great heave of his head, which rocked his body from side to side, he pronounced the words:

"Thank you, Sir."

Mr. Acton got up, took the gold watch from Srijut Sharma's hands and put it back in the socket of the red case. Then he stretched his right hand towards the despatch clerk, with a brisk shake-hand gesture and offered the case to him with his left hand.

Srijut Sharma instinctively took the Sahib's right hand gratefully in his two sweating hands and opened his palms out to receive the case.

"Good luck, Sharma," Mr. Acton said. "Come and see me after your leave is over. And when your son matriculates let me know if I can do something for him."

Dumb, and with bent head, the fumes of his violent emotions rising above the mouth which could have expressed them, he withdrew in the abject manner of his ancestors going out of the presence of feudal lords.

Mr. Acton saw the danger to the watch and went ahead to open the door, so that the clerk could go out without knocking his head against the door or fall down.

As Srijut Sharma emerged from the General Manager's office, involuntary tears flowed from his eyes and his lower lip fell in a pout that somehow controlled him from breaking down completely.

The eyes of the whole office staff were on him.

In a moment, a few of the men clustered around him.

One of them took the case from his hands, opened it and read the inscription aloud:

"In appreciation of the loyal service of Mr. Sharma to Henry King & Co., on his retirement . . ."

The curiosity of his colleagues became a little less enthusiastic as the watch passed from hand to hand.

Unable to stand, because of the wave of dizziness that swirled in his head, Srijut Sudarshan Sharma sat down on his chair with his head hidden in his hands and allowed the tears to roll down. One of his colleagues, Mr. Banaji, the accountant, patted his back understandingly. But the pity was too much for him.

"To be sure, Seth Makhanji, the new partner has a relation, to fill Sharma's position," another said.

"No, no," another refuted him. "No one is required to kill himself with work in our big concern. We are given the Sunday off! And fat pension years. The bosses are full of love for us."

"Damn fine gold watch, but it does not go," said Sriraman, the typist.

Mr. Banaji took the watch from Sriraman and, putting it in the case, placed it before Srijut Sharma, and he signaled to the others to move away.

As Srijut Sharma realized that his colleagues had drifted away, he lifted his head, took the case, as well as his hat, and began to walk away.

Mr. Banaji saw him to the door, his hand on Sharma's back.

"Sahibji," the Parsi accountant said, as the lift came up and the liftman took Srijut Sharma in.

On the way home, Srijut Sharma found that the gold watch only went when it was shaken. Obviously, some delicate part had broken when he had dropped it on Mr. Acton's table. He would get it mended, but he must save all the cash he could get hold of and not go spending it on the luxury of having a watch repaired now. He shouldn't have been weak with his son and given him his old silver watch. But as there would be no office to go to anymore, he would not need to look at the time very much, specially in Jullunder, where time just stood still and no one bothered about keeping appointments.

# Doris Lessing

Although Doris Lessing has lived in England for nearly fifty years, she has drawn heavily in her fiction from her early years in Africa. She was born in Persia (now Iran), 22 October 1919. When she was six, her parents moved to Rhodesia (now Zimbabwe), where they farmed unsuccessfully. Lessing's mother, a former nurse, established her version of a proper British home in what she considered a savage land; Lessing's father, a World War I veteran left crippled, gave into depression and failure. Such a combination made for an unhappy childhood, and Lessing, recalling those years on the remote farm, said that books served as her escape, thus setting her on a path of self-education. She left school at thirteen and home at fifteen to work as a nursemaid. In 1937 she moved to Rhodesia's capital city of Salisbury (now Harare), worked as a telephone operator, married, and had two children. She left her first family in 1943, and two years later married Gottfried Lessing, a German-Jewish refugee and fellow member in the Left Book Club, a Communist organization whose talk about equality and justice attracted her; she later joined the party, but by 1956 she had become disillusioned and rejected it.

Lessing and her son from the second marriage, which also ended in divorce, moved to London in 1949, where she still lives. A year later her first novel, *The Grass Is Singing*—a story about miscegenation in Africa, appeared in British and American editions, and her long and distinguished career as a writer was underway. In addition to nearly twenty novels, the latest in 1999—*Mara and Dann: An Adventure*, Lessing has published several volumes of short fiction, plays, memoirs, poetry, and essays. But it is her fiction for which she is most widely admired, the best known works being the five-volume *Children of Violence* (1952–1969) and *The Golden Notebook* (1962). Contrasting with her earlier work, several novels described as "inner-space fiction," which reflect her longstanding interest in Sufi mysticism, appeared during the 1970s and early 1980s. In 1994 the first volume of her autobiography, *Under My Skin*, was published, and covered the years before her 1949 arrival in London; the second autobiographical volume, *Walking in the Shade*, appeared in 1997. Thirty or so books and hundreds of articles have been published on Lessing's work, and address it from perspectives ranging from feminism to Jungianism.

While the form of Lessing's fiction moves in sundry directions to include social realism, science fiction, fantasy, fable, and so on, the theme remains constant: the urgent need to expand individual consciousness and to view oneself in untried ways. Critics have pointed to her African background as one of the prime forces behind the fiction. She belonged neither to Rhodesia's white colonial layer, which she rejected, nor to the native sphere from which she was excluded. Then as an exile, a colonial in England, forbidden even to return to her homeland in 1956 for political reasons, she remained an outsider, a detached observer. Further, as a woman who repudiated the traditional role assigned her, she was forced to examine her own disconnection and altered idea of responsibility. This isolation and alienation on several fronts, along with self-examination, are explored fully in the Martha Quest novels, *The Children of Violence*, and through the central character in *The Golden Notebook*.

Like the poet in "A Letter from Home," Lessing must have believed that she dared not practice her art publicly in the confining, provincial atmosphere of colonial society. The idea that the artist must leave the colony, whether it was Rhodesia or Australia or Canada, prevailed until after World War II. Today that is no longer the case, and the brilliant poet, whose destruction is revealed so movingly in this letter, would be free to seek a receptive audience at home, then abroad.

# A Letter from Home

. . . *Ja*, but that isn't why I'm writing this time. You asked about Dick. You're worrying about him?—man! But he's got a poetry scholarship from a Texas university and he's lecturing the Texans about letters and life too in Suid Afrika, South Africa to you (forgive the hostility), and his poems are read, so they tell me, wherever the English read poetry. He's fine, man, but I thought I'd tell you about Johannes Potgieter, remember him? Remember the young poet, The Young Poet? He was around that winter you were here. Don't tell me you've forgotten those big melting brown eyes and those dimples. About ten years ago (*ja*, times flies) he got a type of unofficial grace-gift of a job at St. _____ University on the strength of those poems of his, and—God— they were good. Not that you or any other English-speaking *domkop* will ever know, because they don't translate out of Afrikaans. Remember me telling you and everyone else (give me credit for that at least; I give the devil his due, when he's a poet) what a poet he was, how blerry good he was—but several people tried to translate Hans's poems, including me, and failed. Right. *Goed*. Meanwhile a third of the world's population—or is it a fifth, or to put it an- other way, X5Y59 million people—speak English (and it's increasing by six births a minute) but one million people speak Afrikaans, and though I say it in a whisper, man, only a fraction of them can read it, I mean to read it. But Hans is still a great poet. Right.

He wasn't all that happy about being a sort of unofficial laureate at that university. It's no secret some poets don't make laureates. At the end of seven months he produced a book of poems which had the whole God-fearing place sweating and sniffing out heresy of all kinds, sin, sex, liberalism, brother love, and so forth and so on; but of course in a civilized country (I say this under my breath, or I'll get the sack from my university, and I've got four daughters these days, had you forgotten?) no one would see anything in them but good poetry. Which is how Hans saw them, poor innocent soul. He was surprised at what people saw in them, and he was all upset. He didn't like being called all those names, and the good country boys from their fine farms and the smart town boys from their big houses all started looking sideways, making remarks, and our Hans, he was reduced to pap, because he's not a fighter, Hans; he was never a taker of positions on the side of justice, freedom, and the rest, for tell you the truth, I don't think he ever got round to defining them. *Goed.* He resigned, in what might be called a dignified silence, but his friends knew it was just plain cowardice or, if you like, incomprehension about what the fuss was over, and he went to live in Blagspruit in the Orange Free, where his Tantie Gertrude had a house. He helped her in her store. *Ja,* that's what he did. What did we all say to this? Well, what do you think? The inner soul of the artist (et cetera) knows what is best, and he probably *needed* the Orange Free and his Auntie's store for his development. Well, something like that. To tell the truth, we didn't say much; he simply dropped out. And time passed. *Ja.* Then they made me editor of *Onwards,* and thinking about our indigenous poets, I remembered Johannes Potgieter, and wrote "What about a poem from you?"—feeling bad because when I counted up the years, it was eight since I'd even thought of him, even counting those times when one says drunk at dawn: Remember Hans? Now, there was a poet. . . .

No reply, so I let an editorial interval elapse and I wrote again, and I got a very correct letter back. Well phrased. Polite. But not just that, it took me an hour to work out the handwriting—it was in a sort of Gothic print, each letter a work of art, like a medieval manuscript. But all he said, in that beautiful black art-writing was: he was very well, he hoped I was very well, the weather was good, except the rains were late, his Tantie Gertie was dead, and he was running the store. "*Jou vriend,* Johannes Potgieter."

Right. *Goed.* I was taking a trip up to Joburg, so I wrote and said I'd drop in at Blagspruit on my way back, and I got another Manuscript, or Missal, saying he hoped to see me, and he would prepare Esther for my coming. I thought, he's married, poor *kerel,* and it was the first time I'd thought of him as anything but a born bachelor, and I was right—because when I'd done with Joburg, not a moment too soon, and driven down to the Orange Free, and arrived on the doorstep, there was Hans, but not a sign of a wife, and Esther turned out to be—but first I take pleasure in telling you that the beautiful brown-eyed poet with his noble brow and pale dimpled skin was bald—he has a tonsure, I swear it—and he's fat, a sort of smooth pale fat. He's like a monk, lard-colored and fat and smooth. Esther is the cook, or rather, his jailer. She's a Zulu, a great fat woman, and I swear she put the fear of God into me before I even got into the house. Tantie Gertie's house is a square brick four-roomed shack, you know the kind, with an iron roof and verandas—well, what you'd expect in Blagspruit. And Esther stood about six feet high in a white apron and a white *doekie* and she held a lamp up in one great black fist and looked into my face and sighed and went off into her kitchen singing "Rock of Ages." *Ja*, I promise you. And I looked at Hans, and all he said was "It's O.K., man. She likes you. Come in."

She gave us a great supper of roast mutton and pumpkin fritters and samp, and then some preserved fruit. She stood over us, arms folded, as we ate, and when Johannes left some mutton fat, she said in her mellow hymn-singing voice: "Waste not, want not, Master Johannes." And he ate it all up. *Ja*. She told me I should have some more peaches for my health, but I defied her and I felt as guilty as a small kicker, and I could see Hans eyeing me down the table and wondering where I got the nerve. She lives in the *kia* at the back, one small room with four children by various fathers, but no man, because God is more than enough for her now, you can see, with all those kids and Hans to bring up the right way. Auntie's store is a Drapery and General Goods in the main street, called Gertie's Store, and Hans was running it with a colored man. But I heard Esther with my own ears at supper saying to his bowed bald shamed head: "Master Johannes, I heard from the cook at the predikant's house today that the dried peaches have got worms in them." And Hans said: "O.K., Esther, I'll send them up some of the new stock tomorrow."

Right. We spent all that evening talking, and he was the same old Hans. You remember how he used to sit, saying not a blerry word, smiling that sweet dimpled smile of his, listening, listening, and then he'd ask a question, remember? Well, *do* you? Because it's only just now *I'm* beginning to remember. People'd be talking about I don't know what—the Nats or the weather or the grape crop, anything—and just as you'd start to get nervous because he never said anything, he'd lean forward and start questioning, terribly serious, earnest, about some detail, something not quite central, if you know what I mean. He'd lean forward, smiling, smiling, and he'd say: "You really mean that? It rained all morning? It rained all morning? Is that the truth?" That's right, you'd say, a bit uneasy, and he'd say, shaking his head: "God, man, it rained all morning, you say...." And then there'd be a considerable silence till things picked up again. And half an hour later he'd say: "You really mean it? The hanepoort grapes are good this year?"

Right. We drank a good bit of brandewyn that night, but in a civilized way—you know: "Would you like another little drop, Mr. Martin?" "*Ja*, just a small tot, Hans, thank you"—but we got pretty pickled, and when I woke Sunday morning, I felt like death, but Esther was setting down a tray of tea by my bed, all dressed up in her Sunday hat and her black silk saying: "*Goeie more*, Master du Preez, it's nearly time for church," and I nearly said: "I'm not a churchgoer, Esther," but I thought better of it, because it came to me, can it be possible, has our Hans turned a God-fearing man in Blagspruit? So I said, "*Goed*, Esther. Thanks for telling me, and now just get out of here so that I can get dressed." Otherwise she'd have dressed me, I swear it. And she gave me a majestic nod, knowing that God had spoken through her to send me to church, sinner that I was and stinking of cheap *dop* from the night before.

Right. Johannes and I went to *kerk*, he in a black Sunday suit, if you'd believe such a thing, and saying: "Good morning, Mr. Stein. *Goeie more*, Mrs. Van Esslin," a solid and respected member of the congregation, and I thought, poor *kerel*, there but for the grace of God go I, if I had to live in this godforsaken dorp stuck in the middle of the Orange Free State. And he looked like death after the brandewyn, and so did I, and we sat there swaying and sweating in that blerry little church through a sermon an hour and a half long, while all the faithful gave us nasty curious looks. Then we had a cold lunch, Esther having been worshipping at the Kaffir church down in the Location, and we slept it all off and woke covered with flies and sweating, and it was as hot as hell, which is what Blagspruit is, hell. And he'd been there ten years, man, ten years. . . .

Right. It is Esther's afternoon off, and Johannes says he will make us some tea, but I see he is quite lost without her, so I say: "Give me a glass of water, and let's get out from under this iron, that's all I ask." He looks surprised, because his hide is hardened to it, but off we go, through the dusty little garden full of marigolds and zinnias, you know those sun-baked gardens with the barbed wire fences and the gates painted dried-blood color in those little dorps stuck in the middle of the veld, enough to make you get drunk even to think of them, but Johannes is sniffling at the marigolds, which stink like turps, and he sticks an orange zinnia in his lapel, and says: "Esther likes gardening." And there we go along the main street, saying good afternoon to the citizens, for half a mile, then we're out in the veld again, just the veld. And we wander about, kicking up the dust and watching the sun sink, because both of us have just one idea, which is: how soon can we decently start sundowning?

Then there was a nasty stink on the air, and it came from a small bird impaled on a thorn on a thorn tree, which was a butcherbird's cache, have you ever seen one? Every blerry thorn had a beetle or a worm or something stuck on it, and it made me feel pretty sick, coming on top of everything, and I was just picking up a stone to throw at the damned thorn tree, to spite the butcherbird, when I saw Hans staring at a lower part of this tree. On a long black thorn was a great big brown beetle, and it was waving all its six legs and its two feelers in rhythm, trying to claw the thorn out of its middle, or so it looked, and it was writhing and wriggling, so that at last it fell off the thorn, which was at right angles, so to speak, from the soil, and it landed on its back, still waving its legs, trying to up itself. At which Hans bent down to look at it for some time, his two monk's hands on his upper thighs, his bald head sweating and glowing red in the last sunlight. *Then he bent down, picked up the beetle and stuck it back on the thorn.* Carefully, you understand, so that the thorn went back into the hole it had already made. You could see he was trying not to hurt the beetle. I just stood and gaped, like a *domkop*, and for some reason I remembered how one used to feel when he leaned forward and said, all earnest and involved: "You say the oranges are no good this year? Honestly, is that really true?" Anyway, I said: "Hans, man, for God's sake." And then he looked at me, and he said, reproachfully: "The ants would have killed it, just look." Well, the ground was swarming with ants of one kind or another, so there was logic in it, but I said: "Hans, let's drink, man, let's drink."

Well, it was Sunday, and no bars open. I took a last look at the beetle, the black thorn through its oozing middle, waving its black legs at the setting sun, and I said: "Back home, Hans, and to hell with Esther. We're going to get drunk."

Esther was in the kitchen, putting out cold meat and tomatoes, and I said: "Esther, you can take the evening off."

She said: "Master Hans, I have had all the Sunday afternoon off talking to Sister Mary." Hans looked helpless at me, and I said: "Esther, I'm giving you the evening off. Good night,"

And Hans said, stuttering and stammering: "That's right, Esther, I'll give you the evening off. Good night, Esther."

She looked at him. Then at me. Hey, what a woman. Hey, what a queen, man! She said, with dignity: "Good night, Mr. Johannes. Good night, Mr. du Preez." Then she wiped her hands free of evil on her white apron, and she strode off, singing "All things bright and beautiful," and I tell you we felt as if we weren't good enough to wash Esther's *broekies,* and that's the truth.

*Goed.* We got out the brandy, never mind about the cold meat and the tomatoes, and about an hour later I reached my point at last, which was, what about the poems, and the reason I'd taken so long was I was scared he'd say: "Take a look at Blagspruit, man. Take a look. Is this the place for poems, Martin?" But when I asked, he leaned forward and stared at me, all earnest and intent, then he turned his head carefully to the right, to see if the door into the kitchen was shut, but it wasn't; and then left at the window, and that was open too, and then past me at the door to the verandah. Then he got up on tiptoes and very carefully shut all three, and then he drew the curtains. It gave me the *skriks*, man, I can tell you. Then he went to a great old black chest and took out a Manuscript, because it was all in the beautiful black difficult writing, and gave it to me to read. And I sat and slowly worked it out, letter by letter, while he sat opposite, sweating and totting, and giving fearful looks over his shoulders.

What was it? Well, I was drunk, for one thing, and Hans sitting there all frightened scared me, but it was good, it was good, I promise you. A kind of chronicle of Blagspruit it was, the lives of the citizens—well, need I elaborate, since the lives of citizens are the same everywhere in the world, but worse in Suid Afrika, and worse a million times in Blagspruit. The Manuscript gave off a stink of church and right-doing, with the sin and the evil underneath. It had a medieval stink to it, naturally enough, for what is worse than the *kerk* in this our land? But I'm saying this to you, remember, and I never said it, but what is worse than the stink of the *kerk* and the God-fearing in this our feudal land?

But the poem. As far as I can remember, because I was full as a tick, it was a sort of prose chronicle that led up to and worked into the poems; you couldn't tell where they began or ended. The prose was stiff and old-fashioned, and formal, monk's language, and the poems too. But I knew when I read it it was the best I'd read in years—since I read those poems of his ten years before, man, not since then. And don't forget, God help me, I'm an editor now, and I read poems day and night, and when I come on something like Hans's poems that night I have nothing to say but—*Goed.*

Right. I was working away there an hour or more because of that damned black ornamented script. Then I put it down and I said: "Hans, can I ask you a question?" And he looked this way and that over his shoulder first, then leaned forward, the lamplight shining on his pate, and he asked in a low trembling sinner's voice: "What do you want to ask me, Martin?"

I said, "Why this complicated handwriting? What for? It's beautiful, but why this monkey's puzzle?"

And he lowered his voice and said: "It's so that Esther can't read it."

I said; "And what of it, Hans? Why not? Give me some more brandewyn and tell me."

He said: "She's a friend of the predikant's cook, and her sister Mary works in the Mayor's kitchen."

I saw it all. I was drunk, so I saw it. I got up, and I said: "Hans, you're right. You're right a thousand times. If you're going to write stuff like this, as true and as beautiful as God and all his angels, then Esther mustn't read it. But why don't you let me take this back with me and print it in *Onwards*?"

He went white and looked as if I might knife him there and then like a *totsti.* He grabbed the Manuscript from me and held it against his fat chest, and he said; "They mustn't see it."

"You're right," I said, understanding him completely.

"It's dangerous keeping it here," he said, darting fearful looks all around.

"Yes, you're right," I said, and I sat down with a bump in my *rimpie* chair, and I said: "*Ja*, if they found that, Hans . . ."

"They'd kill me," he said.

I saw it, completely.

I was drunk. He was drunk. We put the Manuscript *boekie* on the table and we put our arms around each other and we wept for the citizens of Blagspruit. Then we lit the hurricane lamp in the kitchen, and he took his *boekie* under his arm, and we tiptoed out into the moonlight that stank of marigolds, and out we went down the main street, all dark as the pit now because it was after twelve and the citizens were asleep, and we went staggering down the tarmacked street that shone in the moonlight between low dark houses, and out into the veld. There we looked sorrowfully at each other and wept some sad brandy tears, and right in front of us, the devil aiding us, was a thorn tree. All virgin it was, its big black spikes lifted up and shining in the devil's moon. And we wept a long time more, and we tore out the pages from his Manuscript and we made them into little screws of paper and we stuck them all over the thorns, and when there were none left, we sat under the thorn tree in the moonlight, the black spiky thorns making thin purplish shadows all over us and over the white sand. Then we wept for the state of our country and the state of poetry. We drank a lot more brandy, and the ants came after it and us, so we staggered back down the gleaming sleeping main street of Blagspruit, and that's all I remember until Esther was standing over me with a tin tray that had a teapot, teacup, sugar and some condensed milk, and she was saying: "Master du Preez, where is Master Hans?"

I saw the seven o'clock sun outside the window, and I remembered everything, and I sat up and I said: "My God!"

And Esther said: "God has not been in this house since half-past five on Saturday last." And went out.

Right. I got dressed, and went down the main street, drawing looks from the Monday-morning citizens, all of whom had probably been watching us staggering along last night from behind their black drawn curtains. I reached the veld and there was Hans. A wind had got up, a hot dust-devilish wind, and it blew about red dust and bits of grit, and leaves, and dead grass into the blue sky, and those pale dry bushes that leave their roots and go bouncing and twirling all over the empty sand, like dervishes, round and round, and then up and around, and there was Hans, letting out yelps and cries and shouts, and he was chasing about after screws of paper that were whirling around among all the dust and stuff.

I helped him. The thorn tree had three squirts of paper tugging and blowing from spikes of black thorn, so I collected those, and we ran after the blowing white bits that had the black beautiful script on them, and we got perhaps a third back. Then we sat under the thorn tree, the hard sharp black shadows over us and the sand, and we watched a dust devil whirling columns of yellow sand and his poems up and off into the sky.

I said: "But Hans, you could write them down again, couldn't you? You couldn't have forgotten them, surely?"

And he said: "But, Martin, anyone can read them now. Don't you see that, man? Esther could come out here next afternoon off, and pick any one of those poems up off the earth and read it. Or suppose the predikant or the Mayor got their hands on them?"

Then I understood. I promise you, it had never crossed my *domkop* mind until that moment. I swear it. I simply sat there, sweating out guilt and brandy, and I looked at that poor madman, and then I remembered back ten years and I thought: You idiot. You fool.

Then at last I got intelligent and I said: "But, Hans, even if Esther and the predikant and the Mayor did come out here and pick up your poems, like leaves, off the bushes? They couldn't understand one word, because they are written in that slim black script you worked out for yourself."

I saw his poor crazy face get more happy, and he said: "You think so, Martin? Really? You really think so?"

I said: "*Ja*, it's the truth." And he got all happy and safe, while I thought of those poems whirling around forever, or until the next rainstorm, around the blue sky with the dust and the bits of shining grass.

And I said: "Anyway, at the best only perhaps a thousand, or perhaps two thousand, people would understand that beautiful *boekie*. Try to look at it that way, Hans, it might make you feel better."

By this time he looked fine; he was smiling and cheered up.

Right.

We got up and dusted each other off, and I took him home to Esther. I asked him to let me take the poems we'd rescued back to publish in *Onwards*, but he got desperate again and said: "No, no. Do you want to kill me? Do you want them to kill me? You're my friend, Martin, you can't do that."

So I told Esther that she had a great man in her charge, through whom Heaven Itself spoke, and she was right to take such care of him. But she merely nodded her queenly white-*doekied* head and said: "Good-bye, Master du Preez, and may God be with you."

So I came home to Kapstaad.

A week ago I got a letter from Hans, but I didn't see at once it was from him; it was in ordinary writing, like yours or mine, but rather unformed and wild, and it said: "I am leaving this place. They know me now. They look at me. I'm going north to the river. Don't tell Esther. *Jou vriend*, Johannes Potgieter."

Right.

*Jou vriend,*
Martin du Preez

# Robertson Davies

Canada's venerable man of letters was the son of a Welsh immigrant who prospered as a newspaper publisher. Born on 28 August 1913 into an educated family living in a remote Canadian town, Robertson Davies began writing at an early age and did not stop until his death in December of 1995. He received his preparatory education at an exclusive Canadian boys' school, then graduated from Queen's University in Kingston, Ontario, followed by further study at Oxford in England. Yielding to his passion for the theater, he acted at the Old Vic in London for a season, but returned to Canada in 1940 convinced that an acting career was not for him. At home he edited one of his father's newspapers for nearly twenty years, and at the same time started publishing fiction, sketches, and plays. In 1960 he served as a visiting professor at the University of Toronto, and joined the staff a year later as the master of Massey College, where he remained until 1981. Never retiring, he continued to write and published his last novel, *The Cunning Man*, in 1994. A man of many parts, Davies combined the careers of businessman, journalist, lecturer, scholar, actor, and playwright, but it is as a novelist that he is now most widely known and will likely continue to be.

The dominant theme in Davies's fiction focuses on the individual's pursuit of identity. As well, the novels set out to examine the way a nation, Canada in particular, formulates and claims its identity. The thematic source for much of the writing comes from Carl Jung's work, which Davies studied and admired. The eleven novels are set for the most part in Canada but occasionally move to other parts of the world. Reflecting Davies's wide interests and extensive scholarship, the fiction embodies not only Jungian theories but also such elements as magic, theatrical production, art restoration, academia, music, medicine, and religion. His urbane, witty work also abounds in biting satire, directed especially at Canadians' philistine attitude toward the arts, middle-class pretentiousness, academic eccentricities, and orthodox Christianity. In part the nine novels that comprise what are now called "The Salterton Trilogy," "The Deptford Trilogy," and "The Cornish Trilogy," as well as the last two, provide a social history of Canada from the colonial era to its gradual emergence as a country in its own right.

Davies also had a penchant for telling ghost stories, and a collection of them, *High Spirits*, appeared in 1983, including "The Charlottetown Banquet." Based on a historical incident and personage, this charming tale exemplifies Davies's fictional touch to a large degree—through its elegance and wit, the rich detail, a slight hint of snobbery, and a sheer delight in the good life. Sir John A. Macdonald, born in Scotland in 1815, was the architect of Confederation, which united Canada's scattered parts; in 1867 he became the country's first prime minister and died in office in 1891. In an effort to persuade the maritime colonies to join the Confederation, Macdonald attended the famed dinner at Charlottetown, Prince Edward Island. Davies successfully mixes the historical and supernatural, as well as counterpointing colonial and contemporary Canada.

# The Charlottetown Banquet

The range of guests who come to our fortnightly High Table dinners is wide, and provides us with extraordinarily good company. Sometimes we get a surprise—an economist who turns out to be a poet, for instance. (I mean a poet in the formal sense: all economists are rapt, fanciful creatures; it is necessary to their profession.) Only last Friday we had a visitor whom I found a most delightful and illuminating companion. I shall not tell you what his profession is, or you will immediately identify him, and I shall have betrayed his secret, which is that he is a medium.

He does not like being a medium. He finds it embarrassing. But the gift, like being double-jointed or having the power to wiggle one's ears, can neither be acquired by study nor abdicated by an act of will. His particular power lies in the realm of psychometry; that is to say that sometimes—not always—he finds that when he is near to an object that has strong and remarkable associations, he becomes aware of those associations with an intensity that is troublesome to him. And occasionally psychic manifestations follow.

He confided this to me just as we were leaving the small upstairs dining-room, where we assemble after dinner for conversation and a reasonable consumption of port and Madeira. We were standing at the end of the room by the sideboard, for he had been looking at our College grant-of-arms; he put his hand on the wall to the left of the frame, to enable him to lean forward for a closer look, and then he turned to me, rather white around the mouth, I thought, and said—

"Let's go downstairs. It's terribly close in here."

I thought it was the cigar smoke that was troubling him. Excellent as the Bursar's cigars undoubtedly are, the combustion of a couple of dozen of them within an hour does make the air rather heavy. So I went downstairs with him, and thought no more about the matter.

It must have been a couple of hours later that I was taking a turn around the quad for a breath of air before bed, when I saw something I did not like. The window of the small dining room was lighted up, but not by electricity. It was a low, flickering light that seemed to rise and fall in its intensity, and I thought at once of fire. I dashed up the stairs with a burst of speed that any of the Junior Fellows might envy, and opened the door. Sure enough, there was light in the room.

But—! Now you must understand that we had left the room in the usual sort of disorder; the table had been covered with the debris of our frugal academic pleasures—nutshells, the parings of fruit, soiled wine-glasses, filled ashtrays, crumpled napkins, and all that sort of thing. But now—!

I have never seen the room looking as it looked at that moment. How shall I describe it?

To begin, the table was covered with a cloth of that refulgent blueywhiteness that speaks of the finest linen. And, what is more, there was not a crease in it; obviously it had been ironed on the table. The pattern that was woven into it was of maple leaves, entwined with lilies and roses. At every place—and it was set for twenty-four—was a napkin folded into the intricate shape known to Victorian butlers as Crown Imperial. At either end of the table was a soup tureen, and my heightened senses immediately discerned that the eastern tureen contained Mock Turtle, while that at the western end was filled with a Consommé enriched with a *julienne* of truffles—that is to say, Consommé Britannia. A noble boiled salmon of the Restigouche variety was displayed on one platter, with a vessel of Lobster Sauce in waiting, and on another was a selection of Fillets of the most splendid Nova Scotia mackerel, each gleaming with the pearls of a Sauce Maitre d'Hotel.

And the Entrees! Petites Bouches à la Reine, and Grenadine de Veau with a Pique Sauce Tomate—and none of your nasty bottled tomato sauce, either, but the genuine fresh article. There was a Lapin Sauté which had been made to stand upright, its paws raised as though in delight at its own beauty, and a charming fluff of cauliflower sprigs where its tail had been a few hours before; you could see that it was served au Champignons, for two button mushrooms gleamed where its eyes had once been. There was a Cotellete d'Agneau with, naturally, Petits Pois. There was a Coquette de Volaille, and a Timbale de Macaroni which had been molded into the form of—of all things—a Beaver.

In addition there were roasted turkeys, chickens, a saddle of mutton and a sirloin of beef, and there were boiled turkeys, hams, corned beef and mutton cutlets. And it was all piping hot.

The flickering soft light I had seen through the window came from a gasolier that hung over the table, and through its alabaster globes gleamed the gaslight—surely one of the loveliest forms of illumination ever devised by man.

You have recognized the meal, of course. Every gourmet has that menu by heart. It was the Grand Banquet in Honour of the Colonial Delegates which was held at the Halifax Hotel in Charlottetown on September 12, 1864. This was the authentic food of Confederation. A specimen of the menu, elegantly printed on silk, and the gift of Professor Maurice Careless, one of our Senior Fellows, hangs on the wall of our small dining room, just at the point where our guest, the medium, had laid his hand.

Nor was this all. What I have described to you at some length leapt to my eye in an instant, and my gaze had turned to the sideboard, which was laden with bottles of wine.

And what bottles! Tears came into my eyes, just to look at them. For these were not our ugly modern bottles, with their disagreeable Government stickers adhering to them, and their high shoulders, and their uniformity of shape, and their self-righteous airs, as though in the half-literate, nasal drone of politicians, they were declaiming: "We are the support of paved roads, general education and public health; we are the pillars of society." No, no; these were smaller bottles, in a multiplicity of shapes and colors. There were the slim pale-green maidens of hock; the darkly opalescent romantic ports; the sturdily gay clarets and the high-nosed aristocrats of Burgundy; there were champagnes that almost danced, yet were not gassy impostors; and they were all bottles of the old shapes and the old colors—dark, merry and wicked.

My knees gave a little, and I sat down in the nearest chair.

It was then that I noticed the figure by the sideboard. His back was toward me, and whether he was somewhat clouded in outline, or whether my eyes were dazzled by the table, I cannot say, but I could not quite make him out. He was hovering —I might almost say gloating—over a dozen of sherry. That should have given me a clue, but you will understand that I was not fully myself. And, furthermore, I had at that instant recalled that the menu given to us by Professor Careless was said by him to have been the property of the Honorable George Brown. On such a matter one does not doubt the word of Maurice Careless.

"Mr. Brown! I believe?" I said, in what I hoped was a hospitable tone.

"God forbid that I should cast doubt on any man's belief," said the figure, still with its back to me, "but I cannot claim the distinction you attribute to me." He picked up a bottle of sherry and drew the cork expertly. Then he drew the cork of another, and turned toward me with a wicked chuckle, a bottle in either hand;

"These are Clan Alpine's warriors true,

And, Saxon, I am Roderick Dhu—"

said he, and I was so astonished that I quite overlooked the disagreeable experience of being addressed as a Saxon. For it was none other than Old Tomorrow himself!

Yes, it was Sir John A. Macdonald in his habit as he lived. Or rather, not precisely as we are accustomed to seeing him, but in Victorian evening dress, with a red silk handkerchief thrust into the bosom of his waistcoat. But that head of somewhat stringy ringlets, that crumpled face which seemed to culminate and justify itself in the bulbous, coppery nose, that watery, rolling, merry eye, the accordion pleating of the throat, those moist, mobile lips, were unmistakable.

"If you were expecting Brown, I am truly sorry," he continued. "But, you see, I was the owner of this menu." (He pronounced it, in the Victorian manner, meenoo.) "Brown pocketed it as we left the table. It was a queer little way he had, of picking up odds and ends; we charitably assumed he took them home to his children. But it's mine, right enough. Look, you can see my thumb-mark on it still."

But I was not interested in thumb-prints. I was deep in awe of the shade before me. I started to my feet. In a voice choking with emotion I cried: "The Father of my country!"

"Hookey Walker!" said Sir John, with a wink. "Tuck in your napkin, Doctor, and let us enjoy this admirable repast."

I had no will of my own. I make no excuses. Who, under such circumstances, would have done other than he was bidden? I sat. Sir John, with remarkable grace, uncovered the Mock Turtle, and gave me a full plate. I ate it. Then he gave me a plate of the Consommé Britannia. I ate it. Then I had quite a lot of the salmon. Then a substantial helping of mackerel. I ate busily, humbly, patriotically.

I have always heard of the extraordinary gustatory zest of the Victorians. They ate hugely. But it began to be borne in upon me, as Sir John plied me with one good thing after another, that I was expected to eat all, or at least some, of everything on the table. My gorge rose. But, I said to myself, when will you, ever again, eat such a meal in such company? And my gorge subsided. I began to be aware that my appetite was unimpaired. The food I placed in my mouth, and chewed, and swallowed, seemed to lose substance somewhere just behind my necktie. I had no sense of repletion. And little by little it came upon me that I was eating a ghostly meal, in ghostly company, and that under such circumstances I could go on indefinitely. Not even my jaws ached. But the taste—ah, the taste was as palpable as though the viands were of this earth.

Meanwhile Sir John was keeping pace with me, bite for bite. But rather more than glass for glass. He had asked me to name my poison, which I took to be a Victorian jocularity for choosing my wine, and I had taken a

Moselle—a fine Berncasteler—with the soup and fish, and had then changed to a St. Emilion with the entrees. (It was particularly good with the rabbit, a dish of which I am especially fond; Sir John did not want any, and I ate that rabbit right down to the ground, and sucked its ghostly bones.) But Sir John stuck to sherry. Never have I seen a man put away so much sherry. And none of your whimpering dry sherries, either, but a brown sherry that looked like liquefied plum pudding. He threw it off a glass at a time, and he got through bottle after bottle.

You must not suppose that we ate in silence. I do not report our conversation because it is of slight interest. Just—"Another slice of turkey, my dear Doctor; allow me to give you the liverwing." And—"Sir John, let me press you to a little more of this excellent Timbale de Macaroni; and may I refill your glass. Oh, you've done it yourself." You know the sort of thing; the polite exchanges of men who are busy with their food.

But at last the table was empty, except for bones and wreckage. I sat back, satisfied yet in no way uncomfortable, and reached for a toothpick. It was a Victorian table, and so there were toothpicks of the finest sort—real quill toothpicks such as one rarely sees in these weakly fastidious days. I was ready to put into effect the plan I had been hatching.

In the bad old days, before the academic life claimed me, I was, you must know, a journalist. And here I found myself in a situation of which no journalist would dare even to dream. Across the table from me sat one whose unique knowledge of our country's past was incalculably enhanced by his extraordinary privilege of possessing access to our country's future! Here was one who could tell me what would be the outcome of the present disquiet in Quebec. And then how I should be courted in Ottawa! Would I demand the Order of Canada—the Companionship, not the mere medal—before I deigned to reveal what I knew? And how I should lord it over Maurice Careless! But I at once put this unworthy thought from me. Whom the gods would destroy, they first make mad. I wound myself up to put my leading question.

But, poor creature of the twentieth century that I am, I was mistaken about the nature of our meal.

"Ready for the second course, I think, eh Doctor?" said Sir John, and waved his hand. In a moment, in the twinkling of an eye—the Biblical phrase popped into my mind—the table was completely reset, and before us was spread a profusion of partridges, wild duck, lobster salad, galantines, plum pudding, jelly, pink blancmange, Charlotte Russe, Italian Cream, a Bavarian Cream, a Genoa Cream, plates of pastries of every variety—apple puffs, bouchées, cornucopias, croquenbouche, flans, strawberry tartlets, maids-of-honor, stuffed monkeys, prune flory, tortelli—it was bewildering. And there were ice creams in the Victorian temples of frozen, colored, flavored cornstarch—and there were plum cakes and that now forgotten delicacy called Pyramids.

And fruit! Great towers of fruit, mounting from foundations of apples, through oranges and nectarines to capitals of berries and currants, upon each of which was perched the elegantly explosive figure of a pineapple.

You see, I had forgotten that a proper Victorian dinner had a second course of this nature, so that one might have some relaxation after the serious eating was over.

But Sir John seemed disappointed. "What!" he cried, "no gooseberry fool? And I had been so much looking forward to it!" He proceeded to drown his sorrow in sherry.

I had no fault to find. I began again, eating methodically of every dish, and accepting second helpings of Charlotte Russe and plum cake. During this course I drank champagne only. It was that wonderful Victorian champagne, somewhat sweeter than is now fashionable, and with a caressing, rather than an aggressive, carbonization. I hope I did not drink greedily, but in Sir John's company it was not easy to tell.

I do not mean to give you the impression that Sir John was the worse for his wine. He was completely self-possessed, but I could not help being aware that he had consumed nine bottles of sherry without any assistance from me, and that he showed no sign of stopping. I knew—once again I was in the debt of Professor Careless for this information—that it was sherry he had favored for those Herculean bouts of solitary drinking that are part of his legend. I was concerned, and I suppose my concern showed. Before I could begin my interrogation, might not my companion lose the power of coherent speech? I sipped my champagne and nibbled abstractedly at a stuffed monkey wondering what to do. Suddenly Sir John turned to me.

"Have a weed?" he said. I accepted an excellent cigar from the box he pushed toward me.

"And a b. and s. to top off with?" he continued. Once again I murmured my acquiescence, and he prepared a brandy and soda for me at the sideboard. But for himself he kept right on with the sherry.

"Now, Doctor," said Sir John, "I can see that you have something on your mind. Out with it."

"It isn't very easy to put into words," said I. "Here am I, just as Canada's centennial year is drawing to a close, sitting alone with the great architect of our Confederation. Naturally my mind is full of questions; the problem is, which should come first?"

"Ah, the centennial year," said Sir John. "Well, in my time, you know, we didn't have this habit of chopping history up into century-lengths. It's always the centennial of something."

"But not the centennial of Canada," said I. "You pretend to be indifferent to the growth of the country you yourself brought into being."

"Not indifferent at all," said he. "I've put myself to inconvenience during the past year, dodging all over the continent—*a mari usque ad mare*—to look at this, that and the other thing."

I could not control myself; the inevitable question burst from my lips. "Did you see Expo?" I cried.

"I certainly did," said he, laughing heartily, "and I took special trouble to be there at the end when they were adding up the bill. The deficit was roughly eight times the total budget of this Dominion for the year 1867. You call that a great exposition? Why, my dear Doctor, the only Great Exposition that made any sense at all was the Great Exposition of 1851. It was the only world's fair in history that produced a profit. And why was that? Because it was dominated by that great financier and shrewd man of business Albert the Prince Consort. If you had had any sense you would have put your confounded Expo under the guidance of the Duke of Edinburgh; no prince would have dared to bilk and rook the country as your politicians did, for he would have known that it might cost him his, head. Expo!—" And then Sir John used some genial indecencies which I shall not repeat.

"But Sir John," I protested, "this is a democratic age."

"Democracy, sir, has its limitations, like all political theories," said he, and I remembered that I was talking, after all, to a great Conservative and a titled Canadian. But now, if ever, was the time to come to the point.

"We have hopes that our mighty effort may reflect itself in the future development of our country," said I. "Because you have been so kind as to make yourself palpable to me I am going to ask a very serious question. Sir John, may I inquire what you see in store for Canada, the land which you brought into being, the land which reveres your memory, the land in which your ashes lie and your mighty example is still an inspiration? May I ask what the second century of our Confederation will bring?"

"You may ask, sir," said Sir John; "but it won't signify, you know. I see, Doctor, that I must give you a peep into the nature of the realm of which I am now a part. It is a world of peace, and every man's idea of peace is his own. Consider the life I led: it was one long vexation. It was an obstacle race in which my rivals were people like that tendentious, obstructive ass Brown, that rancorous, dissident ruffian Cartier, even such muttonheaded fellows as Tupper and Mowat. It was a world in which I would be interrupted in the task of writing a flattering letter to an uncomprehending Queen in order to choke off some Member of Parliament who wanted one of his constituents appointed to the post of a lighthouse-keeper. It was a life in which my every generous motive was construed as political artfulness, and my frailties were inflated into examples to scare the children of the Grits. It was, Doctor, the life of a yellow dog. Now—what would peace be to such a man as I was? Freedom, Doctor; freedom from such cares as those; freedom to observe the comedy and tragedy of life without having to take a hand in it. Freedom to do as I please without regard for consequences."

During this long speech Sir John had finished the final bottle of his dozen of sherry. Those which he had drunk before had all floated, each as it was emptied, to the sideboard, where they now stood in a cluster. He picked up the twelfth bottle, and whirled it round his head like an Indian club, closing one eye to take more careful aim.

"You ask about the future of Canada, my dear sir?" he shouted. "Understandably you want to tell the world what I know it to be. But you can't, my dear Doctor, because I haven't taken the trouble to look. And the reason for that, my dear sir, is that I DO NOT GIVE A DAMN!"

And as he uttered these fearful words the Father of My Country hurled that last sherry bottle at the eleven on the sideboard. There was a tremendous smash, the gaslight went out, and I lost consciousness.

How much later it was I cannot tell, but when I was myself again I was walking around the quad, somewhat dazed but strangely elated. For, although I had been baulked in my wish to learn something of the future in this world, had I not been admitted to a precious, soothing, heartlifting secret about the next? To be a Canadian, yet not to have to give a damn—was it not glorious?

And to have eaten the Charlottetown banquet in such company! A smile rose to my lips, and with it the ghost of a hiccup.

# Alan Paton

Alan Paton's first novel, *Cry, the Beloved Country*, has evolved into a legendary work. Its author had lived until the book's publication an ordinary, obscure life. He was born in Pietermaritzburg, South Africa, 11 January 1903, into a middle-class family of British descent. Educated at Maritzburg College and Natal University College, he first taught at Maritzburg, then in 1935 became principal of Diepkloof Reformatory for young black males. In 1948 *Cry, the Beloved Country* appeared in the United States and Great Britain, and immediately received an overwhelming reception. That same year the National Party, the architects of the apartheid system, came to power in South Africa. Paton resigned from the Reformatory to take up writing full time.

His second novel, *Too Late the Phalarope*, appeared in 1953, followed in 1961 by a collection of short stories, *Tales from a Troubled Land*. A third novel, *Ah, But Your Land Is Beautiful* was published in 1981. He also published three biographies of prominent South African figures, as well as books and articles on South African politics and social problems. In addition he wrote three autobiographical works: *For You Departed* (1969), which is a moving tribute to his first wife; *Towards the Mountain* (1980); and *Journey Continued* (1988), which appeared three weeks after Paton died on 12 April 1988.

Called "a reluctant politician," Paton remained in constant opposition to the ruling political party, and to some degree became an international symbol of white South African resistance against apartheid. While this untenable political and social ideology has vanished, it is unlikely that Paton's legacy will fade. *Cry, the Beloved Country* continues to be read, has been translated into several languages, and turned into film twice. And its overriding theme of racial reconciliation remains relevant, even if parts of the book appear dated. While *Too Late the Phalarope* may be the better work from a literary stand-

point, it has never received the attention accorded to the first book. This ne-
glect probably stems mainly from its focus on the Afrikaners. Descendants of
the early Dutch settlers in South Africa for the most part, the Afrikaners have
developed their own language and culture, which are not generally known
abroad. Still, the novel paints in different but equally memorable tones one
more vivid picture of the tragic consequences rendered by racial separation
and hatred.

"A Drink in the Passage" appeared first in *Tales from a Troubled Land*.
Most of the stories in this collection are derived from Paton's experiences at
Diepkloof Reformatory, and recount both the comic and the sad encounters
between black inmates and white staff members. But "A Drink in the Passage" differs in setting and content. While the black artist is a fictional creation, the incident has a factual basis. A friend of Paton's, Todd Matshikiza—
a black musician, told Paton about being invited by a white South African to
his apartment house to share "a drink in the passage," and Paton turned the
strange experience into a short story. In 1960 Paton and Matshikiza collabo-
rated on the musical "Mkhumbane—the story of the village in the gulley," for
which Paton wrote the libretto.

# A Drink in the Passage

In the year 1960 the Union of South Africa celebrated its Golden Jubilee, and there was a nation-wide sensation when the one-thousand-pound prize for the finest piece of sculpture was won by a black man, Edward Simelane. His work, *African Mother and Child*, not only excited the admiration, but touched the conscience or heart or whatever it is, of white South Africa, and was likely to make him famous in other countries.

It was by an oversight that his work was accepted, for it was the policy of the Government that all the celebrations and competitions should be strictly segregated. The committee of the sculpture section received a private reprimand for having been so careless as to omit the words "for whites only" from the conditions, but was told, by a very high personage it is said, that if Simelane's work "was indisputably the best," it should receive the award. The committee then decided that this prize must be given along with the others, at the public ceremony which would bring this particular part of the celebrations to a close.

For this decision it received a surprising amount of support from the white public, but in certain powerful quarters, there was an outcry against any departure from the "traditional policies" of the country, and a threat that many white prize-winners would renounce their prizes. However a crisis was averted, because the sculptor was "unfortunately unable to attend the ceremony."

*"I wasn't feeling up to it," Simelane said mischievously to me. "My parents, and my wife's parents, and our priest, decided that I wasn't feeling up to it.*

From *Tales from a Troubled Land*. Copyright © 1961 by Alan Paton. Used by permission of Andrew Ewing & Associates, Natal, South Africa, on behalf of The Estate of Alan Paton.

*And finally I decided so too. Of course Majosi and Sola and the others wanted me to go and get my prize personally, but I said, 'boys, I'm a sculptor, not a demonstrator.'"*

*"This cognac is wonderful," he said, "especially in these big glasses. It's the first time I've had such a glass. It's also the first time I've drunk a brandy so slowly. In Orlando you develop a throat of iron, and you just put back your head and pour it down, in case the police should arrive."*

*He said to me, "this is the second cognac I've had in my life. Would you like to hear the story of how I had my first?"*

• • • • •

You know the Alabaster Bookshop in von Brandis Street? Well, after the competition they asked me if they could exhibit my *African Mother and Child*. They gave a whole window to it, with a white velvet backdrop, if there is anything called white velvet, and some complimentary words, *black man conquers white world*.

Well somehow I could never go and look in that window. On my way from the station to the *Herald* office, I sometimes went past there, and I felt good when I saw all the people standing there, but I would only squint at it out of the comer of my eye.

Then one night I was working late at the *Herald*, and when I came out there was hardly anyone in the streets, so I thought I'd go and see the window, and indulge certain pleasurable human feelings. I must have got a little lost in the contemplation of my own genius, because suddenly there was a young white man standing next to me.

He said to me, "what do you think of that, mate?" And you know, one doesn't get called "mate" every day.

"I'm looking at it," I said.

*"I live near here," he said, "and I come and look at it nearly every night. You know it's by one of your own boys, don't you? See, Edward Similane."*

*"Yes, I know."*

*"It's beautiful," he said. "Look at that mother's head. She's loving that child, but she's somehow watching too. Do you see that? Like someone guarding. She knows it won't be an easy life."*

*He cocked his head on one side, to see the thing better.*

*"He got a thousand pounds for it," he said. "That's a lot of money for one of your boys. But good luck to him. You don't get much luck, do you?"*

*Then he said confidentially, "Mate, would you like a drink?"*

Well honestly I didn't feel like a drink at that time of night, with a white stranger and all, and me still with a train to catch to Orlando.

*"You know we black people must be out of the city by eleven," I said.*

*"It won't take long. My flat's just round the corner. Do you speak Afrikaans?"*

*"Since I was a child," I said in Afrikaans.*

*"We'll speak Afrikaans then. My English isn't too wonderful. I'm van Rensburg. And you?"*

I couldn't have told him my name. I said I was Vakalisa, living in Orlando.

"Vakalisa, eh? I haven't heard that name before."

By this time he had started off, and I was following, but not willingly. That's my trouble, as you'll soon see. I can't break off an encounter. We didn't exactly walk abreast, but he didn't exactly walk in front of me. He didn't look constrained. He wasn't looking round to see if anyone might be watching.

He said to me, "do you know what I wanted to do?"

"No," I said.

*"I wanted a bookshop, like that one there. I always wanted that, ever since I can remember. When I was small, I had a little shop of my own." He laughed at himself. "Some were real books, of course, but some of them I wrote myself. But I had bad luck. My parents died before I could finish school."*

Then he said to me, "are you educated?"

I said unwillingly, "Yes." Then I thought to myself, how stupid, for leaving the question open.

And sure enough he asked, "Far?"

And again unwillingly, I said, "Far."

He took a big leap and said, "Degree?"

"Yes."

"Literature?"

"Yes."

He expelled his breath, and gave a long "ah." We had reached his building, Majorca Mansions, not one of those luxurious places. I was glad to see that the entrance lobby was deserted. I wasn't at my ease. I don't feel at my ease in such places, not unless I am protected by friends, and this man was a stranger. The lift was at ground level, marked "Whites only. Slegs vir Blankes." Van Rensburg opened the door and waved me in. Was he constrained? To this day I don't know. While I was waiting for him to press the button, so that we could get moving and away from that ground floor, he stood with his finger suspended over it, and looked at me with a kind of honest, unselfish envy.

*"You were lucky," he said. "Literature, that's what I wanted to do."*

He shook his head and pressed the button, and he didn't speak again until we stopped high up. But before we got out he said suddenly, "if I had had a bookshop, I'd have given that boy a window too."

We got out and walked along one of those polished concrete passageways. I suppose you could call it a stoep if it weren't so high up, let's call it a passage. On the one side was a wall, and plenty of fresh air, and far down below von Brandis Street. On the other side were the doors, impersonal doors; you could hear radio and people talking, but there wasn't a soul in sight. I wouldn't like living so high; we Africans like being close to the earth. Van Rensburg stopped at one of the doors, and said to me, "I won't be a minute." Then he went in, leaving the door open, and inside I could hear voices. I thought to myself, he's telling them who's here. Then after a minute or so, he came back to the door, holding two glasses of red wine. He was warm and smiling.

*"Sorry there's no brandy," he said. "Only wine. Here's happiness."*

Now I certainly had not expected that I would have my drink in the passage. I wasn't only feeling what you may be thinking. I was thinking that one of the impersonal doors might open at any moment, and someone might see me in a "white" building, and see me and van Rensburg breaking the liquor laws of the country. Anger could have saved me from the whole embarrassing situation, but you know I can't easily be angry. Even if I could have been, I might have found it hard to be angry with this particular man. But I wanted to get away from there, and I couldn't. My mother used to say to me, when I had said something anti-white, "son, don't talk like that, talk as you are." She would have understood at once why I took a drink from a man who gave it to me in the passage.

*Van Rensburg said to me, "don't you know this fellow Simelane?"*

*"I've heard of him," I said.*

*"I'd like to meet him," he said. "I'd like to talk to him." He added in explana-tion, "you know, talk out my heart to him."*

A woman of about fifty years of age came from the room beyond, bring-ing a plate of biscuits. She smiled and bowed to me. I took one of the biscuits, but not for all the money in the world could I have said to her *"dankie, my nooi,"* or that disgusting *"dankie, missus,"* nor did I want to speak to her in English because her language was Afrikaans, so I took the risk of it and used the word *"mevrou"* for the politeness of which some Afrikaners would knock a black man down, and I said in high Afrikaans, with a smile and a bow too, *"Ek is u dankbaar, Mevrou."*

But nobody knocked me down. The woman smiled and bowed, and van Rensburg, in a strained voice that suddenly came out of nowhere, said, "our land is beautiful. But it breaks my heart."

The woman put her hand on his arm, and said "Jannie, Jannie."

Then another woman and a man, all about the same age, came up and stood behind van Rensburg.

"He's a B.A.," van Rensburg told them. "What do you think of that?"

The first woman smiled and bowed to me again, and van Rensburg said, as though it were a matter for grief, "I wanted to give him brandy, but there's only wine."

The second woman said, "I remember, Jannie. Come with me."

She went back into the room, and he followed her. The first woman said to me, "Jannie's a good man. Strange, but good."

And I thought the whole thing was mad, and getting beyond me, with me a black stranger being shown a testimonial for the son of the house, with these white strangers standing and looking at me in the passage, as though they wanted for God's sake to touch me somewhere and didn't know how, but I saw the earnestness of the woman who had smiled and bowed to me, and I said to her "I can see that, *Mevrou.*"

*"He goes down every night to look at the statue," she said. "He says only God could make something so beautiful, therefore God must be in the man who made it, and he wants to meet him and talk out his heart to him."*

She looked back at the room, and then she dropped her voice a little, and said to me, "can't you see, it's somehow because it's a black woman and a black child?"

And I said to her, "I can see that, *Mevrou.*"

She turned to the man and said of me, "he's a good boy."

Then the other woman returned with van Rensburg, and van Rensburg had a bottle of brandy. He was smiling and pleased, and he said to me, "this isn't ordinary brandy, it's French."

He showed me the bottle, and I, wanting to get the hell out of that place, looked at it and saw it was cognac. He turned to the man and said, "Uncle, you remember? When you were ill? The doctor said you must have good brandy. And the man at the bottlestore said this was the best brandy in the world."

*"I must go," I said. "I must catch that train."*

*"I'll take you to the station," he said. "Don't you worry about that."*

He poured me a drink and one for himself.

"Uncle," he said, "what about one for yourself?"

The older man said, "I don't mind if I do," and he went inside to get himself a glass.

Van Rensburg said, "Happiness," and lifted his glass to me. It was good brandy, the best I've ever tasted. But I wanted to get the hell out of there. I stood in the passage and drank van Rensburg's brandy. Then Uncle came back with his glass, and van Rensburg poured him a brandy, and Uncle raised his glass to me too. All of us were full of goodwill, but I was waiting for the opening of one of those impersonal doors. Perhaps they were too, I don't know. Perhaps when you want so badly to touch someone you don't care. I was drinking my brandy almost as fast as I would have drunk it in Orlando.

"I must go," I said.

Van Rensburg said, "I'll take you to the station." He finished his brandy, and I finished mine too. We handed the glasses to Uncle, who said to me, "Good night my boy." The first woman said "May God bless you," and the other woman bowed and smiled. Then van Rensburg and I went down in the lift to the basement, and got into his car.

*"I told you I'd take you to the station," he said. "I'd take you home, but I'm frightened of Orlando at night."*

We drove up Eloff Street, and he said, "did you know what I meant?" I knew that he wanted an answer to something, and I wanted to answer him, but I couldn't, because I didn't know what that something was. He couldn't be talking about being frightened of Orlando at night, because what more could one mean than just that?

"By what?" I asked.

"You know," he said, "about our land being beautiful?"

Yes, I knew what he meant, and I knew that for God's sake he wanted to touch me too and he couldn't; for his eyes had been blinded by years in the dark. And I thought it was a pity, for if men never touch each other, they'll hurt each other one day. And it was a pity he was blind, and couldn't touch me, for black men don't touch white men any more; only by accident, when they make something like "Mother and Child."

He said to me "what are you thinking?"

I said "many things," and my inarticulateness distressed me, for I knew he wanted something from me. I felt him fall back, angry, hurt, despairing, I didn't know. He stopped at the main entrance to the station, but I didn't tell him I couldn't go in there. I got out and said to him, "thank you for the sociable evening."

*"They liked having you," he said. "Did you see that they did?"*

*I said, "Yes, I saw that they did."*

He sat slumped in his seat, like a man with a burden of incomprehensible, insoluble grief. I wanted to touch him, but I was thinking about the train. He said "good-night" and I said it too. We each saluted the other. What he was thinking, God knows, but I was thinking he was like a man trying to run a race in iron shoes, and not understanding why he cannot move.

When I got back to Orlando, I told my wife the story, and she wept.

•  •  •  •  •

We didn't speak for a long time.

Then I said, "Even the angels would weep."

"Don't weep," he said, "write it."

"Write it," he said eagerly. "Perhaps that way I could make amends."

Then after a time he said to me, "Do you think we'll ever touch each other? Your people and mine? Or is it too late?"

But I didn't give him any answer. For though I may hope, and though I may fear, I don't really know.

PART 2

# Postcolonial Encounters

*Our ancestors are silent. A great something is*
*going to come from the sky and change the*
*face of the earth. We must take an interest in*
*politics. We must become spies on behalf of*
*justice. . . . We must look at the world with new*
*eyes. We must look at ourselves differently.*
*We are freer than we think. We haven't begun*
*to live yet. . . . The whole of human history is an*
*undiscovered continent deep in our souls.*
　　　　　　　　　　—Ben Okri, *The Famished Road*

# Peter Carey

The quest for national identity in a postcolonial nation has steadily played a pivotal role in Peter Carey's highly imaginative fiction. Born 7 May 1943 in a provincial Australian town, Carey has emerged as one of the most important post–World War II Australian writers. He came from a family of aviators and used car salesman—occupations that figure prominently in his fiction. He attended a private secondary school, followed by a year at Monash University in Melbourne. After staying the requisite period in London, Carey settled in Sydney where he worked for an advertising agency, spent intervals in a Queensland commune, and wrote in his spare time. Once he had established himself as a writer he moved to New York City in the early 1990s, where he now lives and writes full time.

Carey's two short-story collections, *The Fat Man in History* (1974) and *War Crimes* (1979), drew immediate attention by departing from social realism and moving into the fantastic to focus on the search for identity. In his first major novel, *Illywhacker* (1985), Carey retells Australian history through the eyes of a con artist (an "illywhacker," according to Australian slang), who claims to be 139 years old. That the narrator is an admitted liar confirms the novel's proposal that Australian history—or perhaps all of traditional colonial and postcolonial history, for that matter—consists of lies. His next novel, *Oscar and Lucinda* (1988), takes nineteenth-century England and Australia as its setting, and once more examines the inherited burden of colonialism.

*The Unusual Life of Tristan Smith* (1994) invents a contemporary postcolonial nation called Efica to represent Australia and to signify its dubious role as an unofficial colony of the United States (called Voorstand in the novel). In *Jack Maggs* (1997), Carey completes the story of the Australian convict Magwitch who appears in Charles Dickens's *Great Expectations*. Although the Dickens character has been renamed Maggs, he still bears similarity to the original. After a calamitous trip back to England to see the young man he has supported and educated over the years, the freed convict gladly returns to Australia and accepts his identity as an Australian. This claim he had denied earlier when he insisted that he was English and did not belong to the "Australian race." The novel appears less inconclusive than the earlier work and may suggest that Carey has at last through a fictional quest discovered the elusive meaning of "Australianness."

Taken from *War Crimes*, "Do You Love Me?" is typical of Carey's work, unfolding in sundry directions and taking undefined courses so that neither a single nor a specific intention emerges. Here are a few possibilities. *Considered from a historical standpoint*: The cartographers could represent medieval mapmakers in the Northern Hemisphere who invented the Great South Land, believing that such a landmass was necessary for the world to maintain its balance. Once Captain Cook explored the antipodes, it turned out to be vastly different in size and location. *Or approached from the act of colonization*: The early mapmakers thought of Australia as an unclaimed land waiting to be discovered and settled by Europeans, even though Australia had been home to the Aborigines for 40,000 years or so. Yet the cartographers remapped the land into a European replica and altered, even obliterated, the original inhabitants' home. *Or read in a modern vein*: Even today the majority of the population ignores most of Australia, shows little love for the harsh land, and huddles in cities along the coast. The bleak desert, the impenetrable mountains, and the shoreline claim reality only on maps, or as symbols for poets. So the questions arise: Can a land that remains unloved truly exist? Can a postcolonial nation be mapped accurately and definitely? *Finally, approached from a philosophical viewpoint*: That human "love" will somehow solve the problems generated by an unloved physical world creates yet another riddle, because this simplistic antidote fails as the story unfolds.

# "Do You Love Me?"

## 1. *THE ROLE OF THE CARTOGRAPHERS*

Perhaps a few words about the role of the Cartographers in our present society are warranted.

To begin with one must understand the nature of the yearly census, a manifestation of our desire to know, always, exactly where we stand. The census, originally a count of the population, has gradually extended until it has become a total inventory of the contents of the nation, a mammoth task which is continuing all the time—no sooner has one census been announced than work on another begins.

The results of the census play an important part in our national life and have, for many years, been the pivot point for the yearly "Festival of the Corn" (an ancient festival, related to the wealth of the earth).

We have a passion for lists. And nowhere is this more clearly illustrated than in the Festival of the Corn which takes place in midsummer, the weather always being fine and warm. On the night of the festival, the householders move their goods and possessions, all furniture, electrical goods, clothing, rugs, kitchen utensils, bathrobes, slippers, cushions, lawnmowers, curtains, doorstops, heirlooms, cameras, and anything else that can be moved into the street so that the census officials may the more easily check the inventory of each household.

The Festival of the Corn is, however, much more than a clerical affair. And, the day over and the night come, the householders invite each other to view their possessions which they refer to, on this night, as gifts. It is like nothing more than a wedding feast—there is much cooking, all sorts of traditional dishes, fine wines, strong liquors, music is played loudly in quiet neighborhoods, strangers copulate with strangers, men dance together, and maidens in yellow robes distribute small barley sugar corn-cobs to young and old alike.

And in all this the role of the Cartographers is perhaps the most important, for our people crave, more than anything else, to know the extent of the nation, to know, exactly, the shape of the coastline, to hear what land may have been lost to the sea, to know what has been reclaimed and what is still in doubt. If the Cartographers' report is good the Festival of the Corn will be a good festival. If the report is bad, one can always sense, for all the dancing and drinking, a feeling of nervousness and apprehension in the revelers, a certain desperation. In the year of a bad Cartographers' report there will always be fights and, occasionally, some property will be stolen as citizens attempt to compensate themselves for their sense of loss.

Because of the importance of their job the Cartographers have become an elite—well-paid, admired, envied, and having no small opinion of themselves. It is said by some that they are overproud, immoral, vain and footloose, and it is perhaps the last charge (by necessity true) that brings about the others. For the Cartographers spend their years traveling up and down the coast, along the great rivers, traversing great mountains and vast deserts. They travel in small parties of three, four, sometimes five, making their own time, working as they please, because eventually it is their own responsibility to see that their team's task is completed in time.

My father, a Cartographer himself, often told me stories about himself or his colleagues and the adventures they had in the wilderness.

There were other stories, however, that always remained in my mind and, as a child, caused me considerable anxiety. These were the stories of the nether regions and I doubt if they were known outside a very small circle of Cartographers and government officials. As a child in a house frequented by Cartographers, I often heard these tales which invariably made me cling closely to my mother's skirts.

It appears that for some time certain regions of the country had become less and less real and these regions were regarded fearfully even by the Cartographers, who prided themselves on their courage. The regions in question were invariably uninhabited, unused for agriculture or industry. There were certain sections of the Halverson Ranges, vast stretches of the Greater Desert, and long pieces of coastline which had begun to slowly disappear like the image on an improperly fixed photograph.

It was because of these nebulous areas that the Fischerscope was introduced. The Fischerscope is not unlike radar in its principle and is able to detect the presence of any object, no matter how dematerialized or insubstantial. In this way the Cartographers were still able to map the questionable pairs of the nether regions. To have returned with blanks on the maps would have created such public anxiety that no one dared think what it might do to the stability of our society. I now have reason to believe that certain areas of the country disappeared so completely that even the Fischerscope could not detect them and the Cartographers, acting under political pressure, used old maps to fake-in the missing sections. If my theory is grounded in fact, and I am sure it is, it would explain my father's cynicism about the Festival of the Corn.

## 2. *THE ARCHETYPAL CARTOGRAPHER*

My father was in his fifties but he had kept himself in good shape. His skin was brown and his muscles still firm. He was a tall man with a thick head of gray hair, a slightly less gray mustache and a long aquiline nose. Sitting on a horse he looked as proud and cruel as Genghis Khan. Lying on the beach clad only in bathers and sunglasses he still managed to retain his authoritative air.

Beside him I always felt as if I had betrayed him. I was slightly built, more like my mother.

It was the day before the festival and we lay on the beach, my father, my mother, my girlfriend and I. As was usual in these circumstances my father addressed all his remarks to Karen. He never considered the members of his own family worth talking to. I always had the uncomfortable feeling that he was flirting with my girlfriends and I never knew what to do about it.

People were lying in groups up and down the beach. Near us a family of five were playing with a large beach ball.

"Look at those fools," my father said to Karen.

"Why are they fools?" Karen asked.

"They're fools," said my father. "They were born fools and they'll die fools. Tomorrow they'll dance in the streets and drink too much."

"So," said Karen triumphantly, in the manner of one who has become privy to secret information. "It will be a good Cartographers' report?"

My father roared with laughter.

Karen looked hurt and pouted. "Am I a fool?"

"No," my father said, "you're really quite splendid."

## 3. *THE MOST FAMOUS FESTIVAL*

The festival, as it turned out, was the greatest disaster in living memory.

The Cartographers' report was excellent, the weather was fine, but somewhere something had gone wrong.

The news was confusing. The television said that, in spite of the good report, various items had been stolen very early in the night. Later there was a news flash to say that a large house had completely disappeared in Howie Street.

Later still we looked out the window to see a huge band of people carrying lighted torches. There was a lot of shouting. The same image, exactly, was on the television and a reporter was explaining that bands of vigilantes were out looking for thieves.

My father stood at the window, a martini in his hand, and watched the vigilantes set alight a house opposite.

My mother wanted to know what we should do.

"Come and watch the fools," my father said, "they're incredible."

## 4. *THE I.C.I. INCIDENT*

The next day the I.C.I. building disappeared in front of a crowd of two thousand people. It took two hours. The crowd stood silently as the great steel and glass structure slowly faded before them.

The staff who were evacuated looked pale and shaken. The caretaker who was amongst the last to leave looked almost translucent. In the days that followed he made some name for himself as a mystic, claiming that he had been able to see other worlds, layer upon layer, through the fabric of the here and now.

## 5. *BEHAVIOR WHEN CONFRONTED WITH DEMATERIALIZATION*

The anger of our people when confronted with acts of theft has always been legendary and was certainly highlighted by the incidents which occurred on the night of the festival.

But the fury exhibited on this famous night could not compare with the intensity of emotion displayed by those who witnessed the earliest scenes of dematerialization.

The silent crowd who watched the I.C.I. building erupted into hysteria when they realized that it had finally gone and wasn't likely to come back.

It was like some monstrous theft for which punishment must be meted out.

They stormed into the Shell building next door and smashed desks and ripped down office partitions. Reporters who attended the scene were rarely impartial observers, but one of the cooler headed members of the press remarked on the great number of weeping men and women who hurled typewriters from windows and scattered files through crowds of frightened office workers.

Five days later they displayed similar anger when the Shell building itself disappeared.

## 6. *BEHAVIOR OF THOSE DEMATERIALIZING*

The first reports of dematerializing people were not generally believed and

were suppressed by the media. But these things were soon common knowledge and few families were untouched by them. Such incidents were obviously not all the same but in many victims there was a tendency to exhibit
extreme aggression towards those around them. Murders and assaults committed by these unfortunates were not uncommon and in most cases they exhibited an almost unbelievable rage, as if they were the victims of a shocking
betrayal.

My friend James Bray was once stopped in the street by a very beautiful
woman who clawed and scratched at his face and said: "You did this to me,
you bastard, you did this to me."

He had never seen her before but he confessed that, in some irrational
way, he felt responsible and didn't defend himself. Fortunately she disappeared before she could do him much damage.

## 7. *SOME THEORIES THAT AROSE AT THE TIME*

1. The world is merely a dream dreamt by god who is waking after a
   long sleep. When he is properly awake the world will disappear completely. When the world disappears we will disappear with it and be
   happy.
2. The world has become sensitive to light. In the same way that prolonged use of say penicillin can suddenly result in a dangerous al-
   lergy, prolonged exposure of the world to the sun has made it
   sensitive to light.

   The advocates of this theory could be seen bustling through the
   city crowds in their long, hooded black robes.
3. The fact that the world is disappearing has been caused by the sloppy
   work of the Cartographers and census takers. Those who filled out
   their census forms incorrectly would lose those items they had neglected to describe. People overlooked in the census by impatient officials would also disappear. A strong pressure group demanded that
   a new census be taken quickly before matters got worse.

## 8. *MY FATHER'S THEORY*

The world, according to my father, was exactly like the human body and had
its own defense mechanisms with which it defended itself against anything
that either threatened it or was unnecessary to it. The I.C.I. building and the
I.C.I. company had obviously constituted some threat to the world or had
simply been irrelevant. That's why it had disappeared and not because some
damn fool god was waking up and rubbing his eyes.

"I don't believe in god," my father said. "Humanity is god. Humanity is
the only god I know. If humanity doesn't need something it will disappear.

People who are not loved will disappear. Everything that is not loved will disappear from the face of the earth. We only exist through the love of others and that's what it's all about."

## 9. *A CONTRADICTION*

"Look at those fools," my father said, "they wouldn't know if they were up themselves."

## 10. *AN UNPLEASANT SCENE*

The world at this time was full of unpleasant and disturbing scenes. One that I recall vividly took place in the middle of the city on a hot, sultry Tuesday afternoon. It was about one-thirty and I was waiting for Karen by the post office when a man of forty or so ran past me. He was dematerializing rapidly. Everybody seemed to be deliberately looking the other way, which seemed to me to make him dematerialize faster. I stared at him hard, hoping that I could do something to keep him there until help arrived. I tried to love him, because I believed in my father's theory. I thought, I must love that man. But his face irritated me. It is not so easy to love a stranger and I'm ashamed to say that he had the small mouth and close-together eyes that I have always disliked in a person. I tried to love him but I'm afraid I failed.

While I watched he tried to hail taxi after taxi. But the taxi drivers were only too well aware of what was happening and had no wish to spend their time driving a passenger who, at any moment, might cease to exist. They looked the other way or put up their NOT FOR HIRE signs.

Finally he managed to way-lay a taxi at some traffic lights. By this time he was so insubstantial that I could see right through him. He was beginning to shout. A terrible thin noise, but penetrating nonetheless. He tried to open the cab door, but the driver had already locked it. I could hear the man's voice, high and piercing: "I want to go home." He repeated it over and over again. "I want to go home to my wife."

The taxi drove off when the lights changed. There was a lull in the traffic. People had fled the corner and left it deserted and it was I alone who saw the man finally disappear.

I felt sick.

Karen arrived five minutes later and found me pale and shaken. "Are you alright?" she said.

"Do you love me?" I said.

## 11. *THE NETHER REGIONS*

My father had an irritating way of explaining things to me I already understood, refusing to stop no matter how much I said "I know" or "You told me before."

Thus he expounded on the significance of the nether regions, adopting the tone of a lecturer speaking to a class of particularly backward children.

"As you know," he said, "the nether regions were amongst the first to disappear and this in itself is significant. These regions, I'm sure you know, are seldom visited by men and only then by people like me whose sole job is to make sure that they're still there. We had no use for these areas, these deserts, swamps, and coastlines which is why, of course, they disappeared. They were merely possessions of ours and if they had any use at all it was as symbols for our poets, writers and film makers. They were used as symbols of lovelessness, loneliness, uselessness and so on. Do you get what I mean?"

"Yes," I said, "I get what you mean."

"But do you?" my father insisted. "But do you really, I wonder." He examined me seriously, musing on the possibilities of my understanding him. "How old are you?"

"Twenty," I said.

"I knew, of course," he said. "Do you understand the significance of the nether regions?"

I sighed, a little too loudly and my father narrowed his eyes. Quickly I said: "They are like everything else. They're like the cities. The cities are deserts where people are alone and lonely. They don't love one another."

"Don't love one another," intoned my father, also sighing. "We no longer love one another. When we realize that we need one another we will stop disappearing. This is a lesson to us. A hard lesson, but, I hope, an effective one."

My father continued to speak, but I watched him without listening. After a few minutes he stopped abruptly: "Are you listening to me?" he said. I was surprised to detect real concern in his voice. He looked at me questioningly. "I've always looked after you," he said, "ever since you were little."

## 12. *THE CARTOGRAPHERS' FALL*

I don't know when it was that I noticed that my father had become depressed. It probably happened quite gradually without either my mother or me noticing it.

Even when I did become aware of it I attributed it to a woman. My father had a number of lovers and his moods usually reflected the success or failure of these relationships.

But I know now that he had heard already of Hurst and Jamov, the first two Cartographers to disappear. The news was suppressed for several weeks and then, somehow or other, leaked to the press. Certainly the Cartographers had enemies amongst the civil servants who regarded them as overproud and overpaid, and it was probably from one of these civil servants that the press heard the news.

When the news finally broke I understood my father's depression and felt sorry for him.

I didn't know how to help him. I wanted, badly, to make him happy. I had never been able to give him anything or do anything for him that he couldn't do better himself. Now I wanted to help him, to show him I understood.

I found him sitting in front of the television one night when I returned from my office and I sat quietly beside him. He seemed more kindly now and he placed his hand on my knee and patted it.

I sat there for a while, overcome with the new warmth of this relationship and then, unable to contain my emotion any more, I blurted out. "You could change your job."

My father stiffened and sat bolt upright. The pressure of his hand on my knee increased until I yelped with pain, and still he held on, hurting me terribly.

"You are a fool," he said, "you wouldn't know if you were up yourself."

Through the pain in my leg, I felt the intensity of my father's fear.

### 13. *WHY THE WORLD NEEDS CARTOGRAPHERS*

My father woke me at 3.00 a.m. to tell me why the world needed Cartographers. He smelled of whisky and seemed, once again, to be very gentle.

"The world needs Cartographers," he said softly, "because if they didn't have Cartographers the fools wouldn't know where they were. They wouldn't know if they were up themselves if they didn't have a Cartographer to tell them what's happening. The world needs Cartographers," my father said, "it fucking well needs Cartographers."

### 14. *ONE FINAL SCENE*

Let me describe a final scene to you: I am sitting on the sofa my father brought home when I was five years old. I am watching television. My father is sitting in a leather armchair that once belonged to his father and which has always been exclusively his. My mother is sitting in the dining alcove with her cards spread across the table, playing one more interminable game of patience.

I glance casually across at my father to see if he is doing anything more than stare into space, and notice, with a terrible shock that he is showing the first signs of dematerializing.

"What are you staring at?" My father, in fact, has been staring at me.

"Nothing."

"Well, don't."

Nervously I return my eyes to the inanity of the television. I don't know what to do. Should I tell my father that he is dematerializing? If I don't tell him will he notice? I feel I should do something but I can feel, already, the anger in his voice. His anger is nothing new. But this is possibly the beginning of a tide of uncontrollable rage. If he knows he is dematerializing, he will think I don't love him. He will blame me. He will attack me. Old as he is, he is still considerably stronger than I am and he could hurt me badly. I stare determinedly at the television and feel my father's eyes on me.

I try to feel love for my father, I try very, very hard.

I attempt to remember how I felt about him when I was little, in the days when he was still occasionally tender towards me.

But it's no good.

Because I can only remember how he has hit me, hurt me, humiliated me and flirted with my girlfriends. I realize, with a flush of panic and guilt, that I don't love him. In spite of which I say: "I love you."

My mother looks up sharply from her cards and lets out a surprised cry.

I turn to my father. He has almost disappeared. I can see the leather of the chair through his stomach.

I don't know whether it is my unconvincing declaration of love or my mother's exclamation that makes my father laugh. For whatever reason, he begins to laugh uncontrollably: "You bloody fools," he gasps, "I wish you could see the looks on your bloody silly faces."

And then he is gone.

My mother looks across at me nervously, a card still in her hand. "Do you love me?" she asks.

# Ngugi wa Thiong'o

Although highly regarded as a novelist in English, Ngugi has chosen in recent years to write for the most part in his African language, Gikuyu. He grew up and attended schools in Kenya, where he was born on 5 January 1938. After graduating from Makere University College in Uganda, he taught literature at the University of Nairobi and established a rural theater company. In 1977 the Kenyan authorities arrested him without charge. Amnesty International declared Ngugi, by then an established novelist, a Prisoner of Conscience and gained his release in 1978. Threatened with further detentions, Ngugi left Kenya with his family in 1982. They now live in the United States, where he is a professor at New York University. His work has been widely translated and has earned him numerous international awards.

While Ngugi's reputation rests primarily on his fiction, his nonfiction not only provides a gloss to the creative work but also stresses the significance of cultural practices and language in the struggle to forge a national identity. For Ngugi the eradication of African language leads to the ruin of African culture. In *Decolonizing the Mind: The Politics of Language in African Literature* (1986), Ngugi bids farewell to English, which he considers a neocolonial tool of dominance that will erase authentic African tradition. His more recent book of essays, *Moving the Center: The Struggle for Cultural Freedom* (1993), continues to stress his commitment to the preservation and reestablishment of Kenyan cultural and linguistic heritage.

In some ways Ngugi's novels form a loose sequence that records Kenya's history from the time of the initial colonial encroachment into the postcolonial era. The first published novel, *Weep Not, Child* (1964), takes place before and during Kenya's War of Independence. A year later his first novel, *The River Between*, appeared, and traces the rivalry between two villages, one that retained its traditions, the other that took up Christianity. *A Grain of Wheat*

(1967) covers the four days leading to independence, and explores Ngugi's claim that the colonizers used Christianity to conquer the land and to persuade the natives to embrace European values. One of his most powerful novels and the last to be written in English, *Petals of Blood* (1977) moves into the postcolonial era and assails the African-led government, exposing and condemning the officials for their cynicism, political posturing, and corruption. Both written in Gikuyu, then "rendered" into English by Ngugi, *Devil on the Cross* (1977—originally titled *Caitani Mutharabain*) and *Matagari* (1987) demonstrate Ngugi's continuing revulsion at the state of affairs in postcolonial Kenya where a privileged few hold the wealth and power, and the majority bear the consequences of an oppressive and exploitative government. Ngugi declared in *Writers in Politics* (1981) that "art for art's sake" has no place in fiction because "the very act of writing is a social act." Still, his fiction, although holding true to this idea, deftly balances the political and the social with the human struggle.

This chapter from *Devil on the Cross* presents one of the scenes from the "Devil's Feast," an event held to crown the foremost exploiter, not only through his past successes but through future proposals as well. The passage also stresses the role of the neocolonial European and American businessmen, who employ the African officials for their own financial gain, thus exploiting the exploiters. Appearing at the end of the selection, Wariinga is the central character, and a victim of both social conditions and male sexism. While the satiric excesses bring to mind Jonathan Swift's writing, the passage contains an African flavor as well through its use of African sayings, language, and character.

# The Testimony of Kîhaahu wa Gatheeca

from *Devil on the Cross*

And these are the experiences of Kîhaahu wa Gatheeca, revealed to those who had gathered at the robber's cave in Ilmorog for the competition in modern theft and robbery.

Kîhaahu was a tall, slim fellow: he had long legs, long arms, long fingers, a long neck and a long mouth. His mouth was shaped like the beak of the kingstock: long, thin and sharp. His chin, his face, his head formed a cone. Everything about him indicated leanness and sharp cunning.

That day, Kîhaahu was dressed in black-and-gray striped trousers, a black tail coat, a white shirt and a black tie. Standing on the platform, he looked like a six-foot praying mantis or mosquito.

Kîhaahu started by clearing his throat, and then he spoke the following words.

"I don't have much to tell. Too much of anything is poison. But a little is often sweet. My aim, or my motto, is to act on my words. My actions are the trumpet that sounds my abilities as a thief and robber. I myself am the best possible illustration of the sayings that we were reminded of earlier today: that tallness is not a misfortune, and a hero is not known by the size of his calves. For, indeed, I am the cock that crows in the morning and silences all the others. I am the lion that roars in the forest, making elephants urinate. I am the eagle that flies in the sky, forcing hawks to seek refuge in their nests. I am the wind that stills all breezes. I am the lightning that dazzles all light. I am the thunder that silences all noise. I am the sun in the heavens during the day. I am the moon, king of the stars, at night. I am the king of kings of modern theft and robbery. Crown me with the golden crown, for it is not too early for the new king to begin his reign.

From *Devil on the Cross* by Ngugi wa Thiong'o. Copyright © 1982 by Ngugi wa Thiong'o. Used by permission of Heinemann Educational Publishers, a division of Reed Educational & Professional Publishing Ltd.

"I am not praising myself for the sake of it. We came here to hold a seminar in modern theft and robbery. I'll sing a song about myself that will move our foreign guests to make me overseer of other overseers, watchdog over other watchdogs, messenger above all other messengers. Say yes, and I'll tell you a story full of wonder.

"Skills like those just mentioned to us by Gitutu wa Gataangguru *ni kama mswagi kwangu*, they are nothing at all. To head societies or companies that purchase land in such a way that one is the first to select all the healthy cows for one's own farm, or in a position to divert public money for one's own use, or to borrow from a bank on the *security* of the society's lands— these are the simple tricks through which I learned how to steal and rob. In English they would be called *amateurish tricks* or beginners' tactics.

"As for my name, I am Kîhaahu wa Gatheeca. My foreign name is Lord Gabriel Bloodwell-Stuart-Jones. To turn to matters of the flesh, I am an elder with only two wives. I married one before I became a man of property; I married the other after acquiring property, when I started receiving invitations to *cocktail parties*. You here don't need to be lectured about the fact that old, scentless perfume is not fit for the modern dance of party talk in foreign languages. If a woman were to be out of step, she might jeopardize your whole future. So my second wife knows English, and she has no job other than decking herself out in expensive clothes and jewelry for *cocktail parties*.

"As for my children, I have quite a few. All of them speak English through the nose, exactly like people born and brought up in England. If you were to hear them speak Gikuyu or Kiswahili, you would laugh until you pissed yourself. *It is so funny*. They speak the two languages as if they were Italian priests newly arrived from Rome—priests without priestly collars. But then the children are mine, and I don't mind that they speak their national languages like Italian foreigners.

"Now for my *sugar girls*. I never run after schoolgirls. Girls like those are danger itself. They may pass on diseases, and I have no time for penicillin injections or for swallowing preventive capsules before the job.

"I like other people's wives. One gets such a glorious feeling of victory. You know, don't you, that that's another kind of stealing? I am particularly good at bourgeois women. They never resist. And they have no pretensions. They want only one thing. Some are not satisfied with one or two shots—this is because their husbands are always at nightclubs with their girlfriends. And again, many of them don't have much work to keep them *busy*: today, they sing only one song—change for good seeds are not all contained in one gourd. A cunt is not salt or soap that will dissolve or disappear after use. I have baptized them Ready-to-Yield. They aren't expensive. But there is one *professional*, who has a row of degrees that stretches from here to there. She left her husband for my sake, and I felt as if I had just returned from a victorious raid. But, of course, I had to give her something in return: 1,500,000 shillings for a ten-acre plot of land that I bought for her at Tigoni, near Limuru. . . . That's why I've always sworn that if I catch my wife loitering on street corners, I'll make her begin to see through her arse!

"As for my car, there's not a single model that I haven't tried. . . . I change cars like clothes. A Mercedes Benz beats them all, but when I get tired of that, I buy a *Citroën* or a *Daimler* or a *Range Rover*. I have also bought toys for my two wives and older children, playthings like Toyotas, Datsuns and Peugeots.

"My *sports*: counting money in the evening, playing golf on Saturdays and Sundays and, of course, playing about with the thighs of the Ready-to-Yield when I have the time.

"I often contrast the way I live today with the way I used to live before I entered the field of theft and robbery, and it seems to me like contrasting sleep with death. Long ago, before Uhuru, I lived with duster and chalk in my hands, teaching children their ABC at Ruuwa-ini *Primary School*. Oh, those were terrible days! I used to eat ugali with salt as soup, or with ten cents' worth of vegetables when a bird of good omen had visited me. I used to cough all day because of the chalk dust that had accumulated in my throat, and I couldn't afford any fat to cool the pain that burned in my chest.

"I don't know, even now, how it came about that one day I opened the classroom window, and I looked outside, and I saw many people of my own generation busy picking fruit from the Uhuru tree. I heard something whisper to me: Kîhaahu, son of Gatheeca, how can you stay here like a fool, your nose clogged with chalk dust, while your contemporaries out there are munching the fruits of freedom? What are you waiting for? What will be left for you after everybody else has grabbed his share? Remember that there are no crumbs to be gathered in the wake of masters of the art of eating.

"And suddenly the scales fell from eyes. I could now see quite clearly. I, son of Gatheeca, threw the chalk through the window, put on my long coat, made the biggest *about turn* of my life and said *bye-bye* to the teaching profession. I too wanted a chance to find out what these fruits of *Uhura wa Mwafrika* tasted like.

"Too much haste often splits the yam. Listen to this. I foolishly rushed for the very first fruit that came my way, like the girl in the story who was tricked by others into picking fruit with her eyes shut and ended up by picking only the raw ones. The fruit tasted bitter in my mouth. Had I picked crab-apples, mistaking them for real apples?

"Let me tell you about the mistake I had made, for we have come here not only to boast about our abilities but to also *share our experience*. While I was still teaching, I had already found out that the biggest thirst in the country was the thirst for education. This thirst for education oppressed the masses, but it was the basis of the wealth of a select few. Even people who could hardly read or write A or B had started their own private secondary schools, and they would get a Mercedes Benz or two out of the enterprise. The buildings were often made of mud, the teachers had been recruited from a junk yard, the desks were made from off-cuts of wood, the stationery had been collected at the road-side, and *still* the schools were able to turn a profit for their owners. I thought that I too, son of Gatheeca, should try to find out for myself the true weight of a coin picked up in that quarter.

"I thought I would start a *nursery school*, because it would not call for heavy investment. I went to a bank and got a loan. My small farm was my security. I looked for and found a building in Nairobi. Then I looked for and found an African girl who had failed her CPE, whom I employed to look after the kids: she would play with them, give them a bit of milk at ten and teach them a few songs. Then I placed a big advertisement in a newspaper, with the following wording:

> *New Black Beauty Nursery School*
> *for Children of VIP Kenyans.*
> *Owned, Managed and Taught*
> *Entirely by Kenyans.*
> *Swahili Language in Use.*
> *Kenyan Songs, Kenyan Lullabies, etc., etc.*
> *Cheap in Fees: Dear in Quality.*
> *Bring One, Bring All,*
> *Sisi Kwa Sisi, Tujenge Kenya Taifa Letu.*

"Well! I never got a single child, not even a disabled one.

"I sat down and wept, remembering the amount of money that I had spent, and knowing very well that the bank might auction the piece of land I had been foolhardy enough to offer as security. I thought and thought hard. Could it be that I had not examined the Uhuru tree properly, so that instead of a sweet berry, I had picked a bitter one? But then I told myself: That which defeats a seeker after money has been turned over and over again.

"I did a bit more research to find out what was really going on. I soon found out that no prominent Kenyan, on acquiring a large farm, would employ a Kenyan as his manager: he would only employ a European foreigner. A prominent Kenyan who was a success at big business would not employ a Kenyan as his manager or accountant: he would only employ a European or an Indian foreigner. When Kenyans conversed, they never used their national languages: they only conversed in foreign languages. Whenever a Kenyan . . . I noted and observed until my vision cleared. *Ugeni juu, Ukenya chini.* That was the basis of profit for the modern Kenyan bourgeois.

"I hurried back to the nursery school before the bank started harassing me. I changed its name. I baptized it: MODERN-DAY NURSERY SCHOOL. Then I looked for a white woman to be the *principal.* Luckily, I found one. She was a decrepit old woman, half-blind and hard of hearing, and she was always falling asleep. She agreed to join the staff of my school and to do her dozing there.

"Next I visited certain Nairobi shops. I bought child mannequins—those plastic human shapes—and I dressed them in expensive clothes. I fixed red wigs to their heads. I put electric machines into their plastic bellies, and then I fixed tiny wheels on the soles of their plastic feet. When I switched on the power, the mannequins would move about the floor like real human children at play. Through the big glass windows of the school building one could see them playing even if one were standing by the roadside. Then I placed another big advertisement in a newspaper:

*Modern-Day Nursery School.*
*Experienced European Principal.*
*Formerly for Europeans Only,*
*Now Open to a Few Kenyans.*
*Foreign Standards as Before.*
*National Languages, National Songs, National Names Banned.*
*Foreign Languages, Foreign Songs, Foreign Toys, etc., etc.*
*English Medium of Instruction.*
*Limited Places.*
*Telephone or Call in Your Car.*
*Color is no Bar. Money is the Bar.*
*Fees High.*

"Oh, then parents started ringing day and night to reserve places for their children. Whenever the phone rang, I would run to wake up the European principal to answer it. But the majority of parents preferred to call in their cars to make sure of a place for their children. And on finding a white woman, and on seeing the mannequins at play through the windows, the parents would pay the fees then and there: they didn't even bother to find out more about the school.

"I took—or, rather, I instructed the principal to take—no more than a hundred children. Each child paid 2,500 shillings a month. I was overjoyed, for that meant that every month I was pocketing 250,000 shillings. After paying the rent and the salaries of the dozing principal and her assistants, I would be left with over 200,000 shillings every month. And please note, all this time I hadn't shed a single drop of sweat, and I hadn't swallowed any dust from chalk and dusters. To me the fruit from that particular tree did not taste bitter—not at all.

"I picked another fruit and yet another. I opened four other nursery schools in Nairobi, using the same trick of employing aged or even crippled white women as principals and buying white mannequins to stand in for real white children. Even here at Ilmorog and Ruuwa-ini I have opened a few nursery schools along the same lines.

"The fruit from that tree was certainly plentiful, and it was very ripe indeed. And sweet—but that's another story! Now, Europeans have told us that it is not good to put all your eggs in one basket. So I thought I should try to find out what the fruits of other trees tasted like. Societies and companies for purchasing farms like those mentioned by Gitutu wa Gataanguru and other ways of stealing and robbing through land speculation have all yielded fruit that I have eaten gladly.

"But the tree from which I've picked fruit riper and sweeter than that on all the other Uhuru trees is—Wait, let me start the story of that special tree right from the beginning, so that all of you can see that I am not a novice when it comes to the art of theft and robbery.

"After I had picked a lot of fruit from the two trees that were watered by the people's thirst for education and their hunger for land, I began to look about me to see which fruits my contemporaries were plucking. I saw that as soon as people accumulated property, they all wanted to enter *Parliament*. With my own eyes, I've seen someone sell his farm and auction his very beautiful wife in order to meet his election expenses. I paused to think: What's in this business, which has become the object of so much in-fighting, to the extent that people are prepared to scatter millions of bank notes about and sell their wives and daughters and farms? Could it be that this tree yields more fruit than all other trees?

"I made up my mind to enter the field of politics and find out for myself: after all, it's only he who sits under the tree who knows what the black tree-ant eats. But since I was also familiar with the saying that too much haste splits the yam, I was determined not to race for a parliamentary seat—those seats, as you know, are very hot and have been the cause of bloodshed—I would go first for a seat on Iciriri *County Council*, Ruuwa-ini *Ward*.

"To say is to do, and it is never too early to market vegetables, before they lose their bloom. I literally poured money into the pockets of those around me. When I mean to do something, I do it in style: I don't hold back. I gathered a choir of Nyakinyua women about me, who sang my praises and invented stories of how I had fought for freedom and had provided people with land and education and other lies like those. I bought colorful uniforms for the Nyakinyua women, with my picture printed on them.

"Then I employed a youth wing, whose task was to destroy the property of my opponents and to beat those who murmured complaints about me. I had five opponents. I took two of them aside and bought them out for 50,000 shillings each. They both made public announcements that they were withdrawing in favor of Gatheeca, the hero. The third opponent refused to be bribed. One night he was kidnapped by two youth wingers and taken to Ruuwa-ini forest, where he was shown the barrel of a gun and told to choose between living and being elected. He wisely opted for life. The fourth one not only refused to be bribed but actually went as far as to shout his defiance even after he had been shown the barrel of a gun. I sent some youth wingers to his home. They broke both his legs.

"The fifth was a clever bastard. He quickly sent round his own thugs, who blocked the road with their car and pointed a gun at me and warned me that should I ever play with their chief, the result would be a tooth for a tooth, an eye for an eye, a leg for a leg, blood for blood. I got the message. My opponent wasn't joking. I gave in. I told them to tell their chief that eaters of other people's wealth usually meet in the field to decide which can out-eat the other. So he should agree to meet me on the election battlefield to put an end to all doubt, once and for all, about who was who. In the meantime, I warned, no eater should threaten the life of another. Money is power, so he should let his money and my money fight it out in the field. In the end we arrived at an understanding: we agreed to let iron and iron clash to see whose weapon could drill a hole in the other.

"So the field was now left open to us two. Money would do the work, show which of us had stolen the most. For my part, I gave instructions that all the taps should be turned on full, so that every beer drinker could drink as much as he wanted, knowing that his vote was cast for the son of Gatheeca. I tell you, there wasn't a single trick I didn't pull, including buying votes. I spent a total of 2,000,000 shillings on that campaign. My opponent was no push-over. He spent 1,500,000. But eventually the seat went to the hero you now see standing before you.

"Even before I had properly taken my seat on the Council, I began to figure out how I could get back the millions I had spent on the campaign. But by now I had learned that enthusiasm for the modern dance is fueled with money. I tried this and that. For a week or two, I hardly slept, for my time was spent seeing this and that councilor. The second campaign cost me another 50,000 shillings. The result was that I was appointed (or perhaps I should say 'elected') *chairman of the Iciciri County Council's Housing Committee*. The committee was responsible for the construction and distribution of council houses and also for the allocation of industrial and business plots to individuals or companies.

"Now I knew that I, son of Gatheeca, had really arrived. My time had come. Public property fattens the wily.

"It happened that now and then the Council would borrow money from the American-owned *World Bank*, or from European and Japanese banks, to finance the construction of cheap houses for the poor. That was a source of real fat. I can remember one time when the Council demolished some shanties at Ruuwa-ini. The plan was to erect a thousand houses there instead. The money was loaned to the Council by an Italian bank. The company that won the tender for building the houses was Italian. But, of course, it had first given me a small back-hander of about 2,000,000 shillings. I put the money in my account and knew that the campaign money had been repaid. Now I waited for the returns on my investment in the elections.

"It was only after the houses had been built that I found what I had been looking for. Anybody who wanted a council house first had to buy me a cup of tea worth 2,000 shillings. I made another 2,000,000 shillings that way, which I stacked away in the bank.

"I hardly need to tell you that after two years, the millions that I'd invested in the election campaign had yielded quite a tidy sum. And, you will note, I hadn't shed a drop of sweat. All my money came from the very people who had voted for me. How? Because it was their tax that would go to pay back the money borrowed from foreign banks.

"What do you think of that? If you were me, would you have stopped nibbling at that fruit, which tasted more luscious than sweetness itself? I never stopped plucking it. I picked one fruit after another. The sweet juice would spill out of the corners of my mouth before I learned to eat more discreetly.

"These days I don't wait for the Council to build houses before I pocket tidbits. I have teamed up with some Italian foreigners and have formed a construction company: *Ruuwa-ini Housing Development Company*. It is my company that usually wins tenders from the Council. But the company also borrows money from banks to construct whole estates, and it's able to sell the houses long before they are even completed. You people! Don't underestimate people's thirst for houses. The company builds houses to suit the different classes. Stone houses, for instance, are not all that profitable. Have you seen those barracks made of mud and wood? If you build shanties like those and then rent them out to workers and peasants, that, I assure you, is where the fat lies.

"I started receiving invitations to become a director of branches of foreign companies. I would buy a *share* here, and there I would pocket *a sitting allowance*, a kind of baksheesh for attending board meetings. From all those sources I was able to take home a few cents at the end of the month—a piece here and a piece there collect in the belly of Kîhaahu wa Gatheeca (despite his slimness) to make a whole number.

"That's why I'm very grateful to the masses of the Kenyan people. For their blindness, their ignorance, their inability to demand their rights are what enable us, the clan of man-eaters, to feed on their sweat without their asking us too many awkward questions.

"But we shouldn't be complacent or imagine that the masses will always be as foolish. It's the possibility that things may change that has prompted some foreigners to appoint me a director of their companies—to protect them from the wrath of the masses of workers and peasants. I don't mind the assignment. It's fairly lucrative.

"That's why, these days, I never pass up an opportunity for making Haraambe donations. I might give 10,000 shillings here, 5,000 or 10,000 there and perhaps 20,000 elsewhere. It depends on my mood. But when I really mean to make an impression on people, I go first to various foreign-owned companies—you all know that they set aside money to bribe the public blind—and I ask them for a donation, 1,000 shillings, ten cents, five cents, anything, then I mount the platform to announce my generosity: 'These hundreds of thousands which I have brought in sacks are from me and my friends.' My Nyakinyua women's choir immediately trills the five ululations for a male child, all in my honor. What did I say? The volume of today's applause depends on the size of the recipients' pockets. Money can flatten mountains. Today who sings in honor of the likes of Kimathi?

"Long may the masses stay as they are, singing praises only to the size of a man's pockets. This will give us more time to live off the fat of the land—and, as you know, that which is safety in the belly never betrays its presence to inquisitive eyes and ears. I personally believe in the principle of governing by holding a carrot in the left hand and a stick in the right. Haraambe donations are our carrot. But there are a few blackguards who have had the audacity to talk about removing the scales from the eyes of the masses. Those who want to awaken the masses should be shown the whip—detention or prison—just like the fellows you all know about. But I normally send my thugs round to those who are obstinate—after plying them, of course, with drugs and alcohol and money—and then they cart their bodies along to the hyenas on Ngong Hills or to the crocodiles in the Athi River to continue their work for the masses inside the belly of a hyena or a crocodile (like the fellows you all know about). I don't believe in this democracy nonsense. In the morning the topic is democracy. In the evening the topic is democracy. Is democracy food and drink? If I could get hold of those kids at the university, together with their pygmy-sized teachers . . . *Wangenijuta* . . . I would load them on to an aeroplane and request them to take their communist nonsense to China or the Soviet Union.

"Sorry, gentlemen! My raging anger with that lot temporarily distracted me from the business in hand. Let me resume my story. *Oh, yes,* I was talking about theft and robbery based on housing. As for me, I'll never abandon theft and robbery that is based on housing. There's nothing on this Earth that generates as much profit as people's hunger and thirst for shelter. So I never want to see this appetite diminish, even by the slightest amount. In fact, I've often stayed awake figuring out ways and means of increasing the whole country's hunger and thirst, because the degree to which there's a property famine determines exactly the level to which the price of houses will rise and hence the level to which profits will climb like flames of fire reaching out for fatty meat. When such a famine becomes intense—of course, we don't call it famine; we

give it gentler names—we, the eaters of the fat of the land, can sit down to de-
vise ways of sharing the fat among ourselves.

"My idea is this. When the famine exceeds the limits of endurance, we
need only build houses the size of a bird's nest. The nests will be constructed
in such a way that they can be folded, the way tents are folded. Anyone who is
desperate for a place to lay his head will be forced to buy a nest from us,
which he will be able to fold and carry on his shoulders or slip into his pocket.
Whenever and wherever darkness catches up with him, he will simply set up
the nest at the roadside and lay down his head. And imagine, the whole night
long he will be saying his prayers, asking Heaven to bless the kindhearted
providers who have built him a shelter for his eyes, his ears, his lips, his
nose. . . .

"Just imagine the money we could make building nests—*one man, one
nest*! Ha, ha, ha! Ha, ha, ha! Every peasant inside a nest . . . ha, ha, ha! Every
worker with just his nose inside a nest! Peasants and workers will be competing with the birds for air space!

"Good people, hand me the crown of victory. Hey! Wait a minute, those
of you who may still be harboring doubts about my abilities: the grass and
rope for building the nests will be imported from America, Europe and Japan,
foreign countries, or we could simply import ready-made nests.

"That's all I have to say. Hand me the crown!"

## THE REBUTTAL

Kîhaahu wa Gatheeca descended from the platform, utterly baffled about why
nobody was applauding him. Before he had reached his seat, Kîhaahu saw
Gitutu wa Gataanguru heaving himself towards the platform. Gitutu was full
of bitterness. His lips were trembling, and saliva dribbled out of the corners of
his mouth.

"*Mr. Chairman*, we didn't come here to hurl insults at one another. We
didn't come here to cast contemptuous innuendoes at one another. We didn't
come here to listen to filth and rubbish. We came to this cave to take part in a
competition to find out which one of us is the most skillful in the art and science of modern theft and robbery. The lucky winner may find himself appointed the watchdog of foreign-owned finance houses and industries, so that
while benefiting his foreign masters, he may also be able to line his own
pockets. Whether one man wins or another is entirely dependent on a bird of
good omen, and we should not anticipate the outcome by way of insults.

"But if this competition is designed to find out who can hurl the filthiest
insults and innuendoes, we should all be told now. Some of us have been circumcised, and we learned a few lessons in abuse and insulting epithets during
the initiation rites.

"And if we have gathered to brag about our ability to use our youth wings to terrorize others, everybody here should know that I, Gitutu wa Gataanguru, have also employed a group of thugs more terrifying than any other youth wing I know. The group undertakes any mission I give it, including removing from the face of this Earth anybody who so much as dares to meddle in my thieving and robbing activities. My thugs, or perhaps I should say my mercenaries, have an enormous appetite for very strong bhang. My present intention is to import European mercenaries from France or Britain.

"But if there's anybody here who's anxious for a duel, I, Gitutu wa Gataanguru am ready with my gun, *wakati wo wote*.

"Why do I say that? The lanky fellow who was standing here, known by the name of Kîhaahu wa Gatheeca, has claimed that I am a mere beginner in the art of theft and robbery. What! Son of Gatheeca! Do you really know who Gitutu wa Gataanguru is, or have you merely heard men mention his name? I swear by the Truth of Truths that you should come and kneel before me at my school—that is, you go back to *Standard One*—so I can teach you the ABC of the kind of theft and robbery that has made my belly the size it is now.

"*Mr. Chairman*, what kind of theft and robbery is it that this long-legged fellow has been bragging about? Bribing opponents to drop out of the running in council elections? It might perhaps make more sense if these had been parliamentary elections! What's the other kind of theft that he bragged about? Buying plastic Europeans and deceiving people into believing that they were real European children?

"Let's go back to the question of how he intends to contribute to the development of theft and robbery in this land. Isn't it laughable that the one idea our long-legged friend can come up with is to build sparrow's nests as houses? Who'd ever agree to buy a nest just to shelter his nose and lips? *Mr. Chairman*, that man who calls himself Gatheeci wa Kihuuhia (or was it Kihihi wa Gatheeci?) wants to rouse the workers and peasants to take up arms against us. The man wants the workers to become so angry that the scales will fall from their eyes, and they will rise up against us with swords and clubs and guns. Doesn't Gatheeci wa Kîhaahu realize that our people are sick to death of taking up arms? I know what it is: the man wants to introduce Chinese-style communism into this country.

"*Mr. Chairman*, my development plans make a thousand times more sense: sell soil in tiny dishes, and trap air so we can sell it in tins or through meters! The workers and peasants would then breathe to order—our order! Grabbing all the soil in the land and all the air about us is the surest way of making workers and peasants obey us for ever, because should they make even the smallest noise, we would only need to turn off the air to bring them to their knees. . . .

"My friends! You'd better show Waceke wa Gatheeca that you are not the kind of people who can be bribed into surrendering your votes with a glass of beer. I hope that wherever he is now seated, Gatheeca now realizes that I, Gitutu wa Gataanguru, am not a man to run away from the battlefield and leave victory to the clan of long-shanks, even if they are experts at breaking the legs of their opponents. The crown of victory is mine!"

Before Gitutu wa Gataanguru could stagger back to his seat, another man had already jumped up. This one did not even bother to mount the platform. Although saliva did not dribble out of the corners of his mouth, as had been the case with Gitutu wa Gataanguru, he too was clearly bitter.

"*Mr. Chairman*, I too would like to put in a word, for it has been said that wisdom locked in the heart never won a law suit. . . . *Sorry!* I'm known as Ithe wa Mbooi. I take it that we have all gathered in this cave to brag and to teach one another more efficient and cunning ways of stealing and robbing from the poor. But the man who was standing up there just now—I mean, the lanky, mosquito-like fellow—has slipped up very badly.

"Son of Gatheeca, don't you feel ashamed? Weren't you embarrassed, standing there in front of us bragging about deceiving people of your class, shamelessly boasting about how you have stolen from people of your class? If we start robbing, thieving and cheating one another, how will our unity as a class take roots?

"For my part, I am dreadfully ashamed, and feel very sad because all my children have attended those so-called modern nursery schools. I have always taken it that my children were attending the same schools as European children. So they were only fake Europeans? They were plastic Europeans in wigs? And to think that I've paid hundreds of thousands of shillings for my children to be in the company of Europeans with plastic skin, stones for bones and electric machines for hearts? What! So when my children come home and tell me that they have been playing with their European friends, all along these friends have been plastic and electric European machines?

"I have never in all my life come across such unspeakable wickedness. Imagine an adult like Kîhaahu wa Gatheeca pocketing other people's money for nothing? So that's why my children can't speak English through the nose like real European children? And to think how often they have made me feel ashamed in front of people of my class because whenever they are spoken to in English, they normally reply in Gikuyu?

"And, you know, their mother, Nyina wa Mbooi, has said to me from time to time: 'Ithe wa Mbooi, I don't think those Europeans are real Englishmen. Why, they are always playing and doing the same thing over and over again: they spend their time running about.' And I would reassure her: 'Nyina wa Mbooi, the English are a hybrid race of whites of different kind—Irish, American, German, French, Scottish—and they are a very highly principled race, not the kind to keep changing from one thing to another, day in, day out. They love games that involve running. Indeed, the English were the people who invented *football* and *rugby* and *cricket*, all based on running. Nyina wa Mbooi, let our children stay at those schools, so that they can learn true English customs. A European is a European even though he may be deformed—what matters is the whiteness of his skin!' And now it turns out it was she who was *right*? It's true indeed that a man believes a woman's word when it's too late.

"*Mr. Chairman*, to thieve, to rob and to cheat the poor is *all right*. Where else would our wealth come from? Nobody worth his salt would ever question such a scheme of things, for that's how the world has always been and that's how it will ever be. But this man who thieves, robs and cheats his own class—what kind of a thief and a robber is he? Isn't it generally agreed that theft like this passes all understanding? And he dares to stand before us to make hollow noises and to demand a crown of victory! A crown of victory indeed! He should go home and put on his mother's crown!

"Kîhaahu, from today onwards my children will never go anywhere near your schools. I'll go straight to Nyina wa Mbooi—she is highly educated, has even been to Cambridge—to tell her to look for an *international* school. Kîhaahu wa Gatheeca, do you hear that? You have had it! You'll never again eat anything that belongs to Ithe wa Mbooi and Nyina wa Mbooi. We shall go to *international* schools for *international* Europeans, where *international* English is spoken, schools without cripples for principals, schools without Europeans made of plastic and with electric hearts and skins whitened with *Ambi* acids. We want an *international* color!"

And before Ithe wa Mbooi had sat down, another man stood up to speak. He was so angry that as he spoke, he gnawed at his fingers and his lips. His belly was so huge that it almost bulged over his knees.

"*Mr. Chairman*, my name is Fathog Marura wa Kimeengemeenge. I don't have much to say. I move that Kîhaahu wa Gatheeca be expelled from this competition. How dare he come here and boast about how he fucks other people's wives? *Mr. Chairman*, my wife has virtually run away from home. Now I know where she goes. Now I know the adulterer who despoils and destroys other people's homes. You, it's you, Kîhaahu! I swear that if I had brought my gun with me—yes, I swear by the woman who bore me—that tonight you would have slept minus that prick that offers Haraambe to other people's wives. I wouldn't have minded, *Mr. Chairman*, if Kîhaahu only fucked the wives of the poor, or schoolgirls from poor homes, but . . . but . . . !"

At that point a lump of pain blocked his throat, and Fathog Marura wa Kimeengemeenge could only bite his lips and fingers helplessly in rage as he sat down. The cave now became a beehive of angry noise. Much of the anger was directed at Kîhaahu wa Gatheeca.

And then Kîhaahu wa Gatheeca stood up and began to defend himself.

"*Mr. Chairman*, I have been abused and insulted by those who have just spoken, and I have listened to their insults patiently. But now I seek and demand protection from the chair. I too am going to speak frankly, come what may. Each man here should go home right now and secure his wife's cunt with a padlock, and then take all the keys to a bank safe, which will keep the keys safe until he is ready to retrieve them, primed by an erection. I'm not the one who has instructed their wives to become sugar mummies, or to join the club of the Ready-to-Yield. But a woman like yours," and here Kîhaahu pointed a finger directly at Marura wa Kimeengemeenge, "I swear by the name of truth that I would never touch such a woman, even were I to find her thighs spread in the middle of the road, or if she and I were shut in a house together with all the lights turned out. I cannot bring myself to compete for it with schoolboys and tourists. . . .

"I should also make the point that nobody here should brag about guns. In my house I have three *rifles* and two *machine guns*, and in the car I keep a *patchet*. And if you think that this coat pocket bulges a little, I'll have you know that it is not for nothing. Wherever I go, I am always armed from head to toe. If anybody wants to come up here and try to disarm me, he'll see stars in daylight. . . .

"*Mr. Chairman*, Gitutu wa Gataanguru has also insulted me. We came here so that each competitor could boast, in any way he chose, about his capacity for theft and robbery. I was only telling the truth, and I wasn't trying to insult anyone. What I said was that robbing the masses by means of speculation in land (the very land they fought for) was a stage through which I too passed before going on to higher things. I no longer deal with land-buying companies and societies. One does not steal and squat to eat the loot in the same place all the time, for the owner will sooner or later catch up with one.

"The only thing I deny with my heart and my life is what Gitutu wa Gataanguru said about the possibility that I might be the cause of the emergence of Chinese-style communism in this country. What, me, accept being ruled by a party of the workers and peasants? Me, accept being ruled by a party dedicated to eradicating the system of theft and robbery on Earth? Me, go back to working with my hands? Eat only what has been produced by my sweat alone, without having access to the products of other people's sweat? Find myself facing duster and chalk again? Forget that, Mr. Gitutu. . . .

"On the contrary, I would say that it is your plan for grabbing all the soil and all the air in the universe that's the *dangerous* one and the one that could spread the disease of Chinese-style communism more quickly. The reason is this: if you prevented people from breathing, what would prevent them from taking up clubs and swords and guns? Isn't that tantamount to showing how much you despise the masses? Better meanness that is covert: better a system of theft that is disguised by lies. Or why do you think that our imperialist friends brought us the Bible? Do you think that they were being foolish when they urged workers and peasants to close their eyes in prayer and told them that earthly things were vain? Why do you think I go to all the church fund-raising Haraambe meetings?

"Gitutu, leave me alone. But if you still want to challenge me to a pistol duel, I would be only too happy to oblige, because your belly would make a perfect target and I'd like to find out if I can deflate it with a bullet or two. But should you prefer a war between our mercenaries, that would also give us a chance to find out which group, yours or mine, smokes the strongest bhang. I too have been circumcised. If you inquire carefully among the women, they will testify that there is no foreskin attached to my cock!

"And lastly I would like to answer the charge of Ithe wa Mbooi, who complained that I rob members of my own class. To him I say this: what kind of thief and robber are you? What is he doing in this competition if he has never learned the elementary truth that there is steel which can easily drill through steel? Let me say this to Ithe wa Mbooi: there are thieves who can out-steal other thieves; there are robbers who can out-rob other robbers; there are kings who can out-rule other kings. If Ithe wa Mbooi doesn't know this, he should pack up at once and go home to help Nyina wa Mbooi peel potatoes by the fireside and chat about ashes and embers. A piece of steel that can drill through steel itself—doesn't that indicate that the steel is of special quality and toughness? What else do you people want? The crown is mine. Let's not waste time. Give me the crown of victory!"

His last speech appeared to have created even more enemies. Several people jumped up at the same time and started shouting at one another, some in support of Kîhaahu or Gitutu or Ithe wa Mbooi, others on the side of Fathog Marura wa Kimeengemeenge. It was as if the cave had become the site of seven markets combined.

And then suddenly silence fell in the cave. Kîhaahu, Gitutu and Ithe wa Mbooi had pulled out their guns.

People silently pushed back their chairs and stood up, each trying to keep out of the way of the bullets. For a minute or so nobody coughed or sneezed; the only noise was the scraping of tables and chairs as the occupants moved away, waiting for the whistling of bullets.

The whole feast would have broken up in disarray had the master of ceremonies not jumped on to the platform before the shoot-out could begin and yelled with all his might until people returned to their seats. Still glaring at one another, Kîhaahu wa Gatheeca, Gitutu wa Gataanguru and Ithe wa Mbooi also resumed their seats. And again, quite suddenly, noise returned to the cave. The master of ceremonies tried to silence the people with a wave of his hand. Then he spoke to them in a soothing, conciliatory tone.

"Put those guns away in your pockets. I ask you with due respect to remember what has brought us together here today. We didn't come here for a duel. We came here with the sole purpose of taking part in a competition in modern theft and robbery. I would also like to remind you that we have guests, seven emissaries from *International Thieves and Robbers*, who are here to monitor all that we say and do. Do you want to strip each other naked in front of our foreign guests? What do you imagine they think of us now, after witnessing this chaos and a threatened shoot-out in broad daylight? Our actions may make them lose faith in us and rethink their position. They must be wondering: Can these people really look after the products of our theft and robbery in their country? Are they really capable of looking after our finance houses and stores and all the industries underwritten by these? Imagine what we would lose if they were to take their leftovers to another village? What a loss for Ilmorog! Who would be to blame except ourselves? Let me be frank with you, for as the saying goes, one man can smear another out of love: too fierce a flame can cheat the fire of its meat. . . .

"I beg you, I beseech you, *tafadhali,* please, be patient. Every competitor will get his chance to give his testimony on this platform and to brag about his artistry in theft and robbery. Let us not look down upon one another. Testimony is testimony. We should not let testimony testify against testimony. There is no hawk too small when it comes to hunting in the modern style.

"But to restore peace to our souls and bodies, I suggest a small break to entertain our bellies, for the belly of a thief and a robber is not so foolish as to keep quiet when there is plenty of food, and it is not easily bribed into silence with a bite or two. You can all buy lunch here in the cave—we have a special *international dish*—or you can go elsewhere in Ilmorog. But I plead with you to hurry up over the eating and drinking so that we can all reassemble here at 2:30. There are plenty of testimonies to come.

"Before we break for lunch, I would like to remind the women here, whether they are wives, mistresses or girlfriends, that after the competition there will be a fashion parade, a chance for you to show off your jewelry, your gold, diamonds, silver, rubies, tanzanites, pearls. We must develop our *culture*, and you know very well that it is the way that women dress and the kind of jewelry they wear that indicates the heights a culture has reached. So when you come back, have ready your necklaces, earrings, rings and brooches, so that we can impress our foreign guests and show them that we too are on the way to modern civilization. So remember, *2:30 sharp! For now, namtakieni, bon appetit, mes amis!*"

The master of ceremonies was given a standing ovation. People were now satisfied, and they started talking lightheartedly. The *Hell's Angels* band started playing some Congolese tunes:

> Babanda nanga bakimi na mobali
> Mobali oyo toto ya matema
> Nakei koluko mobali nangae. . . .

A few people stayed where they were, drinking and discussing the threatened shoot-out. Others moved towards the door.

> Kyrie, kyrie eleison
> Kyrie, kyrie eleison. . . .

Gatuiria took Wariinga by the hand and said: "We should go outside. Let's get out, or this air will suffocate me!"

"Yes, I feel sick," Wariinga replied, standing up. "Let's go outside where we can breathe free air before it is turned into a commodity by Kîhaahu and Gitutu," she added, as they left the cave.

> Kyrie, kyrie eleison
> Kyrie, kyrie eleison. . . .

Mwaura turned towards Muturi and said: "How come you know about the *Devil's Angels*? What's your connection with them?"

Muturi took out the piece of paper which had been handed to Wariinga by the thugs who had ejected her from her house in Nairobi.

"Look at this," Muturi said, as he gave the piece of paper to Mwaura. "I think it belongs to you."

Mwaura read it and frowned. "Where did you get it from?" he asked.

"It was in your car last night," Muturi replied.

Mwaura looked at Muturi with eyes filled with bitter questions: What's Muturi doing here? Who is he hunting down with his restless eyes? Could it be me? Why did he write this, only to pretend that he found it in the car? Or did he want to gauge the expression on my face? Who is Muturi? Who is Wangari? Muturi could not see the bitterness in Mwaura's eyes, for he had, at that moment, turned towards Wangari.

"We should go outside too," Muturi told Wangari.

The *Hell's Angels* band went on playing the same Congolese tune:

> Nakai Koluka banganga
> Po ya Kosongisa mobali nangai. . . .

Mwaura suddenly decided to ask Muturi and Wangari who had sent them to Ilmorog. I must show them that I know about their secret mission, he thought. I must show them that I wasn't fooled by their tall stories last night.

"I say!" he started, and then he suppressed what was in his mind and tried to cover it up with a different question. "Wangari, are you going to deck yourself out with gold and diamonds and pearls and other stones?"

Wangari, Muturi and Mwaura laughed. They left the cave, still laughing. Mwaura felt relieved: what had he been worrying about?

"I would rather put on earrings made of dry maize stems," Wangari answered. "The only problem is that I missed my chance to have my ears pierced."

"Why?" Muturi and Mwaura asked.

"Because ours was not a time for adorning our bodies with flowers and necklaces. Ours was a time for decorating ourselves with bullets in the fight for Kenya's freedom!" Wangari said with pride, because she knew that the deeds of her youth had changed Kenya's history.

Mwaura suddenly stopped laughing. He was troubled. His face darkened. His heart beat as if it were asking him: Could it be that in your *matatu* you were carrying a threat to your own life, like the louse one carries around on one's body?

But Muturi looked at Wangari, his heart overflowing with sudden pride and happiness. Wangari, heroine of our country—all Wangaris, heroines of our land! Should I reveal to her the task that has brought me here today, so that she and I can help each other? No, the time is not yet ripe. I'll observe her a little longer, he muttered to himself, still gazing at Wangari. But afterwards . . . afterwards . . . , he whispered to himself. And then he recalled the braggarts in the cave, and Muturi felt like weeping. "Let's get out of here," he urged Wangari and Mwaura. "Let's leave this place!"

# Margaret Laurence

Considered by many critics to be the premier figure in shaping postwar Canadian literature, Margaret Laurence has gained an international reputation. She was born in a small Manitoba town, 18 July 1926, and lost her mother at age four, her father at age nine; Laurence's aunt, later her stepmother, reared her. After graduating from United College in Winnipeg, she worked as a reporter for the *Winnipeg Citizen*. In 1947 she married Jack Laurence, and three years later they went to Africa, first to Somalia, then to the Gold Coast, where he worked as an engineer. They came back to Canada in 1957, and in 1962 separated. Laurence spent the following years in England until she returned home to serve as writer in residence at the University of Toronto, the first of several such posts. She remained in Canada until her death on 5 January 1987. In addition to writing, Laurence took an active part in public life and lent her prestige to various causes, including nuclear disarmament, environmental issues, and censorship questions.

James King's *The Life of Margaret Laurence* (1997), a biography authorized by Laurence's son and daughter, reveals for the first time officially that she committed suicide after being diagnosed with cancer. In contrast to the public role she had established as a confident, successful writer, the biographer identifies Laurence's struggle with alcoholism, depression, and personal anguish. King traces the writer's tormented self to the early loss of her parents, and reevaluates her fiction as a lifelong way to cope creatively with her own sense of inadequacy. He sees this personal conflict as an important element in Laurence's genius.

Laurence derived her first published fiction from the African experience—a novel, *This Side Jordan* (1960), and a short-story collection, *The Tomorrow-Tamer* (1963). But her reputation rests largely on the Canadian books, known as "the Manawake series": *The Stone Angel* (1964); *A Jest of*

*God* (1966); *The Fire-Dwellers* (1969); *A Bird in the House* (1970); *The Diviners* (1974). Although the link between Africa and Canada at first appears improbable, it has been pointed out that Laurence grasped that both shared a history of colonialism. Consequently, Canadians and Africans judged their behavior by standards imposed from an outside source, and in order to gain their own identity they must decolonize themselves as individuals. She carried over this definition of the postcolonial dilemma into her treatment of women, whom she saw as submissive, powerless, self-deprecating, and uncertain, finally as the pawns of men. "The Manawake series" provides a fictional history of four generations of Canadian women struggling to discover their selfhood, beginning with ninety-year-old Hagar in *The Stone Angel* and leading to the writer Morag in *The Diviners*.

Published in *The Tomorrow-Tamer*, "The Perfume Sea" reflects in near comic tones Laurence's major themes of alienation and survival, themes she refined in the Canadian fiction. The unidentified African nation is most likely Ghana, formed from the Gold Coast, where Laurence and her husband were living on the eve of the colony's independence from Great Britain in 1957. Although dispossessed, the two European outsiders, the surviving "flotsam" of colonialism, find a place and tranquility in the newly established nation. The irony, though, lies in the fact that their acceptance is grounded on a continued imposition of outside values—in this instance European ideas of feminine beauty.

# The Perfume Sea

"No question of it," Mr. Archipelago said, delicately snipping a wisp of hair. "I am flotsam."

"Not jetsam?" Mrs. Webley-Pryce asked, blinking sharply watchful eyes as the scissored shreds fell down onto her face. "I always get the two confused."

Outside, the small town was growing sluggish under the sedative sun of late morning. The one-footed beggar who squatted beside Mr. Archipelago's door had gone to sleep on the splintery wooden steps. Past the turquoise-and-red façade of Cowasjee's Silk Bazaar, in the rancid and shadowy room, the shriveled Parsee sat, only half awake, folding a length of sari-cloth and letting the silk slip through his fingers as he dreamed of a town in India, no less ill-smelling and dirty than this African one, but filled with the faces and speech of home. At the shop of K. Tachie (General Merchant), Tachie himself sat beside his cash register, surrounded by boxes and barrels. Kinglike, he perched on a high stool and roared abuse at his court of counter-clerks, while at the same time he managed to gulp a lurid carbonated grape beverage called Doko-Doko. At the Africa Star Chemists, a young shopgirl dozed, propping her brown arms against a carton of Seven Seas cod-liver oil. Down the street, in the Paradise Chop-Bar, a young man recalled those arms as he sloshed a rag over the tables in preparation for the customers who would soon be lifting the striped bedspread that hung across the doorway and shouting for beer and *kenkey*. In the Government Agent's office, and in the offices of Bridgeford & Knight, Exporters-Importers, Englishmen sighed and wilted and saw from their watches that they could not yet legitimately leave for lunch. Pariah dogs on the road snarled over the corpse of a cat; then, panting, tongues dribbling, defeated by sun, they crawled back to a shaded corner, where their scabrous hides were fondled by an old man in a hashish dream. Footsteps on the cracked and scorching pavement lagged. Even the brisk shoes of white men slackened and slowed. The market women walked tiredly, their head-trays heavy, their bare feet pressing the warm dust into ripples and dunes. Babies slung on their mothers' backs allowed their heads to loll forward and whimpered at the sweat that made sticky their faces. A donkey brayed disconsolately. Voices droned low. Laughter like melted honey poured slowly. Down by the shore, under a few scattered palm trees, the wives of fishermen drowsed over their net-mending. Only the children, the fire and gleam of them greater even than the harsh glint of sun, continued to leap and shout as before.

Mr. Archipelago riffled a comb through the winter straw of the lady's hair, and nuzzled his rotundity against her arm for the lightly spiteful pleasure of feeling her recoil. He moved back a decent pace. Under his white smock, the red and gold brocade waistcoat quivered with his belly's silent laughter.

"Flotsam, dear lady," he said. "I looked it up in the Concise Oxford."

On the other side of the room, Doree glanced up from the lustrous green with which she was enameling the fingernails of her thin white hands, knuckle-swollen from years of cleansing other women's hair. Her mild myopic eyes were impressed, even awed. Her mouth, painted to emulate hardness, opened in a soft spontaneous astonishment.

"Can you beat it?" she said. "He looks up words all the time, and laughs like the dickens. I used to read the telephone book sometimes, in the nights, and wonder about those names and if they all belonged to real people, living somewhere, you know, and doing something. But I never laughed. What'd it say for flotsam, Archipelago?"

Mr. Archipelago beamed. His shiny eyes were green as malachite. He stood on tiptoe, a plump pouter-pigeon of a man, puffing out his chest until the brocade waistcoat swelled. His hair, black as ripe olives, he only touched from time to time with pomade, but it gave the impression of having been crimped and perfumed.

"Wreckage found floating," he said proudly. "It said—'wreckage found floating.'"

"The very thing" Doree cried, clapping her hands, but Mrs. Webley-Pryce looked aloof because she did not understand.

The air in the shop was syrupy with heat and perfume, and the odd puff of breeze that came in through the one window seemed to be the exhalation of a celestial fire-eater. Mrs. Webley-Pryce, feeling the perspiration soaking through her linen dress, wriggled uncomfortably in her chair and tried to close her eyes to the unseemly and possibly septic litter all around her. The shop was not really dirty, although to the fastidious English minds of lady customers it appeared so. Doree swept it faithfully every evening at closing time, but as her sight was so poor and she would not wear glasses, she often missed fragments of hair which gradually mingled with dust and formed themselves into small tangled bails of gray and hazelnut brown and bottled blonde. The curl-papers, too, had an uncanny way of escaping and drifting around the room like leaves fallen from some rare tree. Doree chain-smoked, so the ashtrays were nearly always full. Mr. Archipelago found her cigarette butts charming, each with its orange kiss mark from the wide mouth he had never touched. But the ladies did not share his perception; they pushed the ashtrays away impatiently, hintingly, until with a sigh he emptied them into a wastepaper basket and watched the ashes flutter like gray flakes of dandruff.

Sweat was gathering on Mr. Archipelago's smooth forehead, and his fingers were becoming slippery around the comb and scissors.

"The morning beer," he announced. "It is now time. For you, as well, Mrs. Webley-Pryce?"

"I think not, thanks," she replied coldly. "Nothing before sundown is my rule. Can't you hurry a little, Mr. Archipelago? At this rate it'll be midnight before my perm is finished."

"Pardon, pardon," said Mr. Archipelago, tilting the beer bottle. "One moment, and we fly to work. Like birds on the wing."

Out came the solutions, the flasks of pink and mauve liquid, the odor of ammonia competing with the coarse creamy perfumes. Out came clamps and pins and curlpapers, the jumbled contents of a dozen shelves and cupboards. In the midst of the debris, stirring it all like a magic potion, stood Mr. Archipelago, a fat and frantic wizard, refreshing himself occasionally with Dutch ale. He darted over to the mainstay of his alchemist's laboratory, an elaborate arrangement of electrically heated metal rods, on which he placed the heavy clamps. He waited, arms folded, until the whole dangerous mechanism achieved the dull mysterious fire which was to turn Mrs. Webley-Pryce's base metal, as it were, to gold.

"You should sell that lot," Mrs. Webley-Pryce remarked. "Any museum in Europe would give you a good price."

At once he was on the defensive, his pride hurt.

"Let me tell you, dear lady, there isn't one beauty salon in the whole of Europe could give you a perm like this one does."

"I don't doubt that for one instant," she said with a short laugh.

Doree stood up, an emaciated yellow-and-white bird, a tall gaunt crane, her hair clinging like wet feathers around her squeezed-narrow shoulders. With her long, hesitant stride she walked across the room, and held out her green-lacquered hands.

"Sea pearl," she said. "Kind of different, anyhow. Africa Star Chemists just got it in. Like it?"

Shuddering slightly, Mrs. Webley-Pryce conceded that it was very handsome.

"Pearl reminds me," Mr. Archipelago said, returning to cheerfulness, "the Concise Oxford stated another thing for flotsam."

Mrs. Webley-Pryce looked at him with open curiosity and begged decorously to be told. Mr. Archipelago applied a dab of spit to a finger and casually tested the heat of the clamps.

"Precisely, it said 'oyster-spawn.' Think of that. Oyster-spawn. And that is me, too, eh?"

Doree laughed until she began to cough, and he frowned at her, for they were both worried by this cough and she could not stop smoking for more than an hour at a time.

"I don't see—" Mrs. Webley-Pryce probed.

"A little joke," Mr. Archipelago explained. "Not a very good one, perhaps, but we must do the best with what we have. My father, as I may have told you, was an Armenian sailor."

"Oh yes," Mrs. Webley-Pryce said, disappointed, holding her breath as he placed the first hot clamp on her tightly wound-up hair, "I believe you did mention it. Odd—Archipelago never seems like an Armenian name to me, somehow."

"It isn't."

"Oh?"

Mr. Archipelago smiled. He enjoyed talking about himself. He allowed himself a degree of pride in the fact that no one could ever be sure where the truth ended and the tinted unreality began. With the Englishmen to whom he administered haircuts, Mr. Archipelago talked sparingly. They seemed glum and taciturn to him, or else overly robust, with a kind of dogged heartiness that made him at once wary. But with the lady customers it was a different matter. He had a genuine sympathy for them. He did not chide, even to himself, their hunger. If one went empty for long enough, one became hungry. His tales were the manna with which it was his pleasure to nourish his lady customers. Also, he was shrewd. He knew that his conversation was an attraction, no less than the fact that he was the only hairdresser within a hundred miles; it was his defense against that noxious invention the home-permanent.

"It would have been difficult for my mother to give me my father's name," he said, "as she never knew it. She was—I may have mentioned—an Italian girl. She worked in a wineshop in Genoa. It smelled of Barbera and stale fish and—things you would prefer I did not speak about. I grew up there. That Genoa! Never go there. A port town, a sailors' town. The most saddening city in the world, I think. The ships are always mourning. You hear those wailing voices even in your sleep. The only place I ever liked in all Genoa was the Staglieno cemetery, up on the hills. I used to go there and sit beside the tombs of the rich, a small fat boy with the white marble angels—so compassionate they looked, and so costly—I believed then that each was the likeness of a lady buried beneath. Then I would look over at the fields of rented graves nearby. The poor rent graves for one, two, five years—I can't remember exactly. The body must be taken out if the rent cannot be paid. In death, as in life, the rent must always be paid."

"How horrible," Mrs. Webley-Pryce said. "Look here—are you sure this clamp isn't too hot? I think it's burning my neck. Oh thanks, that's better. It's your mother's name, then?"

Doree glared. Mrs. Webley-Pryce was the wife of the Government Agent, but she had married late and had lived in Africa only one year—she had not yet learned that however eager one might be, the questions must always be judicious, careful. But Mr. Archipelago was bland. He did not mind the curiosity of his lady customers.

"No, dear lady, it is not her name. Why should a person not pick his own name? It sounds Italian. I liked it. It suits me. Do you know what it means?"

"Well, of course," Mrs. Webley-Pryce said uncertainly. "An archipelago is—well, it's—"

"A sea with many islands, according to the Concise Oxford. That has been my life. A sea with many islands."

"This is one of them, I suppose?"

"The most enduring so far," he replied. "Twelve years I have been here."

"Really? That's a long time. You'll go back, though, someday?"

"I have no wish to go back," Mr. Archipelago answered offhandedly. "I would like to die here and be buried in my own garden. Perhaps if I were buried under the wild orchids they would grow better. I have tried every other kind of fertilizer."

"You can't be serious," Mrs. Webley-Pryce protested. "About not going back, I mean."

"Why not? I like it here."

"But it's so far away from everything. So far from home."

"For you, perhaps," Mr. Archipelago said. "But then, you are not a true expatriate. You may stay twenty years, but you are a visitor. Your husband, though—does he anticipate with pleasure the time when he will retire and go back to England?"

She looked at him in surprise.

"No—he dreads it, as a matter of fact. That's understandable, though. His work is here, his whole life. He's been here a long time, too, you know. But it's rather different. He was sent out here. He had to come."

"Did he?"

"Of course," she said. "If a person goes in for colonial administration, he must go to a colony, mustn't he?"

"Indeed he must," Mr. Archipelago said agreeably. "If he goes in for colonial administration, it is the logical step."

"But for a hairdresser," she said, "it's not the sort of place most people would exactly choose—"

"Aha—now we come to it. You are one of those who believe I did not choose to come here, then? That I was, perhaps, forced to leave my own country?"

"I didn't mean that—" Mrs. Webley-Pryce floundered. "And I suppose it's a blessing for the European women that there's someone in a tiny station like this who can do hair—"

"Even if it is only Archipelago with his equipment that belongs in a museum. Well, well. Tell me, madam—what is the current theory about me? It changes, you know. This interests me greatly. No, please—I am not offended. You must not think so. Only curious, just as you are curious about me. Once, I remember, I was said to have been a counterfeiter. Another time, I had deserted my wife and family. Through the years, it has been this and that. Perhaps one of them is true. Or perhaps not. To maintain dignity, one must have at least one secret—don't you agree?"

Mrs. Webley-Pryce gave him a sideways glance.

"I have heard," she admitted, "about there having been some trouble. I'm sure it couldn't have been true, though—"

But Mr. Archipelago neither confirmed nor denied. He tested a curl, and finding it satisfactory, he began to remove the mass of iron from the hair. Mrs. Webley-Pryce, embarrassed by his silence, turned to Doree, who was applying bleach to her own long yellow hair.

"Speaking of names, I've always meant to ask you about yours, Doree. It's rather unusual, isn't it?'

"Yeh," Doree said, through her mane. "I used to be Doreen."

"Oh?" Once more the lilt in the voice of the huntress.

Doree spoke of herself rarely. She did not possess Mr. Archipelago's skill or his need, and when she talked about her own life she usually blurted unwillingly the straight facts because she could not think of anything else to say. Her few fabrications were obvious; she wrenched them out aggressively, knowing no one would believe her. Now she was caught off guard.

"I had my own shop once," she said in her gentle rasping voice. "It had a sign up—DOREEN/BEAUTY INCORPORATED. Classy. Done in those gilt letters. You buy them separately and stick them up. The state of my dough wasn't so classy, though. So when the goddam 'N' fell off, I figured it was cheaper to change my name to fit the sign."

Gratified, Mrs. Webley-Pryce tittered.

"And just where was your shop?"

Now it was Mr. Archipelago's turn to glare. It was permissible to question him minutely, but not Doree. Customers were supposed to understand this rule. He saw Doree's eyes turn vague, and he longed to touch her hand, to comfort and reassure her. But it was better not to do such a thing. He did not want her to misunderstand his devotion, or to be in any way alarmed by a realization of its existence. Instead, he slithered a still-hot clamp down on Mrs. Webley-Pryce's neck, causing a faint smell of singed skin and a gasp of pain.

"It was in Montreal, if you must know," Doree said harshly.

Last time someone asked, the answer was Chicago, and once, daringly, Mexico City. Mr. Archipelago himself did not know. She had simply walked into his shop one day, and where she came from, or why, did not matter to him. When they were alone, he and Doree never questioned each other. Their evening conversation was of the day's small happenings.

"Montreal—" Mrs. Webley-Pryce said thoughtfully. "Perhaps David and I will go to some place like that. There's nothing much left for administrative men in England."

"You're leaving?" Mr. Archipelago asked, startled. "You're leaving Africa?"

"Yes, of course—that's what I meant when I said David dreaded—didn't you know?"

"But—why?" he asked in dismay, for recently she had been patronizing the shop regularly. "Why?"

"Dear me," she said, with an effort at brightness, "you are behind the times, aren't you? Didn't you know this colony will be self-governing soon? They don't want us here any more."

"I knew it was coming," Mr. Archipelago said, "but I had not realized it was so soon. Strange. I read the newspapers. I talk with Mr. Tachie, my landlord, who is a very political man. But—ah well, I tend my garden, and try to get wild orchids to grow here beside the sea, where the soil is really much too sandy for them, and I do the ladies' hair and drink beer and talk to Doree. I think nothing will ever change in this place—so insignificant, surely God will forget about it and let it be. But not so. How many will be going?"

"Oh, I don't know—most of the Europeans in government service—perhaps all. I expect some of those in trade will remain."

Her tone implied that Mr. Archipelago would be left with a collection of lepers, probably hairless.

"There are not enough of them," he murmured, "to keep me in business."

He groped on a shelf for another beer and opened it with perspiring hands. He thought of the sign outside his establishment. Not a gilt-lettered sign, to be sure, but nicely done in black and aquamarine, with elegant spidery letters:

ARCHIPELAGO
English-Style Barber
European Ladies' Hairdresser

"A sea with many islands," he said, addressing only himself. "Sometimes it happens that a person discovers he has built his house upon an island that is sinking."

A large green house by the shore sheltered Mr. Archipelago. Once he had lived there alone, but for the past five years he had not been alone. Doree's presence in his house had been, he knew, a popular topic of discussion at the morning coffee parties in the European cantonment. He did not blame the ladies for talking, but it did give him a certain satisfaction to know that their actual information on the subject was extremely slight. Neither he nor Doree had ever spoken of their domestic arrangements to customers. And their cook-steward, Attah, under the impression that he was protecting his employers' reputations, had never told a living soul that the two shared only living- and dining-rooms and that neither had ever entered the private apartments of the other.

Mr. Archipelago's dwelling was not close either to the white cantonment or to the African houses. It was off by itself, on a jut of land overlooking a small bay. The sprawling overgrown garden was surrounded by a high green wall which enabled Mr. Archipelago in the late afternoons to work outside clad only in his underwear and a round white linen hat. He had no wish to tame the garden, which was a profusion of elephant grass, drooping casuarina trees, frowsy banana palms, slender paw-paw, and all manner of flowering shrubs—hibiscus, purple bougainvillea, and the white rose of Sharon, whose blossoms turned to deep blush as they died. Into this cherished disorder, Mr. Archipelago carefully introduced wild orchids, which never survived for long, and clumps of hardy canna lilies that bloomed pink and ragged. He grew pineapples, too, and daily prodded angrily with his stick at the speared clusters which consistently refused to bear fruit the size of that sold for a mere shilling in the African market. The favorite of his domain, however, was the sensitive plant, an earth vine, which, if its leaves were touched even lightly, would softly and stubbornly close. Mr. Archipelago liked to watch the sensitive plant's closing. Nothing in this world could stop its self-containment; it was not to be bribed or cajoled; it had integrity. But he seldom touched it, for the silent and seemingly conscious inturning of each leaf made him feel clumsy and lacking in manners.

Just as the garden was Mr. Archipelago's special province, so the long verandah was Doree's. Here flew, uncaged, four gray African parrots, their wings tipped with scarlet. Sometimes they departed for a while, and sulked in the branches of the frangipani tree. Doree never attempted to catch them, nor would she even lure them with seeds or snails. Mr. Archipelago believed she almost wished one of them would find itself able to leave the sanctuary and return to the forest. But they had lived inside the verandah for too long. They could not have fended for themselves, and they must have known it. They always came back to be fed.

Mr. Archipelago could well have done without some of the visitors to Doree's menagerie. He did not mind the little geckos that clung transparent to the walls, like lizards of glass, nor the paunchy toads whose tongues hunted the iridescent green flies. But the trays containing all the morsels which Doree imagined to be choice fare for spiders—these sometimes drew scorpions and once a puff-adder. Doree would not kill even the lethal guests. She shooed them carefully out at broom-point, assuring the sweating Mr. Archipelago that they had no wish to harm anyone—they wanted only to be shown how to escape. Perhaps her faith protected her, or her lack of fear, for within her sanctuary no live thing seemed to her to be threatening. In any event, she had never been touched by the venom of wild creatures.

She had a chameleon, too, of which she was extremely fond, an eerie bright green reptile with huge eyes and a long tail curled up like a tape-measure. Mr. Archipelago once ventured to suggest that she might find a prettier pet. Doree's large pale eyes squinted at him reproachfully.

"What do you want me to do, anyway? Conk him on the head because he's not a goddam butterfly?"

Mr. Archipelago, appalled at his blunder, answered humbly.

"Am I God, that I should judge a creature? It is not the chameleon that is ugly, but I, for thinking him so. And now, looking at him more carefully, and seeing his skin grow darker against that dark branch where he is, I can see that he must be appreciated according to his own qualities, and not compared with butterflies, who are no doubt gaudy but who do not possess this interesting ability. You are right—he is beautiful."

"I don't get it," Doree said. "I never said he was beautiful."

"Well, then, I did. I do."

"You're what they call 'round the bend,' Archipelago. Never mind. Maybe so am I."

"We suit each other," he replied.

The evenings were spent quietly. They did not go out anywhere, nor did they entertain. They had always been considered socially non-existent by the European community, while in the Africans' view they were standard Europeans and therefore apart. Mr. Archipelago and Doree did not mind. They preferred their own company. Mr. Archipelago possessed a gramophone which vied in antiquity with the wave-machine. Often after dinner he played through his entire repertoire of fourteen records, mainly Italian opera. He particularly liked to listen to *I Pagliacci,* in order to criticize it.

"Hear that!" he would cry to the inattentive Doree. "How sorry he is for himself! A storm of the heart—what a buffoon. Do you know his real tragedy? Not that he had to laugh when his heart was breaking—that is a commonplace. No—the unfortunate fact is that he really is a clown. Even in his desolation. A clown."

Doree, sitting on the mock-Persian carpet whose richness was not lessened for her by its label "Made in Brussels," would placidly continue to talk to her two favorite parrots. She called them Brasso and Silvo, and Mr. Archipelago understood that this christening was meant as a compliment to him, these being the closest to Italian names she could manage.

After work, Mr. Archipelago's scarlet waistcoat was discarded in favor of an impressive smoking-jacket. It was a pale bluish-green Indian brocade, and the small cockerels on it were worked in threads of gold. Although it was a rather warm garment, Mr. Archipelago suffered his sweat for the sake of magnificence.

"You look just like one of those what-d'you-call-'ems—you know, sultans," Doree had once said admiringly.

He remembered the remark each evening when he donned the jacket. Momentarily endowed with the hauteur of Haroun-al-Raschid, he would saunter nonchalantly through the Baghdad of his own living-room.

Frequently they brought out their perfumes, of which they had a great variety, bottles and flagons of all colors and intricate shapes—crowns and hearts and flowers, diamonded, bubbled, baubled, angular, and smooth. The game was to see how many could be identified by smell alone, the vessel masked, before the senses began to flag. Mr. Archipelago did not love the perfumes for themselves alone, nor even for their ability to cover the coarse reek of life. Each one, sniffed like snuff, conjured up for him a throng of waltzing ladies, whirling and spinning eternally on floors of light, their gray gowns swaying, ladies of gentle dust.

Mr. Archipelago and Doree got along well with their one servant. Attah regularly told them the gossip of the town, although they cared about it not at all. He tended to be cantankerous; he would not be argued with; he served for meals the dishes of his own choice. They accepted him philosophically, but on one point they were adamant. They would not allow Attah's wife and family to live within the walls of the compound. The family lived, instead, in the town. Mr. Archipelago and Doree never ceased to feel sorry about this separation, but they could not help it. They could not have endured to have the voices of children threatening their achieved and fragile quiet.

Outside the green wall, however, and far from the sugared humidity of the small shop, events occurred. Governments made reports and politicians made speeches. Votes were cast. Supporters cheered and opponents jeered. Flags changed, and newspapermen typed furiously, recording history to meet a deadline. Along the shore, loin-clothed fishermen, their feet firm in the wet sand, grinned and shrugged, knowing they would continue to burn their muscles like quick torches, soon consumed, in the sea-grappling that claimed them now as always, but sensing, too, that the land in which they set their returning feet was new as well as old, and that they, unchanged, were new with it.

In the town, the white men began to depart one by one, as their posts were filled by Africans. And in Mr. Archipelago's shop, the whirr of the hair-dryer was heard less and less.

Late one night Doree came downstairs in her housecoat, an unheard-of thing for her. Mr. Archipelago was sitting like a gloomy toad in his high-backed wicker armchair. He glanced up in surprise.

"It's my imagination again," she said. "It's been acting up."

Doree suffered periodic attacks of imagination, like indigestion or migraine. She spoke of it always as though it were an affliction of a specific organ, as indeed it was, for her phrenology charts placed the imagination slightly above the forehead, on the right side. Mr. Archipelago brought another wicker chair for her and gave her a little crème de cacao in her favorite liqueur glass, a blinding snow-shadow blue, frosted with edelweiss.

"It's two months," Doree said, sipping, "since the Webley-Pryces left. I don't know how many are gone now. Almost all, I guess. I heard today that Bridgeford & Knight are putting in an African manager. The last perm we gave was nearly a month ago. This week only three haircuts and one shampoo-and-set. Archipelago—what are we going to do?"

He looked at her dumbly. He could give her no comfort.

"Could we go someplace else?" she went on. "Sierra Leone? Liberia?"

"I have thought of that," he said. "Yes, perhaps we shall have to consider it."

They both knew they did not have sufficient money to take them anywhere else.

"Please—" He hesitated. "You must not be upset, or I cannot speak at all—"

"Go on," she said roughly. "What is it?"

"Did you know," Mr. Archipelago questioned sadly, "that if an expatriate is without funds, he can go to the consulate of his country, and they will send him back?"

She lowered her head. Her yellow hair, loose, fell like unraveled wool around her, scarfing the bony pallor of her face.

"I've heard that—yes."

Mr. Archipelago pushed away his crème de cacao, the sweetness of which had begun to nauseate him. His incongruously small feet in their embroidered slippers pattered across the concrete floor. He returned with Dutch ale.

"I have never asked," he said. "And you have never asked, and now I must break the rule. Could you go back? Could you, Doree, if there was nothing else to do?"

Doree lit a cigarette from the end of the last one.

"No," she replied in a steady, strained voice. "Not even if there was nothing else to do."

"Are you sure?"

"My God—" she said. "Yes, I'm sure all right."

Mr. Archipelago did not ask why. He brought his hands together in a staccato clap.

"Good. We know where we stand. Enough of this, then."

"No," she said. "What about you?"

"It is very awkward," he said, "but unfortunately I cannot go back, either."

She did not inquire further. For her, too, his word was sufficient.

"But, Archipelago, the Africans won't let us stay if we're broke. We're not their responsibility—"

"Wait—" Mr. Archipelago said. "I have just remembered something."

Beside his chair, a carved wooden elephant bore a small table on its back. Mr. Archipelago groped underneath and finally opened a compartment in the beast's belly. He took out an object wrapped in tissue paper.

"I have always liked this elephant," he said. "See—a concealed hiding-place. Very cloak-and-dagger. A treasure—no, a toy—such as Columbus might have brought back from his travels. He was once in West Africa, you know, as a young seaman, at one of the old slave-castles not far from here. And he, also, came from Genoa. Well, well. There the similarity ends. This necklace is one I bought many years ago. I have always saved it. I thought I was being very provident—putting away one gold necklace to insure me against disaster. It is locally made—crude, as you can see, but heavy. Ashanti gold, and quite valuable."

Doree looked at it without interest.

"Very nice," she said. "But we can't live off that forever."

"No, but it will give you enough money to live in the city until you find work. More Europeans will be staying there, no doubt, and we know there are several beauty salons. At least it is a chance. For me, the worst would be for you not to have any chance—"

Mr. Archipelago perceived that he had revealed too much. He squirmed and sweated, fearful that she would misunderstand. But when he looked at her, he saw in her eyes not alarm but surprise.

"The necklace and all—" Doree said slowly. "You'd do that—for me?"

Mr. Archipelago forgot about himself in the urgency of convincing her.

"For you, Doree," he said. "Of course, for you. If only it were more—"

"But—it's everything—"

"Yes, everything," he said bitterly. "All I have to offer. A fragment of gold."

"I want you to know," she said, her voice tough with tears, "I want you to know I'm glad you offered. Now put the necklace back in the elephant and let's leave it there. We may need it worse, later."

"You won't take it?" he cried. "Why not?"

"Because you haven't told me yet what's gonna happen to you," Doree said. "And anyway, I don't want to go to another place."

He could not speak. She hurried on.

"If I wasn't here," she said, with a trembling and apologetic laugh, "who'd remind you to put on your hat in the boiling sun? Who'd guess the perfumes with you?"

"I would miss you, of course," he said in a low voice. "I would miss you a great deal."

She turned on him, almost angrily.

"Don't you think I'd miss you?" she cried. "Don't you know how it would be—for me?"

They stared at each other, wide-eyed, incredulous. Mr. Archipelago lived through one instant of unreasonable and terrifying hope. Then, abruptly, he became once more aware of himself, oddly swathed in Indian brocade and holding in his fat perspiring hands an ale-glass and a gold necklace.

Doree's eyes, too, had become distant and withdrawn. She was twisting a sweat-lank strand of her hair around one wrist.

"We're getting ourselves into a stew over nothing," she said at last. "Nobody's gonna be leaving. Everything will be just the same as always. Listen, Archipelago, I got a hunch we're due for a lucky break. I'm sure of it. Once I met a spiritualist—nice old dame—I really went for that Ouija-board stuff in those days—well, she told me I had natural ability. I had the right kind of an aura. Yeh, sure it's phony, I know that. But my hunches are hardly ever wrong. Shall we shake on it?"

Gravely, they shook hands and drank to the lucky break. Mr. Archipelago began to tell stories about the tourists with whom, as a boy, he used to practice his shaky English, and how nervous they always were of getting goat's milk in their tea.

They talked until the pressure lamp spluttered low and the floor beneath it was littered with the beige and broken wings of moths. Doree went upstairs then, singing a snatch of an African highlife tune in her warm raw voice. But later, Mr. Archipelago, queasy with beer and insomnia, heard once again the sound that used to be so frequent when she first came to this house, her deep and terrible crying in her sleep.

They had had no customers at all for a fortnight, but still they opened the shop each morning and waited until exactly four o'clock to close it. One morning Tachie strolled in, prosperous in a new royal-blue cloth infuriatingly patterned with golden coins. He was a large man; the warm room with its sweet cloying air seemed too small to hold his brown ox-shoulders, his outflung arms, his great drum of a voice.

"Mistah Arch'pelago, why you humbug me? Two month, and nevah one penny I getting. You t'ink I rich too much? You t'ink I no need for dis money?"

Mr. Archipelago, standing beside his idle transmutation machine and sagging gradually like a scarlet balloon with the air sinking out of it, made one unhopeful effort at distracting Tachie.

"Can I offer you a beer, Mr. Tachie? A light refreshing ale at this time of day—"

Tachie grimaced.

"You t'ink I drink beer wey come from my shop an' nevah been pay at all? No, I t'ank you. I no drink dis beer—he too cost, for me. Mistah Arch'pelago, you trouble me too much. What we do, eh?"

Mr. Archipelago's skin looked sallower than usual. His eyes were dull and even his crisp neat hair had become limp. Doree held out large and pitying hands towards him, but she could not speak.

"In life as in death, the rent must be paid," he said. "We have been dreaming, dreaming, while the world moved on, and now we waken to find it so changed we do not know what to do. We wanted only to stay and not to harm anyone, but of course you are right, Mr. Tachie, to remind us it is not enough. One must always have a product to sell that someone wants to buy. We do not have much of anything any more, but we will try to pay our debts before we move on. Perhaps a museum will buy my wave-machine after all."

Doree put her hands over her face, and Tachie, horrified, looked from one to the other, still unable to grasp the actuality of their despair.

"You no got money-at all? De time wey I come for you shop, I anger too much for you. Now angry can no stay for me. My friend, I sorry. Befoah God, I too sorry. But what I can do?"

"It is not your concern," Mr. Archipelago said with dignity. "We do not expect you to let us stay. We are not appealing for charity."

But Tachie could not stop justifying himself.

"I look-a de shop, I see Eur'pean womans all dey gone, I see you no got lucky. But I no savvy propra. I t'ink you got money you put for bank. Now I see wit' my eye you tell me true, you no got nothing. But what I can do? I no be rich man. I got shop, I got dis place. But I got plenty plenty family, all dey come for me, all dey say 'Tachie, why you no give we more?' My own pickin dey trouble me too much. My daughtah Mercy, she big girl, all time she saying 'meka you buy for me one small new cloth, meka you buy powdah for face, meka you buy shoe same city girl dey wear it—' "

Mr. Archipelago peered sharply at Tachie.

"Your daughter—face powder—shoes—she, too, is changed—"

"I tell you true. Mistah Arch'pelago, why you're looking so?"

The balloon that was Mr. Archipelago suddenly became re-inflated. He began to spin on one foot, whistled a Viennese waltz, bounced across the room, grasped Doree's hand, drew her into his comprehension and his laughter. Together they waltzed, absurd, relieved, triumphant.

"Mr. Tachie, you are a bringer of miracles!" Mr. Archipelago cried. "There it was, all the time, and we did not see it. We, even we, Doree, will make history—you will see."

Tachie frowned, bewildered.

"I see it happen so, for white men, wen dey stay too long for dis place. Dey crez'. Mistah Arch'pelago, meka you drink some small beer. Den you head he come fine."

"No, no, not beer," Mr. Archipelago replied, puffing out his waistcoat. "Here—a flask kept for medicinal purposes or special celebrations. A brandy, Mr. Tachie! A brandy for the history-makers!"

He and Doree laughed until they were weak. And Tachie, still not understanding, but pleased that they were in some lunatic fashion pleased, finally laughed with them and consented to drink the unpaid-for brandy.

That evening they painted the new sign. They worked until midnight, with tins and brushes spread out on the dining-room table, while Brasso and Silvo squawked and stared. The sign was black and gilt, done in optimistically plump lettering:

ARCHIPELAGO & DOREE
Barbershop
All-Beauty Salon
African Ladies a Speciality

The men of the town continued, not unnaturally, to have their hair cut by the African barbers who plied their trade under the *niim* tree in the market. The African women, however, showed great interest in the new sign. They gathered in little groups and examined it. The girls who had attended school read the words aloud to their mothers and aunts. They murmured together. Their laughter came in soft gusts, like the sound of the wind through the casuarina branches. But not one of them would enter the shop.

Several times Mr. Archipelago saw faces peeping in at the window, scrutinizing every detail of the room. But as soon as he looked, the curious ones lowered their eyes and quickly walked away.

The hair-straightening equipment (obtained secondhand, and on credit, through Tachie) remained unused. Each day Doree dusted and set back on the counter the unopened packets and jars of dusky powder and cinnamon-brown make-up base which she had hurriedly ordered from the city when she discovered that the Africa Star Chemists, slightly behind the times, sold only shades of ivory and peach.

Another week, and still no customers. Then one morning, as Mr. Archipelago was opening his second bottle of Dutch ale, Mercy Tachie walked in.

"Please, Mr. Archipelago—" she began hesitantly. "I am thinking to come here for some time, but I am not sure what I should do, We have never had such a place in our town before, you see. So all of us are looking, but no one wishes to be the first. Then my father, he said to me today that I should be the first, because if you are having no customers, he will never be getting his money from you."

Mercy was about sixteen. She was clad in traditional cloth, but her face was thickly daubed with a pale powder that obscured her healthy skin. She stood perfectly still in the center of the room, her hands clasped in front of her, her face expressionless. Mr. Archipelago looked in admiration at the placidity of her features, a repose which he knew concealed an extreme nervousness and perhaps even panic, for in her life there had not been many unfamiliar things. He motioned her to a chair, and she sat down woodenly.

"Good," he said. "Doree and I welcome you. Now—can you help us to know, a little, the way you want to look?"

Mercy's splendid eyes were blank no longer; they turned to him appealingly.

"I would like to look like a city girl, please," Mercy Tachie said. "That is what I would like the most."

"A city girl—" Mr. Archipelago ran a finger lightly over the chalky powder on her face. "That is why you wear this mask, eh? Ladies never know when they are beautiful—strange. They must be chic—God is not a good enough craftsman. Fortunate, I suppose, for us. Ah well. Yes, we will make you look like a city girl, if that is what you would like the most."

Confused by his sigh and smile, Mercy felt compelled to explain herself.

"I was going for seven years to the mission school here, you see, and all my life I am never knowing any place outside this town. But someday, maybe, I will be living in some big place, and if so, I would not want to feel like a bushgirl. So I wish to know how it is proper to have my hair, and what to do for the face. You do not think I am foolish?"

Mr. Archipelago shook his bead,

"I think the whole world is foolish," he said. "But you are no more foolish than anyone else, and a great deal less so than many."

Doree, who felt his reply to be unsatisfactory, placed her splay-hands on the girl's dark wiry hair.

"Not to worry," she said. "We'll straighten your hair just enough to set it and style it. We'll take that goop off your face. You got lovely skin—not a wrinkle—you shouldn't cover it up like that. We'll give you a complete make-up job. Doll, you'll be a queen."

And Mercy Tachie, her eyes trusting, smiled.

"Do you think so? Do you really think it will be so?"

The air was redolent once more with the potions and unguents, the lotions and shampoos and lacquers, the nostril-pinching pungency of ammonia

and the fragrance of bottled colognes. The snik-snik-snik of Mr. Archipelago's scissors was the theme of a small-scale symphony; overtones and un-
dertones were provided by the throb of the dryer and the strident
blues-chanting of Doree as she paced the room like a priestess. Mercy began
to relax.

"My friends, they also would like to come here, I think, if they like the
way I will look," she confided. "Mr. Archipelago, you will be staying here?
You will not be leaving now?"

"Perhaps we will be staying," he said. "We must wait and see if your
friends like the way you look."

Mercy pursed her lips pensively.

"Will you not go back, someday," she ventured, "to your own country?
For the sake of your family?"

Doree glared, but Mr. Archipelago was bland. He had never minded the
curiosity of his lady customers.

"The charming questions," he said. "They begin again. Good. No—I
have no family."

"Oh, I thought it must be so!" Mercy cried.

"I beg your pardon?"

Once more she became self-conscious. She folded her hands and looked
at the floor.

"I have heard," she said apologetically, "that you were leaving your own
country many years ago because you had some bad trouble—maybe because
you thought you might go to prison. But I am never believing that story, truly.
Always I think you had some different kind of trouble. My aunt Abenaa, you
know, she lost all her family—husband and three children—when their house
burned down, and after that she left her village and came to live here, in my
father's house, and never again will she go to that village."

"You think it was that way, for me?" he said.

"I think it—yes."

Mr. Archipelago straightened his waistcoat over his belly. In his eyes
there appeared momentarily a certain sadness, a certain regret. But when he
replied, his voice expressed nothing except a faint acceptable tenderness.

"You are kind. Perhaps the kindest of all my ladies."

At last the ritual was accomplished, and Mercy Tachie looked at herself
in the cracked and yellowing wall-mirror. Slowly, she turned this way and
that, absorbing only gradually the details—the soft-curled hair whorled skill-
fully down onto her forehead, the face with its crimson lipstick and its brown
make-up that matched her own skin. Then she smiled.

"O—" she breathed. "It is just like the pictures I have seen in *Drum* magazine—the girls, African girls, who know how everything is done in the new
way. Oh, now I will know, too!"

"Do you think your friends will overcome their shyness now?" Mr. Archipelago asked.

"I will make sure of it," Mercy promised. "You will see."

They sat quietly in the shop after Mercy had left. They felt spent and drained, but filled and renewed as well. Doree stretched her long legs and closed her eyes. Mr. Archipelago bulged in his carved rocking-chair, and cradled to and fro peacefully, his shoes off and his waistcoat unbuttoned.

The crash of noise and voices from outside startled them. They ran to the open door. Spilling down the street was an impromptu procession. Every girl in town appeared to be there, hips and shoulders swaying, unshod feet stepping lightly, hands clapping, cloths of blue and magenta and yellow fluttering around them like the flags of nations while they danced. A few of the older women were there, too, buxom and lively, their excited laughter blaring like a melody of raucous horns. At the front of the parade walked Mercy Tachie in new red high-heel shoes, her head held high to display her proud new hair, her new face slight with pleasure and infinite hope. Beside Mercy, as her guard and her champions, there pranced and jittered half a dozen young men, in khaki trousers and brilliantly flower-printed shirts. One held her hand—he was her own young man. Another had a guitar, and another a gourd rattle. They sang at full strength, putting new words to the popular highlife "Everybody Likes Saturday Night."

> *"Everybody like Mercy Tachie,*
> *Everybody like Mercy Tachie,*
> *Everybody everybody*
> *Everybody everybody*
> *Everybody say she fine pas' all—"*

Mr. Archipelago turned to Doree. Gravely, they shook hands.

"By an act of Mercy," Mr. Archipelago said, "we are saved."

They walked along the shore in the moist and cooling late afternoon. The palm boughs rustled soothingly. The sound reminded Mr. Archipelago of taffeta, the gowns of the whispering ladies, twirling forever in a delicate minuet of dust, the ladies watched over by pale and costly marble angels, the dove-gray and undemanding ladies of his insomnia, eternally solacing, eternally ladies.

He watched Doree. She had discovered a blue crab, clownishly walking sideways, a great round crab with red and comic protruding eyes, and she stooped to examine it more carefully, to enjoy its grotesque loveliness. But it did not know that it need not be afraid, so it ran away.

"Archipelago," Doree said, "now that it's over, and we're here to stay, I guess I oughta tell you."

"No," he said. "There is nothing you need tell me."

"Yes," she insisted. "You know when you asked me if I could go back, and I said I couldn't? Well, I guess I didn't give you the straight goods, in a way—"

"I know," Mr. Archipelago said quietly. "There was no troubled past. I have always known that."

"Have you?" she said, mild-eyed, not really surprised. "How did you know?"

He glanced at her face, at the heavy make-up that covered the aging features, ravaged and virginal.

"Because," he replied slowly, "for me it was the same. I, too, had no past. The white ladies and now the brown ladies—they have never guessed. I did not intend that they should. It is not their concern. But we know, Doree, why we are here and why we stay."

"Yes," she said, "I guess we do know. I guess we both know that. So we don't need to talk about it any more, do we?"

"No," he promised. "No more."

"And whatever happens," she went on, "even if we go broke, you won't get any more fancy ideas about me finding a better job somewhere else?"

"The new sign—" he reminded her. "Have you forgotten what it says?"

"That's right," she said. "'Archipelago & Doree.' Yeh, that's right."

Mr. Archipelago sniffed the brine-laden wind.

"Smell the sea, Doree? A perfume for our collection."

She smiled. "What shall we call it?"

"Oh, nothing too ornate," he said lightly. "Perhaps *eau d'exile* would do."

The sea spray was bitter and salty, but to them it was warm, too. They watched on the sand their exaggerated shadows, one squat and bulbous, the other bone-slight and clumsily elongated, pigeon and crane. The shadows walked with hands entwined like children who walk through the dark.

# Thea Astley

One of Australia's most widely recognized writers, Thea Astley sets her fiction most often in the tropical state of Queensland, where she was born 25 August 1925. She graduated from the University of Queensland in Brisbane, and taught for several years in country schools; these experiences provide the basis for her early novels. In 1948 she married Jack Gregson, a musician, and moved to Sydney. There she taught in public schools until 1967 when she started lecturing on Australian literature at Macquarie University in Sydney. Now retired, she and her husband live near Sydney, and she continues to write, having published her first novel in 1958 and her most recent one in 1996. Astley has received numerous awards for her fourteen novels and two collections of short stories, including the Patrick White Prize in 1989.

Australian readers often consider Astley's fiction as social satire and sometimes object to its acerbic depiction of Australia. From her first novel, *Girl with a Monkey*, to her last one, *The Multiple Effects of Rainshadow*, she has castigated white Australians on matters ranging from their historical treatment of Aboriginals in *A Kindness Cup* (1974) to their inability to appreciate art and the artist in *The Acolyte* (1972). Small town intolerance receives its lumps in novels such as *A Descant for Gossips* (1960) and *An Item from the Late News* (1982). In the two novellas that comprise *Vanishing Points* (1992), Astley targets Australian obsession with development, tourism, and real estate. *A Boat Load of Home Folk* (1968) and *Beachmasters* (1985) take place on South Pacific islands but focus in large part on the questionable behavior of Australians or Europeans.

Although colonial misdeeds and postcolonial provincialism figure prominently in the work, it embodies far more substantial themes. The characters invariably combat what Astley calls "the thundering emptiness of the void" as they seek a spiritual "center," a word that appears again and again in the novels. But this elusive "center" is never reached, and the novels emerge finally as parables of discontent, with Australia or the islands—the people and the land—acting as a sustained metaphor for an unfulfilled spiritual quest. Astley once said that the process of writing fiction started with a metaphor, then enlarged to extend that metaphor. An original writer with a quirky stylistic streak, Astley handles time with great deftness within the narrative, shows remarkable economy in plot structure, invents new ways of using language, exercises a sardonic wit, and carnivalizes Christian ritual. She also captures the tropical landscape and atmosphere flawlessly.

"Chloe of the Dancing Bears" is a chapter from *Beachmasters*, which gives a fictional account of an actual but short-lived revolution on a South Pacific island in the late 1970s when the natives rebelled against British and French rule. Sparingly yet fully covering the details of this gentle uprising in less than two hundred pages, the novel obliquely condemns imperialism and exposes the political bewilderment of the native islanders. At the same time, the narrative expands to reveal the lives, past and present, of assorted Europeans and Australians. These colonial leftovers find themselves on an island that is belatedly entering the postcolonial era, and some have no place else to go. Like Chloe, they have allowed "the island to devour them."

# Chloe of the Dancing Bears
from *Beachmasters*

Chloe of the Dancing Bears was conscious, oh too aware, that her face was disappearing.

Not, she knew, like some of the colonial faces that had the appearance of crumpled brown paper smoothed out hastily for reuse.

No. It was as if, my God, the features, made of some lardy substance, were melting away, a little bit more each time she looked in a mirror, something she rarely did these days on the wrong side of fifty. Eyes, nose, eyebrows, mouth, chin—all, all were changing, the contours altering by agonizing millimeters. There was no bone, no patrician bone, to sustain that fleeting—well, not prettiness but great flower-opened-eye who-me? innocence of the flingabout years when sheer blurred roundness of cheek-curve flowed pleasantly to small chin, slim neck. Now, the curves flattened out, there was a limpness, a sparseness of structure. The hollowing cheeks were only that; the small chin a token thrust at the bottom of a face whose eyes once bluely challenging, clenched too often against sun and island gossip, were becoming vestigial.

Every time the camera trapped her, Augustine Guichet behind the click-button of her Instamatic, she could see, strongly emergent, that slightly idiotic cross-eyed look she had had in her early teens, a look that later muted to a melting blue astigmatic vagueness that wasn't cross-eyed at all, that gave off that impression of vulnerability.

This town.

Well . . . this *town*!

The Dancing Bears was finished.

And so was she. No longer counting in years but decades. Four of those decades since she had sway-bummed down the Boulevard d'Urville, all her clothes rammed into a buckled carry-bag ready to leave, to follow mother and father and two brothers out of town in the first windy scare after Pearl Harbor. Father's plantation at Thresher Bay, so he insisted, like those of all the other east coast planters, would be the first place taken over once the Japanese troops landed, once their wasps of planes had strafed their houses tucked into palm nests like rich egg clusters.

Everyone was getting out—on mission launches, copra boats, government motor-vessels—whatever could be boarded was taken and the boats streamed out down the Channel heading for Port Lena and the evacuation ships leaving for Australia.

Mother kept telling her they weren't running away.

"British don't run, darling," she said.

The night before they left, Chloe had kept leafing sentimentally through the big family photo album they had decided to leave behind as a talisman, leafing despite the early moths worrying the grain of twilight to thud against the lamp and rain wing-dust on snapshots of picnicking planters, the real thing in pith helmets and whites, mustaches bristling over hampers; on graying prints of her waving from the deck of the *Tulagi* as it carried her off to a mainland school; on solemn house-girls in Mother Hubbards, that dreadful ruching and ribbons fluttering from sleeves against the shiny black flesh, making them look . . . well, yes . . . *blacker*. All under the blinking eye of the lamp. "It is," her father added, drawing the blackout canvas, "what is known as a tactical retreat. In any case, the government has advised this. Civilians will only be in the way if the worst happens. We help the forces best by leaving the field clear."

Her two brothers leaned goggle-eyed against her as she turned the pages although they had seen these crummy photos a dozen times, and placed various pointing sticky fingers on smeared snapshots of Chloe in first communion dress standing stiffly outside the mission church at Ebuli along with six cocoa-brown communicants in white voile and veils—and again, blacker, blacker—supplied by the nuns.

There was giggling and kicking and the squashing of moths.

Father cuffed the older boy into a howl.

"Is father going to enlist when we get back?" Chloe asked. "Monsieur Duchard, the young one, is joining the Islands' Defense Unit."

No one replied. Father must be getting terribly old, she had decided then, to be blocked by her innocent question, though now, confronted by the gasping flesh, she realized he would have been only in his middle years.

They were stuck in Port Lena for a week in an old pub on the waterfront with nothing much to do except stare out at the islands floating in the blue and green streaked harbor and watch the residency motor-boat beetling its way each day across to the wharves. Father did a lot of drinking on the hotel terrace over the water which didn't quite reach his whisky while mother spent irritable time fussing after the boys who would keep wandering their boredom along the scrubby waterfront. There would not be a boat, a residency official assured them and three other trapped planter families, for yet another week. After this one. The eyes of the Administrative Officer, Class B, roamed interestedly over Chloe.

She kept her own eyes down.

Then, during the next few days, a fleet of American ships appeared in Meso Bay, a battle formation of aircraft carriers and cruisers and destroyers and the gadflies of landing craft. The dreamy circle of blue water was threatened and crowds of natives clustering along the sand-strip gawked, stunned, as barges grated onto shingle. It was a western takeover and within days artillery units moved to strategic points around Port Lena, batteries were established, sentry posts sprang up at town crossroads, court house and waterfront shacks were appropriated and huge teams of marines commenced building an air-strip. Planters, drinking on the terrace of the Hotel Kokonas, made grumbling noises about their crops. The departure of the evacuees was delayed another two weeks.

No one inquired how the islanders felt about all this. It was assumed they didn't.

After this, Chloe's parents found it difficult to keep track of their daughter.

There were jeep rides to lagoons, drinks at the Bar des Pêcheurs and some long hand-claspings with several smooth-faced boys from upstate New York, Maine and Connecticut. The flotilla bearing fleeing Europeans from the northern islands had trickled its last ship in days ago and the hotel was a muddle of make-shift beds on side verandahs, in dining alcoves and even the office.

Two nights before the *Tulagi* was due to take them off Chloe yielded languidly to the ardent demands of a particularly pink naval lieutenant. By the time dawn had blazed over the world-rim and the lieutenant had sneaked back to his base, Chloe, rumpled and abraded by beach sand, had made a decision.

She announced it to her parents at breakfast between the crumbling French rolls and the coffee.

"I will not be going with you."

It was such a simple statement she could not have imagined the inverse complexity of their anger. This was moderated in the presence of interested hotel guests who had been dying of boredom. Later, in her parents' room lashed by ravings about her age (she was not yet sixteen), her family obligations and in any case the sheer impossibility of bucking colonial administration, she sat creamily content, deaf with discovery. Her parents were forced to abuse her in whispers.

"I am staying," she insisted once more on the last morning among the bloated suitcases and cabin trunks. She seemed to have grown overnight. Her mango blonde hair electrified them. "I have a job to go to. A job here. The Americans need office staff. If you're worried about me," she added, "about *that*,"—her mother winced—"then the nurses will arrange something."

Other planters, bemused by her clear and carrying voice, were eyeing the family across the crowded dining-room.

Her father was choking in the middle of "it is absolutely forbid—" when Chloe solved the problem by rising gracefully and leaving the dining-room, the hotel and lugging her suitcase to the home of a French family in Lena, people who had always disliked him and were staying on. Flummoxed by the shrillings of the *Tulagi*, their squabbling sons and the absorbed attention of fellow evacuees, her parents found there was not time to enlist residency aid. It was then or never. They departed leaving disciplinary threats and the garbled promises of action from the hotelier.

Soon, it was too late for anything to be done.

The war accelerated. The pink lieutenant from upstate New York was killed in Guadalcanal.

Not really marooned, Chloe refused the advice of the Administrative Officer, Class B whom she allowed to become, for practical reasons a quick substitute for the American. Declining a wangled passage on a transport plane to the mainland she managed, instead, to island-hop by U.S. military aircraft onto which she was smuggled by a friend of the lieutenant.

Mataso was a changed town of canvas tents and row upon row of Quonset huts, cinemas, demountable hospitals, a huge PX store, a sophisticated telephone network and radio station, torpedo and patrol boat maintenance shops, air-strips, hangars, offices, tennis courts, sportsgrounds—and where there had been no roads, roads; and where there had been no bridges, bridges. The building binge stretched from the western end of the Channel in a dense fringe of New World chewing-gum know-how almost as far up the east coast as Thresher Bay.

But more. Oh much, Chloe, more!

It was temporary home and base for one hundred thousand servicemen who passed through on their way to the blood-run islands of the north.

Chloe returned briefly to the plantation to defy the exhausted ghosts of her parents and rouse its green honeycomb with a party that drained the last of father's abandoned liquor. The photograph album was lying where she had left it on that last night. Geckoes had fouled the open pages, but she shook the detritus carefully off and in a moment of irrational sentiment took the album back with her to Mataso town.

Chloe's sea-change took a year.

She had persuaded someone anyone, to allow her to work in an army canteen.

If the officers who used her and then rejected her or who loved her and were killed or even simply moved to another area of war, leaned the weight of their passion too heavily on her smooth blunt features, she did not show it. Her stoicism was remarkable. And then her cynicism. Believing it a folly to mingle pleasure with business, she left the canteen and bought a small house on the seaward ledge of the Boulevard d'Urville just opposite the abandoned branch of La Banque de L'Indochine, and with smuggled food gifts from admirers in the big army based opened a small café on the dawn-side of Mataso town.

It soon became more than that.

As naturally as breathing.

Two Eurasian girls helped out both in the restaurant section and the poky bedrooms that looked over the water. The business became more than they could cope with. Chloe was aware of grossness. She had to draw rank distinctions and the little house became an officers-only club which Chloe (feeling the tug of the chain) in a moment of inspired metaphor, named the Dancing Bears.

Every day, every steaming heavy-aired day or night through the next two years she could watch the ships in the Channel or the bomber squadrons that took off from strips in the hills removing her ten-minute lovers, and feel like any classic whore touting for trade. She was always a realist. She was even entertaining an army colonel when his satisfaction coincided with the hitting of a mine by a transport ship coming down Channel to the town wharves. Everything was interrupted.

Perhaps that was the moment her lack of bone commenced failing her.

She was eighteen. She was eight hundred.

She had not done it for money, she kept telling herself.

She had done it for food, for rent, for good times, for clothes, for the memory of mother and father whose pale British ambience had always depleted her.

Almost as suddenly as they had come, the troops pulled out, the hundreds of conscript islanders who had laundered uniforms, cleared bush camp sites, worked with coast-watchers and loosely organized patrol forces, watched their cargo gods vanish. The bone had gone out of the whole war operation too.

Chloe was left with a customerless bordello—well, almost bordello, almost customerless. There were the planters drifting back, the hugger-mugger army of visiting post-war experts: cartographers and botanists, anthropologists and ecologists, forestry advisers, geographers, photographers (one did not count Augustine Guichet, then young and between husbands, pounding masculine and feminine genders and the causes of the French Revolution into unwilling skulls at St. Pierre), geologists, historians, linguists, health inspectors, education experts, housing consultants and colonial politicians. Some of them visited the Dancing Bears—there was little else to visit—and after they had achieved their abrupt and temporary pleasures, Chloe cooked for them, something she did even better. Her whole enterprise teetered between respectability and bawdy. On a holiday in Sydney she married a chef whom she took back to Mataso where he cooked, drank, shouted, bounced the last would-be carnal visitors, showed her three splendid ways of cooking reef fish and left.

After the town died when the flush of post-war enthusiasm for those strategically needed but nuisance outposts of empire faded, and after the decades melted, turning to water in summer after summer, she was simply Chloe Dancing Bears whom all Mataso town knew, whom some of the planters spoke to—usually the French who had a tolerance of what they called the genial sins—and who was cut dead by British wives fed on the long tentacles of legend. Before the final collapse of the flesh there was a second husband, a trawler operator until a Taiwanese boat rammed him off Emba. And there was a lover or two.

Could you call them that?

Chloe scratched a living from a little this, a little that, the café, an occasional land deal, the whoring gone now, *long wé, long wé*, abandoned entirely as a present to herself the year she turned thirty—not that there was much to abandon and not that it was whoring really, just a sad flutter with lonely men who stopped at the Mataso Hotel while they filled in their temporary duty service and their reports in triplicate. A kindness you could call it. And there was a pension of sorts some guilty aging American had arranged coming regular as clockwork, until a year back, was it? Two?

The mind was falling off the bone, as well.

She could suck at memory and it skidded like mango seed.

Augustine Guichet handled time with more aplomb.

"They do not understand, these newcomers," she would say to Chloe sipping coffee on the little Channel verandah of the Dancing Bears, "that they must allow the island to devour them. They try to eat it. That is their mistake."

The two women knew they would never leave.

"I am almost fully digested," Madame Guichet would say. "I await the total absorption."

So when on that heat-sullen morning of distant and fogged explosion, of rifle fire and shouts and later the surge of rebels and sympathizer *colons* along the Boulevard, she heard a frantic beating on the seaward door, her heart paused momentarily with dreadful enquiry.

Was this to be the moment of supreme subsumption?

All her shutters were drawn. She had sat within the sea-light of her shell of a house, warned only yesterday by the most diffident of ni-Kristi—the soft knock on the door, the smiling black face, Pardon, *madame*, tomorrow we make protest march. Tomorrow there will be revolution. You should stay inside inside—aligning that moment with the endurance of an hour past when, between the yells and the random crack of rifles, her walls had shrunk from bashings and a din of obscenities: *wanem ples blong puspus? Oué! Wanem ples blong puspus?*

Not here, she thought. No place now for a fuck. Only a joke, she consoled herself. Oh the winding lengths of oral tradition! The thought stopped her fright even as the voices moved away leaving her to be only Chloe Dancing Bears, a dusty poke-hole for drip-dry trippers off the tour ships, brought to her little café by shreds of rumor, color hunters sadder than herself.

But now this knocking. Its persistence fluttered. A voice filled in the diffidence of the beat.

"Anyone there? Please? Please? Is anyone there?"

Chloe drew back the bolt and opened the door to peer through the screen at Letty Trumble still clutching portions of shopping bag, her hat clownish over a dust-striped face. One of her knees bled quietly through a dangling hem. There was an apologetic blink and her mouthing seemed to transmit words too early or too late for the muscles, like a bad dubbing.

Chloe found herself encompassed with memories.

Here was a mendicant who had waged border war on the Dancing Bears with velvet innuendo, snub, parochial blacklisting. How long since the Bears danced? Twenty years? Oh certainly that. Certainly long before Letty Trumble had set neat sandaled foot on Kristi. Was it merely the folklore analects of those lasciviously slow threshings while the sea rocked at the end of her garden that so agitated Dr. Trumble's wife? That buckled the Dali shopping-bag? That befouled the dress and skewed the hat?

Chloe was arrested on this crest of payback for a decade of tacit insult. As if bone were once more asserting itself, she felt her face harden. Yet—accept, accept, she could hear Augustine Guichet advise, filled with tiddly wisdom. Submission is easier. The triumph is in that.

As the other woman's wretchedness seeped about her, as the insignificance of her enmity became the flaw in Chloe herself, she opened the door wide. She could take the movement no further. Chloe drew in her breath hard and then slowly let it out into the gasp of the morning.

"Quickly," she urged, stepping back into her exhausted kitchen, conscious of the bedrooms, the pleasure domes, opening out their miniscule spaces from the narrow hallway behind. She felt she must resort to platitudes, spread like a volcano crust to soothe Letty Trumble's sobbed explanations with treacherous phrases.

"They're still savages, my dear"—(*my dear!*)—"when it all comes down. My father"—(now who was he?) the words had come automatically—"swore nothing would make any difference, not missions, not schools. And he knew. He knew the islands like his face in the mirror." She didn't believe a word of it.

Her surprise stopped her.

The prim moustached assurance that must have gazed back at him from the shaving glass! His fleshy face and phantom twin both without depth. Not for thirty years had she mentioned him, perhaps even thought of him. For the duty letters she had written early on dear mother and father to somewhere in England had spaced themselves into cards at Christmas and birthdays and finally trickled into silence. On both sides. The plantation had been sold, she heard, and whether the blood-strangers of the mould-spotted album, parents and brothers in their roistering shorts, were alive or dead she did not know, seeing them permanently settled at a cantankerous forty and sub-teens, the sun bouncing off a jelly blue seat onto the verandah of the plantation house, father trapped in mid-shout as he roared at a house-boy, her mother purse-lipped behind a table set with 4 o'clock snorters and translated into an un-blitzed Kensington houselet with her brothers forever in preparatory school.

This day, this sagging boneless day, she could have cried for the loss of all those sun-fired years surging up from her gut.

Locked in, in the little back room, they could only contemplate each other, across deserts.

"Try crying," she suggested to Letty Trumble crumpled in a rattan chair. "I mean with anger."

Letty was too bleared with disaster.

"They attacked me," she kept protesting. "Me. And I've been so kind. And Jim. Always concerned. The groceries. Everywhere. I left them."

Chloe allowed her to ramble. Her own eyes were glued to the trickle of blood that was making a lacy pattern down the front of Letty Trumble's legs.

"There was no where else I could come."

Chloe kept staring at the rosy lace.

"I am truly glad," she couldn't stop herself saying, "to be of some use after all these years."

Letty Trumble remained deaf. "They were screaming at me, screaming, when I came round the back of Bipi. Daniel had lent me his bicycle. Yelling. Screaming filth. There was a stall for emergency supplies and the rest of the place was barred because of the looting down at Fong's. There was glass everywhere, more and more glass, and—"

"But what were they yelling?" Chloe was certain the insult would make them sisters.

The other woman's mouth twisted horribly as if there were an unclean taste. She challenged Chloe's eyes.

"They called me a whore. White whore. Dirty white whore. Give me a drink," she demanded.

Chloe smoothed her satisfaction across her thinning scalp.

She had to turn her laughter away.

"There's only a little brandy. Will that do?"

But Letty was drowning in herself. "They kept yelling that as they dragged on the bike, coming right up into my face and screeching. White whore. On and on. I spat at them. I couldn't help it. I spat. And then they started pushing and shoving and the bicycle was grabbed and banged up and down up and down against the awning posts and I tried to fight them for it. I kept hitting and hitting but they didn't hit back. Just kept laughing at me and I tripped and fell over and then one of the police came up, the rebel police, and he stopped them. Someone stopped them. I don't know. And then he told me to get indoors before he arrested me I was so stupid to be out after all the warnings."

"Here." Chloe set the brandy down in front of Letty Trumble and watched the nervous hands, too white, too veined, shake as they clutched the glass. "They called me that too," she said. "It doesn't matter, you know. It's just a word. It doesn't mean much to them except a—a one-sound explosion of air."

Letty Trumble could not look up at that moment. She gulped the drink in one burning slash at her own throat.

Chloe assessed her resentment at the linkage and savored it. She would not utter defenses, explain that whoring had been over and done with long before, rip down that lewd tapestry that brief twelve years nearly three decades gone had swaddled her in.

"We're all whores," she said, "of a sort. Whatever you like. Living is whoring. Just living. It's taken me years to see that."

Mrs. Trumble, the brandy down, this melting elderly and logical woman before her, still felt as if she were seated on the feather-down edge of some voluptuous bed with the ghosts, the echoes of orgastic cries misting the mirrors, the pink quilts, the silk, the wanton spread-legged dolls lolling on chairs in a bordello of the mind; yet here she was, her feet on cracked linoleum under the grocery caddies labeled *thé, sucre, farine,* an appallingly humble gas-burner stove and a hallway at her back that led to four other rooms whose open doors, she knew, kept nothing to speculate on but dust, sunlight and old furniture.

She looked down at her torn skirt, her torn knees. The blood was staining the straps of her sandals.

Then she cried, gulpingly and long.

Chloe was practical if not warm, her warmth diminished by too many years of lack. She heated water, fetched disinfectant and strapped up the bony knees and hands while tears fell on her head. Inwardly she scoffed at her Magdalene. Between the gulps, she managed to discover more. What had happened to the doctor? The boy? They were hostages, Letty presumed. A jeep had driven them off to Talasa Pati headquarters, Dannie Ching at Bipi told her. He had seen the jeep going past, a hedge of rifles and arrows and the doctor sitting very straight, one arm about his son's shoulders. A quick film clip.

Letty didn't know what to do now. "There is nothing to do," Chloe said, "but wait. It will be all over once they know in Lena. We only have to wait. With each other."

She had to smile at it.

Letty Trumble was a guest at the Dancing Bears.

Confronted by somber reasoning and a woman whose face retained mere flickerings of the prettiness that had been her legend, the meretricious glamour, the nonsense thinking all began to dissipate in the confidence of brandy, the bit of iodine, the firm grip of bandage. What Letty Trumble was beginning to see was another woman like herself, netted in this Pacific backwater and only licked at by memories of tides that now were all at the neap. Or low water. Even that.

She had her own guilty memories. The house, the bedrooms, the woman opposite, all started them like birds: some twilit beach party at Thresher Bay in the dark apses of the buttressed *nabangura* trees, she had once been crushed most willingly against the body of a sodden planter from Port Ebuli and wanted it; or swimming naked, Kendrick guiding her, in a sheltered pool at the Bay of the Two Saints; and then that time in Port Lena when she had gone down to shop—to escape really—for a few days and there had been that busy American biologist with an interest in snails. She didn't think of that time if she could help it, his hot room at the Hotel Kokonas with the fans going and the bed rocking and the clear-eyed look she had to practice for Jim and the winking of a cheap-stoned signet ring the snail man had worn on his little finger that interrupted the clarity of her domestic eye.

Perhaps this woman with the face made ordinary by time, the myth removed as she sat flanked by strip plaster and disinfectant, was right: we are all whores. There is only that fragile differential. And the men as well. Whores. Or worse than that. Her nose was assailed suddenly by the dusty smell of brown flesh and the mouths opening and closing on their tongues, teeth; the shock of the pink.

"Do you mind," she asked, "if I stay?" The word "please" occurred to her. She added it.

Chloe interpreted the hiatus and wanted to bawl out her resentment. Oh the screechings she could vent in this box of drab memories she was trapped in beside the Channel. She could never leave. For where, anyway? It was a struggle to climb over the crest of each year on a scrap income that made her the most permanent of foreigners. She was sustained only by an out-of-place and obstinate dignity and Augustine Guichet's bottle cynicism.

Letty Trumble and Chloe Dancing Bears were looking cautiously into each other's eyes, blue into blue. Outside wind gnawed at a broken shutter and the dry clicks and rappings framed a moment so ordinary that Letty swayed with a surge of lascivious curiosity that rose like confessional bile.

"Tell me," she begged, leaning forward across the table and surprising the other woman. "As we are all whores, tell me."

Chloe knew the surprise dance like fireflies down the dark of her spirit. She gripped the brandy bottle and refilled their glasses.

"If," she insisted with impudent perception, "you tell me."

# Ruth Prawer Jhabvala

Although once considered an Indian writer, Ruth Prawer Jhabvala actually wrote about India as a transplanted European. She was born in Cologne, Germany, on 7 May 1927. Her father, a Jewish lawyer of Polish descent, moved his family to England in 1939; depressed by the deteriorating conditions in Germany, he committed suicide a few years later. Growing up in London, Jhabvala made the transition into a new language, and graduated from the University of London with a degree in English. In 1951 she married a Parsi architect from Delhi, and they moved to India. After twenty-five years in India, Jhabvala took up residence in New York City, where she still lives. Honored widely for her fiction, Jhabvala has received a MacArthur Foundation Fellowship as well as the Booker Prize for *Heat and Dust* in 1975. Writing screenplays for numerous Merchant-Ivory films has complemented her career as a novelist; she has adapted the work of writers such as Henry James, Jean Rhys, and E. M. Forster.

India's Parsi community—into which Jhabvala moved as a young bride—originated in Persia (now Iran) and migrated to India thirteen hundred years ago. Westernized, educated, and most often wealthy, the Parsis remain aloof from ordinary Indian life. While much of Jhabvala's early fiction reflects this isolated community, she gradually broadened her knowledge of Indian culture. Through her husband's architectural firm, she met Punjabi families whose rural background and vigor contrasted dramatically with the more sophisticated Parsis. At the same time, she remained a displaced European refugee adrift in a foreign culture, which, according to Jhabvala, outsiders accept and reject in cycles: embracing the culture with enthusiasm and repudiating it as abominable, then repeating this process endlessly.

These three strands of experience form the basis of much of Jhabvala's early fiction. *To Whom She Will* (1955) and *The Nature of Passion* (1956) both portray Indian family life affectionately—including the arranged marriage, which Jhabvala does not condemn. In contrast, *Esmond in India* (1958) and *A Backward Place* (1965) draw dismal pictures of stranded Europeans in India longing for home. Her best-known novel, *Heat and Dust*, interweaves the story of two expatriates: a lonely English colonial wife in the 1920s and a contemporary visitor to India—a British woman fascinated by the earlier woman's letters, which she attempts to relive. Through this double-layered narrative, Jhabvala not only provides a graphic account of Indian life and its intricacies on varied social levels, but portrays as well alienated Europeans at sea in a complex and impenetrable society to which they will never belong.

In an interview, Jhabvala admitted: "If I must be considered anything, then let it be as one of those European writers who have written about India"—a claim that appears obvious when examining her fiction in retrospect. Beginning with *In Search of Love and Beauty* (1983), Jhabvala moved away from an exclusive representation of the Indian scene. Later novels, such as *Three Continents* (1987) and *Shards of Memory* (1995), employ international settings as well and develop one of Jhabvala's recurring themes: the way unscrupulous gurus from India exploit gullible westerners, who in the course of events reveal their own shortcomings.

That theme figures in "An Experience of India." In this story Jhabvala, as is usually the case, does not outwardly condemn religious charlatans but uses them to reveal the weakness and delusion of the narrator. In the first-person account of her futile search for the mystical "world upon world, all spinning in one great eternal cycle," the narrator finds that India does not answer her personal dilemma. Such an "experience of India" has played out many times both in the colonial and postcolonial era.

# An Experience of India

Today Ramu left. He came to ask for money and I gave him as much as I could. He counted it and asked for more, but I didn't have it to give him. He said some insulting things, which I pretended not to hear. Really I couldn't blame him. I knew he was anxious and afraid, not having another job to go to. But I also couldn't help contrasting the way he spoke now with what he had been like in the past: so polite always, and eager to please, and always smiling, saying "Yes sir," "Yes madam please." He used to look very different too, very spruce in his white uniform and his white canvas shoes. When guests came, he put on a special white coat he had made us buy him. He was always happy when there were guests—serving, mixing drinks, emptying ashtrays— and I think he was disappointed that more didn't come. The Ford Foundation people next door had a round of buffet suppers and Sunday brunches, and perhaps Ramu suffered in status before their servants because we didn't have much of that. Actually, coming to think of it, perhaps he suffered in status anyhow because we weren't like the others. I mean, I wasn't. I didn't look like a proper memsahib or dress like one—I wore Indian clothes right from the start—or ever behave like one. I think perhaps Ramu didn't care for that. I think servants want their employers to be conventional and put up a good front so that other people's servants can respect them. Some of the nasty things Ramu told me this morning were about how everyone said I was just someone from a very low sweeper caste in my own country and how sorry they were for him that he had to serve such a person.

He also said it was no wonder Sahib had run away from me. Henry didn't actually run away, but it's true that things had changed between us. I suppose

India made us see how fundamentally different we were from each other. Though when we first came, we both came we thought with the same ideas. We were both happy that Henry's paper had sent him out to India. We both thought it was a marvelous opportunity not only for him professionally but for both of us spiritually. Here was our escape from that Western materialism with which we were both so terribly fed up. But once he got here and the first enthusiasm had worn off, Henry seemed not to mind going back to just the sort of life we'd run away from. He even didn't seem to care about meeting Indians anymore, though in the beginning he had made a great point of doing so; now it seemed to him all right to go only to parties given by other foreign correspondents and sit around there and eat and drink and talk just the way they would at home. After a while, I couldn't stand going with him anymore, so we'd have a fight and then he'd go off by himself. That was a relief. I didn't want to be with any of those people and talk about inane things in their tastefully appointed air-conditioned apartments.

I had come to India to *be* in India. I wanted to be changed. Henry didn't— he wanted a change, that's all, but not to be changed. After a while because of that he was a stranger to me and I felt I was alone, the way I'm really alone now. Henry had to travel a lot around the country to write his pieces, and in the beginning I used to go with him. But I didn't like the way he traveled, always by plane and staying in expensive hotels and drinking in the bar with the other correspondents. So I would leave him and go off by myself. I traveled the way everyone travels in India, just with a bundle and a roll of bedding that I could spread out anywhere and go to sleep. I went in third-class railway carriages and in those old lumbering buses that go from one small dusty town to another and are loaded with too many people inside and with too much scruffy baggage on top. At the end of my journeys, I emerged soaked in perspiration, soot, and dirt. I ate anything anywhere and always like everyone else with my fingers (I became good at that)—thick, half-raw chapatis from wayside stalls and little messes of lentils and vegetables served on a leaf, all the food the poor eat; sometimes if I didn't have anything, other people would share with me from out of their bundles. Henry, who had the usual phobia about bugs, said I would kill myself eating that way. But nothing ever happened. Once, in a desert fort in Rajasthan, I got very thirsty and asked the old caretaker to pull some water out of an ancient disused well for me. It was brown and sort of foul-smelling, and maybe there was a corpse in the well, who knows. But I was thirsty so I drank it, and still nothing happened.

People always speak to you in India, in buses and trains and on the streets, they want to know all about you and ask you a lot of personal questions. I didn't speak much Hindi, but somehow we always managed, and I didn't mind answering all those questions when I could. Women quite often used to touch me, run their hands over my skin just to feel what it was like I suppose, and they specially liked to touch my hair which is long and blond.

Sometimes I had several of them lifting up strands of it at the same time, one pulling this way and another that way and they would exchange excited comments and laugh and scream a lot; but in a nice way, so I couldn't help but laugh and scream with them. And people in India are so hospitable. They're always saying "Please come and stay in my house," perfect strangers that happen to be sitting near you on the train. Sometimes, if I didn't have any plans or if it sounded as if they might be living in an interesting place, I'd say "All right thanks," and I'd go along with them. I had some interesting adventures that way.

I might as well say straight off that many of these adventures were sexual. Indian men are very, very keen to sleep with foreign girls. Of course men in other countries are also keen to sleep with girls, but there's something specially frenzied about Indian men when they approach you. Frenzied and at the same time shy. You'd think that with all those ancient traditions they have— like the Kama Sutra, and the sculptures showing couples in every kind of position—you'd think that with all that behind them they'd be very highly skilled, but they're not. Just the opposite. Middle-aged men get as excited as a fifteen-year-old boy, and then of course they can't wait, they *jump*, and before you know where you are, in a great rush, it's all over. And when it's over, it's over, there's nothing left. Then they're only concerned with getting away as soon as possible before anyone can find them out (they're always scared of being found out). There's no tenderness, no interest at all in the other person as a person; only the same kind of curiosity that there is on the buses and the same sort of questions are asked, like are you married, any children, why no children, do you like wearing our Indian dress . . . There's one question though that's not asked on the buses but that always inevitably comes up during sex, so that you learn to wait for it: always, at the moment of mounting excitement, they ask "How many men have you slept with?" and it's repeated over and over: "How many? How many?" and then they shout "Aren't you ashamed?" and "Bitch!"—always that one word, which seems to excite them more than any other, to call you that is the height of their lovemaking, it's the last frenzy, the final outrage: "Bitch!" Sometimes I couldn't stop myself but had to burst out laughing.

I didn't like sleeping with all these people, but I felt I had to. I felt I was doing good, though I don't know why, I couldn't explain it to myself. Only one of all those men ever spoke to me: I mean the way people having sex together are supposed to speak, coming near each other not only physically but also wanting to show each other what's deep inside them. He was a middle-aged man, a fellow passenger on a bus, and we got talking at one of the stops the bus made at a wayside tea stall. When he found I was on my way to X and didn't have anywhere to stay, he said, as so many have said before him, "Please come and stay in my house." And I said, as I had often said before, "All right." Only when we got there he didn't take me to his house but to a hotel. It was a very poky place in the bazaar and we had to grope our way up a steep smelly stone staircase and then there was a tiny room with just one string cot and an earthenware water jug in it. He made a joke about there being only one bed. I was too tired to care much about anything. I only wanted to get it over with quickly and go to sleep. But afterward I found it wasn't possible to go to sleep because there was a lot of noise coming up from the street where all the shops were still open though it was nearly midnight. People seemed to be having a good time and there was even a phonograph playing some cracked old love song. My companion also couldn't get to sleep: he left the bed and sat down on the floor by the window and smoked one cigarette after the other. His face was lit up by the light coming in from the street outside and I saw he was looking sort of thoughtful and sad, sitting there smoking. He had rather a good face, strong bones but quite a feminine mouth and of course those feminine suffering eyes that most Indians have.

I went and sat next to him. The window was an arch reaching down to the floor so that I could see out into the bazaar. It was quite gay down there with all the lights; the phonograph was playing from the cold-drink shop and a lot of people were standing around there having highly colored pop drinks out of bottles; next to it was a shop with pink and blue brassieres strung up on a pole. On top of the shops were wrought-iron balconies on which sat girls dressed up in tatty georgette and waving peacock fans to keep themselves cool. Sometimes men looked up to talk and laugh with them and they talked and laughed back. I realized we were in the brothel area; probably the hotel we were in was a brothel too.

I asked "Why did you bring me here?"

He answered "Why did you come?"

That was a-good question. He was right. But I wasn't sorry I came. Why should I be? I said "It's all right. I like it."

He said "She likes it," and he laughed. A bit later he started talking: about how he had just been to visit his daughter who had been married a few months before. She wasn't happy in her in-laws' house, and when he said good-bye to her she clung to him and begged him to take her home. The more he reasoned with her, the more she cried, the more she clung to him. In the end he had had to use force to free himself from her so that he could get away and not miss his bus. He felt very sorry for her, but what else was there for him to do. If he took her away, her in-laws might refuse to have her back again and then her life would be ruined. And she would get used to it, they always did; for some it took longer and was harder, but they all got used to it in the end. His wife too had cried a lot during the first year of marriage.

I asked him whether he thought it was good to arrange marriages that way, and he looked at me and asked how else would you do it. I said something about love and it made him laugh and he said that was only for the films. I didn't want to defend my point of view; in fact, I felt rather childish and as if he knew a lot more about things than I did. He began to get amorous again, and this time it was much better because he wasn't so frenzied and I liked him better by now too. Afterward he told me how when he was first married, he and his wife had shared a room with the whole family (parents and younger brothers and sisters), and whatever they wanted to do, they had to do very quickly and quietly for fear of anyone waking up. I had a strange sensation then, as if I wanted to strip off all my clothes and parade up and down the room naked. I thought of all the men's eyes that follow one in the street, and for the first time it struck me that the expression in them was like that in the eyes of prisoners looking through their bars at the world outside; and then I thought maybe I'm that world outside for them—the way I go here and there and talk and laugh with everyone and do what I like—maybe I'm the river and trees they can't have where they are. Oh, I felt so sorry, I wanted to do so much. And to make a start, I flung myself on my companion and kissed and hugged him hard, I lay on top of him, I smothered him, I spread my hair over his face because I wanted to make him forget everything that wasn't—this room, his daughter, his wife, the women in georgette sitting on the balconies—I wanted everything to be new for him and as beautiful as I could make it. He liked it for a while but got tired quite quickly, probably because he wasn't all that young anymore.

It was shortly after this encounter that I met Ahmed. He was eighteen years old and a musician. His family had been musicians as long as anyone could remember and the alley they lived in was full of other musicians, so that when you walked down it, it was like walking through a magic forest all lit up with music and sounds. Only there wasn't anything magic about the place itself, which was very cramped and dirty; the houses were so old that, whenever there were heavy rains, one or two of them came tumbling down. I was never inside Ahmed's house or met his family—they'd have died of shock if they had got to know about me—but I knew they were very poor and scraped a living by playing at weddings and functions. Ahmed never had any money, just sometimes if he was lucky he had a few coins to buy his betel with. But he was cheerful and happy and enjoyed everything that came his way. He was married, but his wife was too young to stay with him and after the ceremony she had been sent back to live with her father who was a musician in another town.

When I first met Ahmed, I was staying in a hostel attached to a temple that was free of charge for pilgrims; but afterward he and I wanted a place for us to go to, so I wired Henry to send me some more money. Henry sent me the money, together with a long complaining letter that I didn't read all the way through, and I took a room in a hotel. It was on the outskirts of town, which was mostly wasteland except for a few houses and some of these had never been finished. Our hotel wasn't finished either because the proprietor had run out of money, and now it probably never would be for the place had turned out to be a poor proposition; it was too far out of town and no one ever came to stay there. But it suited us fine. We had this one room, painted bright pink and quite bare except for two pieces of furniture—a bed and a dressing table, both of them very shiny and new. Ahmed loved it, he had never stayed in such a grand room before; he bounced up and down on the bed, which had a mattress, and stood looking at himself from all sides in the mirror of the dressing table.

I never in all my life was happy with anyone the way I was with Ahmed. I'm not saying I never had a good time at home; I did. I had a lot of friends before I married Henry and we had parties and danced and drank and I enjoyed it. But it wasn't like with Ahmed because no one was ever as *carefree* as he was, as light and easy and just ready to play and live. At home we always had our problems, personal ones of course, but on top of those there were universal problems—social, and economic, and moral, we really cared about what was happening in the world around us and in our own minds, we felt a responsibility toward being here alive at this point in time and wanted to do our best. Ahmed had no thoughts like that at all; there wasn't a shadow on him. He had his personal problems from time to time, and when he had them, he was very downcast and sometimes he even cried. But they weren't anything really very serious—usually some family quarrel, or his father was angry with him—and they passed away, blew away like a breeze over a lake and left him sunny and sparkling again. He enjoyed everything so much: not only our room, and the bed and the dressing table, and making love, but so many other things like drinking Coca-Cola and spraying scent and combing my hair and my combing his; and he made up games for us to play like indoor cricket with a slipper for a bat and one of Henry's letters rolled up for a ball. He taught me how to crack his toes, which is such a great Indian delicacy, and yelled with pleasure when I got it right; but when he did it to me, I yelled with pain so he stopped at once and was terribly sorry. He was very considerate and tender. No one I've ever known was sensitive to my feelings as he was. It was like an instinct with him, as if he could feel right down into my heart and know what was going on there; and without ever having to ask anything or my ever having to explain anything, he could sense each change of mood and adapt himself to it and feel with it. Henry would always have to ask me "Now what's up? What's the matter with you?" and when we were still all right with each other, he would make a sincere effort to understand. But Ahmed never had to make an effort, and maybe if he'd had to he wouldn't have succeeded because it wasn't ever with his mind that he understood anything, it was always with his feelings. Perhaps that was so because he was a musician and in music everything is beyond words and explanations anyway; and from what he told me about Indian music, I could see it was very, very subtle, there are effects that you can hardly perceive they're so subtle and your sensibilities have to be kept tuned all the time to the finest, finest point; and perhaps because of that the whole of Ahmed was always at that point and he could play me and listen to me as if I were his sarod.

After some time we ran out of money and Henry wouldn't send any more, so we had to think what to do. I certainly couldn't bear to part with Ahmed, and in the end I suggested he'd better come back to Delhi with me and we'd try and straighten things out with Henry. Ahmed was terribly excited by the idea; he'd never been to Delhi and was wild to go. Only it meant he had to run away from home because his family would never have allowed him to go, so one night he stole out of the house with his sarod and his little bundle of clothes and met me at the railway station. We reached Delhi the next night, tired and dirty and covered with soot the way you always get in trains here. When we arrived home, Henry was giving a party, not a big party, just a small informal group sitting around chatting. I'll never forget the expression on everyone's faces when Ahmed and I came staggering in with our bundles and bedding. My blouse had got torn in the train all the way down the side, and I didn't have a safety pin so it kept flapping open and unfortunately I didn't have anything underneath. Henry's guests were all looking very nice, the men in smart bush shirts and their wives in little silk cocktail dresses; and although after the first shock they all behaved very well and carried on as if nothing unusual had happened, still it was an awkward situation for everyone concerned.

Ahmed never really got over it. I can see now how awful it must have been for him, coming into that room full of strange white people and all of them turning around to stare at us. And the room itself must have been a shock to him; he can never have seen anything like it. Actually, it was quite a shock to me too. I'd forgotten that that was the way Henry and I lived. When we first came, we had gone to a lot of trouble doing up the apartment, buying furniture and pictures and stuff, and had succeeded in making it look just like the apartment we have at home except for some elegant Indian touches. To Ahmed it was all very strange. He stayed there with us for some time, and he couldn't get used to it. I think it bothered him to have so many *things* around, rugs and lamps and objets d'art; he couldn't see why they had to be there. Now that I had traveled and lived the way I had, I couldn't see why either; as a matter of fact I felt as if these things were a hindrance and cluttered up not only your room but your mind and your soul as well, hanging on them like weights.

We had some quite bad scenes in the apartment during those days. I told Henry that I was in love with Ahmed, and naturally that upset him, though what upset him most was the fact that he had to keep us both in the apartment. I also realized that this was an undesirable situation, But I couldn't see any way out of it because where else could Ahmed and I go? We didn't have any money, only Henry had, so we had to stay with him. He kept saying that he would turn both of us out into the streets but I knew he wouldn't. He wasn't the type to do a violent thing like that, and besides he himself was so frightened of the streets that he'd have died to think of anyone connected with him being out there. I wouldn't have minded all that much if he *had* turned us out: it was warm enough to sleep in the open and people always give you food if you don't have any. I would have preferred it really because it was so unpleasant with Henry; but I knew Ahmed would never have been able to stand it. He was quite a pampered boy, and though his family were poor, they looked after and protected each other very carefully; he never had to miss a meal or go dressed in anything but fine muslin clothes, nicely washed and starched by female relatives.

Ahmed bitterly repented having come. He was very miserable, feeling so uncomfortable in the apartment and with Henry making rows all the time. Ramu, the servant, didn't improve anything by the way he behaved, absolutely refusing to serve Ahmed and never losing an opportunity to make him feel inferior. Everything went out of Ahmed; he crumpled up as if he were a paper flower. He didn't want to play his sarod and he didn't want to make love to me, he just sat around with his head and his hands hanging down, and there were times when I saw tears rolling down his face and he didn't even bother to wipe them off. Although he was so unhappy in the apartment, he never left it and so he never saw any of the places he had been so eager to come to Delhi for, like the Juma Masjid and Nizamuddin's tomb. Most of the time he was thinking about his family. He wrote long letters to them in Urdu, which I posted, telling them where he was and imploring their pardon for running away; and long letters came back again and he read and read them, soaking them in tears and kisses. One night he got so bad he jumped out of bed and, rushing into Henry's bedroom, fell to his knees by the side of Henry's bed and begged to be sent back home again. And Henry, sitting up in bed in his pajamas, said all right, in rather a lordly way I thought. So next day I took Ahmed to the station and put him on the train, and through the bars of the railway carriage he kissed my hands and looked into my eyes with all his old ardor and tenderness, so at the last moment I wanted to go with him but it was too late and the train pulled away out of the station and all that was left to me of Ahmed was a memory, very beautiful and delicate like a flavor or a perfume or one of those melodies he played on his sarod.

I became very depressed. I didn't feel like going traveling anymore but stayed home with Henry and went with him to his diplomatic and other parties. He was quite glad to have me go with him again; he liked having someone in the car on the way home to talk to about all the people who'd been at the party and compare their chances of future success with his own. I didn't mind going with him; there wasn't anything else I wanted to do. I felt as if I'd failed at something. It wasn't only Ahmed. I didn't really miss him all that much and was glad to think of him back with his family in that alley full of music where he was happy. For myself I didn't know what to do next, though I felt that something still awaited me. Our apartment led to an open terrace and I often went up there to look at the view, which was marvelous. The house we lived in and all the ones around were white and pink and very modern, with picture windows and little lawns in front, but from up here you could look beyond them to the city and the big mosque and the fort. In between there were stretches of wasteland, empty and barren except for an occasional crumbly old tomb growing there. What always impressed me the most was the sky because it was so immensely big and so unchanging in color, and it made everything underneath it—all the buildings, even the great fort, the whole city, not to speak of all the people living in it—seem terribly small and trivial and passing somehow. But at the same time as it made me feel small, it also made me feel immense and eternal. I don't know, I can't explain, perhaps because it was itself like that and this thought—that there *was* something like that—made me feel that I had a part in it, I too was part of being immense and eternal. It was all very vague really and nothing I could ever speak about to anyone; but because of it I thought well maybe there is something more for me here after all. That was a relief because it meant I wouldn't have to go home and be the way I was before and nothing different or gained. For all the time, ever since I'd come and even before, I'd had this idea that there was something in India for me to *gain,* and even though for the time being I'd failed, I could try longer and at last perhaps I would succeed.

I'd met people on and off who had come here on a spiritual quest, but it wasn't the sort of thing I wanted for myself. I thought anything I wanted to find, I could find by myself traveling around the way I had done. But now that this had failed, I became interested in the other thing. I began to go to a few prayer meetings and I liked the atmosphere very much. The meeting was usually conducted by a swami in a saffron robe who had renounced the world, and he gave an address about love and God and everyone sang hymns also about love and God. The people who came to these meetings were mostly middle-aged and quite poor. I had already met many like them on my travels, for they were the sort of people who sat waiting on station platforms and bus depots, absolutely patient and uncomplaining even when conductors and other officials pushed them around. They were gentle people and very clean though there was always some slight smell about them as of people who find it difficult to keep clean because they live in crowded and unsanitary places where there isn't much running water and the drainage system isn't good. I loved the expression that came into their faces when they sang hymns. I wanted to be like them, so I began to dress in plain white saris and I tied up my hair in a plain knot and the only ornament I wore was a string of beads not for decoration but to say the names of God on. I became a vegetarian and did my best to cast out all the undesirable human passions, such as anger and lust. When Henry was in an irritable or quarrelsome mood, I never answered him back but was very kind and patient with him. However, far from having a good effect, this seemed to make him worse. Altogether he didn't like the new personality I was trying to achieve but sneered a lot at the way I dressed and looked and the simple food I ate. Actually, I didn't enjoy this food very much and found it quite a trial eating nothing but boiled rice and him sitting opposite me having his cutlets and chops.

The peace and satisfaction that I saw on the faces of the other hymn singers didn't come to me. As a matter of fact, I grew rather bored. There didn't seem much to be learned from singing hymns and eating vegetables. Fortunately just about this time someone took me to see a holy woman who lived on the roof of an old over-crowded house near the river. People treated her like a holy woman but she didn't set up to be one. She didn't set up to be anything really, but only stayed in her room on the roof and talked to people who came to see her. She liked telling stories and she could hold everyone spellbound listening to her, even though she was only telling the old mythological stories they had known all their lives long, about Krishna, and the Pandavas, and Rama and Sita. But she got terribly excited while she was telling them, as if it wasn't something that had happened millions of years ago but as if it was all real and going on exactly now. Once she was telling about Krishna's mother who made him open his mouth to see whether he had stolen and was eating up her butter. What did she see then, inside his mouth?

"Worlds!" the holy woman cried. "Not just this world, not just one world with its mountains and rivers and seas, no, but world upon world, all spinning in one great eternal cycle in this child's mouth, moon upon moon, sun upon sun!"

She clapped her hands and laughed and laughed, and then she burst out singing in her thin old voice some hymn all about how great God was and how lucky for her that she was his beloved. She was dancing with joy in front of all the people. And she was just a little shriveled old woman, very ugly with her teeth gone and a growth on her chin: but the way she carried on it was as if she had all the looks and glamour anyone ever had in the world and was in love a million times over. I thought, well whatever it was she had, obviously it was the one thing worth having and I had better try for it.

I went to stay with a guru in a holy city. He had a house on the river in which he lived with his disciples. They lived in a nice way: they meditated a lot and went out for boat rides on the river and in the evenings they all sat around in the guru's room and had a good time. There were quite a few foreigners among the disciples, and it was the guru's greatest wish to go abroad and spread his message there and bring back more disciples. When he heard that Henry was a journalist, he became specially interested in me. He talked to me about the importance of introducing the leaven of Indian spirituality into the lump of Western materialism. To achieve this end, his own presence in the West was urgently required, and to ensure the widest dissemination of his message he would also need the full support of the mass media. He said that since we live in the modern age, we must avail ourselves of all its resources. He was very keen for me to bring Henry into the ashram, and when I was vague in my answers—I certainly didn't want Henry here nor would he in the least want to come—he became very pressing and even quite annoyed and kept returning to the subject.

He didn't seem a very spiritual type of person to me. He was a hefty man with big shoulders and a big head. He wore his hair long but his jaw was clean-shaven and stuck out very large and prominent and gave him a powerful look like a bull. All he ever wore was a saffron robe and this left a good part of his body bare so that it could be seen at once how strong his legs and shoulders were. He had huge eyes, which he used constantly and apparently to tremendous effect, fixing people with them and penetrating them with a steady beam. He used them on me when he wanted Henry to come, but they never did anything to me. But the other disciples were very strongly affected by them. There was one girl, Jean, who said they were like the sun, so strong that if she tried to look back at them something terrible would happen to her like being blinded or burned up completely.

Jean had made herself everything an Indian guru expects his disciples to be. She was absolutely humble and submissive She touched the guru's feet when she came into or went out of his presence, she ran eagerly on any errand he sent her on. She said she gloried in being nothing in herself and living only by his will. And she looked like nothing too, sort of drained of everything she might once have been. At home her cheeks were probably pink but now she was quite white, waxen, and her hair too was completely faded and colorless. She always wore a plain white cotton sari and that made her look paler than ever, and thinner too, it seemed to bring out the fact that she had no hips and was utterly flat-chested. But she was happy—at least she said she was—she said she had never known such happiness and hadn't thought it was possible for human beings to feel like that. And when she said that, there was a sort of sparkle in her pale eyes, and at such moments I envied her because she seemed to have found what I was looking for. But at the same time I wondered whether she really had found what she thought she had, or whether it wasn't something else and she was cheating herself, and one day she'd wake up to that fact and then she'd feel terrible.

She was shocked by my attitude to the guru—not touching his feet or anything, and talking back to him as if he were just an ordinary person. Sometimes I thought perhaps there was something wrong with me because everyone else, all the other disciples and people from outside too who came to see him, they all treated him with this great reverence and their faces lit up in his presence as if there really was something special. Only I couldn't see it. But all the same I was quite happy there—not because of him, but because I liked the atmosphere of the place and the way they all lived. Everyone seemed very contented and as if they were living for something high and beautiful. I thought perhaps if I waited and was patient, I'd also come to be like that. I tried to meditate the way they all did, sitting cross-legged in one spot and concentrating on the holy word that had been given to me. I wasn't ever very successful and kept thinking of other things. But there were times when I went up to sit on the roof and looked out over the river, the way it stretched so calm and broad to the opposite bank and the boats going up and down it and the light changing and being reflected back on the water: and then, though I wasn't trying to meditate or come to any higher thoughts, I did feel very peaceful and was glad to be there.

The guru was patient with me for a long time, explaining about the importance of his mission and how Henry ought to come here and write about it for his paper. But as the days passed and Henry didn't show up, his attitude changed and he began to ask me questions. Why hadn't Henry come? Hadn't I written to him? Wasn't I going to write to him? Didn't I think what was being done in the ashram would interest him? Didn't I agree that it deserved to be brought to the notice of the world and that to this end no stone should be left unturned? While he said all this, he fixed me with his great eyes and I squirmed—not because of the way he was looking at me, but because I was embarrassed and didn't know what to answer. Then he became very gentle and said never mind, he didn't want to force me, that was not his way, he wanted people slowly to turn toward him of their own accord, to open up to him as a flower opens up and unfurls its petals and its leaves to the sun. But next day he would start again, asking the same questions, urging me, forcing me, and when this had gone on for some time and we weren't getting anywhere, he even got angry once or twice and shouted at me that I was obstinate and closed and had fenced in my heart with seven hoops of iron. When he shouted, everyone in the ashram trembled and afterward they looked at me in a strange way. But an hour later the guru always had me called back to his room and then he was very gentle with me again and made me sit near him and insisted that it should be I who handed him his glass of milk in preference to one of the others, all of whom were a lot keener to be selected for this honor than I was.

Jean often came to talk to me. At night I spread my bedding in a tiny cubbyhole that was a disused storeroom, and just as I was falling asleep, she would come in and lie down beside me and talk to me very softly and intimately. I didn't like it much, to have her so close to me and whispering in a voice that wasn't more than a breath and which I could feel, slightly warm, on my neck; sometimes she touched me, putting her hand on mine ever so gently so that she hardly was touching me but all the same I could feel that her hand was a bit moist and it gave me an unpleasant sensation down my spine. She spoke about the beauty of surrender, of not having a will and not having thoughts of your own. She said she too had been like me once, stubborn and ego-centered, but now she had learned the joy of yielding, and if she could only give me some inkling of the infinite bliss to be tasted in this process—

here her breath would give out for a moment and she couldn't speak for ecstasy, I would take the opportunity to pretend to fall asleep, even snoring a bit to make it more convincing; after calling my name a few times in the hope of waking me up again, she crept away disappointed. But next night she'd be back again, and during the day too she would attach herself to me as much as possible and continue talking in the same way.

It got so that even when she wasn't there, I could still hear her voice and feel her breath on my neck. I no longer enjoyed anything, not even going on the river or looking out over it from the top of the house. Although they hadn't bothered me before, I kept thinking of the funeral pyres burning on the bank, and it seemed to me that the smoke they gave out was spreading all over the sky and the river and covering them with a dirty yellowish haze. I realized that nothing good could come to me from this place now. But when I told the guru that I was leaving, he got into a great fury. His head and neck swelled out and his eyes became two coal-black demons rolling around in rage. In a voice like drums and cymbals, he *forbade* me to go. I didn't say anything but I made up my mind to leave next morning. I went to pack my things. The whole ashram was silent and stricken, no one dared speak. No one dared come near me either till late at night when Jean came as usual to lie next to me. She lay there completely still and crying to herself. I didn't know she was crying at first because she didn't make a sound, but slowly her tears seeped into her side of the pillow and a sensation of dampness came creeping over to my side of it. I pretended not to notice anything.

Suddenly the guru stood in the doorway. The room faced an open courtyard and this was full of moonlight that illumined him and made him look enormous and eerie. Jean and I sat up. I felt scared, my heart beat fast. After looking at us in silence for a while, he ordered Jean to go away. She got up to do so at once. I said "No, stay," and clung to her hand but she disengaged herself from me and, touching the guru's feet in reverence, she went away. She seemed to dissolve in the moonlight outside, leaving no trace. The guru sat beside me on my bedding spread on the floor. He said I was under a delusion, that I didn't really want to leave; my inmost nature was craving to stay by him—he knew, he could hear it calling out to him. But because I was afraid, I was attempting to smother this craving and to run away. "Look how you're trembling," he said. "See how afraid you are." It was true, I was trembling and cowering against the wall as far away from him as I could get. Only it was impossible to get very far because he was so huge and seemed to spread and fill the tiny closet. I could feel him close against me, and his pungent male smell, spiced with garlic, overpowered me.

"You're right to be afraid," he said: because it was his intention, he said, to batter and beat me, to smash my ego till it broke and flew apart into a million pieces and was scattered into the dust. Yes, it would be a painful process and I would often cry out and plead for mercy, but in the end—ah, with what joy I would step out of the prison of my own self, remade and reborn! I would fling myself to the ground and bathe his feet in tears of gratitude. Then I would be truly his. As he spoke, I became more and more afraid because I felt, so huge and close and strong he was, that perhaps he really had the power to do to me all that he said and that in the end he would make me like Jean.

I now lay completely flattened against the wall, and he had moved up and was squashing me against it. One great hand traveled up and down my stomach, but its activity seemed apart from the rest of him and from what he was saying. His voice became lower and lower, more and more intense. He said he would teach me to obey, to submit myself completely, that would be the first step and a very necessary one. For he knew what we were like, all of us who came from Western countries: we were self-willed, obstinate, *licentious.* On the last word his voice cracked with emotion, his hand went further and deeper. *Licentious,* he repeated, and then, rolling himself across the bed so that he now lay completely pressed against me, he asked "How many men have you slept with?" He took my hand and made me hold him: how huge and hot he was! He pushed hard against me. "How many? Answer me!" he commanded, urgent and dangerous. But I was no longer afraid: now he was not an unknown quantity nor was the situation any longer new or strange. "Answer me, answer me!" he cried, riding on top of me, and then he cried "Bitch!" and I laughed in relief.

I quite liked being back in Delhi with Henry. I had lots of baths in our marble bathroom, soaking in the tub for hours and making myself smell nice with bath salts. I stopped wearing Indian clothes and took out all the dresses I'd brought with me. We entertained quite a bit, and Ramu scurried around in his white coat, emptying ashtrays. It wasn't a bad time. I stayed around all day in the apartment with the air-conditioner on and the curtains drawn to keep out the glare. At night we drove over to other people's apartments for buffet suppers of boiled ham and potato salad; we sat around drinking in their living rooms, which were done up more or less like ours, and talked about things like the price of whiskey, what was the best hill station to go to in the summer, and servants. This last subject often led to other related ones like how unreliable Indians were and how it was impossible ever to get anything done. Usually this subject was treated in a humorous way, with lots of funny anecdotes to illustrate, but occasionally someone got quite passionate; this happened usually if they were a bit drunk, and then they went off into a long thing about how dirty India was and backward, riddled with vile superstitions—evil, they said—corrupt—corrupting. Henry never spoke like that—maybe because he never got drunk enough—but I know he didn't disagree with it. He disliked the place very much and was in fact thinking of asking for an assignment elsewhere. When I asked where, he said the cleanest place he could think of. He asked how would I like to go to Geneva. I knew I wouldn't like it one bit, but I said all right. I didn't really care where I was. I didn't care much about anything these days. The only positive feeling I had was for Henry. He was so sweet and good to me. I had a lot of bad dreams nowadays and was afraid of sleeping alone, so he let me come into his bed even though he dislikes having his sheets disarranged and I always kick and toss about a lot. I lay close beside him, clinging to him, and for the first time I was glad that he had never been all that keen on sex. On Sundays we stayed in bed all day reading the papers and Ramu brought us nice English meals on trays. Sometimes we put on a record and danced together in our pajamas. I kissed Henry's cheeks, which were always smooth—he didn't need to shave very often—and sometimes his lips, which tasted of toothpaste.

Then I got jaundice. It's funny, all that time I spent traveling about and eating anything anywhere, nothing happened to me, and now that I was living such a clean life with boiled food and boiled water, I got sick. Henry was horrified. He immediately segregated all his and my things, and anything that I touched had to be sterilized a hundred times over. He was forever running into the kitchen to check up whether Ramu was doing this properly. He said jaundice was the most catching thing there was, and though he went in for a whole course of precautionary inoculations that had to be specially flown in from the States, he still remained in a very nervous state. He tried to be sympathetic to me, but couldn't help sounding reproachful most of the time. He had sealed himself off so carefully, and now I had let this in. I knew how he felt, but I was too ill and miserable to care. I don't remember ever feeling so ill. I didn't have any high temperature or anything, but all the time there was this terrible nausea. First my eyes went yellow, then the rest of me as if I'd been dyed in the color of nausea, inside and out. The whole world went yellow and sick. I couldn't bear anything: any noise, any person near me, worst of all any smell. They couldn't cook in the kitchen anymore because the smell of cooking made me scream. Henry had to live on boiled eggs and bread. I begged him not to let Ramu into my bedroom for, although Ramu always wore nicely laundered clothes, he gave out a smell of perspiration that was both sweetish and foul and filled me with disgust. I was convinced that under his clean shirt he wore a cotton vest, black with sweat and dirt, which he never took off but slept in at night in the one-room servant quarter where he lived crowded together with all his family in a dense smell of cheap food and bad drains and unclean bodies.

I knew these smells so well—I thought of them as the smells of India, and had never minded them; but now I couldn't get rid of them, they were like some evil flood soaking through the walls of my air-conditioned bedroom. And other things I hadn't minded, had hardly bothered to think about, now came back to me in a terrible way so that waking and sleeping I saw them. What I remembered most often was the disused well in the Rajasthan fort out of which I had drunk water. I was sure now that there had been a corpse at the bottom of it, and I saw this corpse with the flesh swollen and blown but the eyes intact: they were huge like the guru's eyes and they stared, glazed and jellied, into the darkness of the well. And worse than seeing this corpse, I could taste it in the water that I had drunk—that I was still drinking—yes, it was now, at this very moment, that I was raising my cupped hands to my mouth and feeling the dank water lap around my tongue. I screamed out loud at the taste of the dead man and I called to Henry and clutched his hand and begged him to get us sent to Geneva quickly, quickly. He disengaged his hand—he didn't like me to touch him at this time—but he promised. Then I grew calmer, I shut my eyes and tried to think of Geneva and of washing out my mouth with Swiss milk.

I got better, but I was very weak. When I looked at myself in the mirror, I started to cry. My face had a yellow tint, my hair was limp and faded; I didn't look old but I didn't look young anymore either. There was no flesh left, and no color. I was drained, hollowed out. I was wearing a white nightdress and that increased the impression. Actually, I reminded myself of Jean. I thought, so this is what it does to you (I didn't quite know at that time what I meant by it—jaundice in my case, a guru in hers; but it seemed to come to the same). When Henry told me that his new assignment had come through, I burst into tears again; only now it was with relief. I said let's go now, let's go quickly. I became quite hysterical so Henry said all right; he too was impatient to get away before any more of those bugs he dreaded so much caught up with us. The only thing that bothered him was that the rent had been paid for three months and the landlord refused to refund. Henry had a fight with him about it but the landlord won. Henry was furious but I said never mind, let's just get away and forget all about all of them. We packed up some of our belongings and sold the rest; the last few days we lived in an empty apartment with only a couple of kitchen chairs and a bed. Ramu was very worried about finding a new job.

Just before we were to leave for the airport and were waiting for the car to pick us up, I went on the terrace. I don't know why I did that, there was no reason. There was nothing I wanted to say good-bye to, and no last glimpses I wanted to catch. My thoughts were all concentrated on the coming journey and whether to take airsickness pills or not. The sky from up on the terrace looked as immense as ever, the city as small. It was evening and the light was just fading and the sky wasn't any definite color now: it was sort of translucent like a pearl but not an earthly pearl. I thought of the story the little saintly old woman had told about Krishna's mother and how she saw the sun and the moon and world upon world in his mouth. I liked that phrase so much—world upon world—I imagined them spinning around each other like glass spheres in eternity and everything as shining and translucent as the sky I saw above me. I went down and told Henry I wasn't going with him. When he realized and this took some time—that I was serious, he knew I was mad. At first he

was very patient and gentle with me, then he got in a frenzy. The car had already arrived to take us. Henry yelled at me, he grabbed my arm and began to
pull me to the door. I resisted with all my strength and sat down on one of the
kitchen chairs. Henry continued to pull and now he was pulling me along
with the chair as if on a sleigh. I clung to it as hard as I could but I felt terribly
weak and was afraid I would let myself be pulled away. I begged him to leave
me. I cried and wept with fear—fear that he would take me, fear that he
would leave me.

Ramu came to my aid. He said it's all right Sahib, I'll look after her. He
told Henry that I was too weak to travel after my illness but later, when I was
better, he would take me to the airport and put me on a plane. Henry hesitated.
It was getting very late, and if he didn't go, he too would miss the plane.
Ramu assured him that all would be well and Henry need not worry at all. At
last Henry took my papers and ticket out of his inner pocket. He gave me instructions how I was to go to the air company and make a new booking. He
hesitated a moment longer—how sweet he looked all dressed up in a suit and
tie ready for traveling, just like the day we got married—but the car was hoot-
ing furiously downstairs and he had to go. I held on hard to the chair. I was
afraid if I didn't I might get up and run after him. So I clung to the chair, trembling and crying. Ramu was quite happily dusting the remaining chair. He
said we would have to get some more furniture. I think he was glad that I had
stayed and he still had somewhere to work and live and didn't have to go
tramping around looking for another place. He had quite a big family to
support.

I sold the ticket Henry left with me but I didn't buy any new furniture
with it. I stayed in the empty rooms by myself and very rarely went out. When
Ramu cooked anything for me, I ate it, but sometimes he forgot or didn't have
time because he was busy looking for another job. I didn't like living like that
but I didn't know what else to do. I was afraid to go out: everything I had once
liked so much—people, places, crowds, smells—I now feared and hated. I
would go running back to be by myself in the empty apartment. I felt people
looked at me in a strange way in the streets; and perhaps I was strange now
from the way I was living and not caring about what I looked like anymore; I
think I talked aloud to myself sometimes—once or twice I heard myself
doing it. I spent a lot of the money I got from the air ticket on books. I went to
the bookshops and came hurrying back carrying armfuls of them. Many of
them I never read, and even those I did read, I didn't understand very much. I
hadn't had much experience in reading these sort of books—like the Upan-
ishads and the Vedanta Sutras—but I liked the sound of the words and I liked
the feeling they gave out. It was as if I were all by myself on an immensely
high plateau breathing in great lungfuls of very sharp, pure air. Sometimes the
landlord came to see what I was doing. He went around all the rooms, peering
suspiciously into corners, testing the fittings. He kept asking how much

longer I was going to stay; I said till the three months' rent was up. He brought prospective tenants to see the apartment, but when they saw me squatting on the floor in the empty rooms, sometimes with a bowl of half-eaten food that Ramu had neglected to clear away, they got nervous and went away again rather quickly. After a time the electricity got cut off because I hadn't paid the bill. It was very hot without the fan and I filled the tub with cold water and sat in it all day. But then the water got cut off too. The landlord came up twice, three times a day now. He said if I didn't clear out the day the rent was finished he would call the police to evict me. I said it's all right, don't worry, I shall go. Like the landlord, I too was counting the days still left to me. I was afraid what would happen to me.

Today the landlord evicted Ramu out of the servant quarter. That was when Ramu came up to ask for money and said all those things. Afterward I went up on the terrace to watch him leave. It was such a sad procession. Each member of the family carried some part of their wretched household stock, none of which looked worth taking. Ramu had a bed with tattered strings balanced on his head. In two days' time I too will have to go with my bundle and my bedding. I've done this so often before—traveled here and there without any real destination—and been so happy doing it; but now it's different. That time I had a great sense of freedom and adventure. Now I feel compelled, that I *have* to do this whether I want to or not. And partly I don't want to, I feel afraid. Yet it's still like an adventure, and that's why besides being afraid I'm also excited, and most of the time I don't know why my heart is beating fast, is it in fear or in excitement, wondering what will happen to me now that I'm going traveling again.

# R. K. Narayan

Probably the most Indian of all Indian novelists in English, R. K. Narayan has faithfully re-created daily life in South India, where he was born in Madras on 10 October 1906. Educated in English-language preparatory schools, Narayan graduated from Maharajah's College in Mysore and, following in his father's footsteps, entered teaching; determined, however, to become an English-language novelist, Narayan soon gave up the profession. After his marriage he worked as a reporter for a Madras newspaper. This experience, Narayan recalls in his memoir, *My Days* (1974), brought him into contact with a variety of people and provided material that he would use later in his fiction. In 1935 his first novel, *Swami and Friends*, was published in England after being rejected by several publishers and finally recommended by Graham Greene, who was impressed by Narayan's narrative technique. A second novel, *The Dark Room*, appeared in 1938. A year later his wife died of typhoid, leaving an infant daughter. In *The English Teacher* (1945) Narayan tells the story of a young man whose wife dies, and traces how the bereaved husband handles his grief through mystical communication with his dead wife. Narayan admits in *My Days* that the novel is "autobiographical in content, very little part of it being fiction." He never remarried, and has continued to live in Mysore except for occasional travels abroad. A private man, Narayan rarely grants interviews, avoids literary gatherings, and seldom comments on his own work.

Narayan has published fourteen novels and several volumes of short stories. He has also published numerous essays and sketches, as well as English translations of Indian mythological works, *The Ramayana* (1972) and *The Mahabharata* (1978). But it is mainly for his fiction that he has gained an international reputation. Some of his most widely known novels are *The Financial Expert* (1952), *The Guide* (1958), *The Vendor of Sweets* (1967), and *A*

*Tiger for Malgudi* (1982). In 1993 three novellas appeared under the title *The Grandmother's Tale.*

Much of the fiction takes place in the South Indian town of Malgudi and its environs, which is the author's creation but has become a reality for his readers. The human comedy that Narayan depicts blends the realism of Western fiction with the mythology of traditional India. The conflicts his characters face and the way they overcome them Narayan treats with narrative simplicity and a keen understanding of human foibles. He has never given into fashionable trends in fictional technique, and he rarely brings into play the political and social upheavals that have beset postcolonial India. Narayan's last full-length fiction, *The World of Nagaraj* (1990), focuses on a would-be writer and a mythological storyteller. It could be read as a contemplation of Narayan's own career, its struggles, successes, misgivings. For, like the novel's mythological character Narada, Narayan has told stories all his life—and to what purpose, he might be asking.

One of Narayan's most admired short stories, "A Horse and Two Goats," takes place outside of Malgudi in the South Indian countryside. It illustrates effectively Narayan's subtlety in character development, creation of setting, and plot structure, as well as the way in which he draws Indian tradition into the story. The meeting between the Indian peasant and the American tourist—a comic postcolonial encounter—allows Narayan to frame the contrasts between East and West. This is a recurring theme in English fiction about India since Rudyard Kipling wrote "And never the twain shall meet."

# A Horse and Two Goats

Of the seven hundred thousand villages dotting the map of India, in which the majority of India's five hundred million live, flourish, and die, Kritam was probably the tiniest, indicated on the district survey map by a microscopic dot, the map being meant more for the revenue official out to collect tax than for the guidance of the motorist, who in any case could not hope to reach it since it sprawled far from the highway at the end of a rough track furrowed up by the iron-hooped wheels of bullock carts. But its size did not prevent its giving itself the grandiose name Kritam, which meant in Tamil "coronet" or "crown" on the brow of this subcontinent. The village consisted of fewer than thirty houses, only one of them built with brick and cement. Painted a brilliant yellow and blue all over with gorgeous carvings of gods and gargoyles on its balustrade, it was known as the Big House. The other houses, distributed in four streets, were generally of bamboo thatch, straw, mud, and other unspecified material. Muni's was the last house in the fourth street, beyond which stretched the fields. In his prosperous days Muni had owned a flock of forty sheep and goats and sallied forth every morning driving the flock to the highway a couple of miles away. There he would sit on the pedestal of a clay statue of a horse while his stock grazed around. He carried a crook at the end of a bamboo pole and snapped foliage from the avenue trees to feed his flock; he also gathered faggots and dry sticks, bundled them, and carried them home for fuel at sunset.

His wife lit the domestic fire at dawn, boiled water in a mud pot, threw into it a handful of millet flour, added salt, and gave him his first nourishment for the day. When he started out, she would put in his hand a packed lunch, once again the same millet cooked into a little ball, which he could swallow with a raw onion at midday. She was old, but he was older and needed all the attention she could give him in order to be kept alive.

His fortunes had declined gradually, unnoticed. From a flock of forty which he drove into a pen at night, his stock had now come down to two goats, which were not worth the rent of a half rupee a month the Big House charged for the use of the pen in their backyard. And so the two goats were tethered to the trunk of a drumstick tree which grew in front of his hut and from which occasionally Muni could shake down drumsticks. This morning he got six. He carried them in with a sense of triumph. Although no one could say precisely who owned the tree, it was his because he lived in its shadow.

She said, "If you were content with the drumstick leaves alone, I could boil and salt some for you."

"Oh, I am tired of eating those leaves. I have a craving to chew the drumstick out of sauce, I tell you."

"You have only four teeth in your jaw, but your craving is for big things. All right, get the stuff for the sauce, and I will prepare it for you. After all, next year you may not be alive to ask for anything. But first get me all the stuff, including a measure of rice or millet, and I will satisfy your unholy craving. Our store is empty today. Dhall, chili, curry leaves, mustard, coriander, gingelley oil, and one large potato. Go out and get all this." He repeated the list after her in order not to miss any item and walked off to the shop in the third street.

He sat on an upturned packing case below the platform of the shop. The shopman paid no attention to him. Muni kept clearing his throat, coughing, and sneezing until the shopman could not stand it any more and demanded, "What ails you? You will fly off that seat into the gutter if you sneeze so hard, young man." Muni laughed inordinately, in order to please the shopman, at being called "young man." The shopman softened and said, "You have enough of the imp inside to keep a second wife busy, but for the fact the old lady is still alive." Muni laughed appropriately again at this joke. It completely won the shopman over; he liked his sense of humor to be appreciated. Muni engaged his attention in local gossip for a few minutes, which always ended with a reference to the postman's wife, who had eloped to the city some months before.

The shopman felt most pleased to hear the worst of the postman, who had cheated him. Being an itinerant postman, he returned home to Kritam only once in ten days and every time managed to slip away again without passing the shop in the third street. By thus humoring the shopman, Muni could always ask for one or two items of food, promising repayment later. Some days the shopman was in a good mood and gave in, and sometimes he would lose his temper suddenly and bark at Muni for daring to ask for credit.

This was such a day, and Muni could not progress beyond two items listed as essential components. The shopman was also displaying a remarkable memory for old facts and figures and took out an oblong ledger to support his observations. Muni felt impelled to rise and flee. But his self-respect kept him in his seat and made him listen to the worst things about himself. The shopman concluded, "If you could find five rupees and a quarter, you will have paid off an ancient debt and then could apply for admission to swarga. How much have you got now?"

"I will pay you everything on the first of the next month."

"As always, and whom do you expect to rob by then?"

Muni felt caught and mumbled, "My daughter has sent word that she will be sending me money."

"Have you a daughter?" sneered the shopman. "And she is sending you money! For what purpose, may I know?"

"Birthday, fiftieth birthday," said Muni quietly.

"Birthday! How old are you?"

Muni repeated weakly, not being sure of it himself, "Fifty." He always calculated his age from the time of the great famine when he stood as high as the parapet around the village well, but who could calculate such things accurately nowadays with so many famines occurring? The shopman felt encouraged when other customers stood around to watch and comment. Muni thought helplessly, My poverty is exposed to everybody. But what can I do?

"More likely you are seventy," said the shopman. "You also forget that you mentioned a birthday five weeks ago when you wanted castor oil for your holy bath."

"Bath! Who can dream of a bath when you have to scratch the tank-bed for a bowl of water? We would all be parched and dead but for the Big House, where they let us take a pot of water from their well." After saying this Muni unobtrusively rose and moved off.

He told his wife, "That scoundrel would not give me anything. So go out and sell the drumsticks for what they are worth."

He flung himself down in a corner to recoup from the fatigue of his visit to the shop. His wife said, "You are getting no sauce today, nor anything else. I can't find anything to give you to eat. Fast till the evening, it'll do you good. Take the goats and be gone now," she cried and added, "Don't come back before the sun is down." He knew that if he obeyed her she would somehow conjure up some food for him in the evening. Only he must be careful not to argue and irritate her. Her temper was undependable in the morning but improved by evening time. She was sure to go out and work—grind corn in the Big House, sweep or scrub somewhere, and earn enough to buy foodstuff and keep a dinner ready for him in the evening.

Unleashing the goats from the drumstick tree, Muni started out, driving them ahead and uttering weird cries from time to time in order to urge them on. He passed through the village with his head bowed in thought. He did not want to look at anyone or be accosted. A couple of cronies lounging in the temple corridor hailed him, but he ignored their call. They had known him in the days of affluence when he lorded over a flock of fleecy sheep, not the miserable gawky goats that he had today. Of course he also used to have a few goats for those who fancied them, but real wealth lay in sheep; they bred fast and people came and bought the fleece in the shearing season; and then that famous butcher from the town came over on the weekly market days bringing him betel leaves, tobacco, and often enough some bhang, which they smoked in a hut in the coconut grove, undisturbed by wives and well-wishers. After a smoke one felt light and elated and inclined to forgive everyone including that brother-in-law of his who had once tried to set fire to his home. But all this seemed like the memories of a previous birth. Some pestilence afflicted his stock (he could of course guess who had laid his animals under a curse), and even the friendly butcher would not touch one at half the price . . . and now here he was left with the two scraggy creatures. He wished someone would rid him of their company, too. The shopman had said that he was seventy. At seventy, one only waited to be summoned by God. When he was dead what would his wife do? They had lived in each other's company since they were children. He was told on their day of wedding that he was ten years old and she was eight. During the wedding ceremony they had had to recite their respective ages and names. He had thrashed her only a few times in their career, and later she had the upper hand. Progeny, none. Perhaps a large progeny would have brought him the blessing of the gods. Fertility brought merit. People with fourteen sons were always so prosperous and at peace with the world and themselves. He recollected the thrill he had felt when he mentioned a daughter to that shopman; although it was not believed, what if he did not have a daughter?—his cousin in the next village had many daughters, and any one of them was as good as his; he was fond of them all and would buy them sweets if he could afford it. Still, everyone in the village whispered behind their backs that Muni and his wife were a barren couple. He avoided looking at anyone; they all professed to be so high up, and everyone else in the village had more money than he. "I am the poorest fellow in our caste and no wonder that they spurn me, but I won't look at them either," and so he passed on with his eyes downcast along the edge of the street, and people left him also very much alone, commenting only to the extent, "Ah, there he goes with his two goats; if he slits their throats, he may have more peace of mind." "What has he to worry about anyway? They live on nothing and have none to worry about." Thus people commented when he passed through the village. Only on the outskirts did he lift his head and look up. He urged and bullied the goats until they meandered along to the foot of the horse statue on the edge of the village. He sat on its pedestal for the rest of the day. The advantage of this was that he could watch the highway and see the lorries and buses pass through to the hills, and it gave him a sense of belonging to a larger world. The pedestal of the statue was broad enough for him to move around as the sun traveled up and westward; or he could also crouch under the belly of the horse, for shade.

The horse was nearly life-size, moulded out of clay, baked, burnt, and brightly colored, and reared its head proudly, prancing its forelegs in the air and flourishing its tail in a loop; beside the horse stood a warrior with scythe-like mustachios, bulging eyes, and aquiline nose. The old image-makers believed in indicating a man of strength by bulging out his eyes and sharpening his mustache tips, and also decorated the man's chest with beads which looked today like blobs of mud through the ravages of sun and wind and rain (when it came), but Muni would insist that he had known the beads to sparkle like the nine gems at one time in his life. The horse itself was said to have been as white as a dhobi-washed sheet, and had had on its back a cover of pure brocade of red and black lace, matching the multicolored sash around the waist of the warrior. But none in the village remembered the splendor as no one noticed its existence. Even Muni, who spent all his waking hours at its foot, never bothered to look up. It was untouched even by the young vandals of the village who gashed tree trunks with knives and tried to topple off milestones and inscribed lewd designs on all walls. This statue had been closer to the population of the village at one time, when this spot bordered the village; but when the highway was laid through (or perhaps when the tank and wells dried up completely here) the village moved a couple of miles inland.

Muni sat at the foot of the statue, watching his two goats graze in the arid soil among the cactus and lantana bushes. He looked at the sun; it was tilted westward no doubt, but it was not the time yet to go back home; if he went too early his wife would have no food for him. Also he must give her time to cool off her temper and feel sympathetic, and then she would scrounge and manage to get some food. He watched the mountain road for a time signal. When the green bus appeared around the bend he could leave, and his wife would feel pleased that he had let the goats feed long enough.

He noticed now a new sort of vehicle coming down at full speed. It looked like both a motor car and a bus. He used to be intrigued by the novelty of such spectacles, but of late work was going on at the source of the river on the mountain and an assortment of people and traffic went past him, and he took it all casually and described to his wife, later in the day, everything he saw. Today, while he observed the yellow vehicle coming down, he was wondering how to describe it later to his wife, when it sputtered and stopped in front of him. A red-faced foreigner, who had been driving it, got down and went round it, stooping, looking, and poking under the vehicle; then he straightened himself up, looked at the dashboard, stared in Muni's direction, and approached him. "Excuse me, is there a gas station nearby, or do I have to wait until another car comes—" He suddenly looked up at the clay horse and cried, "Marvelous," without completing his sentence. Muni felt he should get up and run away, and cursed his age. He could not readily put his limbs into action; some years ago he could outrun a cheetah, as happened once when he went to the forest to cut fuel and it was then that two of his sheep were mauled—a sign that bad times were coming. Though he tried, he could not easily extricate himself from his seat, and then there was also the problem of the goats. He could not leave them behind.

The red-faced man wore khaki clothes—evidently a policeman or a soldier. Muni said to himself, He will chase or shoot if I start running. Some dogs chase only those who run—O Siva, protect me. I don't know why this man should be after me. Meanwhile the foreigner cried, "Marvelous!" again, nodding his head. He paced around the statue with his eyes fixed on it. Muni sat frozen for a while, and then fidgeted and tried to edge away. Now the other man suddenly pressed his palms together in a salute, smiled, and said, "Namaste! How do you do?"

At which Muni spoke the only English expressions he had learnt, "Yes, no." Having exhausted his English vocabulary, he started in Tamil: "My name is Muni. These two goats are mine, and no one can gainsay it—though our village is full of slanderers these days who will not hesitate to say that what belongs to a man doesn't belong to him." He rolled his eyes and shuddered at the thought of evil-minded men and women peopling his village.

The foreigner faithfully looked in the direction indicated by Muni's fingers, gazed for a while at the two goats and the rocks, and with a puzzled expression took out his silver cigarette case and lit a cigarette. Suddenly remembering the courtesies of the season, he asked, "Do you smoke?" Muni answered "Yes, no." Whereupon the red-faced man took a cigarette and gave it to Muni, who received it with surprise, having had no offer of a smoke from anyone for years now. Those days when he smoked bhang were gone with his sheep and the large-hearted butcher. Nowadays he was not able to find even matches, let alone bhang. (His wife went across and borrowed a fire at dawn from a neighbor.) He had always wanted to smoke a cigarette; only once did the shopman give him one on credit, and he remembered how good it had tasted. The other flicked the lighter open and offered a light to Muni. Muni felt so confused about how to act that he blew on it and put it out. The other, puzzled but undaunted, flourished his lighter, presented it again, and lit Muni's cigarette. Muni drew a deep puff and started coughing; it was racking, no doubt, but extremely pleasant. When his cough subsided he wiped his eyes and took stock of the situation, understanding that the other man was not an Inquisitor of any kind. Yet, in order to make sure, he remained wary. No need to run away from a man who gave him such a potent smoke. His head was reeling from the effect of one of those strong American cigarettes made with roasted tobacco. The man said, "I come from New York," took out a wallet from his hip pocket, and presented his card.

Muni shrank away from the card. Perhaps he was trying to present a warrant and arrest him. Beware of khaki, one part of his mind warned. Take all the cigarettes or bhang or whatever is offered, but don't get caught. Beware of khaki. He wished he weren't seventy as the shopman had said. At seventy one didn't run, but surrendered to whatever came. He could only ward off trouble by talk. So he went on, all in the chaste Tamil for which Kritam was famous. (Even the worst detractors could not deny that the famous poetess Avaiyar was born in this area, although no one could say whether it was in Kritam or Kuppam, the adjoining village.) Out of this heritage the Tamil language gushed through Muni in an unimpeded flow. He said, "Before God, sit, Bhagwan, who sees everything, I tell you, sir, that we know nothing of the case. If the murder was committed, whoever did it will not escape. Bhagwan is all-seeing! Don't ask me about it. I know nothing." A body had been found mutilated and thrown under a tamarind tree at the border between Kritam and Kuppam a few weeks before, giving rise to much gossip and speculation. Muni added an explanation. "Anything is possible there. People over there will stop at nothing." The foreigner nodded his head and listened courteously though he understood nothing.

"I am sure you know when this horse was made," said the red man and smiled ingratiatingly.

Muni reacted to the relaxed atmosphere by smiling himself, and pleaded, "Please go away, sir, I know nothing. I promise we will hold him for you if we see any bad character around, and we will bury him up to his neck in a coconut pit if he tries to escape; but our village has always had a clean record. Must definitely be the other village."

Now the red man implored, "Please, please, I will speak slowly, please try to understand me. Can't you understand even a simple word of English? Everyone in this country seems to know English. I have gotten along with English everywhere in this country, but you don't speak it. Have you any religious or spiritual scruples against English speech?"

Muni made some indistinct sounds in his throat and shook his head. Encouraged, the other went on to explain at length, uttering each syllable with care and deliberation. Presently he sidled over and took a seat beside the old man, explaining, "You see, last August, we probably had the hottest summer in history, and I was working in shirt-sleeves in my office on the fortieth floor of the Empire State Building. We had a power failure one day, you know, and there I was stuck for four hours, no elevator, no air conditioning. All the way in the train I kept thinking, and the minute I reached home in Connecticut, I told my wife, Ruth, 'We will visit India this winter, it's time to look at other civilizations.' Next day she called the travel agent first thing and told him to fix it, and so here I am. Ruth came with me but is staying back at Srinagar, and I am the one doing the rounds and joining her later."

Muni looked reflective at the end of this long oration and said, rather feebly, "Yes, no," as a concession to the other's language, and went on in Tamil, "When I was this high"—he indicated a foot high—"I had heard my uncle say . . ."

No one can tell what he was planning to say, as the other interrupted him at this stage to ask, "Boy, what is the secret of your teeth? How old are you?"

The old man forgot what he had started to say and remarked, "Sometimes we too lose our cattle. Jackals or cheetahs may sometimes carry them off, but sometimes it is just theft from over in the next village, and then we will know who has done it. Our priest at the temple can see in the camphor flame the face of the thief, and when he is caught . . ." He gestured with his hands a perfect mincing of meat.

The American watched his hands intently and said, "I know what you mean. Chop something? Maybe I am holding you up and you want to chop wood? Where is your axe? Hand it to me and show me what to chop. I do enjoy it, you know, just a hobby. We get a lot of driftwood along the backwater near my house, and on Sundays I do nothing but chop wood for the fireplace. I really feel different when I watch the fire in the fireplace, although it may take all the sections of the Sunday *New York Times* to get a fire started." And he smiled at this reference.

Muni felt totally confused but decided the best thing would be to make an attempt to get away from this place. He tried to edge out, saying, "Must go home," and turned to go. The other seized his shoulder and said desperately, "Is there no one, absolutely no one here, to translate for me?" He looked up and down the road, which was deserted in this hot afternoon; a sudden gust of wind churned up the dust and dead leaves on the roadside into a ghostly column and propelled it towards the mountain road. The stranger almost pinioned Muni's back to the statue and asked, "Isn't this statue yours? Why don't you sell it to me?"

The old man now understood the reference to the horse, thought for a second, and said in his own language, "I was an urchin this high when I heard my grandfather explain this horse and warrior, and my grandfather himself was this high when he heard his grandfather, whose grandfather . . ."

The other man interrupted him. "I don't want to seem to have stopped here for nothing. I will offer you a good price for this," he said, indicating the horse. He had concluded without the least doubt that Muni owned this mud horse. Perhaps he guessed by the way he sat on its pedestal, like other souvenir sellers in this country presiding over their wares.

Muni followed the man's eyes and pointing fingers and dimly understood the subject matter and, feeling relieved that the theme of the mutilated body had been abandoned at least for the time being, said again, enthusiastically, "I was this high when my grandfather told me about this horse and the warrior, and my grandfather was this high when he himself . . ." and he was getting into a deeper bog of reminiscence each time he tried to indicate the antiquity of the statue.

The Tamil that Muni spoke was stimulating even as pure sound, and the foreigner listened with fascination. "I wish I had my tape-recorder here," he said, assuming the pleasantest expression. "Your language sounds wonderful. I get a kick out of every word you utter, here"—he indicated his ears—"but you don't have to waste your breath in sales talk. I appreciate the article. You don't have to explain its points."

"I never went to a school, in those days only Brahmin went to schools, but we had to go out and work in the fields morning till night, from sowing to harvest time . . . and when Pongal came and we had cut the harvest, my father allowed me to go out and play with others at the tank, and so I don't know the Parangi language you speak, even little fellows in your country probably speak the Parangi language, but here only learned men and officers know it. We had a postman in our village who could speak to you boldly in your language, but his wife ran away with someone and he does not speak to anyone at all nowadays. Who would if a wife did what she did? Women must be watched; otherwise they will sell themselves and the home." And he laughed at his own quip.

The foreigner laughed heartily, took out another cigarette, and offered it to Muni, who now smoked with ease, deciding to stay on if the fellow was going to be so good as to keep up his cigarette supply. The American now stood up on the pedestal in the attitude of a demonstrative lecturer and said, running his finger along some of the carved decorations around the horse's neck, speaking slowly and uttering his words syllable by syllable, "I could give a sales talk for this better than anyone else. . . . This is a marvelous combination of yellow and indigo, though faded now. . . . How do you people of this country achieve these flaming colors?"

Muni, now assured that the subject was still the horse and not the dead body, said, "This is our guardian, it means death to our adversaries. At the end of Kali Yuga, this world and all other worlds will be destroyed, and the Redeemer will come in the shape of a horse called Kalki; this horse will come to life and gallop and trample down all bad men." As he spoke of bad men the figures of his shopman and his brother-in-law assumed concrete forms in his mind, and he reveled for a moment in the predicament of the fellow under the horse's hoof: served him right for trying to set fire to his home. . . .

While he was brooding on this pleasant vision, the foreigner utilized the pause to say, "I assure you that this will have the best home in the U.S.A. I'll push away the bookcase, you know I love books and am a member of five book clubs, and the choice and bonus volumes mount up to a pile really in our living room, as high as this horse itself. But they'll have to go. Ruth may disapprove, but I will convince her. The TV may have to be shifted, too. We can't have everything in the living room. Ruth will probably say what about when we have a party? I'm going to keep him right in the middle of the room. I don't see how that can interfere with the party—we'll stand around him and have our drinks."

Muni continued his description of the end of the world. "Our pundit discoursed at the temple once how the oceans are going to close over the earth in a huge wave and swallow us—this horse will grow bigger than the biggest wave and carry on its back only the good people and kick into the floods the evil ones—plenty of them about—" he said reflectively. "Do you know when it is going to happen?" he asked.

The foreigner now understood by the tone of the other that a question was being asked and said, "How am I transporting it? I can push the seat back and make room in the rear. That van can take in an elephant"—waving precisely at the back of the seat.

Muni was still hovering on visions of avatars and said again, "I never missed our pundit's discourses at the temple in those days during every bright half of the month, although he'd go on all night, and he told us that Vishnu is the highest god. Whenever evil men trouble us, he comes down to save us. He has come many times. The first time he incarnated as a great fish, and lifted the scriptures on his back when the flood and sea waves . . ."

"I am not a millionaire, but a modest businessman. My trade is coffee."

Amidst all this wilderness of obscure sound Muni caught the word "coffee" and said, "if you want to drink 'kapi,' drive further up, in the next town, they have Friday market and there they open 'kapi-otels'—I learn from passers-by. Don't think I wander about. I go nowhere and look for nothing." His thoughts went back to the avatars. "The first avatar was in the shape of a little fish in a bowl of water, but every hour it grew bigger and bigger and became in the end a huge whale which the seas could not contain, and on the back of the whale the holy books were supported, saved, and carried." Once he had launched on the first avatar, it was inevitable that he should go on to the next, a wild boar on whose tusk the earth was lifted when a vicious conqueror of the earth carried it off and hid it at the bottom of the sea. After describing this avatar Muni concluded, "God will always save us whenever we are troubled by evil beings. When we were young we staged at full moon the story of the avatars. That's how I know the stories; we played them all night until the sun rose, and sometimes the European collector would come to watch, bringing his own chair. I had a good voice and so they always taught me songs and gave me the women's roles. I was always Goddess Lakshmi, and they dressed me in a brocade sari, loaned from the Big House . . ."

The foreigner said, "I repeat I am not a millionaire. Ours is a modest business; after all, we can't afford to buy more than sixty minutes of TV time in a month, which works out to two minutes a day, that's all, although in the course of time we'll maybe sponsor a one-hour show regularly if our sales graph continues to go up . . ."

Muni was intoxicated by the memory of his theatrical days and was about to explain how he had painted his face and worn a wig and diamond earrings when the visitor, feeling that he had spent too much time already, said, "Tell me, will you accept a hundred rupees or not for the horse? I'd love to take the whiskered soldier also but no space for him this year. I'll have to cancel my air ticket and take a boat home, I suppose, Ruth can go by air if she likes, but I will go with the horse and keep him in my cabin all the way if necessary." And he smiled at the picture of himself voyaging across the seas hugging this horse. He added, "I will have to pad it with straw so that it doesn't break . . ."

"When we played *Ramayana,* they dressed me as Sita," added Muni. "A teacher came and taught us the songs for the drama and we gave him fifty rupees. He incarnated himself as Rama, and he alone could destroy Ravana, the demon with ten heads who shook all the worlds; do you know the story of *Ramayana?*"

"I have my station wagon as you see. I can push the seat back and take the horse in if you will just lend me a hand with it."

"Do you know *Mahabharata?* Krishna was the eighth avatar of Vishnu, incarnated to help the Five Brothers regain their kingdom. When Krishna was a baby he danced on the thousand-hooded giant serpent and trampled it to death; and then he suckled the breasts of the demoness and left them flat as a disc, though when she came to him her bosoms were large, like mounds of earth on the banks of a dug-up canal." He indicated two mounds with his hands.

The stranger was completely mystified by the gesture. For the first time he said, "I really wonder what you are saying because your answer is crucial. We have come to the point when we should be ready to talk business."

"When the tenth avatar comes, do you know where you and I will be?" asked the old man.

"Lend me a hand and I can lift off the horse from its pedestal after picking out the cement at the joints. We can do anything if we have a basis of understanding."

At this stage the mutual mystification was complete, and there was no need even to carry on a guessing game at the meaning of words. The old man chattered away in a spirit of balancing off the credits and debits of conversational exchange, and said in order to be on the credit sale, "Oh, honorable one, I hope God has blessed you with numerous progeny. I say this because you seem to be a good man, willing to stay beside an old man and talk to him, while all day I have none to talk to except when somebody stops by to ask for a piece of tobacco. But I seldom have it, tobacco is not what it used to be at one time, and I have given up chewing. I cannot afford it nowadays." Noting the other's interest in his speech, Muni felt encouraged to ask, "How many children have you?" with appropriate gestures with his hands.

Realizing that a question was being asked, the red man replied, "I said a hundred," which encouraged Muni to go into details' "How many of your children are boys and how many girls? Where are they? Is your daughter married? Is it difficult to find a son-in-law in your country also?"

In answer to these questions the red man dashed his hand into his pocket and brought forth his wallet in order to take immediate advantage of the bearish trend in the market. He flourished a hundred-rupee currency note and said, "Well, this is what I meant."

The old man now realized that some financial element was entering their talk. He peered closely at the currency note, the like of which he had never seen in his life; he knew the five and ten by their colors although always in other people's hands, while his own earning at any time was in coppers and nickels. What was this man flourishing the note for? Perhaps asking for change. He laughed to himself at the notion of anyone coming to him for changing a thousand- or ten-thousand-rupee note. He said with a grin, "Ask our village headman, who is also a moneylender; he can change even a lakh of rupees in gold sovereigns if you prefer it that way; he thinks nobody knows, but dig the floor of his puja room and your head will reel at the sight of the hoard. The man disguises himself in rags just to mislead the public. Talk to the headman yourself because he goes mad at the sight of me. Someone took away his pumpkins with the creeper and he, for some reason, thinks it was me and my goats . . . that's why I never let my goats be seen anywhere near the farms." His eyes traveled to his goats nosing about, attempting to wrest nutrition from minute greenery peeping out of rock and dry earth.

The foreigner followed his look and decided that it would be a sound policy to show an interest in the old man's pets. He went up casually to them and stroked their backs with every show of courteous attention. Now the truth dawned on the old man. His dream of a lifetime was about to be realized. He understood that the red man was actually making an offer for the goats. He had reared them up in the hope of selling them some day and, with the capital, opening a small shop on this very spot. Sitting here, watching towards the hills, he had often dreamt how he would put up a thatched roof here, spread a gunny sack out on the ground, and display on it fried nuts, colored sweets, and green coconut for the thirsty and famished wayfarers on the highway, which was sometimes very busy. The animals were not prize ones for a cattle show, but he had spent his occasional savings to provide them some fancy diet now and then, and they did not look too bad. While he was reflecting thus, the red man shook his hand and left on his palm one hundred rupees in tens now, suddenly realizing that this was what the old man was asking. "It is all for you or you may share it if you have a partner."

The old man pointed at the station wagon and asked, "Are you carrying them off in that?"

"Yes, of course," said the other, understanding the transportation part of it.

The old man said, "This will be their first ride in a motor car. Carry them off after I get out of sight, otherwise they will never follow you, but only me even if I am traveling on the path to Yama Loka." He laughed at his own joke, brought his palms together in a salute, turned around and went off, and was soon out of sight beyond a clump of thicket.

The red man looked at the goats grazing peacefully. Perched on the pedestal of the horse, as the westerly sun touched off the ancient faded colors of the statue with a fresh splendor, he ruminated, "He must be gone to fetch some help, I suppose!" and settled down to wait. When a truck came downhill, he stopped it and got the help of a couple of men to detach the horse from its pedestal and place it in his station wagon. He gave them five rupees each, and for a further payment they siphoned off gas from the truck, and helped him to start his engine.

Muni hurried homeward with the cash securely tucked away at his waist in his dhoti. He shut the street door and stole up softly to his wife as she squatted before the lit oven wondering if by a miracle food would drop from the sky. Muni displayed his fortune for the day. She snatched the notes from him, counted them by the glow of the fire, and cried, "One hundred rupees! How did you come by it? Have you been stealing?"

"I have sold our goats to a red-faced man. He was absolutely crazy to have them, gave me all this money and carried them off in his motor car!"

Hardly had these words left his lips when they heard bleating outside. She opened the door and saw the two goats at her door. "Here they are!" she said. "What's the meaning of all this?"

He muttered a great curse and seized one of the goats by its ears and shouted, "Where is that man? Don't you know you are his? Why did you come back?" The goat only wriggled in his grip. He asked the same question of the other, too. The goat shook itself off. His wife glared at him and declared, "If you have thieved, the police will come tonight and break your bones. Don't involve me, I will go away to my parents. . . ."

# Patricia Grace

Noted in particular for her sharply defined short stories about Maori life, Patricia Grace is one of the most prominent Maori writers in English. She was born in Wellington, New Zealand, in 1937, grew up there, attended convent schools, and graduated from Wellington Teachers' College. She taught in primary and secondary schools for several years in various parts of New Zealand. In addition to several volumes of short stories, she has published three novels and books for children. Grace has received numerous awards and grants from New Zealand agencies and universities, and has served as a Writing Fellow at Victoria University, Wellington.

In her first volume of short stories, *Wairiki* (1975), Grace contrasts traditional Maori life with the dominant white society through her accent on the Maori extended family, closeness to the land, and self-sufficiency. The selections in *Electric City and Other Stories* (1987) tend to be stronger, revealing more fully how the colonizers' values and customs have encroached on Maori practices. A sense of displacement and loss runs through these narratives, as the Maoris leave the land for the city, embrace foreign customs, face family disintegration, and turn away from their true consciousness.

Grace's first novel, *Mutuwhenua: The Moon Sleeps* (1978), tells of a mixed marriage between a Maori woman and a man of European descent, and focuses on how they must adjust to reconcile each other's cultural backgrounds. Her second novel, *Potiki* (1987), takes up the conflict that arises when white developers try to acquire ancestral land belonging to the Maoris. The company's representative Dolman (called "Dollarman" by the Maori community) pressures the villagers to sell their land, including the meeting house and cemetery, so that his company can turn the area into an amusement park. Grace's most complex work, *Potiki* makes rich use of Maori mythology and tradition. In 1991 *Selected Stories* appeared and in 1992 a third novel, *Cousins*.

Although focusing on the conflict between cultures, Grace's work avoids a confrontational tone. She views Maori culture in its social and spiritual context, and hopes for a reconciliation between that culture and the one imposed by the European settlers. A writer who handles complex themes that could be shrill, Grace manages indirectness and subtlety in large part through a subdued English prose that has been compared in its rhythm and nuance to Maori speech.

Loss of innocence lies at the heart of "The Hills," which is told by a young male Maori. It is a protest story about a postcolonial encounter all too common in settler countries such as New Zealand, Canada, Australia, and South Africa. The story achieves its effectiveness not through anger but through its faultless narrative voice and controlled unfolding of events.

# The Hills

I like it when I get to the top of the road and I look out and see the mist down over the hills. It's like a wrapped parcel and you know there's something good inside.

And I like being funny. When someone says something I like to have something funny to say back, because I like people to laugh, and I like laughing too. A funny man, that's me.

"Man" might not be quite the right word—but "boy" isn't right either. "Boy" means little kid, "boy" means dirty with a filthy mind. It means "smart-arse." A "boy" is a servant and a slave.

Well I've been grubby and smart all right but never a servant or a slave. Mum bossing me and getting me to mow grass and mop floors doesn't make me a slave or a servant. That's just something for me to moan about because I don't like doing my share. Anyway, I'm not a slave or a servant. I'm just myself. One day I'll call myself a man, and I won't just be an old "boy" like my father.

He's gone. I've got an uncle that I really like, Mum's brother, and he's funny too. Jokes don't stop him being a man.

Some teachers don't like my jokes and they think I'm a pain, but I get on all right with a few. Once when I was in the third form I drew a neat mustache on myself. I got told off and had to go and have a wash, and I got picked on by that teacher all the time after that.

When I was in the fifth I grew a real mustache and trimmed it up, and I had about six hairs of a beard as well. Well my form teacher got screwed up about it and ordered it all off. "The mower's broken down," I said, and I got into a heap of trouble. Anyhow I think someone must have stuck up for me somewhere along the line. I got moved to another class and nothing more was said about my whiskers.

They're not sharp hills, or pointy. They're bums and boobs, with cracks and splits. They're fat and folding. I like it when the wrapping comes off.

One day I wore a big long coat to school. It was an old coat but hadn't been worn much. It was just a coat that my old man had left behind, the type of coat that a lot of men wore then. Gaberdine, my mother said. She said I looked like a drongo.

The first thing the coat made me feel like doing was marching. I don't know why, because it wasn't like an army coat at all. It was big for me and down to my shins. I marched along the street and when I saw Wasi and Georgina I stopped and saluted and they fell in behind. Good on them. Off we marched for a while, until Wasi started talking about something interesting. We stopped acting up and strolled along the way we usually did.

Then when I got to school I thought I could be a flasher. So at each change of class I walked last into the room and went "Zoonk!" I didn't flash anything of course, except for gray shirt, gray jersey and a pair of baggy cords. Some laughed and some didn't. One of the teachers grinned and yelled out "Police!," and the whole class cracked up. I liked that. I had a good laugh too. Sometimes you just need a change from gray shirt, gray jersey, pair of baggy cords.

When the mist comes down to cover the hills I don't think gray. I think of parcels and colored wrapping, and clothes and tits and bums. Then I have a good laugh at myself and think that I'm only a boy after all. I don't mean a servant or a slave or a smart brat. I just mean "boy" in a different, youngish way.

Then something can happen to you that's too much for a boy. You can't be a boy any more afterwards. And when it's gone for good, and you're sure it's gone you can feel sorry. It wasn't you that did it or wanted it. It was something done to you.

You get used to the police, stopping, searching, hassling you around. They say something smart and you say something smart back. But you know you shouldn't get too smart. You have to hold back. You know they don't like you to be clever because it makes them scared. So you let them mouth off and you have to bite your tongue, which isn't easy for someone like me with jokes on his lip all the time. But after they've gone you can have a bit of a laugh—name please where are you going where've you been do you know so and so where do you live whose shoes you got on up against the car search search.

Mum doesn't like me drinking. She says there's nothing wrong with the old man, only drinking. He's all right she reckons, kind, tidy, just useless and a drunk, and she's glad he's gone. We get on better without him, she says. But anyway my mates and I enjoy drinking and parties, and I tell Mum she shouldn't worry about me.

When school finished last year, me, Wasi, Georgina, Steven, Louanna, and Georgie's brother and a few others went to the pub to celebrate. Louanna and Steve weren't coming back to school. I thought I might leave too but hadn't made up my mind. Georgie's brother was the only one old enough to be in the pub. We didn't have much money but Lou and Steve had enough to shout a couple of rounds. It was good. We were having a good time.

Then Steve went out to the toilet and didn't come back. Wasi went to have a look, and when he came back he said that the cops were outside talking to Steve.

Lou and Wasi and I went out to have a look, and on the way we were cracking jokes about Steve leaving school and going straight to Rock College. Ha, ha. There was a cop car outside with two cops in it but no Steven.

We looked round but couldn't see him, had another look in the toilets and he wasn't there, so we went back outside.

I went over to the car and looked in the window. I knew Steven wasn't in the car but I said, "Have you got our mate Steven in there?" Then I was slammed in the head with the door, jerked to my feet with my arm up behind, and hung over the bonnet of the car. They went down and through my pockets and one of them said, "Take him in."

"You can't do that. What for?" That was Louanna yelling at them.

"Get home, girlie," one of them said. He threw me in the car and started up.

Louanna started booting the car and shouting, "What about me, look what I'm doing."

"Shove off," one of them said, and away we went.

"What for?" I said. I'd got over the bang on the face by then, and just thought that it was the same game, only rougher than usual. They'd drop me off any minute as long as I didn't get too smart.

"Shut your black face," one of them said. "You'll know soon enough."

Well some are polite and some aren't, even though they are mostly all playing the same game.

"Abusive language," the other one said, "and resisting arrest."

I was drunk enough to say, "I thought it was for under-age drinking."

"That too," they said.

And then I was just drunk enough to say that anyway, they were the ones being abusive telling me to shut my black face.

"Why?" the same one said. "You've got a black face, haven't you? You're a black, aren't you?"

Well he had me there. If I pointed that I was brown it was like denying blackness, like saying you're halfway to white.

"It's not an offense, is it?" I asked.

"No offense me saying what you are then, is it?" the smart one said.

I could see they weren't going to let me out of the car. Sometimes the game can be quite amusing, something for a laugh later, but I was slacked off with their game this time.

At the station I was charged and asked a whole lot of questions. I just answered the questions and tried to point out that I wasn't drinking when they saw me, I wasn't in the pub when they saw me. I was sober by then. Anyhow the sooner I got out the better, I thought, so I decided I should keep my mouth shut.

The smart one went out for a minute or two then came back in. He held the door open and jerked his head, so I followed him through into another room where I was grabbed and searched again. Then suddenly I was thrown across a bench, my trousers were pulled down and I was searched up the behind.

That's what I meant when I said something can happen, and you can't be what you were after that. I said "searched" but I didn't know at the time that what they were doing was part of a search. I thought I was being raped. I didn't know then—or if I'd heard of it I'd forgotten—that people sometimes hid things up there.

Afterwards I remember feeling sick, and going out and my mates being out there waiting, and us all going to Georgie and her brother's place. I remember crying. They all thought I'd been beaten up and I didn't tell them any different.

They wanted to ring my mother but I said no. I didn't want her to know. Steve and Lou were staring at me. I don't know what I looked like.

"What do you want? What will we do?" Louanna asked.

"I want to have a bath," I said. "I want to go to sleep."

I stayed in the bath a long time, and when I got into bed I stayed awake a long time.

In the morning Georgie said, "We rang your Mum just to tell her you were staying the night." She waited a while. And then she said, "You sore?" so I told them what happened.

But I didn't tell Mum when I got home. I told her I'd been caught under age in the pub and had to go to court. She banged me on the arm and then she cried.

Later that day I went outside and walked up the street, and when I got to the top of the road I wouldn't look out at the hills. The hills could've been clear, or the mist could've been down or it could've been just lifting off. I turned and went back home. I remember wondering if I would ever look there again.

# Ben Okri

Ben Okri mixes the grotesque and the fantastic with actuality to depict life in politically unstable Nigeria, where he was born in the capital city of Lagos in 1959. Growing up in an educated family, he read widely from his father's library of Western classics and especially favored mythology—African, European, and classical. He has noted that this independent reading made him realize how all cultures shared strong similarities, an awareness that plays a significant role in his work. Okri was unable to get a place in a Nigerian university, so at eighteen he went to England where he attended the University of Essex. At age twenty-one, he published his first novel, *Flowers and Shadows* (1980), and a year later his second novel, *The Landscapes Within*. He now lives in London, but makes frequent trips back to Africa. Although he finds the stays at home stimulate his work, he said in an interview in *Contemporary Authors* "that living there could lead to an excess of reality that could kill the imagination, because when reality is more imaginative than the imagination, what job does the imagination have to do?"

Although living abroad, Okri draws from the African experience. On one level, the work could be described as a fictional account of Nigeria's tribulations, a postcolonial nation that has faced political and social turmoil for the past thirty or so years. In contrast to this circumscribed approach, however, the fiction may be considered as a more expansive version of postcolonial history by telling the story of any number of countries caught up in chaos after independence. That Okri often disregards reality in favor of the fantastic makes place inconsequential. Instead, imagination lies at the center of his work. What transpires within the characters as they face the forces of tyranny amid their everyday lives lends the narrative its conflict. Okri's work has often been compared to that of the South American magic realist Gabriel García Márquez, but this parallel makes it no less African. Okri said in the *Con-*

*temporary Authors* interview that he looks at the world "from the inside of the African world view. . . . It's a kind of realism, but a realism with many more dimensions."

In 1991 he received the Booker Prize for *The Famished Road*, which relates the story of an *abiku*, a spirit child named Azaro. A sequel to this novel, *Songs of Enchantment*, was published in 1993. His latest novel, *Dangerous Love* (1996), is a reworking of the earlier book *The Landscapes Within*; again devoted to portraying the upheaval of Nigerian life, the narrative also focuses on the role of the artist. A prolific writer, Okri has also published two books of short stories, *Incidents at the Shrine* (1986) and *Stars of the New Curfew* (1988), as well as a volume of poetry, *An African Elegy* (1992), and a number of uncollected poems and short stories.

Chapter 12 from *The Famished Road* recounts one evening in the life of Akaro, the first-person narrator who is no ordinary child but one who dwells as much in the spirit world as in the natural world—a condition that is accepted in the African system of belief. For Okri nothing is too repulsive to turn into musical prose, whether bloodied heads or shattered glass or the reek of sewers. On one hand, Akaro offers an accurate report of the brutality committed by the goons whom the political opposition has hired to wreck the photographer's studio, because he has dared to take pictures of their past savagery. Then the neighbors, also considered disloyal to the political party, are attacked. At the same time, Akaro views the violence in mythical terms. That the narrative's actuality and its unreality do not collapse on one another is remarkable.

# From *The Famished Road*

A few days later I came upon Madame Koto and the three men. They were standing near a tree. They were involved in a passionate argument. Madame Koto looked fat and haggard. She didn't have the white beads round her neck. When she saw me she stopped arguing. She made a movement towards me and a fear I couldn't understand made me run.

"Catch him!" she cried.

The three men started after me, but without much conviction. They soon gave up the chase. I didn't stop till I was near our compound.

I sat on the cement platform. Chickens roamed the street. Two dogs circled one another and when the afternoon seemed at its hottest one of the dogs succeeded in mounting the other. It was only when children gathered around them that it occurred to me that the two dogs were stuck. The dogs couldn't separate themselves and the children laughed. They threw stones at the dogs and the pain forced them to come unstuck and they ran, howling, in opposite directions.

I sat watching the listless motions of the world. The bushes simmered in the heat. Birds settled on our roof. Dust rose from numerous footsteps and became inseparable from the blinding heat. My sweat was dry. The flies came. The wind stirred and turned into little whirlwinds; dust and bits of paper and rubbish spiraled upwards. Children ran round the whirlwinds and only their piercing cries carried, along with the birdsong, over the somnolent air of the world.

Everything blazed in the bright liquid heat. Sounds had their edges softened. Beggars dragged themselves past. Roving cobblers and tailors came

around the compounds. Men who sold charms and slippers made in the desert
and bamboo artifacts and bright red mats also came round. Then a goatherd
led his goats down the street. The goats shat and left their smells in the air, unmoved by the wind. I got bored watching the ordinary events of the world.
Flashes from the photographer's glass cabinet called me. I went over and
looked at the pictures. They hadn't been changed. I went to the photographer's room. I knocked and no one answered. I knocked again and the door
was opened cautiously. The photographer's face appeared at my level. He was
crouching and he said, in a voice spiked with fear:

"Go away!"

"Why?"

"Because I don't want people to know I'm in."

"Why not?"

"Just go!"

"What if I don't go?"

"I will knock your head and you won't sleep for seven days."

I thought about it.

"Go!" he cried.

"What about the men?"

"What men?"

"The three men?"

"Have you seen them?" he asked in a different voice.

"Yes."

"Where?"

"They were talking with Madame Koto."

"That witch! What were they talking about?"

"I don't know."

"When did you see them?"

"Not long ago."

He shut the door quickly, locked it, and then opened it again.

"Go!" he said. "And if you see them again come and tell me immediately."

"What will you do?"

"Kill them or run."

He shut the door finally. I stood there for a while. The image of his frightened face lingered in my mind. Then I left his compound and went and sat on
our cement platform and kept a steady watch over all movements along the
street. The sun made the air and the earth shimmer and as I kept watch I perceived, in the crack of a moment, the recurrence of things unresolved—histories, dreams, a vanished world of great old spirits, wild jungles, tigers with
eyes of diamonds roaming the dense foliage. I saw beings who dragged
clanking chains behind them, bleeding from their necks. I saw men and
women without wings, sitting in rows, soaring through the empty air. And I

saw, flying towards me in widening dots from the center of the sun, birds and horses whose wings spanned half the sky and whose feathers had the candency of rubies. I shut my eyes; my being whirled; my head tumbled into a well; and I only opened my eyes again, to stop the sensation of falling, when I heard the shattering of glass. The noise woke up the afternoon.

Across the street three men were smashing the photographer's glass cabinet with clubs. Then they hurriedly removed the pictures on display. People of the street, awoken by the noise, came to their housefronts. The men, in a flash, had snatched the pictures and had gone into the photographer's compound. The people who came out looked up and down the street and saw nothing unusual. The action had moved to the photographer's room. I rushed across the street.

When I got to the room his door was wide open and the men weren't there. Neither was the photographer. His window was wide open, but it was too high for me to look out of; I ran to the backyard. I saw no one. But I noticed that the backyard led to other backyards. I followed a route past the bucket latrine alive with flies and maggots. The smell was so bad I almost fainted. Another path led to the swamp and marshes and the forest of massive iroko and obeche and mahogany trees. There were deep footprints in the soft soil behind the houses. I followed the footprints, sinking in the mud till the soft soil shaded into marshes. There was rubbish everywhere. Strange flowers and wild grass and evil-looking fungal growths were profuse over the marshes. Bushes were luxuriant in unexpected places. A wooden footbridge was being constructed to the other side. The footprints merged into many others on the soft soil. Some of them went into the marshes. I looked around, couldn't find anyone, and gave up the search. I went back home, washed the mud off my feet, and resumed watch over the street. Nothing unusual happened.

In the evening Mum returned and was surprised to see me.

"So you stayed home? Good boy. I thought by now you would have wandered to Egypt," she said.

She was back earlier than usual because she hadn't gone to the market that day. She had gone hawking. Her face was sun-shadowed.

That night I was listening in my childhood hour of darkness. I was listening to Mum's voice and Dad's songs, listening to stories of recurrence told down through generations of defiant mouths. In that hour laced with ancient moonlight, I was listening to tales of inscrutable heroes who turned into hard gods of chaos and thunder—when dread paid us a visit. The night brought the dread. It announced itself through piercing voices from the street, crying out in lamentation at the repetition of an old cycle of ascending powers.

We rushed out into the blue memory of a street crowded with shadows. Wild men were wreaking devastation on windows, wooden doors, and human bodies. We rushed out into the haze, into the smell of burning hair, into the acrid yellow smoke from the barber's shop, into the noises of corrupted ritual chants and caterwauling and machetes giving off electric sparks, crying for medicinal war.

The voices howling for vengeance stamped the street. The green bodies bristling with antimony sweated animal blood from their naked chests. They were a river of wild jaguars. Their deep earth songs overwhelmed the wind and came from everywhere, from the stars and the broken flowers. They chanted for destruction. Their whooping filled the night. Their sweating bodies flashed in the lamplight. Their murderous utterances washed over our forgetfulness.

It was impossible to tell who they were. Their chants erupted from crowds gathered outside compounds, from people who we thought were familiar, whose shadows changed beside us into a dreaded heat, whose screechings broke into weird bird-cries. Even amongst us people were answering the call of old bloodknots and secret tidal curfews.

In great numbers the thugs and ordinary familiar people alike poured over the road of our vulnerability, wounding the night with axes, rampaging our sleep, rousing the earth, attacking compounds, tearing down doors, destroying rooftops. In the wound of our cries we did not know who our enemies were. From the darkness figures with flaming faces attacked us, descended on us with sticks, stones, whips, and wires. It was some time before we realized that we were in the grip of an act of vengeance, a night reprisal, with the darkness as our antagonist. One by one the lamps were extinguished.

The darkness conquered our voices. A great cry, as of a terrifying commander ordering his troops, sprang into the air. There was the silence of deep rivers. Everything became still. It was as if the night had withdrawn its violence into itself. The wind breathed over the houses and howled gently through the trees. The whisperings of spirits flowed on the wind. The voices of water and slow footsteps floated towards us. It was as if the wind itself were preparing for a final onslaught.

Then the stillness was broken by the panic of the innocent. There was another cry, not of our antagonists, but of a woman who had seen something wonderful and monstrous. The cry started it all. The innocents turned and with one mind tried to flee back to their rooms. The panic crossed our paths, and collided our bodies in the solid darkness. All over, women wailed for their children. I moved amongst the shadows and ran out into the homeland of darkness, across the street. I thought I was headed for safety. I couldn't see where I was going. Then voices all around me began shouting:

"Kill the photographer!"

"Beat his photographs out of him!"

"Finish him off!"

"Blind him."

"Blind our enemies!"

"Destroy them!"

"Teach them a lesson."

"Show them power!"

"Break their fingers."

"Crack their heads!"

"Crush the photographer."

"And leave his body in the street."

"Let the birds eat him!"

"For mocking our party."

"Our power!"

"Our Leader!"

Their chants intensified. Their footsteps became voices, became one, and then multiplied, like fire. The dead rose under the weight of such footsteps, under such voices, under such intent. I banged my head against something solid, scraped my elbow against the jaws of the dead, clawed my way through jagged rust, and discovered I had reached the safety of the burnt van. I hid in the driver's seat and watched, in that night of blue memories, the drama of the Living that only the Dead can understand.

I couldn't see anything. But from across the street I heard, first in a whisper, then loudly under the spell of grief:

"Azaro! Azaro! Where are you?"

It was Mum.

"Azaro! Azaro!"

Then there was silence. In my childhood hour of darkness, I listened to Mum waiting for my response. But the night and the wind defeated us. From mouth to mouth, from one side of the street to the other, I listened with horror as the wind blew the name.

"AZARO! AZARO!"

The wind passed the name on. The name flowed to our part of the street and then towards Madame Koto's bar. The name surrounded me, wavering above the burnt van in a thousand quivering voices, as if God were calling me with the mouths of violent people.

Even the dead played with my name that night.

I listened in my childhood hour as the name eventually flowed towards the photographer's compound and echoed faintly down the passage before passing away into silence. I did not hear Mum's voice afterwards.

As I sat in the car, overcome with fear, I saw the dead rising. I saw them rising at the same moment that the second wave of havoc started with the chants of the antagonists. The dead joined the innocents, mingled with the thugs, merged with the night, and plundered the antagonists with the cries of the wounded. The dead uttered howls of mortal joy and they found the livid night a shrine glistening with fevers. They reveled in that night of mirrors, where bodies shimmered with blood and silver. The dead shook off their rust of living and seized up steel. Their lips quivered with the defiance of the innocents, with the manipulations of politicians and their interchangeable dreams, and with the insanity of thugs who don't even know for which parties they commit their atrocities.

It was a night without memory. It was a night replaying its corrosive recurrence on the road of our lives, on the road which was hungry for great transformations.

The dead, slowly awakening the sleep of the road, were acrobats of violence. They somersaulted with new political dreams amongst men, women, and children. I heard several voices, without fear or beyond it, uttering a new rallying call. Then I heard fighting. I heard the bright howls of resistance, footsteps running into the darkness, flashing steel on solid bodies, chests painted with antimony being beaten down, and women with mortars for pounding yam pounding on shadows. I heard strong men bewildered by the mutinous wind, deep voices crying out the names of hard gods. I realized that the antagonists were being repulsed. The people from the photographer's compound were in the vanguard. The dead were curiously on the side of the innocents. Voices I knew bravely cried:

"Fight them back!"

"Fight for your freedom!"

"Stone them!"

"They poisoned us with milk."

"And words."

"And promises"

"And they want to rule our country!"

"Our lives!"

"And now they attack us!"

"On our own street!"

"Fight them without fear!"

Machetes burst into flame. Chants were reversed in syllables. Spells were broken on the jagged teeth of night. The antagonists attempted a last desperate rally.

"Pour petrol on the house!"

"Burn it down!"

"Burn out the photographer!"

"Burn out Azaro!"

I trembled in the van. Someone hurled a firebrand at the photographer's compound. The dead caught it and ate up the flames. Someone threw another brand in the air. It landed on the van, and spluttered out on the bonnet. Something crawled up my legs. Smoke drifted in from a side window. The van was alive with spiders and worms. I started to get out of the van. I had got my head out of the other window when I heard a great deafening blast from the photographer's compound. After the blast there was a profound silence. The wind whistled over the noise.

And then the shadows, the footsteps, the green bodies, the fierce jaguars, the disaster-mongers, the fire-breathers, the rousers of the dead, and the rampagers of sleep, became fleeing footfalls scattered by the wind and the great detonation. The dark walls of their bodies disintegrated. The voices were not so menacing any more, but full of fear.

Another gunshot, not aimed in any particular direction, but cracking the air as though a star had exploded over our street, made the escaping stampede of antagonists more desperate. I could hear them falling over one another, running into the terrors of their own making, colliding into their own shadows, into the luminous bodies in the dark. I could hear them screaming the names of their mothers, calling for their wives, wondering who would take care of their children, as the innocents crashed their heads with bottles, as the men of the street rained an insistent beat of clubs on their retreat, and as they fell under the anger of lacerating claws and blunt-edged cutlasses.

New forces had joined the night, converted the night, made it the ally of the innocents. When the tidal force had retreated, the agitation quelled, when the antagonists had started their trucks and taken off at Madame Koto's end of the street—the hosts of the dead descended into the open bleeding mouth of the earth. I saw them from the van. I watched the world dissolving into a delirium of stories. The dead descended into the forgetfulness of our blue memories, with their indigo eyes and their silver glances.

The inhabitants of the street regained the night. Voices were reawakened. Lamps came on one after another. People tentatively gathered at compound-fronts. The only thing that was missing was the photographer to record the events of the night and make them real with his magic instrument. I got out of the van and fled across the street, into the despairing arms of Mother.

In the morning we learned about the wounded, about the woman slashed across the face with a knife, the man whose head was raw with the blunt vengeance of a machete, the people whose noses were cut open with broken bottles, those flagellated with wires, the man who had lost half an ear, the woman whose back was burnt. Against the innocents who were wounded, we heard of the death of an antagonist. We also heard one party claim that the atrocities had been committed by the other.

The energies that went into fighting back exhausted the street. We did not celebrate our resistance. We knew that the troubles were incomplete, that the reprisals had been deferred to another night, when we would have forgotten. The inhabitants of the street, frightened and angry, set up vigilantes. They were armed with knives, clubs, and dane guns. We waited for new forms of iron to fall on us. We waited for a long time. Nothing happened the way we expected. After two weeks, the vigilantes disbanded. We sank back into our usual lives.

The photographer vanished altogether. His room had been wrecked. His door was broken down, his clothes shredded, his mattress slashed, his available pictures and negatives destroyed, and some of his cameras broken up. His landlord, who had no sympathy for heroes, went around looking for him, demanding that his door be repaired.

We feared that the photographer had been murdered. His glass cabinet remained permanently shattered. It looked misbegotten. It became a small representation of what powerful forces in society can do if anyone speaks out against their corruptions. And because the photographer hadn't been there to record what had happened that night, nothing of the events appeared in the newspapers. It was as if the events were never real. They assumed the status of rumor.

At first the street suffered fear. Stall-owners stopped selling things in the evenings. The street seemed darker than usual at night. People became so cautious that no one opened their doors merely because they were knocked on. Those who usually went out drinking, and who returned late, took to getting drunk in their rooms, and singing into the nights.

After a while, when nothing happened, when no reprisals fell on us, it seemed that nothing significant had happened. Some of us began to distrust our memories. We began to think that we had collectively dreamt up the fevers of that night. It wouldn't be the first or the last time. Meanwhile, the river of wild jaguars flowed below the surface of our hungry roads.

On many of those nights, in my childhood hours, Mum told me stories of aquamarine beginnings. Under the white eye of the moon, under the indigo sky, in the golden lights of survival in our little room, I listened to the wisdom of the old songs which Dad rendered in his cracked fighting voice. Mesmerized by the cobalt shadows, the paradoxical ultramarine air, and the silver glances of the dead, I listened to the hard images of joy. I listened also to the songs of work and harvest and the secrets of heroes.

Outside, the wind of recurrence blew gently over the earth.

# Bapsi Sidhwa

The inventor of English-language fiction in Pakistan, Bapsi Sidhwa was born in Lahore, India, 11 August 1938, before the city became part of Pakistan in 1947. The child of a wealthy Parsi family, Sidhwa contracted polio at age two and was tutored privately. A voracious reader, especially of British literature, Sidhwa early on wanted to be a writer. Instead she entered an arranged marriage when she was nineteen, and bore three children. Living in Bombay as an upper-class wife and mother, she did start to write. Following seven years of rejections from British and American publishers, Sidhwa's second novel, *The Crow-Eaters*, was finally published in 1978. The first novel she wrote, *The Bride*, appeared in 1983. Divorced and remarried, Sidhwa moved to the United States in the early 1980s, settled in Houston, Texas, and took U.S. citizenship in 1992. In 1994 she received the Lila Wallace-Reader's Digest Fund Award for her fiction.

To say that Sidhwa invented the English novel in Pakistan is no exaggeration. When she began writing, the newly formed country—whose official language is Urdu—had no established tradition in English-language fiction, and probably had little desire for one. Although warned by publishers that Western readers would reject fiction about such a remote and foreign place, Sidhwa proved that a perceptive writer could succeed. That her work has gained wide recognition stems in large part from its gentle earthiness, the shrewd characterization, the comic elements, and its humane record of an encounter with colonialism and its aftermath.

*The Bride* grew from a story Sidhwa heard on a family vacation in Pakistan's Himalayas. A young woman from the city had entered an arranged marriage with a tribal man; unable to withstand the harshness dealt to women, she escaped, then was killed by her husband and his relatives. Through retelling the girl's story, Sidhwa makes a strong statement about the way women are treated on the subcontinent. This stand influences much of her fiction and has led some critics to stress its feminist stance. Taking up a far different subject, Sidhwa portrays in *The Crow-Eaters* the Parsi community in Lahore before independence through a sometimes irreverent but consistently gentle account of the Parsis' customs, religious beliefs, and sensibility. Sidhwa in her third novel, *Ice-Candy-Man* (1988; published in the United States as *Cracking India*, 1991), thrusts the Lahore Parsis into the violence that marked independence in 1947 when India was "cracked" to create Pakistan. In *An American Brat* (1993) Sidhwa documents the experience of immigration by following Feroza, a Parsi girl from Lahore, through her uncertain beginnings in the United States and her eventual adjustment. Although rebelling against the strictures set for Pakistani women, Feroza confirms that she can retain her roots and at the same time embrace the newly discovered country.

"Ranna's Story" stands by itself in *Cracking India*, which for the most part chronicles the violence of Partition from the viewpoint of a seven-year-old female narrator—significantly the age of Sidhwa herself when she witnessed the events in Lahore, one of the centers of violence. When India gained independence from Great Britain in 1947, the leaders decided to divide the subcontinent into two nations: India—a home for the Hindus; Pakistan—a home for the Muslims. This idealistic but impractical political act demanded the uprooting of millions of people and set into motion a bloody struggle for land and possessions. Hindus and Sikhs murdered Muslims, and in turn Muslims murdered them. The number of deaths has never been determined but has been estimated at nearly a million. In this dramatic episode of survival, the Muslim peasant boy Ranna finds himself the victim of a bitter postcolonial encounter.

# Ranna's Story
## from *Cracking India*

Late that afternoon the clamor of the monsoon downpour suddenly ceased. Chidda raised her hands from the dough she was kneading and, squatting before the brass tray, turned to her mother-in-law. Sitting by his grandmother, Ranna sensed their tension as the old woman stopped chaffing the wheat. She slowly pushed back her age-brittle hair and, holding her knobby fingers immobile, grew absolutely still.

Chidda stood in their narrow doorway, her eyes nervously scouring the courtyard. Ranna clung to her shalwar, peering out. His cousins, almost naked in their soaking rags, were shouting and splashing in the slush in their courtyard. "Shut up. Oye!" Chidda shouted in a voice that rushed so violently from her strong chest that the children quieted at once and leaned and slid uneasily against the warm black hides of the buffaloes tethered to the rough stumps. The clouds had broken and the sun shot beams that lit up the freshly bathed courtyard.

The other members of the household, Ranna's older brothers, his uncles, aunts and cousins, were quietly filing into the courtyard. When she saw Khatija and Parveen, Chidda strode to her daughters and pressed them fiercely to her body. The village was so quiet it could be the middle of the night, and from the distance, buffeting the heavy, moisture-laden air, came the wails and the hoarse voices of men shouting.

Already their neighbors' turbans skimmed the tall mud ramparts of their courtyard, their bare feet squelching on the path the rain had turned into a muddy channel.

I can imagine the old mullah, combing his faded beard with trembling fingers as he watches the villagers converge on the mosque with its uneven green dome. It is perched on an incline; and seen from there the fields, flooded with rain, are the same muddy color as the huts. The mullah drags his cot forward as the villagers, touching their foreheads and greeting him somberly, fill the prayer ground. The *chaudhry* joins the mullah on his charpoy. The villagers sit on their haunches in uneven rows lifting their confused and frightened faces. There is a murmur of voices. Conjectures. First the name of one village and then of another. The Sikhs have attacked Kot-Rahim. No, it sounds closer . . . It must be Makipura.

The *chaudhry* raises his heavy voice slightly: "Dost Mohammad and his party will be here soon . . . We'll know soon enough what's going on."

At his reassuring presence the murmuring subsides and the villagers nervously settle down to wait. Some women draw their veils across their faces and, shading their bosoms, impatiently shove their nipples into the mouths of whimpering babies. Grandmothers, mothers and aunts rock restive children on their laps and thump their foreheads to put them to sleep. The children, conditioned to the numbing jolts, grow groggy and their eyes become unfocused. They fall asleep almost at once.

Half an hour later the scouting party, drenched and muddy, the lower halves of their faces wrapped in the ends of their turbans, pick their way through the squatting villagers to the *chaudhry*.

Removing his wet puggaree and wiping his head with a cloth the mullah hands him, Dost Mohammad turns on his haunches to face the villagers. His skin is gray, as if the rain has bleached the color. Casting a shade across his eyes with a hand that trembles slightly, speaking in a matter-of-fact voice that disguises his ache and fear, he tells the villagers that the Sikhs have attacked at least five villages around Dehra Misri, to their east. Their numbers have swollen enormously. They are like swarms of locusts, moving in marauding bands of thirty and forty thousand. They are killing all Muslims. Setting fires, looting, parading the Muslim women naked through the streets—raping and mutilating them in the center of villages and in mosques. The Bias, flooded by melting snow and the monsoon, is carrying hundreds of corpses. There is an intolerable stench where the bodies, caught in the bends, have piled up.

"What are the police doing?" a man shouts. He is Dost Mohammad's cousin. One way or another the villagers are related.

"The Muslims in the force have been disarmed at the orders of a Hindu Sub-Inspector; the dog's penis!" says Dost Mohammad, speaking in the same flat monotone. "The Sikh and Hindu police have joined the mobs."

The villagers appear visibly to shrink—as if the loss of hope is a physical thing. A woman with a child on her lap slaps her forehead and begins to wail: *"Hai! Hai!"* The other women join her: *"Hai! Hai!"* Older women, beating their breasts like hollow drums, cry, "Never mind us . . . save the young girls! The children! *Hai! Hai!*"

Ranna's two-toothed old grandmother, her frail voice quavering bitterly, shrieks: "We should have gone to Pakistan!"

It was hard to believe that the decision to stay was taken only a month ago. Embedded in the heart of the Punjab, they had felt secure, inviolate. And to uproot themselves from the soil of their ancestors had seemed to them akin to tearing themselves, like ancient trees, from the earth.

And the messages filtering from the outside had been reassuring. Gandhi, Nehru, Jinnah, Tara Singh were telling the peasants to remain where they were. The minorities would be a sacred trust . . . The communal trouble was being caused by a few mischief-makers and would soon subside—and then there were their brothers, the Sikhs of Dera Tek Singh, who would protect them.

But how many Muslims can the Sikh villagers befriend? The mobs, determined to drive the Muslims out, are prepared for the carnage. Their ranks swollen by thousands of refugees recounting fresh tales of horror they roll towards Pir Pindo like the heedless swells of an ocean.

The *chaudhry* raises his voice: "How many guns do we have now?"

The women grow quiet.

"Seven or eight," a man replies from the front.

There is a disappointed silence. They had expected to procure more guns, but every village is holding on to its meager stock of weapons.

"We have our axes, knives, scythes and staves!" a man calls from the back. "Let those bastards come. We're ready!"

"Yes . . . we're as ready as we'll ever be," the *chaudhry* says, stroking his thick mustache. "You all know what to do . . ."

They have been over the plan often enough recently. The women and girls will gather at the *chaudhry's*. Rather than face the brutality of the mob they will pour kerosene around the house and burn themselves. The canisters of kerosene are already stored in the barn at the rear of the *chaudhry's* sprawling mud house. The young men will engage the Sikhs at the mosque, and at other strategic locations, for as long as they can and give the women a chance to start the fire.

A few men from each family were to shepherd the younger boys and lock themselves into secluded back rooms, hoping to escape detection. They were peaceable peasants, not skilled in such matters, and their plans were sketchy and optimistic. Comforted by each other's presence, reluctant to disperse, the villagers remained in the prayer yard as dusk gathered about them. The distant wailing and shouting had ceased. Later that night it rained again, and comforted by its seasonal splatter the tired villagers curled up on their mats and slept.

The attack came at dawn. The watch from the mosque's single minaret hurtled down the winding steps to spread the alarm. The panicked women ran to and fro screaming and snatching up their babies, and the men barely had time to get to their posts. In fifteen minutes the village was swamped by the Sikhs—tall men with streaming hair and thick biceps and thighs, waving full-sized swords and sten-guns, roaring, *"Bola so Nihal! Sat Siri Akal!"*

They mowed down the villagers in the mosque with the sten-guns. Shouting *"Allah-o-Akbar!"* The peasants died of sword and spear wounds in the slushy lanes and courtyards, the screams of women from the *chaudhry's* house ringing in their ears, wondering why the house was not burning.

Ranna, abandoned by his mother and sisters halfway to the *chaudhry's* house, ran howling into the courtyard. Chidda had spanked his head and pushed him away, shrieking, "Go to your father! Stay with the men!"

Ranna ran through their house to the room the boys had been instructed to gather in. Some of his cousins and uncles were already there. More men stumbled into the dark windowless room—then his two older brothers. There must be at least thirty of them in the small room. It was stifling. He heard his father's voice and fought his way towards him. Dost Mohammad shouted harshly: "Shut up! They'll kill you if you make a noise."

The yelling in the room subsided. Dost Mohammad picked up his son, and Ranna saw his uncle slip out into the gray light and shut the door, plunging the room into darkness. Someone bolted the door from inside, and they heard the heavy thud of cotton bales stacked against the door to disguise the entrance. With luck they would remain undetected and safe.

The shouting and screaming from outside appeared to come in waves: receding and approaching. From all directions. Sometimes Ranna could make out the words and even whole sentences. He heard a woman cry, "Do anything you want with me, but don't torment me . . . For God's sake, don't torture me!" And then an intolerable screaming. "Oh God!" a man whispered on a sobbing intake of breath. "Oh God, she is the mullah's daughter!" The men covered their ears—and the boys' ears—sobbing unaffectedly like little children.

A teenager, his cracked voice resounding like the honk of geese, started wailing: "I don't want to die . . . I don't want to die!" Catching his fear, Ranna and the other children set to whimpering: "I don't want to die . . . Abba, I don't want to die!"

"Hush," said Dost Mohammad gruffly. "Stop whining like girls!" Then, with words that must have bubbled up from a deep source of strength and compassion, with infinite gentleness, he said, "What's there to be afraid of? Are you afraid to die? It won't hurt any more than the sting of a bee." His voice, unseasonably lighthearted, carried a tenderness that soothed and calmed them. Ranna fell asleep in his father's arms.

Someone was banging on the door, shouting: "Open up! Open up!"

Ranna awoke with a start. Why was he on the floor?

Why were there so many people about in the dark? He felt the stir of men getting to their feet. The air in the room was oppressive: hot and humid and stinking of sweat. Suddenly Ranna remembered where he was and the darkness became charged with terror.

"We know you're in there. Come on, open up!" The noise of the banging was deafening in the pitch-black room, drowning the other children's alarmed cries.

"Allah! Allah! Allah!" an old man moaned nonstop.

"Who's there?" Dost Mohammad called; and putting Ranna down, stumbling over the small bodies, made his way to the door. Ranna, terrified, groping blindly in the dark, tried to follow.

"We're Sikhs!"

There was a pause in which Ranna's throat dried up. The old man stopped saying "Allah." And in the deathly stillness, his voice echoing from his proximity to the door Dost Mohammad said, "Kill us . . . Kill us all . . . but spare the children."

"Open at once!"

"I beg you in the name of all you hold sacred, don't kill the little ones," Ranna heard his father plead. "Make them Sikhs . . . Let them live . . . they are so little . . ."

Suddenly the noon light smote their eyes. Dost Mohammad stepped out and walked three paces. There was a sunlit sweep of curved steel. His head was shorn clear off his neck. Turning once in the air, eyes wide open, it tumbled in the dust. His hands jerked up slashing the air above the bleeding stump of his neck.

Ranna saw his uncles beheaded. His older brothers, his cousins. The Sikhs were among them like hairy vengeful demons, wielding bloodied swords, dragging them out as a sprinkling of Hindus, darting about at the fringes, their faces vaguely familiar, pointed out and identified the Mussulmans by name. He felt a blow cleave the back of his head and the warm flow of blood. Ranna fell just inside the door on a tangled pile of unrecognizable bodies. Someone fell on him, drenching him in blood.

Every time his eyes open the world appears to them to be floating in blood. From the direction of the mosque come the intolerable shrieks and wails of women. It seems to him that a woman is sobbing just outside their courtyard: great anguished sobs—and at intervals she screams: "You'll kill me! *Hai Allah* . . . Y'all will kill me!"

Ranna wants to tell her, "Don't be afraid to die . . . It will hurt less than the sting of a bee." But he is hurting so much . . . Why isn't he dead? Where are the bees? Once he thought he saw his eleven-year-old sister, Khatija, run stark naked into their courtyard: her long hair disheveled, her boyish body bruised, her lips cut and swollen and a bloody scab where her front teeth were missing.

Later in the evening he awoke to silence. At once he became fully conscious. He wiggled backwards over the bodies and slipping free of the weight on top of him felt himself sink knee-deep into a viscous fluid. The bodies blocking the entrance had turned the room into a pool of blood.

Keeping to the shadows cast by the mud walls, stepping over the mangled bodies of people he knew, Ranna made his way to the *chaudhry's* house. It was dark inside. There was a nauseating stench of kerosene mixed with the smell of spilt curry. He let his eyes get accustomed to the dimness. Carefully he explored the rooms cluttered with smashed clay pots, broken charpoys, spilled grain and chapatties. He had not realized how hungry he was until he saw the pile of stale bread. He crammed the chapatties into his mouth.

His heart gave a lurch. A woman was sleeping on a charpoy. He reached for her and his hand grasped her clammy inert flesh. He realized with a shock she was dead. He walked round the cot to examine her face. It was the *chaudhry's* older wife. He discovered three more bodies. In the dim light he turned them over and peered into their faces searching for his mother.

When he emerged from the house it was getting dark. Moving warily, avoiding contact with the bodies he kept stumbling upon, he went to the mosque.

For the first time he heard voices. The whispers of women comforting each other—of women softly weeping. His heart pounding in his chest he crept to one side of the arching mosque entrance. He heard a man groan, then a series of animal-like grunts.

He froze near the body of the mullah. How soon he had become accustomed to thinking of people he had known all his life as bodies. He felt on such easy terms with death. The old mullah's face was serene in death, his beard pale against the brick plinth. The figures in the covered portion at the rear of the mosque were a dark blur. He was sure he had heard Chidda's voice. He began inching forward, prepared to dash across the yard to where the women were, when a man yawned and sighed, "*Wah Guru!*"

"*Wah Guru! Wah Guru!*" responded three or four male voices, sounding drowsy and replete. Ranna realized that the men in the mosque were Sikhs. A wave of rage and loathing swept his small body. He knew it was wrong of the Sikhs to be in the mosque with the village women. He could not explain why: except that he still slept in his parents' room.

"Stop whimpering, you bitch, or I'll bugger you again!" a man said irritably.

Other men laughed. There was much movement. Stifled exclamations and moans. A woman screamed, and swore in Punjabi. There was a loud cracking noise and the rattle of breath from the lungs. Then a moment of horrible stillness.

Ranna fled into the moonless night. Skidding on the slick wet clay, stumbling into the irrigation ditches demarcating the fields, he ran in the direction of his Uncle Iqbal and his Noni *chachi's* village. He didn't stop until deep inside a thicket of sugarcane he stumbled on a slightly elevated slab of drier ground. The clay felt soft and caressing against his exhausted body. It was a safe place to rest. The moment Ranna felt secure his head hurt and he fainted.

Ranna lay unconscious in the cane field all morning. Intermittent showers washed much of the blood and dust off his limbs. Around noon two men walked into the cane field, and at the first rustle of the dried leaves Ranna became fully conscious.

Sliding on his butt to the lower ground, crouching amidst the pricking tangle of stalks and dried leaves, Ranna followed the passage of the men with his ears. They trampled through the field, selecting and cutting the sugarcane with their kirpans, talking in Punjabi. Ranna picked up an expression that warned him that they were Sikhs. Half-buried in the slush he scarcely breathed as one of the men came so close to him that he saw the blue check on his lungi and the flash of a white singlet. There was a crackling rustle as the man squatted to defecate.

Half an hour later when the men left, Ranna moved cautiously towards the edge of the field. A cluster of about sixty Sikhs in lungis and singlets, their carelessly knotted hair snaking down their backs, stood talking in a fallow field to his right. At some distance, in another field of young green shoots, Sikhs and Hindus were gathered in a much larger bunch. Ranna sensed their presence behind him in the fields he couldn't see. There must be thousands of them, he thought. Shifting to a safe spot he searched the distance for the green dome of his village mosque. He had traveled too far to spot it. But he knew where his village lay and guessed from the coiling smoke that his village was on fire.

Much later, when it was time for the evening meal, the fields cleared. He could not make out a single human form for miles. As he ran again towards his aunt's village the red sun, as if engorged with blood, sank into the horizon.

All night he moved, scuttling along the mounds of earth protecting the waterways, running in shallow channels, burrowing like a small animal through the standing crop. When he stopped to catch his breath, he saw the glow from burning villages measuring the night distances out for him.

Ranna arrived at his aunt's village just after dawn. He watched it from afar, confused by the activity taking place around five or six huge lorries parked in the rutted lanes. Soldiers, holding guns with bayonets sticking out of them, were directing the villagers. The villagers were shouting and running to and fro, carrying on their heads charpoys heaped with their belongings. Some were herding their calves and goats towards the trucks. Others were dumping their household effects in the middle of the lanes in their scramble to climb into the lorries.

There were no Sikhs about. The village was not under attack. Perhaps the army trucks were there to evacuate the villagers and take them to Pakistan.

Ranna hurtled down the lanes, weaving through the burdened and distraught villagers and straying cattle, into his aunt's hut. He saw her right away, heaping her pots and pans on a cot. A fat roll of winter bedding tied with a string lay to one side. He screamed: "Noni *chachi*! It's me!"

*"For a minute I thought: Who is this filthy little beggar?"* Noni *chachi* says, when she relates her part in the story. *"I said: Ranna? Ranna? Is that you? What're you doing here!"*

The moment he caught the light of recognition and concern in her eyes, the pain in his head exploded and he crumpled at her feet unconscious.

*"It is funny,"* Ranna says. *"As long as I had to look out for myself I was all right. As soon as I felt safe I fainted."*

Her hands trembling, his *chachi* washed the wound on his head with a wet rag. Clots of congealed blood came away and floated in the pan in which she rinsed the cloth. *"I did not dare remove the thick scabs that had formed over the wound,"* she says. *"I thought I'd see his brain!"* The slashing blade had scalped him from the rise in the back of his head to the top, exposing a wound the size of a large bald patch on a man. She wondered how he had lived; found his way to their village. She was sure he would die in a few moments. Ranna's *chacha* Iqbal, and other members of the house gathered about him. An old woman, the village *dai*, checked his pulse and his breath and, covering him with a white cloth, said: "Let him die in peace!"

A terrifying roar, like the warning of an alarm, throbs in his ears. He sits up on the charpoy, taking in the disorder in the hastily abandoned room. The other cot, heaped with his aunt's belongings, lies where it was. He can see the bedding roll abandoned in the courtyard. Clay dishes, mugs, chipped crockery, and hand fans lie on the floor with scattered bits of clothing. Where are his aunt and uncle? Why is he alone? And in the fearsome noise drawing nearer, he recognizes the rhythm of the Sikh and Hindu chants.

Ranna leapt from the cot and ran through the lanes of the deserted village. Except for the animals lowing and bleating and wandering ownerless on the slushy paths there was no one about. Why hadn't they taken him with them?

His heart thumping, Ranna climbed to the top of the mosque minaret. He saw the mob of Sikhs and Hindus in the fields scuttling forward from the horizon like giant ants. Roaring, waving swords, partly obscured by the veil of dust raised by their trampling feet, they approached the village.

Ranna flew down the steep steps. He ran in and out of the empty houses looking for a place to hide. The mob sounded close. He could hear the thud of their feet, make out the words of their chants. Ranna slipped through the door into a barn. It was almost entirely filled with straw. He dived into it.

He heard the Sikhs' triumphant war cries as they swarmed into the village. He heard the savage banging and kicking open of doors: and the quick confused exchange of shouts as the men realized that the village was empty.

They searched all the houses, moving systematically, looting whatever they could lay their hands on.

Ranna held his breath as the door to the barn opened.

"Oye! D'you think the Musslas are hiding here?" a coarse voice asked.

"We'll find out," another voice said.

Ranna crouched in the hay. The men were climbing all over the straw, slashing it with long sweeps of their swords and piercing it with their spears.

Ranna almost cried out when he felt the first sharp prick. He felt steel tear into his flesh. As if recalling a dream, he heard an old woman say: He's lost too much blood. Let him die in peace.

Ranna did not lose consciousness again until the last man left the barn.

And while the old city in Lahore, crammed behind its dilapidated Mogul gates, burned, thirty miles away Amritsar also burned. No one noticed Ranna as he wandered in the burning city. No one cared. There were too many ugly and abandoned children like him scavenging in the looted houses and the rubble of burnt-out buildings.

His rags clinging to his wounds, straw sticking in his scalped skull, Ranna wandered through the lanes stealing chapatties and grain from houses strewn with dead bodies, rifling the corpses for anything he could use. He ate anything. Raw potatoes, uncooked grains, wheat flour, rotting peels and vegetables.

No one minded the semi-naked specter as he looked in doors with his knowing, wide-set peasant eyes as men copulated with wailing children—old and young women. He saw a naked woman, her light Kashmiri skin bruised with purple splotches and cuts, hanging head down from a ceiling fan. And looked on with a child's boundless acceptance and curiosity as jeering men set her long hair on fire. He saw babies, snatched from their mothers, smashed against walls and their howling mothers brutally raped and killed.

Carefully steering away from the murderous Sikh mobs he arrived at the station on the outskirts of the city. It was cordoned off by barbed wire, and beyond the wire he recognized a huddle of Muslim refugees surrounded by Sikh and Hindu police. He stood before the barbed wire screaming, *"Amma! Amma!* Noni *chachi!* Noni *chachi!"*

A Sikh sepoy, his hair tied neatly in a khaki turban, ambled up to the other side of the wire. "Oye! What're you making such a racket for? Scram!" he said, raising his hand in a threatening gesture.

Ranna stayed his ground. He could not bear to look at the Sikh. His stomach muscles felt like choked drains. But he stayed his ground: *"I was trembling from head to toe,"* he says.

*"O me-kiya!* I say!" the sepoy shouted to his cronies standing by an opening in the wire. "This little motherfucker thinks his mother and aunt are in that group of Musslas."

"Send him here," someone shouted.

Ranna ran up to the men.

"Don't you know? Your mother married me yesterday," said a fat-faced, fat-bellied Hindu, his hairy legs bulging beneath the shorts of his uniform. "And your *chachi* married Makhan Singh," he said, indicating a tall young sepoy with a shake of his head.

"Let the poor bastard be," Makhan Singh said. "Go on: run along." Taking Ranna by his shoulder he gave him a shove.

The refugees in front watched the small figure hurtle towards them across the gravelly clearing. A middle-aged woman without a veil, her hair disheveled, moved forward holding out her arms.

The moment Ranna was close enough to see the compassion in her stranger's eyes, he fainted.

With the other Muslim refugees from Amritsar, Ranna was herded into a refugee camp at Badami Baug. He stayed in the camp, which is quite close to our Fire Temple, for two months, queuing for the doled-out chapatties, befriended by improvident refugees, until chance—if the random queries of five million refugees seeking their kin in the chaos of mammoth camps all over West Punjab can be called anything but chance—reunited him with his Noni *chachi* and Iqbal *chacha*.

# V. S. Naipaul

Although considered one of the finest and most versatile postcolonial writers, V. S. Naipaul has also met with severe criticism by those who condemn as biased his fictional and nonfictional reportage on the former colonies. He is a transplanted colonial himself—an ambiguity that haunts his writing. Of East Indian descent, he was born on 17 August 1932 in Trinidad. His grandfather had come to the West Indies as an indentured laborer, one of the thousands who left India to replace Africans in the cane fields when slavery was abolished. Most of the Indians stayed on and attempted to re-create their society in the new land; Naipaul, though, grew up in a family that was shedding Indian tradition. Encouraged by his father, a journalist and aspiring fiction writer, Naipaul read extensively in English literature. After completing preparatory school in Trinidad, he moved on to University College, Oxford, in 1950 to earn a degree in English. Except for visits to the West Indies and extended travels abroad, Naipaul has continued to live in England. The author of eleven novels, a short-story collection, and several volumes of history, travel, and essays, Naipaul has received numerous honors for his work, including the 1971 Booker Prize for *In a Free State* and a knighthood in 1990.

His collection of short stories, *Miguel Street* (1959), and early novels, *The Mystic Masseur* (1957) and *The Suffrage of Elvira* (1958), treat Trinidadian society and politics with a satiric edge that is blunted by the comic elements and sheer delight in the characters and situations. These qualities were perfected in *A House for Mr. Biswas* (1961), which loosely traces his father's experiences and presents a fondly recalled way of life among the East Indian descendants in Trinidad. Two other Trinidadian novels, *The Mimic Men* (1967) and *Guerillas* (1975), treat postcolonial politics and its practitioners in greater depth and with increased disillusionment. Perhaps his most penetrating examination of the postcolonial condition prevails in *A Bend in the River*

(1979). Set in an unnamed African country with its central characters displaced East Indians who have grown up in Africa, the novel seems prophetic twenty or so years later. At the same time, the book has been called patronizing and even racist.

In *The Middle Passage* (1962) Naipaul questions the right way to portray the outcome of colonialism through writing and asks: "How can the history of this futility be written?" Through his fiction and travel books, Naipaul has attempted to answer the question—to the satisfaction of some readers and to the disapproval of others. The travel books, in particular, have generated controversy. His observation of Islam in *Among the Believers* (1982) and *Beyond Belief: Islamic Excursions Among the Converted Peoples* (1998) has intrigued Western readers and infuriated many Muslims. Similarly, the travel books about India, *An Area of Darkness* (1964) and *India: A Wounded Civilization* (1977), were not generally appreciated by Indians, who forgave the author to some extent when the more positive account appeared in 1990, *India, A Million Mutinies Now*.

"Prelude: An Inheritance" is the first chapter of Naipaul's *A Way in the World* (1994). Not a narrative in the traditional sense, the novel's core is the author's personal experience as a postcolonial, Trinidadian of East Indian descent who moves to England, the former seat of empire. Once there he does not escape colonialism but spends his life trying to grasp its history and to comprehend what happened in its wake, then writing about his discoveries. *A Way in the World* links personal observations with chapters on the progress of Spanish and British imperialists in the Caribbean and other figures. The lover of beauty, the insignificant Leonard Side, who appears in this selection, represents those who were absorbed into the empire and who through their encounter with postcolonialism are left with only "a fragment" of their background, only "a fragment of the truth."

# Prelude: An Inheritance
from *A Way in the World*

I left home more than forty years ago. I was eighteen. When I went back, after six years—and slowly: a two-week journey by steamer—everything was strange and not strange: the suddenness of night, the very big leaves of some trees, the shrunken streets, the corrugated-iron roofs. You could walk down a street and hear the American advertising jingles coming out of the Rediffusion sets in all the little open houses. Six years before I had known the jingles the Rediffusion sets played; but these jingles were all new to me and were like somebody else's folksong now.

All the people on the streets were darker than I remembered: Africans, Indians, white, Portuguese, mixed Chinese. In their houses, though, people didn't look so dark. I suppose that was because on the streets I was more of a looker, half a tourist, and when I went to a house it was to be with people I had known years before. So I saw them more easily.

To go back home was to play with impressions in this way, the way I played with the first pair of glasses I had, looking at a world now sharp and small and not quite real, now standard size and real but blurred; the way I played with my first pair of dark glasses, moving between dazzle and coolness; or the way, on this first return, when I was introduced to air-conditioning, I liked to move from the coolness of an air-conditioned room to the warmth outside, and back again. I was in time, over the years, and over many returns, to get used to what was new; but that shifting about of reality never really stopped. I could call it up whenever I wished. Up to about twenty years ago whenever I went back I could persuade myself from time to time that I was in a half-dream, knowing and not knowing. It was a pleasant feeling; it was a little like the sensations that came to me as a child when, once in the rainy season, I had "fever."

It was at a time like that, a time of "fever," during a return, that I heard about Leonard Side, a decorator of cakes and arranger of flowers. I heard about him from a school teacher.

The school she taught at was a new one. Beyond the suburbs of the town, and in what had been country and plantations right up to the end of the war. The school grounds still looked like a piece of cleared sugar-cane or coconut estate. There wasn't even a tree. The plain two-story concrete building— green roof, cream-colored walls—stood by itself in the openness and the glare.

The teacher said, "The work we were doing in those early days was a little bit like social work, with girls from laboring families. Some of them had brothers or fathers or relations who had gone to jail; they talked about this in the most natural way. One day, at a staff meeting in that very hot school with the glare all around, one of the senior teachers, a Presbyterian Indian lady, suggested that we should have a May Day fair, to introduce the girls to that idea. Everybody agreed, and we decided that the thing to do would be to ask the girls to make flower displays or arrangements, and to give a prize to the girl who did the best display.

"If you had a prize you had to have a judge. If you didn't have a good judge the idea wouldn't work. Who was this judge to be? The people we taught were very cynical. They got it from their families. Oh, they were very respectful and so on, but they thought that everybody and everything was crooked, and in their heart of hearts they looked down on the people above them. So we couldn't have a judge from the government or the Education Department or anybody too famous. This didn't leave us with too many names.

"One of the junior teachers, very young, a country girl herself, fresh from the GTC, the Government Training College, then said that Leonard Side would make the perfect judge.

"Who was Leonard Side?

"The girl had to think. Then she said, 'He work all his life in flowers.'

"Well. But then somebody else remembered the name. She said Leonard Side gave little courses at the WAA, the Women's Auxiliary Association, and people there liked him. That was the place to find him.

"The Women's Auxiliary Association had been founded during the war and was modeled on the WVS in England. They had a building in Parry's Corner, which was in the heart of the city. There was everything in Parry's Corner, a garage for buses, a garage for taxis, a funeral parlor, two cafés, a haberdasher and dry-goods shop, and a number of little houses, some of them offices, some of them dwelling-places; and the well-known Parry family owned it all.

"It was easy for me to go to Parry's Corner, and I offered to go and talk to

Leonard Side. The WAA was in a very small building from the Spanish time. The flat front wall—a thick rubble wall, plastered and painted, with rusticated stone slabs at either end—rose up directly from the pavement, so that you stepped from the narrow pavement straight into the front room. The front door was bang in the middle of the pavement wall, and there was a little curtained window on either side. Door and windows had yellow-brown jalousies, linked wooden cross slats you could lift all at once and use an iron pin to close.

"A brown woman was sitting at a desk, and on the dusty wall—dust catching on the unevenness of the plastered rubble wall—were Information Office posters from England. The Tower of London, the English countryside.

"I said, 'They tell me I could find Mr. Side here.'

" 'He over there, across the road,' the woman at the desk said.

"I crossed the road. As always at this time of day, the asphalt was soft and black, as black as the oil-stained concrete floor of the big shed of a garage where the Parry buses were. The building I entered was a modern one, with gray-washed decorated concrete blocks mimicking chipped stone. It was a very clean and plain kind of place, like a doctor's office.

"I said to the girl sitting at the table, 'Mr. Side?'

"She said, 'Go right in.'

"I went through to the inner room, and there I could hardly believe what I saw. A dark Indian man was doing things with his fingers to a dead body on a table or slab in front of him. I had gone to Parry's Funeral Parlor. It was a famous place; it advertised every day on the radio with organ music. I suppose Leonard Side was dressing the body. 'Dressing'—I just knew the word. I had had no idea what it meant. I was too frightened and shocked to say anything. I ran out of the room, and the front room, and got out into the open again. The man ran out after me, calling in a soft voice, 'Miss, Miss.'

"And really he was quite a good-looking man, in spite of the hairy fingers I had seen dressing the dead body on the table. He was very pleased to be asked to judge the girls' flower competition. He even said he wanted to give the first prize. He said that if we allowed him he would make a special posy. And he did, too. A little posy of pink rosebuds. Our May Day fair was a great success.

"A year passed. Fair time came again, and I had to go again and look for Leonard Side. This time I wasn't going to forget: I wasn't going to the funeral parlor. The only place I was going to meet Leonard Side was the Women's Association. I went there late one afternoon after school, about five. The little Spanish-style house was full of women, and in the inside room Leonard Side was doing things with dough, using those hairy fingers to knead dough. Using those fingers to work in a little more milk, then a little more butter.

"He was teaching the women how to make bread and cake. After he had finished doing the dough, he began to teach them how to ice a cake, forcing with those hairy fingers colored icing out of the special cones or moulds he had. He pressed on and then into the moulds with his hairy fingers, and out came a pink or green rosebud or a flower, which he then fixed with icing-flecked fingers on to the soft iced cake. The women said ooh and aah, and he, very happy with his audience and his work, worked on, like a magician.

"But I didn't like seeing those fingers doing this kind of work, and I liked it less when, at the end, with those same fingers he offered the women little things he had iced, to eat on the spot, as a treat. He liked offering these little treats. They were offered almost like a wafer in church, and the women, concentrating, ate and tasted with a similar kind of respect.

"The third year came. This time I thought I wouldn't go to Parry's Corner to meet Leonard Side. I thought I would go to his house instead. I had found out where he lived. He lived in St. James, quite near where I lived. That was a surprise: that he should have been so close, living that life, and I shouldn't have known.

"I went after school. I was wearing a slender black skirt and a white shirty top and I was carrying a bag with school books. I blew the horn when I stopped. A woman came out to the front gallery, bright in the afternoon light, and she said, 'Come right in.' Just like that, as though she knew me.

"When I went up the steps to the front gallery she said, 'Come in, Doctor. Poor Lenny. He so sick, Doctor.'

"Doctor—that was because of the car and blowing the horn, and the bag, and the clothes I was wearing. I thought I would explain later, and I followed her through this little old St. James wood house to the back room. There I found Leonard Side, very sick and trembling, but dressed for a meeting with the doctor. He was in a shiny brass fourposter with a flowered canopy, and he was in green silk pajamas. His little hairy fingers were resting on the satin or silk spread he was using as a coverlet. He had laid himself out with great care, and the coverlet was folded back neatly.

"There were crepe-paper flowers in a brass vase on a thin-legged side table or vase-stand, and there were satiny cushions and big bows on two simple cane-bottomed bentwood chairs. I knew at once that a lot of that satin and silk had come from the funeral parlor, and was material for the coffins and the laying out of the bodies.

"He was a Mohammedan, everyone knew. But he was so much a man of his job—laying out Christian bodies, though nobody thought of it quite like that—that in that bedroom of his he even had a framed picture of Christ in Majesty, radiating light and gold, and lifting a finger of blessing.

"The picture was centrally placed above the door and leaned forward so much that the blessing of the finger would have seemed aimed at the man on the bed. I knew that the picture wasn't there for the religion alone: it was also for the beauty, the colors, the gold, the long wavy hair of Christ. And I believe I was more shocked than when I saw him dressing the body and later when I saw him using the same fingers to knead dough and then to squeeze out the terrible little blobs of icing.

"It was late afternoon, warm still, and through the open window came the smell of the cesspits of St. James, the cesspits of those dirt yards with the separate little wood houses, two or three to a lot, with runnels of filth from the latrines, runnels that ran green and shiny and then dried away in the dirt; with the discolored stones where people put out their washing to bleach; with irregular little areas where the earth was mounded up with dust and sand and gravel, and where fruit trees and little shrubs grew, creating the effect not of gardens but of little patches of waste ground where things grew haphazardly.

"When I looked at those hairy fingers on the coverlet and thought about the house and the woman who had called me in—his mother—I wondered about this life and felt sorry and frightened for him. He was sick now; he wanted help. I didn't have the heart to talk to him about the girls and the May Day fair, and I left the house and never saw him again.

"It was his idea of beauty that upset me, I suppose. That idea of beauty had taken him to the job in the funeral parlor, and had got him to deck out his bedroom in the extravagant way he had. That idea of beauty—mixing roses and flowers and nice things to eat with the idea of making the dead human body beautiful too—was contrary to my own idea. The mixing of things upset me. It didn't upset him. I had thought something like that the very first time I had seen him, when he had left his dead body and run out after me to the street, saying, 'Miss, Miss,' as though he couldn't understand why I was leaving.

"He was like so many of the Indian men you see on the streets in St. James, slender fellows in narrow-waisted trousers and open-necked shirts. Ordinary, even with the good looks. But he had that special idea of beauty.

"That idea of beauty, surprising as it was, was not a secret. Many people would have known about it—like the junior teacher who had brought his name up at the staff meeting, and then didn't know how to describe him. He would have been used to people treating him in a special way: the women in the classes clapping him, other people mocking him or scorning him, and people like me running away from him because he frightened us. He frightened me because I felt his feeling for beauty was like an illness; as though some unfamiliar, deforming virus had passed through his simple mother to him, and was even then—he was in his mid-thirties—something neither of them had begun to understand."

This was what I heard, and the teacher couldn't tell me what had happened to Leonard Side; she had never thought to ask. Perhaps he had joined the great migration to England or the United States. I wondered whether in that other place Leonard Side had come to some understanding of his nature; or whether the thing that had frightened the teacher had, when the time of revelation came, also frightened Leonard Side.

He knew he was a Mohammedan, in spite of the picture of Christ in his bedroom. But he would have had almost no idea of where he or his ancestors had come from. He wouldn't have guessed that the name Side might have been a version of Sayed, and that his grandfather or great-grandfather might have come from a Shia Muslim group in India. From Lucknow, perhaps; there was even a street in St. James called Lucknow Street. All Leonard Side would have known of himself and his ancestors would have been what he had awakened to in his mother's house in St. James. In that he was like the rest of us.

With learning now I can tell you more or less how we all came to be where we were. I can tell you that the Amerindian name for that land of St. James would have been Cumucurapo, which the early travelers from Europe turned to Conquerabo or Conquerabia. I can look at the vegetation and tell you what was there when Columbus came and what was imported later. I can reconstruct the plantations that were laid out on that area of St. James. The recorded history of the place is short, three centuries of depopulation followed by two centuries of resettlement. The documents of the resettlement are available in the city, in the Registrar-General's Office. While the documents last we can hunt up the story of every strip of occupied land.

I can give you that historical bird's eye view. But I cannot really explain the mystery of Leonard Side's inheritance. Most of us know the parents or grandparents we come from. But we go back and back, forever; we go back all of us to the very beginning; in our blood and bone and brain we carry the memories of thousands of beings. I might say that an ancestor of Leonard Side's came from the dancing groups of Lucknow, the lewd men who painted their faces and tried to live like women. But that would only be a fragment of his inheritance, a fragment of the truth. We cannot understand all the traits we have inherited. Sometimes we can be strangers to ourselves.

# PART 3

# Immigrant Encounters

*But lets just suppose. What if the whole deal—orientation, knowing where you are, and so on—what if it's all a scam? What if all of it—home, kinship, the whole enchilada—is just the biggest, most truly global, and centuries-oldest piece of brainwashing? Suppose that it's only when you dare to let go that your real life begins? . . . Suppose you've got to go through the feeling of being lost, into the chaos and beyond; you've got to accept the loneliness, the wild panic of losing your moorings, the vertiginous terror of the horizon spinning round and round like the edge of a coin tossed in the air.*
—Salman Rushdie, *The Ground Beneath Her Feet*

# Rohinton Mistry

Although living in Canada since 1975 and taking citizenship, Rohinton Mistry continues to write about India. He was born into a Bombay Parsi family in 1952. After graduating from the University of Bombay with a degree in mathematics, he and his wife immigrated to Canada. In Toronto he worked in a bank and studied at the University of Toronto, receiving in 1984 a degree in literature and philosophy. Determined to become a full-time writer, he left the bank in 1985. Two years later he published his first book in Canada, *Tales from Firozsha Baag*, which appeared in the United States in 1989 as *Swimming Lessons, and Other Stories from Firozsha Baag*. The collection was well received in both countries, and reviewers compared it to James Joyce's *Dubliners* and to the work of the widely admired Indian writer, R. K. Narayan.

In 1991 his first novel appeared, *Such a Long Journey*. Set in the Indira Gandhi years, the narrative follows the misadventures of Gustad Noble, an unassuming bank clerk who gets entangled in a scheme to divert government funds. Once the naïve Noble realizes that he has been duped his life changes irrevocably. Not only does he grasp that he is a hapless victim of forces over which he has no control, but he also learns that his government and its leaders are duplicitous and manipulative. Along with the political overtones, the novel captures the diversity of contemporary Indian life, creates poignant characters, and serves up comic situations. Much the same could be said of his second, more ambitious novel, *A Fine Balance* (1995). Set in 1975 during Indira Gandhi's declared "State of Emergency," the story traces the tribulations and triumphs of four unlikely people sharing an apartment: a widowed seamstress, a student, and two village tailors. The setting moves from an unnamed city by the sea, reminiscent of Bombay, to the mountains and finally to an obscure village. Along the way the whole tapestry of Indian life unfolds to present a complex story that is at once affectionate and comic in its treatment of the apartment dwellers' relationships and horrifying in the degradation and wretchedness they endure.

A crumbling Bombay apartment house serves as the setting for the collection from which "Swimming Lessons" comes. Unlike the novels, the stories are not linked to the larger Indian scene, but comprise a group of finely drawn miniatures that interweave the lives of Firozsha Baag's occupants, and recall their joys, sorrows and fears, their hopes and dreams and disillusionments. In "Swimming Lessons," the first-person narrator, an Indian immigrant in a Canadian apartment house, suggests that people in a cold country far removed from tropical Bombay sometimes behave in much the same manner as those in the stories he has written. He also provides a firsthand, honest account of the immigrant encounter. At the same time, Mistry takes a narrative leap and reports on how his book about Firozsha Baag is received at home.

# Swimming Lessons

The old man's wheelchair is audible today as he creaks by in the hallway: on some days it's just a smooth whirr. Maybe the way he slumps in it, or the way his weight rests has something to do with it. Down to the lobby he goes, and sits there most of the time, talking to people on their way out or in. That's where he first spoke to me a few days ago. I was waiting for the elevator, back from Eaton's with my new pair of swimming-trunks,

"Hullo," he said. I nodded, smiled.

"Beautiful summer day we've got."

"Yes," I said, "it's lovely outside."

He shifted the wheelchair to face me squarely. "How old do you think I am?"

I looked at him blankly, and he said, "Go on, take a guess."

I understood the game; he seemed about seventy-five although the hair was still black, so I said, "Sixty-five?" He made a sound between a chuckle and a wheeze: "I'll be seventy-seven next month." Close enough.

I've heard him ask that question several times since, and everyone plays by the rules. Their faked guesses range from sixty to seventy. They pick a lower number when he's more depressed than usual. He reminds me of Grandpa as he sits on the sofa in the lobby, staring out vacantly at the parking lot. Only difference is, he sits with the stillness of stroke victims, while Grandpa's Parkinson's disease would bounce his thighs and legs and arms all over the place. When he could no longer hold the *Bombay Samachar* steady enough to read, Grandpa took to sitting on the verandah and staring emptily at the traffic passing outside Firozsha Baag. Or waving to anyone who went by in the compound: Rustomji, Nariman Hansotia in his 1932 Mercedes-Benz, the fat ayah Jaakaylee with her shopping-bag, the *kuchrawalli* with her basket and long bamboo broom.

The Portuguese woman across the hall has told me a little about the old man. She is the communicator for the apartment building. To gather and disseminate information, she takes the liberty of unabashedly throwing open her door when newsworthy events transpire. Not for Portuguese Woman the furtive peerings from thin cracks or spyholes. She reminds me of a character in a movie, *Barefoot in the Park* I think it was, who left empty beer cans by the landing for anyone passing to stumble and give her the signal. But PW does not need beer cans. The gutang-khutang of the elevator opening and closing is enough.

The old man's daughter looks after him. He was living alone till his stroke, which coincided with his youngest daughter's divorce in Vancouver. She returned to him and they moved into this low-rise in Don Mills. PW says the daughter talks to no one in the building but takes good care of her father.

Mummy used to take good care of Grandpa, too, till things became complicated and he was moved to the Parsi General Hospital. Parkinsonism and osteoporosis laid him low. The doctor explained that Grandpa's hip did not break because he fell, but he fell because the hip, gradually growing brittle, snapped on that fatal day. That's what osteoporosis does, hollows out the bones and turns effect into cause. It has an unusually high incidence in the Parsi community, he said, but did not say why. Just one of those mysterious things. We are the chosen people where osteoporosis is concerned. And divorce. The Parsi community has the highest divorce rate in India. It also claims to be the most westernized community in India. Which is the result of the other? Confusion again, of cause and effect.

The hip was put in traction. Single-handed, Mummy struggled valiantly with bedpans and dressings for bedsores which soon appeared like grim specters on his back. Mamaiji, bent double with her weak back, could give no assistance. My help would be enlisted to roll him over on his side while Mummy changed the dressing. But after three months, the doctor pronounced a patch upon Grandpa's lungs, and the male ward of Parsi General swallowed him up. There was no money for a private nursing home. I went to see him once, at Mummy's insistence. She used to say that the blessings of an old person were the most valuable and potent of all, they would last my whole life long. The ward had rows and rows of beds; the din was enormous, the smells nauseating, and it was just as well that Grandpa passed most of his time in a less than conscious state.

But I should have gone to see him more often. Whenever Grandpa went out, while he still could in the days before Parkinsonism, he would bring back pink and white sugar-coated almonds for Percy and me. Every time I remember Grandpa, I remember that; and then I think: I should have gone to see him more often. That's what I also thought when our telephone-owning neighbor, esteemed by all for that reason, sent his son to tell us the hospital had phoned that Grandpa died an hour ago.

*The postman rang the doorbell the way he always did, long and continuous; Mother went to open it, wanting to give him a piece of her mind but thought better of it, she did not want to risk the vengeance of postmen, it was so easy for them to destroy letters; workers nowadays thought no end of themselves, strutting around like peacocks, ever since all this Shiv Sena agitation about Maharashtra for Maharashtrians, threatening strikes and Bombay* bundh *all the time, with no respect for the public; bus drivers and conductors were the worst, behaving as if they owned the buses and were doing favors to commuters, pulling the bell before you were in the bus, the driver purposely braking and moving with big jerks to make the standees lose their balance, the conductor so rude if you did not have the right change.*

*But when she saw the airmail envelope with a Canadian stamp her face lit up, she said wait to the postman, and went in for a fifty paisa piece, a little* baksheesh *for you, she told him, then shut the door and kissed the envelope, went in running, saying my son has written, my son has sent a letter, and Father looked up from the newspaper and said, don't get too excited, first read it, you know what kind of letters he writes, a few lines of empty words, I'm fine, hope you are all right, your loving son—that kind of writing I don't call letter-writing.*

*Then Mother opened the envelope and took out one small page and began to read silently and the joy brought to her face by the letter's arrival began to ebb; Father saw it happening and knew he was right, he said read aloud, let me also hear what our son is writing this time, so Mother read: My dear Mummy and Daddy, Last winter was terrible, we had record breaking low temperatures all through February and March, and the first official day of spring was colder than the first official day of winter had been, but it's getting warmer now. Looks like it will be a nice warm summer. You asked about my new apartment. It's small, but not bad at all. This is just a quick note to let you know I'm fine, so you won't worry about me. Hope everything is okay at home.*

*After Mother put it back in the envelope, Father said everything about his life is locked in silence and secrecy, I still don't understand why he bothered to visit us last year if he had nothing to say, every letter of his has been a quick note so we won't worry—what does he think we worry about, his health, in that country everyone eats well whether they work or not, he should be worrying about us with all the black market and rationing, has he forgotten already how he used to go to the ration-shop and wait in line every week; and what kind of apartment description is that, not bad at all; and if it is a*

*Canadian weather report I need from him, I can go with Nariman Hansotia from A Block to the Cawasji Framji Memorial Library and read all about it, there they get newspapers from all over the world.*

The sun is hot today. Two women are sunbathing on the stretch of patchy lawn at the periphery of the parking lot. I can see them. clearly from my kitchen. They're wearing bikinis and I'd love to take a closer look. But I have no binoculars. Nor do I have a car to saunter out to and pretend to look under the hood. They're both luscious and gleaming. From time to time they smear lotion over their skin, on the bellies, on the inside of the thighs, on the shoulders. Then one of them gets the other to undo the string of her top and spread some there. She lies on her stomach with the straps undone. I wait. I pray that the heat and haze make her forget, when it's time to turn over, that the straps are undone.

But the sun is not hot enough to work this magic for me. When it's time to come in, she flips over, deftly holding up the cups, and reties the top. They arise, pick up towels, lotions and magazines, return to the building.

This is my chance to see them closer. I race down the stairs to the lobby. The old man says hullo. "Down again?"

"My mailbox," I mumble.

"It's Saturday," he chortles. For some reason he finds it extremely funny. My eye is on the door leading in from the parking lot.

Through the glass panel I see them approaching. I hurry to the elevator and wait. In the dimly lit lobby I can see their eyes are having trouble adjusting after the bright sun. They don't seem as attractive as they did from the kitchen window. The elevator arrives and I hold it open, inviting them in with what I think is a gallant flourish. Under the fluorescent glare in the elevator I see their wrinkled skin, aging hands, sagging bottoms, varicose veins. The lustrous trick of sun and lotion and distance has ended.

I step out and they continue to the third floor. I have Monday night to look forward to, my first swimming lesson. The high school behind the apartment building is offering, among its usual assortment of macramé and ceramics and pottery classes, a class for non-swimming adults.

The woman at the registration desk is quite friendly. She even gives me the opening to satisfy the compulsion I have about explaining my non-swimming status.

"Are you from India?" she asks. I nod. "I hope you don't mind my asking, but I was curious because an Indian couple, husband and wife, also registered a few minutes ago. Is swimming not encouraged in India?"

"On the contrary," I say. "Most Indians swim like fish. I'm an exception to the rule. My house was five minutes walking distance from Chaupatty beach in Bombay. It's one of the most beautiful beaches in Bombay, or was, before the filth took over, Anyway, even though we lived so close to it, I never learned to swim. It's just one of those things."

"Well," says the woman, "that happens sometimes. Take me, for instance I never learned to ride a bicycle. It was the mounting that used to scare me, I was afraid of falling." People have lined up behind me. "It's been very nice talking to you," she says, "hope you enjoy the course."

The art of swimming had been trapped between the devil and the deep blue sea. The devil was money, always scarce, and kept the private swimming clubs out of reach; the deep blue sea of Chaupatty beach was gray and murky with garbage, too filthy to swim in. Every so often we would muster our courage and Mummy would take me there to try and teach me. But a few minutes of paddling was all we could endure. Sooner or later something would float up against our legs or thighs or waists, depending on how deep we'd gone in, and we'd be revulsed and stride out to the sand.

Water imagery in my life is recurring. Chaupatty beach, now the high-school swimming pool. The universal symbol of life and regeneration did nothing but frustrate me. Perhaps the swimming pool will overturn that failure.

When images and symbols abound in this manner, sprawling or rolling across the page without guile or artifice, one is prone to say, how obvious, how skilless; symbols, after all, should be still and gentle as dewdrops, tiny, yet shining with a world of meaning. But what happens when, on the page of life itself, one encounters the ever-moving, all-engirdling sprawl of the filthy sea. Dewdrops and oceans both have their rightful places; Nariman Hansotia certainly knew that when he told his stories to the boys of Firozsha Baag.

The sea of Chaupatty was fated to endure the finales of life's everyday functions. It seemed that the dirtier it became, the more crowds it attracted: street urchins and beggars and beachcombers looking through the junk that washed up. (Or was it the crowds that made it dirtier?—another instance of cause and effect blurring and evading identification.)

Too many religious festivals also used the sea as repository for their finales. Its use should have been rationed, like rice and kerosene. On Ganesh Chaturthi, clay idols of the god Ganesh, adorned with garlands and all manner of finery, were carried in processions to the accompaniment of drums and a variety of wind instruments. The music got more frenzied the closer the procession got to Chaupatty and to the moment of immersion.

Then there was Coconut Day, which was never as popular as Ganesh Chaturthi. From a bystander's viewpoint, coconuts chucked into the sea do not provide as much of a spectacle. We used the sea, too, to deposit the leftovers from Parsi religious ceremonies, things such as flowers, or the ashes of the sacred sandalwood fire, which just could not be dumped with the regular garbage but had to be entrusted to the care of Avan Yazad, the guardian of the sea. And things which were of no use but which no one had the heart to destroy were also given to Avan Yazad. Such as old photographs.

After Grandpa died, some of his things were flung out to sea. It was high tide; we always checked the newspaper when going to perform these disposals; an ebb would mean a long walk in squelchy sand before finding water. Most of the things were probably washed up on shore. But we tried to throw them as far out as possible, then waited a few minutes; if they did not float back right away we would pretend they were in the permanent safekeeping of Avan Yazad, which was a comforting thought. I can't remember everything we sent out to sea, but his brush and comb were in the parcel, his *kusti,* and some Kemadrin pills, which he used to take to keep the Parkinsonism under control.

Our paddling sessions stopped for lack of enthusiasm on my part. Mummy wasn't too keen either, because of the filth. But my main concern was the little guttersnipes, like naked fish with little buoyant penises, taunting me with their skills, swimming underwater and emerging unexpectedly all around me, or pretending to masturbate—I think they were too young to achieve ejaculation. It was embarrassing. When I look back, I'm surprised that Mummy and I kept going as long as we did.

I examine the swimming-trunks I bought last week. Surf King, says the label, Made in Canada-Fabriqué Au Canada. I've been learning bits and pieces of French from bilingual labels at the supermarket too. These trunks are extremely sleek and streamlined hipsters, the distance from waistband to pouch tip the barest minimum. I wonder how everything will stay in place, not that I'm boastful about my endowments. I try them on, and feel that the tip of my member lingers perilously close to the exit. Too close, in fact, to conceal the exigencies of my swimming lesson fantasy: a gorgeous woman in the class for non-swimmers, at whose sight I will be instantly aroused, and she, spying the shape of my desire, will look me straight in the eye with her intentions; she will come home with me, to taste the pleasures of my delectable Asian brown body whose strangeness has intrigued her and unleashed uncontrollable surges of passion inside her throughout the duration of the swimming lesson.

I drop the Eaton's bag and wrapper in the garbage can. The swimming trunks cost fifteen dollars, same as the fee for the ten weekly lessons. The garbage bag is almost full. I tie it up and take it outside. There is a medicinal smell in the hallway; the old man must have just returned to his apartment.

PW opens her door and says, "Two ladies from the third floor were lying in the sun this morning. In bikinis."

"That's nice," I say, and walk to the incinerator chute. She reminds me of Najamai in Firozsha Baag, except that Najamai employed a bit more subtlety while going about her life's chosen work.

PW withdraws and shuts her door.

*Mother had to reply because Father said he did not want to write to his son till his son had something sensible to write to him, his questions had been ignored long enough, and if he wanted to keep his life a secret, fine, he would get no letters from his father.*

*But after Mother started the letter he went and looked over her shoulder, telling her what to ask him, because if they kept on writing the same questions, maybe he would understand how interested they were in knowing about things over there; Father said go on, ask him what his work is at the insurance company, tell him to take some courses at night school, that's how everyone moves ahead over there, tell him not to be discouraged if his job is just clerical right now, hard work will get him ahead, remind him he is a Zoroastrian: manashni, gavashni, kunashni, better write the translation also: good thoughts, good words, good deeds—he must have forgotten what it means, and tell him to say prayers and do kusti at least twice a day.*

*Writing it all down sadly, Mother did not believe he wore his sudra and kusti anymore, she would be very surprised if he remembered any of the prayers; when she had asked him if he needed new sudras he said not to take any trouble because the Zoroastrian Society of Ontario imported them from Bombay for their members, and this sounded like a story he was making up, but she was leaving it in the hands of God, ten thousand miles away there was nothing she could do but write a letter and hope for the best.*

*Then she sealed it, and Father wrote the address on it as usual because his writing was much neater than hers, handwriting was important in the address and she did not want the postman in Canada to make any mistake, she took it to the post office herself, it was impossible to trust anyone to mail it ever since the postage rates went up because people just tore off the stamps for their own use and threw away the letter, the only safe way was to hand it over the counter and make the clerk cancel the stamps before your own eyes.*

Berthe, the building superintendent, is yelling at her son in the parking lot. He tinkers away with his van. This happens every fine-weathered Sunday. It must be the van that Berthe dislikes because I've seen mother and son together in other quite amicable situations.

Berthe is a big Yugoslavian with high cheekbones. Her nationality was disclosed to me by PW. Berthe speaks a very rough-hewn English, I've overheard her in the lobby scolding tenants for late rents and leaving dirty lint screens in the dryers. It's exciting to listen to her, her words fall like rocks and boulders and one can never tell where or how the next few will drop. But her Slavic yells at her son are a different matter, the words fly swift and true, well-aimed missiles that never miss. Finally, the son slams down the hood in disgust, wipes his hands on a rag, accompanies mother Berthe inside.

Berthe's husband has a job in a factory. But he loses several days of work every month when he succumbs to the booze, a word Berthe uses often in her

Slavic tirades on those days, the only one I can understand, as it clunks down heavily out of the tight-flying formation of Yugoslavian sentences. He lolls around in the lobby, submitting passively to his wife's tongue-lashings. The bags under his bloodshot eyes, his stringy mustache, stubbled chin, dirty hair are so vulnerable to the poison-laden barbs (poison works the same way in any language) emanating from deep within the powerful watermelon bosom. No one's presence can embarrass or dignify her into silence.

No one except the old man who arrives now. "Good morning," he says, and Berthe turns, stops yelling, and smiles. Her husband rises, positions the wheelchair at the favorite angle. The lobby will be peaceful as long as the old man is there.

It was hopeless. My first swimming lesson. The water terrified me. When did that happen, I wonder, I used to love splashing at Chaupatty, carried about by the waves. And this was only a swimming pool. Where did all that terror come from? I'm trying to remember.

Armed with my Surf King I enter the high school and go to the pool area. A sheet with instructions for the new class is pinned to the bulletin board. All students must shower and then assemble at eight by the shallow end. As I enter the showers three young boys, probably from a previous class, emerge. One of them holds his nose. The second begins to hum, under his breath: Paki Paki, smell like curry. The third says to the first two: pretty soon all the water's going to taste of curry. They leave.

It's a mixed class, but the gorgeous woman of my fantasy is missing. I have to settle for another, in a pink one-piece suit, with brown hair and a bit of a stomach. She must be about thirty-five. Plain-looking.

The instructor is called Ron. He gives us a pep talk, sensing some nervousness in the group. We're finally all in the water, in the shallow end. He demonstrates floating on the back, then asks for a volunteer. The pink one-piece suit wades forward. He supports her, tells her to lean back and let her head drop in the water.

She does very well. And as we all regard her floating body, I see what was not visible outside the pool: her bush, curly bits of it, straying out at the pink Spandex V. Tongues of water lapping against her delta, as if caressing it teasingly, make the brown hair come alive in a most tantalizing manner. The crests and troughs of little waves, set off by the movement of our bodies in a circle around her, dutifully irrigate her; the curls alternately wave free inside the crest, then adhere to her wet thighs, beached by the inevitable trough. I could watch this forever, and I wish the floating demonstration would never end.

Next we are shown how to grasp the rail and paddle, face down in the water. Between practicing floating and paddling, the hour is almost gone. I have been trying to observe the pink one-piece suit, getting glimpses of her straying pubic hair from various angles. Finally, Ron wants a volunteer for the last demonstration, and I go forward. To my horror he leads the class to the deep end. Fifteen feet of water. It is so blue, and I can see the bottom. He picks up a metal hoop attached to a long wooden stick. He wants me to grasp the hoop, jump in the water, and paddle, while he guides me by the stick. Perfectly safe, he tells me. A demonstration of how paddling propels the body.

It's too late to back out; besides, I'm so terrified I couldn't find the words to do so even if I wanted to. Everything he says I do as if in a trance. I don't remember the moment of jumping. The next thing I know is, I'm swallowing water and floundering, hanging on to the hoop for dear life. Ron draws me to the rails and helps me out. The class applauds.

We disperse and one thought is on my mind: what if I'd lost my grip? Fifteen feet of water under me. I shudder and take deep breaths. This is it. I'm not coming next week. This instructor is an irresponsible person. Or he does not value the lives of non-white immigrants. I remember the three teenagers. Maybe the swimming pool is the hangout of some racist group, bent on eliminating all non-white swimmers, to keep their waters pure and their white sisters unogled.

The elevator takes me upstairs. Then gutang-khutang. PW opens her door as I turn the corridor of medicinal smells. "Berthe was screaming loudly at her husband tonight," she tells me.

"Good for her," I say, and she frowns indignantly at me.

The old man is in the lobby. He's wearing thick wool gloves. He wants to know how the swimming was, must have seen me leaving with my towel yesterday. Not bad, I say.

"I used to swim a lot. Very good for the circulation." He wheezes. "My feet are cold all the time. Cold as ice. Hands too."

Summer is winding down, so I say stupidly, "Yes, it's not so warm any more."

The thought of the next swimming lesson sickens me. But as I comb through the memories of that terrifying Monday, I come upon the straying curls of brown pubic hair. Inexorably drawn by them, I decide to go.

It's a mistake, of course. This time I'm scared even to venture in the shallow end. When everyone has entered the water and I'm the only one outside, I feel a little foolish and slide in.

Instructor Ron says we should start by reviewing the floating technique. I'm in no hurry. I watch the pink one-piece pull the swim-suit down around her cheeks and flip back to achieve perfect flotation. And then reap disappointment. The pink Spandex triangle is perfectly streamlined today, nothing strays, not a trace of fuzz, not one filament, not even a sign of post-depilation irritation. Like the airbrushed parts of glamour magazine models. The barrenness of her impeccably packaged apex is a betrayal. Now she is shorn like the other women in the class. Why did she have to do it? The weight of this disappointment makes the water less manageable, more lung-penetrating. With trepidation, I float and paddle my way through the remainder of the hour, jerking my head out every two seconds and breathing deeply, to continually shore up a supply of precious, precious air without, at the same time, seeming too anxious and losing my dignity.

I don't attend the remaining classes. After I've missed three, Ron the instructor telephones. I tell him I've had the flu and am still feeling poorly, but I'll try to be there the following week.

He does not call again. My Surf King is relegated to an unused drawer. Total losses: one fantasy plus thirty dollars. And no watery rebirth. The swimming pool, like Chaupatty beach, has produced a stillbirth. But there is a difference. Water means regeneration only if it is pure and cleansing. Chaupatty was filthy, the pool was not. Failure to swim through filth must mean something other than failure of rebirth—failure of symbolic death? Does that equal success of symbolic life? death of a symbolic failure? death of a symbol? What is the equation?

*The postman did not bring a letter but a parcel, he was smiling because he knew that every time something came from Canada his baksheesh was guaranteed, and this time because it was a parcel Mother gave him a whole rupee, she was quite excited, there were so many stickers on it besides the stamps, one for Small Parcel, another Printed Papers, a red sticker saying Insured, she showed it to Father, and opened it, then put both hands on her cheeks, not able to speak because the surprise and happiness was so great, tears came to her eyes and she could not stop smiling, till Father became impatient to know and finally got up and came to the table.*

*When he saw it he was surprised and happy too, he began to grin, then hugged Mother saying our son is a writer, and we didn't even know it, he never told us a thing, here we are thinking he is still clerking away at the insurance company, and he has written a book of stories, all these years in school and college he kept his talent hidden, making us think he was just like one of the boys in the Baag, shouting and playing the fool in the compound, and now what a surprise; then Father opened the book and began reading it, heading back to the easy chair, and Mother so excited, still holding his arm, walked with him, saying it was not fair him reading it first, she wanted to read it too, and they agreed that he would read the first story, then give it to her so she could also read it, and they would take turns in that manner.*

*Mother removed the staples from the padded envelope in which he had mailed the book, and threw them away, then straightened the folded edges of the envelope and put it away safely with the other envelopes and letters she had collected since he left.*

The leaves are beginning to fall. The only ones I can identify are maple.

The days are dwindling like the leaves. I've started a habit of taking long walks every evening. The old man is in the lobby when I leave, he waves as I go by. By the time I'm back, the lobby is usually empty.

Today I was woken up by a grating sound outside that made my flesh crawl. I went to the window and saw Berthe raking the leaves in the parking lot. Not in the expanse of patchy lawn on the periphery, but in the parking lot proper. She was raking the black tarred surface. I went back to bed and dragged a pillow over my head, not releasing it till noon.

When I return from my walk in the evening, PW, summoned by the elevator's gutang-khutang, says, "Berthe filled six big black garbage bags with leaves today."

"Six bags!" I say. "Wow!"

Since the weather turned cold, Berthe's son does not tinker with his van on Sundays under my window. I'm able to sleep late

Around eleven, there's a commotion outside. I reach out and switch on the clock radio. It's a sunny day, the window curtains are bright. I get up, curious, and see a black Olds Ninety-Eight in the parking lot, by the entrance to the building. The old man is in his wheelchair, bundled up, with a scarf wound several times round his neck as though to immobilize it, like a surgical collar. His daughter and another man, the car-owner, are helping him from the wheelchair into the front seat, encouraging him with words like: that's it, easy does it, attaboy. From the open door of the lobby, Berthe is shouting encouragement too, but hers is confined to one word: yah, repeated at different levels of pitch and volume, with variations on vowel-length. The stranger could be the old man's son, he has the same jet black hair and piercing eyes.

Maybe the old man is not well, it's an emergency. But I quickly scrap that thought—this isn't Bombay, an ambulance would have arrived. They're probably taking him out for a ride. If he is his son, where has he been all this time, I wonder.

The old man finally settles in the front seat, the wheelchair goes in the trunk, and they're off. The one I think is the son looks up and catches me at the window before I can move away, so I wave, and he waves back.

In the afternoon I take down a load of clothes to the laundry room. Both machines have completed their cycles, the clothes inside are waiting to be transferred to dryers. Should I remove them and place them on top of a dryer, or wait? I decide to wait. After a few minutes, two women arrive, they are in bathrobes, and smoking. It takes me a while to realize that these are the two disappointments who were sunbathing in bikinis last summer.

"You didn't have to wait, you could have removed the clothes and carried on, dear," says one. She has a Scottish accent. It's one of the few I've learned to identify. Like maple leaves.

"Well," I say, "some people might not like strangers touching their clothes."

"You're not a stranger, dear," she says, "you live in this building, we've seen you before."

"Besides, your hands are clean," the other one pipes in. "You can touch my things any time you like."

Horny old cow. I wonder what they've got on under their bathrobes, Not much, I find, as they bend over to place their clothes in the dryers.

"See you soon," they say, and exit, leaving me behind in an erotic wake of smoke and perfume and deep images of cleavages. I start the washers and depart, and when I come back later, the dryers are empty.

PW tells me, "The old man's son took him out for a drive today. He has a big beautiful black car."

I see my chance, and shoot back: "Olds Ninety-Eight."

"What?"

"The car," I explain, "it's an Oldsmobile Ninety-Eight."

She does not like this at all, my giving her information. She is visibly nettled, and retreats with a sour face.

*Mother and Father read the first five stories, and she was very sad after reading some of them, she said he must be so unhappy there, all his stories are about Bombay, he remembers every little thing about his childhood, he is thinking about it all the time even though he is ten thousand miles away, my poor son, I think he misses his home and us and everything he left behind, because if he likes it over there why would he not write stories about that, there must be so many new ideas that his new life could give him.*

*But Father did not agree with this, he said it did not mean that he was unhappy, all writers worked in the same way, they used their memories and experiences and made stories out of them, changing some things, adding some, imagining some, all writers were very good at remembering details of their lives.*

*Mother said, how can you be sure that he is remembering because he is a writer, or whether he started to write because he is unhappy and thinks of his past, and wants to save it all by making stories of it, and Father said that is not a sensible question, anyway, it is now my turn to read the next story.*

The first snow has fallen, and the air is crisp. It's not very deep, about two inches, just right to go for a walk in. I've been told that immigrants from hot countries always enjoy the snow the first year, maybe for a couple of years more, then inevitably the dread sets in, and the approach of winter gets them fretting and moping. On the other hand, if it hadn't been for my conversation with the woman at the swimming registration desk, they might now be saying that India is a nation of non-swimmers.

Berthe is outside, shoveling the snow off the walkway in the parking lot. She has a heavy, wide pusher which she wields expertly.

The old radiators in the apartment alarm me incessantly. They continue to broadcast a series of variations on death throes, and go from hot to cold and cold to hot at will, there's no controlling their temperature. I speak to Berthe about it in the lobby. The old man is there too, his chin seems to have sunk deeper into his chest, and his face is a yellowish gray.

"Nothing, not to worry about anything," says Berthe, dropping rough-hewn chunks of language around me. "Radiator no work, you tell me. You feel cold, you come to me, I keep you warm," and she opens her arms wide, laughing. I step back, and she advances, her breasts preceding her like the gallant prows of two ice-breakers. She looks at the old man to see if he is ap-preciating the act: "You no feel scared, I keep you safe and warm."

But the old man is staring outside, at the flakes of falling snow. What thoughts is he thinking as he watches them? Of childhood days, perhaps, and snowmen with hats and pipes, and snowball fights, and white Christmases, and Christmas trees? What will I think of, old in this country, when I sit and watch the snow come down? For me, it is already too late for snowmen and snowball fights, and all I will have is thoughts about childhood thoughts and dreams, built around snowscapes and winter-wonderlands on the Christmas cards so popular in Bombay; my snowmen and snowball fights and Christmas trees are in the pages of Enid Blyton's books, dispersed amidst the adventures of the Famous Five, and the Five Find-Outer, and the Secret Seven. My snowflakes are even less forgettable than the old man's, for they never melt.

It finally happened. The heat went. Not the usual intermittent coming and going, but out completely. Stone cold. The radiators are like ice. And so is everything else. There's no hot water. Naturally. It's the hot water that goes through the rads and heats them. Or is it the other way around? Is there no hot water because the rads have stopped circulating it? I don't care, I'm too cold to sort out the cause and effect relationship. Maybe there is no connection at all.

I dress quickly, put on my winter jacket, and go down to the lobby. The elevator is not working because the power is out, so I take the stairs. Several people are gathered, and Berthe has announced that she has telephoned the office, they are sending a man. I go back up the stairs. It's only one floor, the elevator is just a bad habit. Back in Firozsha Baag they were broken most of the time. The stairway enters the corridor outside the old man's apartment, and I think of his cold feet and hands. Poor man, it must be horrible for him without heat.

As I walk down the long hallway, I feel there's something different but can't pin it down. I look at the carpet, the ceiling, the wallpaper: it all seems the same. Maybe it's the freezing cold that imparts a feeling of difference.

PW opens her door: "The old man had another stroke yesterday. They took him to the hospital."

The medicinal smell. That's it. It's not in the hallway any more.

*In the stories that he'd read so far Father said that all the Parsi families were poor or middle-class, but that was okay; nor did he mind that the seeds for the stories were picked from the sufferings of their own lives; but there should also have been something positive about Parsis, there was so much to be proud of: the great Tatas and their contribution to the steel industry or Sir Dinshaw Petit in the textile industry who made Bombay the Manchester of the East, or Dadabhai Naoroji in the freedom movement, where he was the first to use the word* swaraj, *and the first to be elected to the British Parliament where he carried on his campaign; he should have found some way to bring some of these wonderful facts into his stories, what would people reading these stories think, those who did not know about Parsis—that the whole community was full of cranky, bigoted people; and in reality it was the richest, most advanced and philanthropic community in India, and he did not need to tell his own son that Parsis had a reputation for being generous and family-oriented. And he could have written something also about the historic background, how Parsis came to India from Persia because of Islamic persecution in the seventh century, and were the descendants of Cyrus the Great and the magnificent Persian Empire. He could have made a story of all this, couldn't he?*

*Mother said what she liked best was his remembering everything so well, how beautifully he wrote about it all, even the sad things, and though he changed some of it, and used his imagination, there was truth in it.*

*My hope is, Father said, that there will be some story based on his Canadian experience, that way we will know something about our son's life there, if not through his letters then in his stories; so far they are all about Parsis and Bombay and the one with a little bit about Toronto, where a man perches on top of the toilet, is shameful and disgusting, although it is funny at times and did make me laugh, I have to admit, but where does he get such an imagination from, what is the point of such a fantasy; and Mother said that she would also enjoy some stories about Toronto and the people there; it puzzles me, she said, why he writes nothing about it, especially since you say that writers use their own experience to make stories out of.*

*Then Father said this is true, but he is probably not using his Toronto experience because it is too early; what do you mean, too early, asked Mother and Father explained it takes a writer about ten years time after an experience before he is able to use it in his writing, it takes that long to be absorbed internally and understood, thought out and thought about, over and over again, he haunts it and it haunts him if it is valuable enough, till the writer is comfortable with it to be able to use it as he wants; but this is only one theory I read somewhere, it may or may not be true.*

*That means, said Mother, that his childhood in Bombay and our home here is the most valuable thing in his life now, because he is able to remember it all to write about it, and you were so bitterly saying he is forgetting where he came from; and that may be true, said Father, but that is not what the theory means, according to the theory he is writing of these things because they are far enough in the past for him to deal with objectively, he is able to achieve what critics call artistic distance, without emotions interfering; and what do you mean emotions, said Mother, you are saying he does not feel anything for his characters, how can he write so beautifully about so many sad things without any feelings in his heart?*

*But before Father could explain more, about beauty and emotion and inspiration and imagination, Mother took the book and said it was her turn now and too much theory she did not want to listen to, it was confusing and did not make as much sense as reading the stories, she would read them her way and Father could read them his.*

My books on the windowsill have been damaged. Ice has been forming on the inside ledge, which I did not notice, and melting when the sun shines in. I spread them in a corner of the living room to dry out.

The winter drags on. Berthe wields her snow pusher as expertly as ever, but there are signs of weariness in her performance. Neither husband nor son is ever seen outside with a shovel. Or anywhere else, for that matter. It occurs to me that the son's van is missing, too.

The medicinal smell is in the hall again, I sniff happily and look forward to seeing the old man in the lobby. I go downstairs and peer into the mailbox, see the blue and magenta of an Indian aerogramme with Don Mills, Ontario, Canada in Father's flawless hand through the slot.

I pocket the letter and enter the main lobby. The old man is there, but not in his usual place. He is not looking out through the glass door. His wheelchair is facing a bare wall where the wallpaper is torn in places. As though he is not interested in the outside world any more, having finished with all that, and now it's time to see inside. What does he see inside, I wonder? I go up to him and say hullo. He says hullo without raising his sunken chin. After a few seconds his gray countenance faces me. "How old do you think I am?" His eyes are dull and glazed; he is looking even further inside than I first presumed.

"Well, let's see, you're probably close to sixty-four."

"I'll be seventy-eight next August." But he does not chuckle or wheeze. Instead, he continues softly, "I wish my feet did not feel so cold all the time. And my hands." He lets his chin fall again.

In the elevator I start opening the aerogramme, a tricky business because a crooked tear means lost words. Absorbed in this while emerging, I don't notice PW occupying the center of the hallway, arms folded across her chest: "They had a big fight. Both of them have left."

I don't immediately understand her agitation. "What . . . who?"

"Berthe. Husband and son both left her. Now she is all alone."

Her tone and stance suggest that we should not be standing here talking but do something to bring Berthe's family back. "That's very sad," I say, and go in. I picture father and son in the van, driving away, driving across the snow-covered country, in the dead of winter, away from wife and mother; away to where? how far will they go? Not son's van nor father's booze can take them far enough. And the further they go the more they'll remember, they can take it from me.

*All the stories were read by Father and Mother, and they were sorry when the book was finished, they felt they had come to know their son better now, yet there was much more to know, they wished there were many more stories; and this is what they mean, said Father, when they say that the whole story can never be told, the whole truth can never be known; what do you mean, they say, asked Mother, who they, and Father said writers, poets, philosophers. I don't care what they say, said Mother, my son will write as much or as little as he wants to, and if I can read it I will be happy.*

*The last story they liked the best of all because it had the most in it about Canada, and now they felt they knew at least a little bit, even if it was a very little bit, about his day-to-day life in his apartment; and Father said if he continues to write about such things he will become popular because I am sure they are interested there in reading about life through the eyes of an immigrant, it provides a different viewpoint; the only danger is if he changes and becomes so much like them that he will write like one of them and lose the important difference.*

The bathroom needs cleaning. I open a new can of Ajax and scour the tub. Sloshing with mug from bucket was standard bathing procedure in the bathrooms of Firozsha Baag, so my preference now is always for a shower. I've never used the tub as yet; besides, it would be too much like Chaupatty or the swimming pool, wallowing in my own dirt. Still, it must be cleaned.

When I've finished, I prepare for a shower. But the clean gleaming tub and the nearness of the vernal equinox give me the urge to do something different today. I find the drain plug in the bathroom cabinet, and run the bath.

I've spoken so often to the old man, but I don't know his name. I should have asked him the last time I saw him, when his wheelchair was facing the bare wall because he had seen all there was to see outside and it was time to see what was inside. Well, tomorrow. Or better yet, I can look it up in the directory in the lobby. Why didn't I think of that before? It will only have an initial and a last name, but then I can surprise him with: hullo Mr. Wilson, or whatever it is.

The bath is full. Water imagery is recurring in my life: Chaupatty beach, swimming pool, bathtub. I step in and immerse myself up to the neck. It feels good. The hot water loses its opacity when the chlorine, or whatever it is, has cleared. My hair is still dry. I close my eyes, hold my breath, and dunk my head. Fighting the panic I stay under and count to thirty. I come out, clear my lungs and breathe deeply.

I do it again. This time I open my eyes under water, and stare blindly without seeing, it takes all my will to keep the lids from closing. Then I am slowly able to discern the underwater objects. The drain plug looks different, slightly distorted; there is a hair trapped between the hole and the plug, it waves and dances with the movement of the water. I come up, refresh my lungs, examine quickly the overwater world of the washroom, and go in again. I do it several times, over and over. The world outside the water I have seen a lot of, it is now time to see what is inside.

The spring session for adult non-swimmers will begin in a few days at the high school. I must not forget the registration date.

The dwindled days of winter are now all but forgotten; they have grown and attained a respectable span. I resume my evening walks, it's spring, and a vigorous thaw is on. The snowbanks are melting, the sound of water on its gushing, gurgling journey to the drains is beautiful. I plan to buy a book of trees, so I can identify more than the maple as they begin to bloom.

When I return to the building, I wipe my feet energetically on the mat because some people are entering behind me, and I want to set a good example. Then I go to the board with its little plastic letters and numbers. The old man's apartment is the one on the corner by the stairway, that makes it number 201. I run down the list, come to 201, but there are no little white plastic letters beside it. Just the empty black rectangle with holes where the letters would be squeezed in. That's strange. Well, I can introduce myself to him, then ask his name.

However, the lobby is empty. I take the elevator, exit at the second floor, wait for the gutang-khutang. It does not come: the door closes noiselessly, smoothly. Berthe has been at work, or has made sure someone else has. PW's cue has been lubricated out of existence.

But she must have the ears of a cockroach. She is waiting for me. I whistle my way down the corridor. She fixes me with an accusing look. She waits till I stop whistling, then says: "You know the old man died last night."

I cease groping for my key. She turns to go and I take a step towards her, my hand still in my trouser pocket. "Did you know his name?" I ask, but she leaves without answering.

*Then Mother said, the part I like best in the last story is about Grandpa, where he wonders if Grandpa's spirit is really watching him and blessing him, because you know I really told him that, I told him helping an old suffering person who is near death is the most blessed thing to do, because that person will ever after watch over you from heaven, I told him this when he was disgusted with Grandpa's urine-bottle and would not touch it, would not hand it to him even when I was not at home.*

*Are you sure, said father, that you really told him this, or you believe you told him because you like the sound of it, you said yourself the other day that he changes and adds and alters things in the stories but he writes it all so beautifully that it seems true, so how can you be sure; this sounds like another theory said Mother, but I don't care, he says I told him and I believe now I told him, so even if I did not tell him then it does not matter now.*

*Don't you see, said Father, that you are confusing fiction with facts, fiction does not create facts, fiction can come from facts, it can grow out of facts by compounding, transposing, augmenting, diminishing, or altering them in any way; but you must not confuse cause and effect, you must not confuse what really happened with what the story says happened, you must not lose your grasp on reality, that way madness lies.*

*Then Mother stopped listening because, as she told Father so often, she was not very fond of theories, and she took out her writing pad and started a letter to her son; Father looked over her shoulder, telling her to say how proud they were of him and were waiting for his next book, he also said, leave a little space for me at the end, I want to write a few lines when I put the address on the envelope.*

# Chitra Banerjee Divakaruni

The immigrant encounter with the new world forms the core of Chitra Banerjee Divakaruni's fiction. Born in Calcutta in 1956, she came to the United States when she was nineteen to further her education. After earning a master's degree from Wright State University, she completed a doctorate at the University of California, Berkeley. Divakaruni now teaches creative writing at Foothill College in Los Altos Hills, California. She also serves as president of MAITRI, a helpline that assists South Asian women who face domestic violence or other abusive circumstances. Known initially as a poet, Divakaruni published her first book of poetry, *Dark Like the River*, in 1987, and has published three additional volumes, with the most recent, *Leaving Yuba City*, appearing in 1997. Her work as a poet carries over into the fiction, which is characterized by an exquisite prose.

The woman as immigrant dominates Divakaruni's first collection of short stories, *Arranged Marriage* (1995). Except for the opening India-based selection that sets the mood and establishes the recurring theme, each story takes place in various parts of the United States. They all focus on female experience and explore the subtle psychological dominance and the plain physical brutality frequently directed toward South Asian women, whose subjugation is sanctioned by India's patriarchal system. This traditional bias, Divakaruni suggests in these narratives, too often carries over into the immigrant experience as both the women and the men struggle to adjust in a new society that makes demands they are unprepared to meet. Too often the women bear the brunt of masculine frustration.

Divakaruni's first novel, *The Mistress of Spices* (1997), blends the immediacy of urban America—in this case Oakland, California—with the timeless mythology of ancient India. Tilo, the central character, tells how she trained as "a mistress of spices" in a faraway land, then was assigned to a shabby section of Oakland to run a modest shop that stocks various Asian items and a boundless assortment of spices. As this ancient and stooped Indian woman tells her story, it strikes the reader that she may be an outrageous liar. At the same time that this mystical handler of spices engages in flights of imagination, she confronts through various customers the harsh reality that immigrants face in an indifferent city. Eventually, Tilo herself must cope with the hazards of the outside world. Through this elaborate metaphor determined by spices, Divakaruni shows how it is possible for the individual to succeed in what she calls "dissolving boundaries"—a necessity in the immigrant encounter. In her second novel, *Sister of My Heart* (1999), Divakaruni strays from a serious treatment of the immigration theme to tell the melodramatic story of two unrelated women brought up as sisters in a crumbling Calcutta mansion. Although they both eventually come to the United States, their immigration story rings false.

No idealized version of the immigrant experience, "Silver Pavements, Golden Roofs" from *Arranged Marriage* presents an honest and brutal picture of what it must be like to live as an outsider in an alien society. At first it may seem that the dreams of the immigrant girl Jayanti from Calcutta have been shattered when she finds herself isolated in a dreary Chicago apartment with her defeated aunt and bitter, abusive uncle. Yet in spite of the obstacles, the disappointments, and the humiliation she will most likely meet in the months ahead, the knowledge gained as she stands in the falling snow will aid her in "dissolving boundaries."

# Silver Pavements, Golden Roofs

I've looked forward to this day for so long that when I finally board the plane I can hardly breathe. In my hurry I bump into the air hostess who is at the door welcoming us, her brilliant pink smile an exact match for her brilliant pink nails.

"Sorry," I say, "so very very sorry," like the nuns had taught me to in those old, high-ceilinged classrooms cooled by the breeze from the convent *neem* trees. And I am. She is so blond, so American.

"No problem," she replies, her smile as golden as the wavy hair that falls in perfect curls to her shoulder. I have never heard the expression before. *No problem,* I whisper to myself as I make my way down the aisle, in love with the exotic syllables. *No problem.* I finger my long hair, imprisoned in the customary tight braid that reaches below my waist. It feels coarse and oily. As soon as I get to Chicago, I promise myself, I will have it cut and styled.

The air inside the plane smells different from the air I've known all my life in Calcutta, moist and weighted with the smell of mango blossoms and bus fumes and human sweat. This air is dry and cool and leaves a slight metallic aftertaste on my lips. I lick at them, wanting to capture that taste, make it part of me forever.

The little tray of food is so pretty, so sanitary. The knife and fork seated in their own plastic packet, the monogrammed paper napkin. I want to save even the shiny tinfoil that covers the steaming dish. I feel sadness for my friends—Prema, Vaswati, Sabitri—who will never see any of this. I picture them standing outside Ramu's *pakora* stall, munching on the spicy batter-dipped onion rings that our parents have expressly forbidden us to eat, looking up for a moment, eyes squinched against the sun, at the tiny silver plane. I pick up the candy in its crackly pink wrap from the dessert dish, *Almond Roca,* I read, and run my fingers over its nubby surface. I slip it into my purse, then take it out, laughing at my silliness. I am going to the land of Almond Rocas, I remind myself. The American chocolate melts in my month, just as sweet as I thought it would be.

But then the worries come.

I hardly know Aunt Pratima, my mother's younger sister with whom I am to stay while I attend college. And her husband, whom I am to call Bikram-uncle—I don't know him at all. They left India a week after their wedding (I was eight then) and have not been back since. Aunt is not much of a letter writer; every year at Bijoya she sends us a card stating how much she misses us, and that's all. In response to my letter asking for permission to stay with her, she wrote back only, *yes of course, but we live very simply.*

I wasn't quite sure what to make of it. All the women I know—my mother, her friends, my other aunts—are avid talkers, filling up lazy heat-hazed afternoons with long, gossipy tales while they drink tea and chew on betel leaves and laugh loud enough to scare away the *ghu-ghu* birds sleeping under the eaves. I couldn't ask my mother—she'd been against my coming to America and would surely use that letter to strengthen her arsenal. So I told myself that was how Americans (Aunt Pratima had lived there long enough to qualify as one) expressed themselves. Economically. And that second part, about living simply—she was just being modest. We all knew that Bikram-uncle owned his own auto business.

Now I look down on the dazzle-bright clouds packed tight as snow cones, deceptively solid. (But I know they are only mist and gauze, unable to save us should an engine fail and the plane plummet downward.) I pull my blue silk sari, which I bought specially for this trip, close around me. The air feels suddenly stale, heavy with other people's exhalations. I think, *What if Uncle and Aunt don't like me? What if I don't like them?* I remember the only picture I've seen of them, the faded sepia marriage photo where they gazed into the camera, stoic and unsmiling, their heavy garlands pulling at their necks. (Why had they never sent any other pictures?) What if they hadn't re-ally wanted me to come and were only being polite? (Americans, I'd heard, liked their privacy. They liked their lives to be smooth and uninterrupted by the claims of relatives.) What if they're not even at the airport? What if they're there but I don't recognize them? I imagine myself stranded, my suitcases strewn around me, the only one left in a large, echoing building after all the happily reunited families have gone home. Maybe I should have listened to Mother after all, I say to myself. Should have let her arrange that marriage for me with Aunt Sarita's neighbor's nephew. Saying it makes the fear something I can see and breathe, like the gray fog that hangs above the smoking section of the aircraft, where someone has placed me by mistake.

Later, of course, I will laugh at my foolishness. Aunt and Uncle are there, just as Aunt had promised, and I pick them out right away (how can I not?) from among the swirl of smart business suits and shiny leather briefcases, the elegant skirts that swing above stiletto-thin high heels.

Bikram-uncle is a short, stocky man dressed in greasy mechanic's overalls that surprise me. He has a belligerent mustache and very dark skin and a scar that runs up the side of his neck. (Had it been hidden in the wedding photo under the garlands?) I am struck at once by how ugly he is—the garlands had hidden that as well—how unlike Aunt, who stoops a bit to match her husband's height, her fine, nervous hands worrying the edge of her shawl as she scans the travelers emerging from Immigration.

I touch their feet like a good Indian girl should, though I am somewhat embarrassed. Everyone in the airport is watching us, I'm sure of it. Aunt is embarrassed too, and shifts her weight from leg to leg. Then she kisses me on both cheeks, but a little hesitantly—I get the feeling she hasn't done something like this in a long time.

"O Jayanti!" she says. "I am having no idea you are growing so beautiful. And so fair-skinned. And you such a thin thin girl with scabby knees when I left India. It is making me very happy." Her voice is soft and uncertain, as though she rarely speaks above a whisper, but her eyes are warm, flecked with bits of light.

I don't know what Uncle thinks. This makes me smile too widely and speak too fast and thank them too effusively for taking me in. I start to take out letters and packets from my carry-on bag.

"This is from Mother," I tell Aunt. "This fat one wrapped in twine is from Grandfather. And here's a jar of the lemon-mango pickle you used to like so much—Great-aunt Rama made it herself when she heard—"

Bikram-uncle interrupts. Unlike Aunt, who speaks refined Bengali, he uses a staccato American English. His accent jars my ears. I have trouble understanding it.

"Can we get going? I got to be back at work. You women can chat all day once you get home."

His voice isn't unkind. Still I feel reprimanded, as though I am a little girl again, and spitefully I wonder how a marriage could ever have been arranged between a man like Bikram-uncle and my aunt, who comes from an old and wealthy landowning family.

The overalls are part of the problem. They make him seem so—I hesitate to use the word, but only briefly—*low-class.* Why, even Mr. Bhalani, who owned the Lakshmi Motor Works near the Mint, always wore a starched white linen suit and a diamond on his little finger. Now as I stare from the back of the car at the fold of neck that overlaps the grimy collar of Uncle's overalls, I feel that something is very wrong.

But only for a moment. Outside, America is whizzing by the fogged-up

car window, blurry silhouettes of brick and stone and tall black glass that glint
in the sun, making me dizzy. I wipe the moisture from the pane with the edge
of my sari.

"What's this?" I ask. "And this?"

"The central post office," Aunt replies, laughing a little at my excitement.
"The Sears Tower." But a lot of the time she says, "I am not knowing this
one." Uncle busies himself with swerving in and out of traffic, humming
along with the song on the radio.

The apartment is another disappointment, not at all what an American
home should be like. I've seen the pictures in *Good Housekeeping* and *Sunset*
at the USIS library, and once our neighbor Aditi brought over the photos her
*chachaji* had sent from Akron, Ohio. I remember clearly the neat red brick
house with matching flowery drapes, the huge, perfectly mowed lawn green
like it had been painted, the shiny concrete driveway on which sat two shiny
motorcars. And Akron isn't even as big as Chicago. And Aditi's *chachaji* only
works in an office, selling insurance.

This apartment smells of stale curry. It is crowded with faded, over-
stuffed sofas and rickety end tables that look like they've come from a larger
place. A wadded newspaper is wedged under one of the legs of the dining
table. Uncle and Aunt are watching me, his eyes defiant, hers anxious. I shift
my gaze to the dingy walls hung with prints of landscapes, cattle standing
under droopy weeping willows looking vaguely bored, (surely they are not
Aunt's choice?) and try to keep my face polite. My monogrammed leather
cases are an embarrassment in this household. I push them under the bed in
the tiny room I am to occupy—it is the same size as my bathroom at home. I
remember that cool green mosaic floor, the clawfooted marble bathtub from
colonial days, the large window that looks out on my mother's crimson and
gold dahlias, and want to cry. But I tell Aunt that I will be very comfortable
here, and I thank her for the rose she has put in a jelly jar and placed on the
windowsill.

Aunt cooks happily all afternoon. Whenever I offer help she says, "No
no, you just sit and rest your feet and tell me what all's going on at home."

Dinner turns out to be an elaborate affair—a spicy almond-chicken curry
arranged over hot rice, a spinach-lentil *dal,* a yogurt cucumber *raita,* fried
potato *pakoras,* crisp golden *papads,* and sweet white *kheer*—which has
taken hours to prepare—for dessert. I have a guilty feeling that Aunt and
Uncle don't usually eat this way, and as we sit down I glance at Uncle for con-
firmation. But he has already started on the food. He eats quickly and with
concentration, without raising his head. When he wants more he points
silently, and Aunt hurries to serve him. He has taken a shower and put on the
muslin *kutta-pajama* I brought him as a gift from India. With his hair brushed

back wetly and *chappals* on his feet, he could be any Indian man sitting down to his dinner after a hard day's work. As I watch Aunt ladle more *dal* onto his plate, I have a strange sense of disorientation, and for a moment I wonder whether I've left Calcutta at all.

"I think he is liking you," whispers Aunt Pratima when we are alone in the kitchen. She stops spooning dessert into bowls to touch me lightly on the wrist, her face bright. "See how he is wearing the clothes you brought for him? Most nights he does not even change out of his overalls, let alone take a shower."

I am dubious. Uncle's attitude toward me, as far as I can tell, is one of testy tolerance. But I give Aunt a hug and hope, for her sake, that she is right. And as I help her pour tea into chipped cups of fine bone china that look like they might have once been part of her dowry, I make a special effort. I offer Uncle my most charming smile.

"I can't believe I'm finally here in the U.S.," I tell him. "I've heard so much about Chicago—Lake Michigan, which is surely big as an ocean, the Egyptian museum with mummies three thousand years old, and is it true that the big downtown stores have real silver mannequins in their windows?"

Uncle grunts noncommittally, regarding the teacups with disfavor. He stomps into the kitchen where I hear him rummage in the refrigerator.

"I can't wait to see it all!" I call after him. "I'm so glad I have the summer, though of course I'm looking forward to starting at the university in September!"

"You will do well, I know." Aunt nods encouragingly. "You are such a smart girt to be getting into this university where people from all over the world are trying to become students. Soon you will have many many American friends, and—"

"Don't be too sure of that," Bikram-uncle breaks in, startling me. His voice is harsh, raspy. He stands in the kitchen doorway, drinking from a can which glints in his fist. "Things here aren't as perfect as people at home like to think. We all thought we'd become millionaires. But it's not so easy."

"Please," Aunt says, but he seems not to hear her. He tips his head back to swallow, and the scar on his neck glistens pinkly like a live thing. *Budweiser,* I read as he sets the can down, and am shocked to realize he's drinking beer. At home in Calcutta none of the family touches alcohol, not even cousin Ramesh, who attends St. Xavier's College and sports a navy-blue blazer and a British accent. Mother has always told me what a disgusting habit it is, and she's right. I remember Grandfather's village at harvest time, the farmhands lying in ditches, drunk on palm-toddy, flies buzzing around their faces. I try not to let my distaste show on my face.

Now Uncle's tone is dark and raw. The bitterness in it coats my mouth like the *karela* juice Mother used to give me to cool my liver.

"The Americans hate us. They're always putting as down because we're dark-skinned foreigners, *kala admi.* Blaming us for the damn economy, for taking away their jobs. You'll see it for yourself soon enough."

What has made him detest this country so much?

I look beyond Uncle's head at the window. All I can see is a dark rectangle. But I know the sky outside is filled with strange and beautiful stars, and I am suddenly angry with him for trying to ruin it all for me. I take a deep breath. I tell myself, I'll wait to make up my own mind.

At night I lie in my lumpy bed under a coarse green blanket. I try to sleep, but the night noises that still seem unfamiliar after a week—the desperate *whee-whee* of a siren, the wind sighing as it coils about the house—keep me awake. Small sounds filter, too, through the walls from Aunt's bedroom. And though they are quite innocent—the bedsprings creaking as someone turns over in sleep, footsteps and then the hum of the exhaust as the bathroom light is switched on—each time I stiffen with embarrassment. I cannot stop thinking of Uncle and Aunt. I would rather think only of Aunt, but like the shawls of the bride and groom at an Indian wedding ceremony, their lives are inextricably knotted together. I try to imagine her arriving in this country, speaking only a little English, red-veiled, wearing the heavy, elaborate jewelry I've seen in the wedding photo. (What happened to it all? Now Aunt only wears a thin gold chain and the tiniest of pearls in her ears.) Her shock at discovering that her husband was not the owner of an automobile empire (as the matchmaker had assured her family) but only a mechanic who had a dingy garage in an undesirable part of town.

I haven't seen Uncle's shop yet. Of course I haven't seen anything else either, but as soon as the weather—which has been a bone-chilling gray—improves, I plan to. I've already called the people at Midwest Bus Tours, which picks up passengers from their homes for an extra five dollars. But I have a feeling I'll never get to see the shop, and so—again spitefully —I make it, in my head, a cheerless place that smells of sweat and grease, where the hiss of hydraulics and the clanging of tools mix with the curses of mechanics who are all as surly as Bikram-uncle.

But soon, with the self-absorption of the young, I move on the wings of imagination to more exciting matters. In my Modern Novel class at the university, I sit dressed in a plaid skirt and a matching sweater. My legs, elegant in knee-high boots like the ones I have seen on one of the afternoon TV shows that Aunt likes, are casually crossed. My bobbed hair swings around my face as I spiritedly argue against the handsome professor's interpretation of Dreiser's philosophy. I discourse brilliantly on the character of Sister Carrie until he is convinced, and later we go out for dinner to a quiet little French restaurant. Candlelight shines on the professor's reddish hair, on his gold spectacle frames. On the rims of our wineglasses. Chopin plays in the background as he confesses his admiration, his love for me. He slips onto my finger a ring with stones that sparkle like his eyes and tells me of the trips we will go on around the world, the books we will co-author when I am his wife. (No arranged marriage like Aunt's for me!) After dinner he takes me to his apartment overlooking the lake, where fairy lights twinkle and shiver on the water. He pulls me down, respectfully but ardently, on the couch. His lips are hot against my throat, his . . .

But here my imagination, conditioned by a lifetime of maternal censorship, shuts itself down.

After lunch the next day I walk out onto the narrow balcony. It is still cold, but the sun is finally out. The sky stretches over me, a sheet of polished metal. The skyscrapers of downtown Chicago float glimmering in the distance, enchanted towers out of an old storybook. The air is so new and crisp that it makes me suddenly happy, full of hope.

As a child in India, sometimes I used to sing a song. *Will I marry a prince from a far-off magic land, where the pavements are silver and the roofs all gold?* My girlfriends and I would play skipping games to its rhythm, laughing carelessly, thoughtlessly. And now here I am. *America*, I think, and the word opens inside me like a folded paper flower placed in water, filling me until there is no room to breathe.

The apartment with its faded cushions and its crookedly hung pictures seems newly oppressive when I go back inside. Aunt is in the kitchen—where I have noticed she spends most of her time—chopping vegetables.

"Can we go for a walk?" I ask. "Please?"

Aunt looks doubtful. "It is being very cold outside," she tells me.

"Oh no," I assure her. "I was just out on the balcony and it's lovely, it really is."

"Your uncle does not like me to go out. He is telling me it is dangerous."

"How can it be dangerous?" I say. It's just a ploy of his to keep her shut up in the house and under his control. He would like to do the same with me, only I won't let him. I pull her by the hand to the window. "Look," I say. The streets are clean and empty and very wide. A gleaming blue car speeds by. A bus belches to a stop and two laughing girls get down,

I can feel Aunt weakening. But she says, "Better to wait. This weekend he is taking us to the mall. So many big big shops there, you'll like it. He says he will buy pizza for dinner. Do you know pizza? Is it coming to India yet?"

I want to tell her that the walls are closing in on me. My brain is dying. Soon I will turn into one of those mournful-eyed cows in the painting behind the sofa.

"Just a short walk for some exercise," I say. "We'll be back long before Uncle. He need not even know."

Maybe Aunt Pratima hears the longing in my voice. Maybe it makes her feel guilty. She lifts her thin face. When she smiles, she seems not that much older than me.

"In the village before marriage I was always walking everywhere—it was so nice, the fresh air, the sky, the ponds with lotus flowers, the dogs and goats and chickens all around. Of course, here we cannot be expecting such country things. . . ."

I wait.

"No harm in it, I am thinking," she finally says. "As long as we are staying close to the house. As long as we are coming back in time to fix a nice dinner for your uncle."

"Just a half-hour walk," I assure her. "We'll be back in plenty of time."

As we walk down the dim corridor that smells, just like the apartment, of stale curry (do the neighbors mind?), she adds, a bit apologetically, "Please do not be saying anything to Uncle. It will make him angry." She shakes her head. "He worries too much since . . ."

I want to ask her since what, but I sense she doesn't want to talk about it. I give her a bright smile.

"I won't say a word to Uncle. It'll be our secret."

In coats and saris we walk down the street. A few pedestrians stare at us silently as they sidle past. I miss the bristle of the Calcutta streets a little, the hawkers with their bright wares, the honking buses loaded with people, the rickshaw-wallahs calling out *make way*, but I say, "It's so neat and quiet, isn't it?"

"Every Wednesday the cleaning truck is coming with big brushes to sweep the streets," Aunt tells me proudly.

The sun has ducked behind a cloud, and it is colder than I had thought. When I look up the April light is a muted glare that hurts my eyes.

"It is probably snowing later today," Aunt says.

"That's wonderful! You know, I've only seen snow in movies! It always looked so pretty and delicate. I didn't think I'd get to see any this late in the year. . . ."

Aunt pulls her shapeless coat tighter around her. "It is not that great," she says. Her tone is regretful, as though she is sorry to disillusion me. "It melts inside the collar of your jacket and drips down your back. Cars are skidding when it turns to ice. And see how it looks like afterward...." She kicks at the brown slush on the side of the road with a force that surprises me.

I like my aunt though, the endearing way in which her eyes widen like a little girl's when she asks a question, the small frown line between her eyebrows when she listens, the sudden, liquid shift of her features when she smiles. I remember that she'd been considered a beauty back home, someone who deserved the good luck of having a marriage arranged with a man who lived in America.

As we walk, the brisk, invigorating air seems to loosen something inside of Aunt, She talks and talks. She asks about the design on my sari, deep rose-embroidered peacocks dancing against a cream background. Is this being the latest fashion in India? (She uses the word *desh*, country, to refer to India, as though it were the only one in the world.) "I am always loving Calcutta, visiting your mother in that beautiful old house with marble fountains and lions." She wants to know what movies are showing at the Roxy. Do children still fly the moon-shaped kites at the Maidan and do the street vendors still sell puffed rice spiced with green chilies? How about Victoria Memorial with the black angel on top of the white marble dome, is it still the same? Is it true that New Market with all those charming little clothing stores has burnt down? Have I been on the new subway she has read about in *India Abroad?* The words pour from her in a rush. "Imagine all those tunnels under the city, you could be getting lost in there and nobody will be finding you if you do not want them to." I hear the hunger in her voice. And so I hold back my own eagerness to learn about America and answer her the best I can.

The street has narrowed now and the apartment buildings look run-down, even to me, with peeling walls and patchy yellow spots on lawns where the snow has melted. There are chain-link fences and garbage on the pavement. Broken-down cars, their rusted hoods gaping, sit in several front yards. The sweet stench of rot rises from the drains. I am disconcerted. I thought I had left all such smells behind in Calcutta.

"Shouldn't we be going back, Aunt?" I ask, suddenly nervous.

Aunt Pratima looks around blindly.

"Yes yes, my goodness, is it that late already? Look at that black sky. It is so nice to be talking to someone about home that I am forgetting the time completely."

We start back, lifting up our saris to walk faster, our steps echoing along the empty sidewalk, and when we go back a bit Aunt stops and looks up and down the street without recognition, her head pivoting loosely like a lost animal's.

Then we see the boys. Four of them, playing in the middle of the street with cans and sticks. They hadn't been there before, or maybe it is a different street we are on now. The boys look up and I see that their sallow faces are grime streaked. Their blond hair hangs limply over their foreheads, and their eyes are pale and slippery, like pebbles left underwater for a long time. They may be anywhere from eight to fourteen—I can't tell their ages as I would with boys back home. They scare me on this deserted street although surely there's no reason for fear. They're just boys after all, with thin wrists that stick out from the sleeves of too-small jackets, standing under a tree on which the first leaves of spring are opening a pale and delicate green. I glance at Aunt Pratima for reassurance, but the skin on her face stretches tightly across her sharp, fragile cheekbones.

The boys bend their heads together, consulting, then the tallest one takes a step toward us and says, "Nigger." He says it softly, his upper lip curling away from his teeth. The word arcs through the empty street like a rock, an impossible word which belongs to another place and time. In the mouth of a red-faced gin-and-tonic drinking British official, perhaps, in his colonial bungalow, or a sneering overseer out of *Uncle Tom's Cabin* as he plies his whip in the cotton fields. But here is this boy, younger than my cousin Anup, saying it as easily as one might say *thank you* or *please.* Or *no problem.*

Now the others take up the word, chanting it in high singsong voices that have not broken yet, *nigger, nigger,* until I want to scream, or weep. Or laugh, because can't they *see* that I'm not black at all but an Indian girl of good family? When our chauffeur Gurbans Singh drives me down the Calcutta streets in our silver-colored Fiat, people stop to whisper, *Isn't that Jayanti Ganguli, daughter of the Bhavanipur Gangulis?*

I don't see which boy first picks up the fistful of slush, but now they're all throwing it at us. It splatters on our coats and runs down our saris, leaving long streaks. I take a step toward the boys. I'm not sure what I'll do when I get to them—shake them? explain the mistake they've made? smash their faces into the pavement?—but Aunt holds tight to my arm.

"No, Jayanti, no."

I try to pull free but she is surprisingly strong, or perhaps I'm not trying hard enough. Perhaps I'm secretly thankful that she's begging me—*Let's go home, Jayanti*—so that I don't have to confront those boys with more hate in their eyes than boys should ever have. There is slush on Aunt's face; her trembling lips are ash-colored. She's sobbing, and when I put out my hand to comfort her I realize that I too am sobbing. Half running, tripping on the wet saris which slap at our legs, we retreat down the street. The voices follow us for a long time. *Nigger, nigger.* Slush-voices, trickling into us even when we've finally found the right road back to our building, which had been only one street away all the time. Even when in the creaking elevator we tidy each other as best we can, wiping at faces, brushing off coats, holding each other's shivering hands, looking away from each other's eyes.

The light has burned out in the passage outside the door. Aunt Pratima fumbles in her purse for the key, saying, "It was here, I am keeping it right here, where can it *go?*"

In their thin Indian shoes, my feet are colder than I have ever imagined possible. My teeth chatter as I say, "It's all right, calm down, Auntie, we'll find it."

But Aunt's voice quavers higher and higher, a bucking, runaway voice. She turns her purse upside down and shakes it, coins and wrappers and pens and safety pins tumbling out and skittering to the edges of the passage. Then she gets down on all fours on the mangy brown carpet to grope through them.

That is when Bikram-uncle opens the door. He is still wearing his grease-stained overalls. "What the hell is going on?" he says, looking down at Aunt. Standing across from him, I look down too, and see what he must be seeing, the parting in Aunt Pratima's tightly pulled-back hair, the stretched line of the scalp pointing grayly at her lowered forehead like an accusation.

"Where the hell have you been?" Bikram-uncle asks, more loudly this time. "Get in here right now."

I kneel and help Aunt gather up some of her things, leaving the rest behind.

Inside, Bikram-uncle yells, "Haven't I *told* you not to walk around this trashy neighborhood? Haven't I *told* you it wasn't safe? Don't you remember what happened to my shop last year, how they smashed everything? And still you had to go out, had to give them the chance to do *this* to you." He draws in a ragged breath, like a sob. "My God, look at you."

I try not to stare at Aunt's mud-splotched cheek, her ruined coat, her red-rimmed, pleading glance. But I can't drag my eyes away. Once when I was little, I'd looked down into an old well behind Grandfather's house and seen my face, pale and distorted, reflected in the brackish water. I have that same dizzying sensation now. *Is this what my life too will be like?*

"It was my fault," I say. "Aunt didn't want to go."

But no one hears me.

Aunt takes a hesitant, sideways step toward Uncle. It is a small movement, something an injured animal might make toward its keeper. "They were only children," she says in a wondering tone.

"Bastards," cries Uncle, his voice choking, his accent suddenly thick and Indian. "Bloody bastards. I want to kill them, all of them." His entire face wavers, as though it will collapse in on itself. He raises his arm.

"No," I shout. I run toward them. But my body moves slowly, as though underwater. Perhaps it cannot believe that he will really do it.

When the back of his hand catches Aunt Pratima across the mouth, I flinch as if his knuckles had made that thwacking bone sound against my own flesh. My mouth fills with an ominous salt taste.

*Will I marry a prince from a far-off magic land?*

I put out my hand to shield Aunt, but Uncle is quicker. He has her already tight in his grasp. I look about wildly for something—perhaps a chair to bring crashing down on his head. Then I hear him,

"Pratima," he cries in a broken voice, "Pratima, Pratima." He touches her face, his fingers groping uncertainly like a blind man's, his whole body shaking.

"Hush, Ram," says my aunt. "Hush." She strokes his hair as though he were a child, and perhaps he is.

"Pratima, how could I. . . ."

"Shhh, I am understanding."

"Something exploded in my head . . . it was like that time at the shop . . . remember . . . how the fire they started took everything. . . ."

"Don't be thinking of it now, Ram," says Aunt Pratima. She pulls his head down to her breast and lays her cheek on his hair. Her fingers caress the scar on his neck. Her face is calm, almost happy. She—they—have forgotten me.

I feel like an intruder, a fool. How little I've understood. As I turn to tip-toe away to my room, I hear my uncle say, "I tried so hard, Pratima. I wanted to give you so many things—but even your jewelry is gone." Grief scrapes at his voice. "This damn country, like a *dain*, a witch—it pretends to give and then snatches everything back."

And Aunt's voice, pure and musical with the lilt of a smile in it, "O Ram, I am having all I need."

Now it is night but no one has thought to turn on the family room lights. Bikram-uncle sits in front of the TV, his feet up on the rickety coffee table. He is finishing his third beer. The can gleams faintly as it catches the uneven blue flickers from the tube. I feel I should say something to him, but he is not looking at me, and I don't know what to say. Aunt Pratima is in the kitchen preparing dinner as though this were an evening like all others. I should go and help her. But I remain in my chair in the corner of the room. I am not sure how to face her either, how to start talking about what has happened. (In my head I am trying to make sense of it still.) Am I to ignore it all (*can* I?)—the hate-suffused faces of the boys, the swelling spreading its dark blotch across Aunt's jaw, the memory of Uncle's head pressed trembling to her breast? *Home*, I whisper desperately, *homehomehome*, and suddenly, intensely, I want my room in Calcutta, where things were so much simpler. I want the high mahogany bed in which I've slept as long as I can remember, the comforting smell of sun-dried cotton sheets to pull around my head. I want my childhood again. But I am too far away for the spell to work, for the words to take me back, even in my head.

Then out of the corner of my eye I catch a white movement. It is snowing. I step outside onto the balcony, drawing my breath in at the silver marvel of it, the fat flakes cool and wet against my face as in a half-forgotten movie. It is cold, so cold that I can feel the insides of my nostrils stiffening. The air—there is no smell to it at all—carves a freezing path all the way into my chest. But I don't go back inside. The snow has covered the dirty cement pavements, the sad warped shingles of the rooftops, has softened, forgivingly, the rough noisy edges of things. I hold out my hands to it, palms down, shivering a little.

The snow falls on them, chill, stinging all the way to the bone. But after a while the excruciating pain fades. I am thinking of hands. The pink-tipped blond hand of the air hostess as she offers me a warm towelette that smells like unknown flowers. The boy's grimy one pushing back his limp hair, then tightening into a fist to throw a lump of slush. Uncle's with its black nails, its oddly defenseless scraped knuckles, arcing through the air to knock Aunt's head sideways. And Aunt's hand, stroking that angry pink scar. Threading her long elegant fingers (the fingers, still, of a Bengali aristocrat's daughter) through his graying hair to pull him to her. All these American hands that I know will keep coming back in my dreams.

*Will I marry a prince from a far-off magic land*
*Where the pavements are silver and the roofs all gold?*

When I finally look down, I notice that the snow has covered my own hands so they are no longer brown but white, white, white. And now it makes sense that the beauty and the pain should be part of each other. I continue holding them out in front of me, gazing at them, until they're completely covered. Until they do not hurt at all.

# Bharati Mukherjee

"I see myself as an American writer in the tradition of other American writers whose parents or grandparents had passed through Ellis Island," Bharati Mukherjee wrote in the introduction to her 1985 collection of short stories, *Darkness*. That identification is a metaphorical one, considering that Mukherjee was born of Brahmin parents in Calcutta, 27 July 1940, and did not come to the United States until 1961. Yet her work has gradually moved away from India to embrace other places and other stories, so that she has indeed become less of an "Indian writer in English" and more of an "American writer." While growing up in a traditional Indian household, Mukherjee also experienced Western culture: first when her father took the family to Europe for three years when she was eight; then in the Anglicized and elite girls' school, which she attended in Calcutta on their return. After graduating with a bachelor's degree from the University of Calcutta and a master's from the University of Baroda, Mukherjee entered the University of Iowa Writers' Workshop on a scholarship, where she received an MFA in creative writing, followed by a doctorate in comparative literature. In Iowa she married American-born Clark Blaise, and they settled in Canada and took citizenship there. Mukherjee and her family moved back to the United States in 1981, and became U.S. citizens. She now teaches at the University of California, Berkeley.

Mukherjee's first novel, *The Tiger's Daughter* (1971), depicts the alienation of an American-educated Indian woman returning to Calcutta with her American husband. Dislocated, the central character feels like an expatriate in her own homeland. The second novel, *Wife* (1975), also examines alienation and dislocation, but in contrasting terms as it reveals how a Calcutta-born woman transplanted to the United States turns to destructive behavior when she is unable to cope with the pain of immigration. A move toward Americanization on Mukherjee's part is detectable in her next novel, *Jasmine*

(1989), which also concentrates on the emotional reaction of the immigrant but explores the condition in a much wider sphere. While in the earlier novels, Mukherjee reproduced the cadences and oddities of Indians speaking English, she celebrates the American idiom in *Jasmine* and does so admirably. In fact, the Americanization of Mukherjee's diction has become a distinguishing characteristic of her style, and is immediately evident in the short stories and subsequent novels.

Although the central character in *The Holder of the World* (1993) moves from Salem, Massachusetts, into seventeenth-century India, the work is more American than Indian in its context. The book also displays the most original form of any of Mukherjee's work so far, especially in its handling of time. The narrator is a present-day American whose research uncovers the story and whose voice allows Mukherjee enormous freedom. A haunted past and a quest for personal identity dominates *Leave It to Me* (1997) as it follows a young woman's search for her true parents. Set for the most part in contemporary San Francisco, the narrative catches the distinguishing characteristics of that city and its people.

The two short-story collections, *Darkness* (1985) and *The Middleman and Other Stories* (1988), capture the drama of immigration through narratives about Indian women adrift in America, as well as through other stories that explore in varied and inventive ways the immigrant encounter and its accompanying personal displacement. One such story, "Buried Lives" from *The Middleman*, follows a would-be Sri Lankan immigrant on his way to Canada. Although the rigors of his disconnected journey have likely been endured by many like him, the final lines seem to question the reality of his experience.

# Buried Lives

One March midafternoon in Trincomalee, Sri Lanka, Mr. N.K.S. Venkatesan, a forty-nine-year-old school-teacher who should have been inside a St. Joseph's Collegiate classroom explicating Arnold's "The Buried Life" found himself instead at a barricaded intersection, axe in hand and shouting rude slogans at a truckload of soldiers.

Mr. Venkatesan was not a political man. In his neighborhood he was the only householder who hadn't contributed, not even a rupee, to the Tamil Boys Sporting Association, which everyone knew wasn't a cricket club so much as a recruiting center for the Liberation Tigers. And at St. Joe's, he hadn't signed the staff petition abhorring the arrest at a peaceful anti-Buddhist demonstration of Dr. Pillai, the mathematics teacher. Venkatesan had rather enjoyed talking about fractals with Dr. Pillai, but he disapproved of men with family responsibilities sticking their heads between billy clubs as though they were still fighting the British for independence.

Fractals claimed to predict, mathematically, chaos and apparent randomness. Such an endeavor, if possible, struck Mr. Venkatesan as a virtually holy quest, closer to the spirit of religion than of science. What had once been Ceylon was now Sri Lanka.

Mr. Venkatesan, like Dr. Pillai, had a large family to look after: he had parents, one set of grandparents, an aunt who hadn't been quite right in the head since four of her five boys had signed up with the Tigers, and three much younger, unmarried sisters. They lived with him in a three-room flat above a variety store. It was to protect his youngest sister (a large, docile girl who, before she got herself mixed up with the Sporting Association, used to embroider napkin-and-tablecloth sets and sell them to a middleman for export to fancy shops in Canada) that he was marching that afternoon with two hundred baby-faced protesters.

Axe under arm—he held the weapon as he might an umbrella—Mr. Venkatesan and his sister and a frail boy with a bushy mustache on whom his sister appeared to have a crush, drifted past looted stores and charred vehicles. In the center of the intersection, a middle-aged leader in camouflage fatigues and a black beret stood on the roof of a van without tires, and was about to set fire to the national flag with what looked to Mr. Venkatesan very much like a Zippo lighter.

"Sir, you have to get in the mood," said his sister's boyfriend. The mustache entirely covered his mouth. Mr. Venkatesan had the uncanny sensation of being addressed by a thatch of undulating bristles. "You have to let yourself go, sir."

This wasn't advice; this was admonition. Around Mr. Venkatesan swirled dozens of hyperkinetic boys in white shirts, holding bricks. Fat girls in summer frocks held placards aloft. His sister sucked on an ice cream bar. Every protester seemed to twinkle with fun. He didn't know how to have fun, that was the trouble. Even as an adolescent he'd battened down all passion; while other students had slipped love notes into expectant palms, he'd studied, he'd passed exams. Dutifulness had turned him into a pariah.

"Don't think you chaps invented civil disobedience!"

He lectured the boyfriend on how his generation—meaning that technically, he'd been alive though hardly self-conscious—had cowed the British Empire. The truth was that the one time the police had raided the Venkatesans' flat—he'd been four, but he'd been taught anti-British phrases like "the salt march" and "*satyagraha*" by a cousin ten years older—he had saluted the superintendent smartly even as constables squeezed his cousin's wrists into handcuffs. That cousin was now in San Jose, California, minting lakhs and lakhs of dollars in computer software.

The boyfriend, still smiling awkwardly, moved away from Mr. Venkatesan's sister. His buddies, Tigers in berets, were clustered around a vendor of spicy fritters.

"Wait!" the sister pleaded, her face puffy with held-back tears.

"What do you see in that callow, good-for-nothing bloke?" Mr. Venkatesan asked.

"Please, please leave me alone," his sister screamed. "Please let me do what I want."

What if *he* were to do what he wanted! Twenty years ago when he'd had the chance, he should have applied for a Commonwealth Scholarship. He should have immured himself in a leafy dormitory in Oxford. Now it was too late. He'd have studied law. Maybe he'd have married an English girl and loitered abroad. But both parents had died, his sisters were mere toddlers, and he was obliged to take the lowest, meanest teaching job in the city.

"I want to die," his sister sobbed beside him.

"Shut up, you foolish girl."

The ferocity of her passion for the worthless boy, who was, just then, biting into a greasy potato fritter, shocked him. He had patronized her when she had been a plain, pliant girl squinting at embroidered birds and flowers. But now something harsh and womanly seemed to be happening inside her.

"Forget those chaps. They're nothing but troublemakers." To impress her, he tapped a foot to the beat of a slogan bellowing out of loudspeakers.

Though soldiers were starting to hustle demonstrators into double-parked paddy wagons, the intersection had taken on the gaudiness of a village fair. A white-haired vendor darted from police jeep to jeep hawking peanuts in paper cones. Boys who had drunk too much tea or soda relieved themselves freely into poster-clogged gutters. A dozen feet up the road a housewife with a baby on her hip lobbed stones into storefronts. A band of beggars staggered out of an electronics store with a radio and a television. No reason not to get in the mood.

"Blood for blood," he shouted, timidly at first. "Blood begets blood."

"Begets?" the man beside him asked. "What's that supposed to mean?" In his plastic sandals and cheap drawstring pajamas, the man looked like a coolie or laborer.

He turned to his sister for commiseration. What could she expect him to have in common with a mob of uneducated men like that? But she'd left him behind. He saw her, crouched for flight like a giant ornament on the hood of an old-fashioned car, the March wind stiffly splaying her sari and long hair behind her.

"Get down from that car!" he cried. But the crowd, swirling, separated him from her. He felt powerless; he could no longer watch over her, keep her out of the reach of night sticks. From on top of the hood she taunted policemen, and not just policemen but everybody—shopgirls and beggars and ochre-robed monks—as though she wasn't just a girl with a crush on a Tiger but a monster out of one's most splenetic nightmares.

Months later, in a boardinghouse in Hamburg, Mr. Venkatesan couldn't help thinking about the flock of young monks pressed together behind a police barricade that eventful afternoon. He owed his freedom to the monks because, in spite of their tonsure scars and their vows of stoicism, that afternoon they'd behaved like any other hot-headed Sri Lankan adolescents. If the monks hadn't chased his sister and knocked her off the pale blue hood of the car, Mr. Venkatesan would have stayed on in Sri Lanka, in Trinco, in St. Joe's teaching the same poems year after year, a permanent prisoner.

What the monks did was unforgivable. Robes plucked knee-high and celibate lips plumped up in vengeful chant, they pulled a girl by the hair, and they slapped and spat and kicked with vigor worthy of newly initiated Tigers.

It could have been another girl, somebody else's younger sister. Without thinking, Mr. Venkatesan rotated a shoulder, swung an arm, readied his mind to inflict serious harm.

It should never have happened. The axe looped clumsily over the heads of demonstrators and policemen and fell, like a captured kite, into the hands of a Home Guards officer. There was blood, thick and purplish, spreading in jagged stains on the man's white uniform. The crowd wheeled violently. The drivers of paddy wagons laid panicky fingers on their horns. Veils of tear gas blinded enemies and friends. Mr. Venkatesan, crying and choking, ducked into a store and listened to the thwack of batons. When his vision eased, he staggered, still on automatic pilot, down side streets and broke through garden hedges all the way to St. Joseph's unguarded backdoor.

In the men's room off the Teacher's Common Room he held his face, hot with guilt, under a rusty, hissing faucet until Father van der Haagen, the Latin and Scriptures teacher, came out of a stall.

"You don't look too well. Sleepless night, eh?" the Jesuit joked. "You need to get married, Venkatesan. Bad habits can't always satisfy you."

Mr. Venkatesan laughed dutifully. All of Father van der Haagen's jokes had to do with masturbation. He didn't say anything about having deserted his sister. He didn't say anything about having maimed, maybe murdered, a Home Guards officer. "Who can afford a wife on what the school pays?" he joked back. Then he hurried off to his classroom.

Though he was over a half-hour late, his students were still seated meekly at their desks.

"Good afternoon, sir." Boys in monogrammed shirts and rice-starched shorts shuffled to standing positions.

"Sit!" the schoolmaster commanded. Without taking his eyes off the students, he opened his desk and let his hand locate *A Treasury of the Most Dulcet Verses Written in the English Language*, which he had helped the headmaster to edit though only the headmaster's name appeared on the book.

Matthew Arnold was Venkatesan's favorite poet. Mr. Venkatesan had talked the Head into including four Arnold poems. The verses picked by the Head hadn't been "dulcet" at all, and one hundred and three pages of the total of one hundred and seventy-four had been given over to upstart Trinco versifiers' martial ballads.

Mr. Venkatesan would have nursed a greater bitterness against the Head if the man hadn't vanished, mysteriously, soon after their acrimonious coediting job.

One winter Friday the headmaster had set out for his nightly after-dinner walk, and he hadn't come back. The Common Room gossip was that he had been kidnapped by a paramilitary group. But Miss Philomena, the female teacher who was by tradition permitted the use of the Head's private bathroom, claimed the man had drowned in the Atlantic Ocean trying to sneak into Canada in a boat that ferried, for a wicked fee, illegal aliens. Stashed in the bathroom's air vent (through which sparrows sometimes flew in and bothered her), she'd spotted, she said, an oilcloth pouch stuffed with foreign cash and fake passports.

In the Teacher's Common Room, where Miss Philomena was not popular, her story was discounted. But at the Pillais's home, the men teachers had gotten together and toasted the Head with hoarded bottles of whiskey and sung many rounds of "For He's a Jolly Good Fellow," sometimes substituting "smart" for "good." By the time Mr. Venkatesan had been dropped home by Father van der Haagen, who owned a motorcycle, night had bleached itself into rainy dawn. It had been the only all-nighter of Mr. Venkatesan's life and the only time he might have been accused of drunkenness.

The memory of how good the rain had felt came back to him now as he glanced through the first stanza of the assigned Arnold poem. What was the function of poetry if not to improve the petty, cautious minds of evasive children? What was the duty of the teacher if not to inspire?

He cleared his throat, and began to read aloud in a voice trained in elocution.

> Light flows our war of mocking words, and yet,
> Behold, with tears mine eyes are wet!
> I feel a nameless sadness o'er me roll.
> Yes, yes, we know that we can jest,
> We know, we know that we can smile!
> But there's a something in this breast,
> To which thy light words bring no rest,
> And thy gay smiles no anodyne.
> Give me thy hand, and hush awhile,
> And turn those limpid eyes on mine,
> And let me read there, love! thy inmost soul.

"Sir," a plump boy in the front row whispered as Venkatesan finally stopped for breath.

"What is it now?" snapped Venkatesan. In his new mood Arnold had touched him with fresh intensity, and he hated the boy for deflating illusion. "If you are wanting to know a synonym for 'anodyne,' then look it up in the *Oxford Dictionary*. You are a lazy donkey wanting me to feed you with a silver spoon. All of you, you are all lazy donkeys."

"No, sir." The boy persisted in spoiling the mood.

It was then that Venkatesan took in the boy's sweaty face and hair. Even the eyes were fat and sweaty.

"Behold, sir," the boy said. He dabbed his eyelids with the limp tip of his school tie. "Mine eyes, too, are wet."

"You are a silly donkey," Venkatesan yelled. "You are a beast of burden.

You deserve the abuse that you get. It is you emotional types who are selling this country down the river."

The class snickered, unsure what Mr. Venkatesan wanted of them. The boy let go of his tie and wept openly. Mr. Venkatesan hated himself. Here was a kindred soul, a fellow lover of Matthew Arnold, and what had he done other than indulge in gratuitous cruelty? He blamed the times. He blamed Sri Lanka.

It was as much this classroom incident as the fear of arrest for his part in what turned out to be an out-of-control demonstration that made Mr. Venkatesan look into emigrating. At first, he explored legal channels. He wasted a month's salary bribing arrogant junior-level clerks in four consulates—he was willing to settle almost anywhere except in the Gulf Emirates—but every country he could see himself being happy and fulfilled in turned him down.

So all through the summer he consoled himself with reading novels. Adventure stories in which fearless young Britons—sailors, soldiers, missionaries—whacked wildernesses into submission. From lending libraries in the city, he checked out books that were so old that they had to be trussed with twine. On the flyleaf of each book, in fading ink, was an inscription by a dead or retired British tea planter. Like the blond heroes of the novels, the colonials must have come to Ceylon chasing dreams of perfect futures. He, too, must sail dark, stormy oceans.

In August, at the close of a staff meeting, Miss Philomena announced coyly that she was leaving the island. A friend in Kalamazoo, Michigan, had agreed to sponsor her as a "domestic."

"It is a ploy only, man," Miss Philomena explained. "In the autumn, I am signing up for post-graduate studies in a prestigious educational institution."

"You are cleaning toilets and whatnot just like a servant girl? Is the meaning of 'domestic' not the same as 'servant'?"

Mr. Venkatesan joined the others in teasing Miss Philomena, but late that night he wrote away to eight American universities for applications. He took great care with the cover letters, which always began with "Dear Respected Sir" and ended with "Humbly but eagerly awaiting your response." He tried to put down in the allotted blanks what it felt like to be born so heartbreakingly far from New York or London. *On this small dead-end island, I feel I am a shadow-man, a nothing. I feel I'm a stranger in my own room. What consoles me is reading. I sink my teeth into fiction by great Englishmen such as G.A. Henty and A.E.W. Mason. I live my life through their imagined lives. And when I put their works down at dawn I ask myself, Hath not a Tamil eyes, heart, ears, nose, throat, to adapt the words of the greatest Briton. Yes, I am a Tamil. If you prick me, do I not bleed? If you tickle me, do I not laugh? Then, if I dream, will you not give me a chance, respected Sir, as only you can?*

In a second paragraph he politely but firmly indicated the size of scholarship he would require, and indicated the size of apartment he (and his sisters) would require. He preferred close proximity to campus, since he did not intend to drive.

But sometime in late April, the school's porter brought him, rubber-banded together, eight letters of rejection.

"I am worthless," Mr. Venkatesan moaned in front of the porter. "I am a donkey."

The porter offered him aspirins. "You are unwell, sahib."

The schoolteacher swallowed the tablets, but as soon as the servant left, he snatched a confiscated Zippo lighter from his desk and burned the rejections.

When he got home, his sister's suitor was on the balcony, painting placards, and though he meant to say nothing to the youth, meant to admit no flaw, no defeat, his body betrayed him with shudders and moans.

"Racism!" the youth spat as he painted over a spelling error that, even in his grief, Mr. Venkatesan couldn't help pointing out. "Racism is what's slamming the door in your face, man! You got to improvise your weapons!"

Perhaps the boy was not a totally unworthy suitor. He let the exclamations play in his head, and soon the rejections, and the anxiety that he might be stuck on the futureless island fired him up instead of depressing him. Most nights he lay in bed fully dressed—the police always raided at dawn—and thought up a hundred illegal but feasible ways to outwit immigration officials.

The least wild schemes he talked over with Father van der Haagen. Long ago and in another country, Father van der Haagen had surely given in to similar seductions. The Jesuit usually hooted, "So you want to rot in a freezing, foreign jail? You want your lovely sisters to walk the streets and come to harm?" But, always the expatriate ended these chats with his boyhood memories of skating on frozen Belgian rivers and ponds. Mr. Venkatesan felt he could visualize snow, but not a whole river so iced up that it was as solid as a grand trunk highway. In his dreams, the Tamil schoolteacher crisscrossed national boundaries on skates that felt as soft and comforting as cushions.

In August his sister's suitor got himself stupidly involved in a prison break. The sister came to Mr. Venkatesan weeping. She had stuffed clothes and her sewing basket into a camouflage satchel. She was going into the northern hills, she said. The Tigers could count on the tea pickers.

"No way," Mr. Venkatesan exploded. When he was safely in America's heartland, with his own wife and car and all accoutrements of New World hearth and home, he wanted to think of his Trinco family (to whom he meant to remit generous monthly sums) as being happy under one roof, too. "You are not going to live with hooligan types in jungles."

"If you lock me in my room, I'll call the police. I'll tell them who threw the axe at the rally."

"Is that what they teach you in guerrilla camps? To turn on your family?" he demanded.

The sister wept loudly into her sari. It was a pretty lilac sari, and he remembered having bought it for her seventeenth birthday. On her feet were fragile lilac slippers. He couldn't picture her scrambling up terraced slopes of tea estates in that pretty get-up. "Nobody has to teach me," she retorted.

In her lilac sari, and with the white fragrant flower wreath in her hair, she didn't look like a blackmailer. It was the times. She, her boyfriend, he himself, were all fate's victims.

He gave in. He made her promise, though, that in the hills she would marry her suitor. She touched his feet with her forehead in the traditional farewell. He heard a scooter start up below. So the guerrilla had been waiting. She'd meant to leave home, with or without his permission. She'd freed herself of family duties and bonds.

Above the motor scooter's sputter, the grateful boyfriend shouted, "Sir, I will put you in touch with a man. Listen to him and he will deliver you." Then the dust cloud of destiny swallowed up the guerrilla bride-to-be and groom.

The go-between turned out to be a clubfooted and cauliflower-eared middle-aged man. The combination of deformities, no doubt congenital, had nevertheless earned him a reputation for ferocity and an indifference to inflicted suffering. He appeared on the front porch early one Saturday afternoon. He didn't come straight to the point. For the first half-hour he said very little and concentrated instead on the sweet almond-stuffed turnovers that the Venkatesan family had shaped and fried all day for a religious festival they'd be attending later that afternoon.

"You have, perhaps, some news for me?" Mr. Venkatesan asked shyly as he watched the man help himself to a chilled glass of mango fool. "Some important information, no?"

"Excuse me, sir," the man protested. "I know that you are a teacher and that therefore you are in the business of improving the mind of man. But forthrightness is not always a virtue. Especially in these troubled times."

The man's furtiveness was infectious, and Mr. Venkatesan, without thinking, thinned his voice to a hiss. "You are going over my options with me, no?"

"Options!" the man sneered. Then he took out a foreign-looking newspaper from a shopping bag. On a back page of the paper was a picture of three dour sahibs fishing for lobster. "You get my meaning, sir? They have beautiful coves in Nova Scotia. They have beautiful people in the Canadian Maritimes."

On cushiony skates and with clean, cool winds buoying him from behind, Mr. Venkatesan glided all the way into Halifax, dodging posses of border police. He married a girl with red, dimpled cheeks, and all winter she made love to him under a quilt. Summers he set lobster traps. Editors of quarterlies begged to see his poetry.

"Beautiful people, Canadians," he agreed.

"Not like the damn Americans!" The go-between masticated sternly. "They are sending over soldiers of fortune and suchlike to crush us."

Mr. Venkatesan, wise in ways of middlemen, asked, "This means you're not having a pipeline to America?"

The agent dipped into a bowl of stale fried banana chips.

"No matter. The time has come for me to leave."

The next day, Sunday, the man came back to find out how much Mr. Venkatesan might be willing to pay for a fake passport / airline tickets / safe houses en route package deal. Mr. Venkatesan named a figure.

"So you are not really anxious to exit?" the man said.

Mr. Venkatesan revised his figure. He revised the figure three more times before the go-between would do anything more human than sigh at him.

He was being taken by a mean, mocking man who preyed on others' dreams. He was allowing himself to be cheated. But sometime that spring the wish to get away—to flee abroad and seize the good life as had his San Jose cousin—had deepened into sickness. So he was blowing his life's savings on this malady. So what?

The man made many more trips. And on each trip, as Mr. Venkatesan sat the man down on the best rattan chair on the balcony, through the half-open door that led into the hallway he saw the women in his family gather in jittery knots. They knew he was about to forsake them.

Every brave beginning, in these cramped little islands, masked a secret betrayal. To himself, Mr. Venkatesan would always be a sinner.

Mr. Venkatesan threw himself into the planning. He didn't trust the man with the cauliflower ears. Routes, circuitous enough to fool border guards, had to be figured out. He could fly to Frankfurt via Malta, for instance, then hole up in a ship's cargo hold for the long, bouncy passage on Canadian seas. Or he could take the more predictable (and therefore, cheaper but with more surveillance) detours through the Gulf Emirates.

The go-between or travel agent took his time. Fake travel documents and work permits had to be printed up. Costs, commissions, bribes had to be calculated. On each visit, the man helped himself to a double peg of Mr. Venkatesan's whiskey.

In early September, three weeks after Mr. Venkatesan had paid in full for a roundabout one-way ticket to Hamburg and for a passport impressive with fake visas, the travel agent stowed him in the damp, smelly bottom of a fisherman's dinghy and had him ferried across the Palk Strait to Tuticorin in the palm-green tip of mainland India.

Tuticorin was the town Mr. Venkatesan's ancestors had left to find their

fortunes in Ceylon's tea-covered northern hills. The irony struck him with
such force that he rocked and tipped the dinghy, and had to be fished out of
the sea.

The Friends of the Tigers were waiting in a palm grove for him. He saw
their flashlights and smelled their coffee. They gave him a dry change of
clothes, and though both the shirt and the jacket were frayed, they were styl-
ishly cut. His reputation as an intellectual and killer (he hoped it wasn't true)
of a Buddhist policeman had preceded him. He let them talk; it was not
Venkatesan the schoolmaster they were praising, but some mad invention.
Where he was silent from confusion and fatigue, they read cunning and intensity. He was happy to put himself in their hands; he thought of them as fate's
helpers, dispatched to see him through his malady. That night one of them
made up a sleeping mat for him in the back room of his shuttered grocery
store. After that they passed him from back room to back room. He spent
pleasant afternoons with them drinking sweet, frothy coffee and listening to
them plan to derail trains or blow up bus depots. They read his frown as skep-
ticism and redoubled their vehemence. He himself had no interest in destruction, but he listened to them politely.

When it was safe to move on, the Friends wrote out useful addresses in
Frankfurt, London, Toronto, Miami. "Stay out of refugee centers," they advised. But an old man with broken dentures who had been deported out of
Hamburg the year before filled him in on which refugee centers in which
cities had the cleanest beds, just in case he was caught by the wily German
police. "I shan't forget any of you," Mr. Venkatesan said as two Friends saw
him off at the train station. The train took him to Madras; in Madras he
changed trains for Delhi where he boarded an Aeroflot flight for Tashkent.
From Tashkent he flew to Moscow. He would like to have told the story of his
life to his two seat mates—already the break from family and from St. Joe's
seemed the stuff of adventure novels—but they were two huge and grim
Uzbeks with bushels of apricots and pears wedged on the floor, under the
seat, and on their laps. The cabin was noisier than the Jaffna local bus with
squawking chickens and drunken farmers. He communed instead with
Arnold and Keats. In Moscow the airport officials didn't bother to look too
closely at his visa stamps, and he made it to Berlin feeling cocky.

At Schönefeld Airport, three rough-looking Tamil men he'd not have
given the time of day to back home in Trinco grappled his bags away from
him as soon as he'd cleared customs. "This is only a piss stop for you, you
lucky bastard," one of them said. "You get to go on to real places while hard-
working fuckers like us get stuck in this hellhole."

He had never heard such language. Up until a week ago, he would have
denied the Tamil language even possessed such words. The man's coarseness

shocked Mr. Venkatesan, but this was not the moment to walk away from accomplices.

The expatriate Tamils took him, by bus, to a tenement building—he saw only Asians and Africans in the lobby—and locked him from the outside in a one-room flat on the top floor. An Algerian they did business with, they said, would truck him over the border into Hamburg. He was not to look out the window. He was not to open the door, not even if someone yelled, "Fire!" They'd be back at night, and they'd bring him beer and rolls.

Mr. Venkatesan made a slow show of getting money out of his trouser pocket—he didn't have any East German money, only rupees and the Canadian dollars he'd bought on the black market from the travel agent in Trinco—but the Tamils stopped him. "Our treat," they said. "You can return the hospitality when *we* make it to Canada."

Late in the evening the three men, stumbling drunk and jolly, let themselves back into the room that smelled of stale, male smells. The Algerian had come through. They were celebrating. They had forgotten the bread but remembered the beer.

That night, which was his only night in East Germany, Mr. Venkatesen got giggly drunk. And so it was that he entered the free world with a hangover. In a narrow, green mountain pass, trying not to throw up, he said goodbye to his Algerian chauffeur and how-do-you-do to a Ghanaian-born Berliner who didn't cut the engine of his BMW during the furtive transfer.

He was in Europe. Finally. The hangover made him sentimental. Back in Trinco the day must have deepened into dusk. In the skid of tires, he heard the weeping of parents, aunts, sisters. He had looked after them as long as he could. He had done for himself what he should have ten years before. Now he wanted to walk where Shelley had walked. He wanted to lie where consumptive Keats had lain and listened to his nightingale sing of truth and beauty. He stretched out in the seat. When Mr. Venkatesan next opened his eyes, the BMW was parked in front of a refugee center in Hamburg.

"End of trip," the black Berliner announced in jerky English. "*Auf Wiedersehen.*"

Mr. Venkatesan protested that he was not a refugee. "I am paid up in full to Canada. You are supposed to put me in touch with a ship's captain."

The black man snickered, then heaved Mr. Venkatesan's two shiny new bags out on the street. "Good-bye. *Danke.*"

Mr. Venkatesan got out of the private taxi.

"Need a cheap hotel? Need a lawyer to stay deportation orders?"

A very dark, pudgy man flashed a calling card in his face. The man looked Tamil, but not anxious like a refugee. His suit was too expensive. Even his shirt was made of some white-on-white fancy material, though his cuffs and collar were somewhat soiled.

Mr. Venkatesan felt exhilarated. Here was another of fate's angels come to minister him out of his malady.

"The name is Rammi. G. Rammi, Esquire. One-time meanest goddamn solicitor in Paramaribo, Suriname. I am putting myself at your service."

He allowed the angel to guide him into a *rijstafel* place and feed him for free.

Mr. Venkatesan ate greedily while the angel, in a voice as uplifting as harp music, instructed him on the most prudent conduct for undocumented transients. By the end of the meal, he'd agreed to pay Rammi's cousin, a widow, a flat fee for boarding him for as long as it took Rammi to locate a ship's captain whose business was ferrying furtive cargoes.

Rammi's cousin, Queenie, lived in a row house by the docks. Rammi had the cabdriver let them off a block and a half from Queenie's. He seemed to think cabdrivers were undercover immigration cops, and he didn't want a poor young widow bringing up a kid on dole getting in trouble for her charity.

Though Queenie had been telephoned ahead from a pay phone, she was dressed in nothing more formal than a kimono when she opened her slightly warped front door and let the men in. The kimono was the color of parrots in sunlight and reminded Mr. Venkatesan of his last carefree years, creeping up on and capturing parrots with his bare hands. In that glossy green kimono, Queenie the landlady shocked him with her beauty. Her sash was missing, and she clenched the garment together at the waist with a slender, nervous fist. Her smooth gold limbs, her high-bouncing bosom, even the stockingless arch of her instep had about them so tempting a careless sensuality that it made his head swim.

"I put your friend in Room 3A," Queenie said. "3B is less crowded but I had to put the sick Turk in it." She yelled something in German which Mr. Venkatesan didn't understand, and a girl of eight or nine came teetering out of the kitchen in adult-sized high heels. She asked the girl some urgent questions. The girl said no to all of them with shakes of her braided head.

"We don't want the fellow dying on us," Rammi said. Then they said something more in a Caribbean patois that Mr. Venkatesan didn't catch. "God knows we don't want complications." He picked up the two bags and started up the stairs. 3A was a smallish attic room blue with unventilated smoke, fitted with two sets of three-tier bunks. There were no closets, no cupboards, and on the bunk that Rammi pointed out as his, no bed linen. Four young men of indistinguishable nationality—Asia and Africa were their continents—were playing cards and drinking beer.

"Okay, 'bye," Rammi said. He was off to scout ship captains.

When Rammi left, despite the company, Mr. Venkatesan felt depressed, lonely. He didn't try to get to know where the men were from and where they were headed which was how he'd broken the ice in back room dormitories in

Tuticorin. One man spat into a brass spittoon. What did he have in common with these transients except the waiting?

By using his bags as a stepladder, he was able to clamber up to his allotted top bunk. For a while he sat on the bed. The men angled their heads so they could still stare at him. He lay down on the mattress. The rough ticking material of the pillow chafed him. He sat up again. He took his jacket and pants off and hung them from the foot rail. He slipped his wallet, his passport, his cloth bag stuffed with foreign cash, his new watch—a farewell present from Father van der Haagen—between the pillow and the mattress. He was not about to trust his cell mates. A little after the noon hour all four men got dressed in gaudy clothes and went out in a group. Mr. Venkatesan finally closed his eyes. A parrot flew into his dream. Mr. Venkatesan thrilled to the feathery feel of its bosom. He woke up only when Queenie's little girl charged into the room and ordered him down for lunch. She didn't seem upset about his being in underwear. She leaped onto the middle bunk in the tier across the room and told him to hurry so the food wouldn't have to be rewarmed. He thought he saw the flash of a man's watch in her hand.

Queenie had made him a simple lunch of lentil soup and potato croquettes, and by the time he got down to the kitchen it was no longer warm. Still he liked the spiciness of the croquettes and the ketchup was a tasty European brand and not the watery stuff served back home.

She said she'd already eaten, but she sat down with a lager and watched him eat. With her he had no trouble talking. He told her about St. Joe and Father van der Haagen. He told her about his family, leaving out the part about his sister running wild in the hills with hooligans, and got her to talk about her family too.

Queenie's grandfather had been born in a Sinhalese village the name of which he hadn't cared to pass on—he'd referred to it only as "hellhole"—and from which he'd run away at age seventeen to come as an indentured laborer to the Caribbean. He'd worked sugar cane fields in British Guiana until he'd lost a thumb. Then he'd moved to Suriname and worked as an office boy in a coconut oil processing plant, and wooed and won the only daughter of the proprietor, an expatriate Tamil like him who, during the War, had made a fortune off the Americans.

He tried to find out about her husband, but she'd say nothing other than that he'd been, in her words, "a romantic moron," and that he'd hated the hot sun, the flat lands, the coconut palms, the bush, her family, her family's oil factory. He'd dreamed, she said, of living like a European.

"You make me remember things I thought I'd forgotten." She flicked her lips with her tongue until they shone.

"You make me think of doing things I've never done." He gripped the edge of the kitchen table. He had trouble breathing. "Until dinnertime," he said. Then he panted back up to his prison.

But Mr. Venkatesan didn't see Queenie for dinner. She sent word through the girl that she had a guest—a legitimate guest, a tourist from Lübeck, not an illegal transient—that evening. He felt no rage at being dumped. A man without papers accepts last-minute humiliations. He called Rammi from the pay phone in the hall.

That night Mr. Venkatesan had fun. Hamburg was not at all the staid city of burghers that Father van der Haagen had evoked for him in those last restless days of waiting in the Teachers' Common Room. Hamburg was a carnival. That night, with Rammi as his initiator into fun, he smoked his first joint and said, after much prodding, "*sehr schön*" to a skinny girl with a Mohawk haircut.

The tourist from Lübeck had been given the one nice room. Queenie's daughter had shown Mr. Venkatesan the room while the man was checking in. It was on the first floor and had a double bed with a *duvet* so thick you wanted to sink into it. The windows were covered with *two* sets of curtains. The room even had its own sink. He hadn't seen the man from Lübeck, only heard him on the stairs and in the hall on his way to and from the lavatory walking with an authoritative, native-born German tread. Queenie hadn't instructed him to stay out of sight. Secretiveness he'd learned from his bunk mates. They could move with great stealth. Mr. Venkatesan was beginning to feel like a character in Anne Frank's diary. The men in 3A stopped wearing shoes indoors so as not to be heard pacing by the tourist from Lübeck.

The tourist went out a lot. Sometimes a car came for him. From the Tourist Office, Mr. Venkatesan imagined. How nice it would be to tour the city, take a boat trip! Meantime he had to eat his meals upstairs. That was the sad part. Otherwise he felt he had never been so happy.

Every morning as soon as he got the chance he called Rammi, though he was no longer keen for Rammi to find a crooked captain. He called because he didn't want Rammi to catch on that he was feeling whatever it was that he was feeling for Queenie. Like Rammi, he didn't want complications. What he did was remind Rammi that he wouldn't go into the hold of a ship that dumped its cargo into the Atlantic. He told Rammi that both in Trinco and in Tuticorin he'd heard stories of drowned Tamils.

Mr. Venkatesan's roommates stopped going out for meals. They paid Queenie's girl to buy them cold meats and oranges from the corner store. The only thing they risked going out for was liquor. He gathered from fragments of conversation that they were all sailors, from Indonesia and Nigeria, who'd jumped ship in Hamburg harbor. Whenever they went out, he could count on the girl prowling the attic room. He let her prowl. It was almost like having Queenie in the room.

There was only one worry. The girl lifted things—small things—from under pillows. Sometimes she played under the beds where he and the other men stored their suitcases, and he heard lids swish open or closed. He didn't think the things she stole were worth stealing. He'd seen her take a handful of pfennigs from a jacket pocket once, and another time envelopes with brilliant stamps from places like Turkey and Oman. What she seemed to like best to pilfer were lozenges, even the medicated kind for sore throat. It was as if covetousness came upon her, out of the blue, making her pupils twitch and glow.

He didn't mind the loss to his roommates. But he worried that they'd get her in trouble by sending her to the store. He would have to stop her. He would have to scold her as a father might or should without messing things up with Queenie.

One morning Queenie showed up in 3A herself. "I have good news," she whispered. Two of the four men were still in bed. Mr. Venkatesan could tell they hated having a grown woman in their room. "Rammi should have word for you tonight. I'm meeting him to find out more." The morning light, streaming in through a cracked stained-glass panel in the window, put such a heavenly sheen on her face that Mr. Venkatesan blurted out in front of his roommates, "I love you, I love you."

Queenie laughed. "Hush," she said. "You're not there yet. You don't want to wake up our Teuton. I need the legitimate business too."

It seemed to Mr. Venkatesan like an invitation. He followed her down into the front hall in his night clothes. In Tamil movies heroes in his position would have been wearing brocade smoking jackets. It didn't matter. He had made his declaration. Now fate would have to sink the crooked captain and his boat.

Queenie fussed with a pink, plastic clip in her hair. She knotted and re-knotted the wispy silk square around her throat. She tapped the longest fingernail he'd ever seen on the butterfly buckle of her belt. She was teasing him. She was promising he wouldn't really have to go. He wanted to stay, Anne Frank or not.

"Tonight should be a champagne night," she grinned. He saw the tensing of a dainty calf muscle as she straightened a stocking. "I'll see to coffee," she said.

Upstairs the man from Lübeck had hot water running in the bathroom sink. The pipes moaned. It was best to hide out in the kitchen until the man was back in his own room. Mr. Venkatesan joined Queenie's daughter at the dinette table. She had lozenges spread out on the tablecloth, like a sun spiked with long rays. She didn't look like a thief. She looked like a child he might have fathered if he'd married the bride his mother had picked for him in the days he'd still been considered a good catch. He hadn't married. Something dire had shown up in the conjunction of their horoscopes.

What if, just what if, what had seemed disastrous to the astrologer at the time had really been fate's way of reserving him for a better family with Queenie and this child in Hamburg?

"I'll sell you some," the child said. "I have English toffees too."

"Where?" He wanted to see her whole loot.

She ducked and brought out an old milk bottle from under the table. He saw the toffees in their red and blue wrapping papers. He saw a Muslim's worry beads. Some things in the bottle were shiny—he made out two rings among the keys and coins and coat buttons. There were two ID cards in the bottle. She reached for the cards. She had to have stolen one of the cards from a man in Room 3A. In the ID picture, which was amateurishly doctored, the roommate looked like a playboy sheik, and not at all like a refugee without travel papers. He grabbed the roommate's card from her. It wouldn't hurt to have the fellow in his debt. The other card belonged to a very blond, very German man.

The child was shrewd. "I didn't steal anything," she snapped. "I don't know how the stuff got in that jar."

She tossed the blond man's ID to him to get rid of it, and he caught it as he had paper flowers, silk squares, and stunned rabbits hurled to front-row boys by magicians on fete days in his kindergarten. He had loved the magicians. They alone had given him what he'd wanted.

As in dreams, the burly blond man materialized out of thin air and blocked the doorway. The man had on a touristy shirt and short pants, but he didn't have the slack gait of a vacationer. He had to be the man who lived in the nice upstairs room, the man who slept under the cozy duvet, who brushed his teeth in a clean, pink sink he didn't have to share, the man from whom transients like Mr. Venkatesan himself had to hide out. This man yelled something nasty in German to Queenie's daughter.

The child cowered.

The man yelled again. Mr. Venkatesan started to back away. Minute by minute the man ballooned with rage.

"No *deutsch*," Mr. Venkatesan mumbled.

"You filthy swine," the man shouted in English. "We don't want you making filthy our Germany." He threw five passports down on the kitchen table and spat on the top one. "The girl, she stole something from each of you scums," he hooted.

Mr. Venkatesan recognized his in the heap of travel documents. The child must have stolen it. The child must have filched it from under his pillow while he'd slept. She was a child possessed with covetousness. Now, because of her sick covetousness, he would rot in jail. He yanked the girl by her braids and shook her. The girl made her body go limp, taking away all pleasure in hate and revenge. The tourist from Lübeck ignored the screaming child. He got on the pay phone, the one Mr. Venkatesan called Rammi on every morning. Mr. Venkatesan heard the word "*Polizei!*" He was almost fifty. By fifty a man ought to stop running. Maybe what seemed accidental now—Queenie's daughter's kleptomania blowing away his plans for escape—wasn't accidental. He remembered what had consoled Dr. Pillai at the time of his arrest. Fractals. Nothing was random, the math teacher used to say. Nothing, not even the curliness of a coastline and the fluffiness of a cloud.

Mr. Venkatesan thought about the swoops and darts of his fate. He had started out as a teacher and a solid citizen and ended up as a lusty criminal. He visualized fate now as a buzzard. He could hear the whir of fleshy wings. It hopped off a burning car in the middle of a Trinco intersection.

Then, suddenly, Queenie the beauteous, the deliverer of radiant dreams, burst through the door of the kitchen. "Leave him alone!" she yelled to the man from Lübeck. "You're harassing my fiancé! He's a future German citizen. He will become my husband!"

# Buchi Emecheta

An examination of the role of African women is the central concern of Buchi Emecheta's fiction. While growing up in Lagos, Nigeria, where she was born on 21 July 1944, she confronted the African tradition that favored males and placed a low value on girls and women. Another aspect of her heritage with a more positive effect was the love of oral storytelling, and it is to this custom that Emecheta traces her own longing to tell stories. Rebelling against the bias toward girls, Emecheta managed to get an education usually reserved for the boys in the family. She left school at sixteen to marry, and two years later she and her husband went to London with their two infant children. Meeting with racial prejudice and poverty, they struggled to survive: the husband a failing student who refused to work, Emecheta a mother—three more children were born in London—and sole supporter of the family. Four years later the marriage failed, and twenty-two year old Emecheta remained alone in London with five children to support. During this difficult period, she completed a degree in sociology and wrote fiction. *The New Statesman* helped launch her writing career when it published some of her work in 1972. Except for intervals spent in Nigeria, Emecheta has continued to live in London.

*In the Ditch* (1972) and *Second-Class Citizen* (1974) tell the story of Adah, an African woman left with her children to survive in London. The second novel has more narrative force than the first book as it recalls Adah's Nigerian upbringing, the move to London, her husband's dominance, and the dissolution of their marriage. In the next two novels, *The Bride Price* (1976) and *The Slave Girl* (1977), Emecheta moves away from fictionalized autobiography to explore Nigerian society and to show how its rigid social structures oppress women. *Joys of Motherhood* (1979), which is considered one of Emecheta's best novels, reveals through the depiction of a polygamous marriage how women bear the brunt of a sanctioned domination by men. In *Double-Yoke*

(1982), she challenges the prejudices against educated women by picturing male-female relations at a Nigerian university. *Destination Biafra* (1982) and *The Rape of Shavi* (1983) take a radical turn from her previous work. The first one provides a fictional account of the Biafran war that follows its actual course faithfully, and has as its hero a woman who joins the army. The other novel takes a leap into allegory to explore the complex relationship between Europe and Africa, and in the process recounts the European subjugation of the continent. In *Gwendolen* (1989, also known as *The Family*), Emecheta returns to London's black ghetto to tell the story of an incest victim—one more shape of female domination. The family is West Indian, not African as in the earlier novels. Her most recent work is *Kehende* (1994).

Even though Emecheta has been called by some critics the most important African woman writer, she has enraged certain readers, mainly African males, by her emphasis on the condition of women. The detractors have called her a traitor to her own culture and have accused her of misrepresenting the Nigerian community. Although Emecheta declines to be called a feminist writer, most of her work has pointed toward the reinvention of social and sexual attitudes—and perhaps not just in African society.

Emecheta's first published work in *The New Statesman* consisted of a series of "observations" that re-created day to day life among welfare recipients as seen through the eyes of an African immigrant named Adah. Her first novel, *In the Ditch* (1972), is a collection of these pieces. Adah in one of the sketches, "The Ministry's Visiting Day," suffers the humiliation dealt to the poor, but at the same time harbors ambiguous feelings toward her fellow dwellers "in the ditch."

# The Ministry's Visiting Day
from *In the Ditch*

Adah jumped from her bed to the screams of Mrs. Cox.

"Leave that milk alone!" the voice outside shouted.

Adah rushed out of her flat; the little boy had done it again. It was very funny really. The little boy's unwashed face peered at Adah and his little pinkish-white body tried desperately to wriggle out of Mrs. Cox's big hand.

"If you steal her milk again, I'll get the law on you," Mrs. Cox howled, and the little boy shrank, his bright eyes gleaming with terror. When she let him go, he dashed blindly into his home. He banged the door so loudly that Mrs. Cox and Adah jumped.

"Thank you," said Adah, as she bent down to pick up her bottles of milk. This was a daily occurrence at the Mansions. If you were late in collecting your bottles of milk in the mornings, they simply disappeared. Nobody sympathized with you when you lost your milk, you just had to keep a good lookout. That was one of the unwritten laws of the Mansions.

"Wake up," she shouted to her children who were still in bed. Still feeling too lazy to go all the way up, she yelled at the sleeping kids once more.

Just then, there was a clip and a clap from the letter-box. A brown envelope flew down, lifelessly, like a hen's feather. Official sort of envelope. Adah stared at it lazily, guessed that it was from the children's school. The people at that school never had anything good to tell her. Maybe a school officer would be calling on her to tell her that Titi would not eat her baked beans and watery salad. Or that Vicky was bored with his schoolwork the month before. Whatever it was it could wait right there on the mat. She did not want her whole day ruined by some woolly complaints.

She went upstairs quickly. Her two boys had wet their beds. The smell was heavy. Bubo was shivering, his brown, bony, naked body shaking as if doing an African dance. "You've done it again," Adah remonstrated.

"Yes, Mum, I was asleep, and I done it," explained the boy innocently. To him the reason was logical enough, he did it because he was asleep.

"Well, tomorrow try to wake up when you want to do it; after all, there is a potty under your bed. You must learn to use it."

"Yes, Mum, I would, but it's too cold to get out of bed, and the floor is so cold too."

Well, what could she say to that? The children had no night clothes. The Ministry would glare if she asked for money to buy night clothes. She was supposed to buy such things from her allowance. She would not blame the kids. She would not blame them about wetting their beds any more. She would just have to live with it. The more one blamed kids for bed-wetting and things, the jumpier they would get. If only she could get enough money to buy them warm clothes, if only she could have enough heating in the bedrooms. Then she remembered the brown envelope on the mat. Carol, the Family Adviser, had promised to write to the Ministry for her, to ask for a shoe allowance. That letter on the mat might be from them. She raced down, with silent prayers on her lips, her heart beating so fast she thought it would burst. She picked up the envelope with shaking hands. Yes, it was from them all right.

"One of my officers will call on you today, the 17th. I am sorry I cannot be more specific about the time."

"I do wish these people would say what time they would be visiting," Adah thought. Still, there was now a slight hope that the kids would have decent shoes for the next three months. The night clothes? No, she wouldn't mention those, otherwise the officer would think her greedy. The trouble was that she needed so many things. Bedding, beds, money for the payments on the gas cooker she had foolishly bought when she was working.

"Hurry up," she sang happily to her children. Happy. The kids would at least have shoes and wellingtons. God bless Carol.

The children had custard for breakfast. There was some rice from the day before, and some of them had that too. Blast balanced meals! You can think of balancing meals when you have enough food. In any case the kids' diet would balance at school all right. For herself, she would pay a visit to Carol and she would be sure of getting a nice strong cup of coffee with milk in it. The milk in the coffee should balance her for the day, or balance her enough till the kids came home from school. Then she would eat more rice. Rice tasted good. It is cheap, it is filling.

She hurried the kids. They dressed quickly. "Please wait for me, I shan't be long," read the note she left at her door for the social security officer should he call when she was away. She took the kids to school, grabbed a gallon of paraffin from the owner of the shop down the road. She promised to pay the following week. That was all right—she was an old and well-known customer. She cleaned her flat quickly, dusted the few wooden pieces of furniture, and then lighted the heater with the paraffin she had bought on credit. Get warm now, pay later.

At ten o'clock, she was so hungry that she decided to cook the rice she had kept for the evening. She would just take a few spoonfuls, she promised herself. After all rice made her fat, she should watch her waistline. Well, when the rice was cooked, she forgot about her waistline, she forgot that the portion she cooked was for six. She finished the lot. Anyway that would make her cheerful and alert when the man called. She would go on a diet the following week. She was sure of losing at the very least two whole pounds. Then she would be really beautiful. She would have her bath, she decided. The rice had given her so much energy. The gas meter? Well, next week the Ministry would give her some money for the shoes, so she could afford a luxurious bath while waiting. That would be an extra bath for the week. She only allowed herself three baths a week to save gas. After the bath, she was pleased with herself. She thought she looked and smelt nice. "At least the officer won't think I'm filthy."

There was a bang at the door. Oh, it must be him, please God, let it be him. The paraffin made her place a cozy picture, but alas, it was burning low fast. Oh, it was not him. It was Whoopey.

"Hello, Adah," said Whoopey. She had a squeaky voice, Whoopey had. "Adah, I have some'nk to tell yer. There are some old clothes just arrived at Carol's. She's only got them this morning. You mustn't miss them, they'll be ever so nice for your kids. I should run and get them now, go on!"

"But I can't," wailed Adah wringing her hands. "The almighty Ministry men are descending on me today. I can't leave the house. I might miss them."

"Are they? I say . . . you do look nice. Just for them? Cor, blimey."

"Well, since they told me they'd be coming, I thought I'd clean up a bit. You know, just to look nice, you know what I mean." Adah found herself apologizing for having had a bath and put on clean clothes so early in the morning. That was part of living in the ditch. Everybody knew what the other was doing. To have a bath and put on clean clothes was very uncommon. At that time in the morning, when the kids had all gone to school, mums were free to chat on the balconies with bunches of curlers on their heads, old tattered slippers on their feet. You got dressed only when you wanted to take one of "yours" to see the doctor or the dentist.

"Watch it, those men do take advantage, you know," said Whoopey nodding her small head vigorously like an African lizard resting in the shade.

"I will be very careful," promised Adah. She too had heard funny stories about the social security officers. But at the Mansions, one of the most difficult things to do was to tell what was fantasy and what was fact. Whoopey looked sincere enough, so perhaps there was some truth in them—there might well be.

Whoopey sighed. "My advice is, don't bother to heat up the sitting-room for them. They'll think you're well off. Why don't you be your age, girl? What do you think you're doing? You're poor, let the buggers know you're poor, and that's that. What are the sods coming for, anyway?"

"To give us money for shoes," replied Adah in a weak voice.

"*Those* lousy men! If your house is warm and you look nice, they'll think you get extra income from God knows where, and may not approve your grant, you know. You have to whine all the time, and make a song and dance of the fact that you're unsupported. The more trouble you make, the more grant you get. If you want to be la-di-da and ladylike with them, you'll get nothing. We are poor, and the bastards want us to look poor. Don't bother yourself at all, and, Adah—good luck. I'll be around in case he makes a grab at you. Just give out a loud yell. You do look nice, I must say. Put ashes on your face and head . . ." Whoopey's voice floated down the balcony.

Adah listened to every sound that came from outside, but no one knocked. One o'clock, and still no social security officer. She was getting hungry again. That was the trouble with being at home and unhappy. You kept wanting to eat all the time. Anyway there was nothing in the house to eat as she still had to do her shopping. She looked at the heater and knew that her paraffin was wasting. What a bloody waste. She was crying now. The man would not come. By three o'clock the social security officers would be drinking their coffee and tea, laughing over the day's experiences. Adah did not like the way the less fortunate were treated. But she would not judge the officers, not really. They expected everyone on the dole to be at home, despite the fact that most of them were women with young children. She had been unable to do her shopping for fear of missing the social security officer, so she had stayed at home and eaten more than she could afford. The paraffin was now low. Wearily, she bent down and turned off the heater. The man might come tomorrow. She would have to borrow another half-a-crown to buy more paraffin for the oil heater. She would probably feel she ought to have another bath too.

She dragged herself out aimlessly on to the balcony, and saw Carol talking to Mrs. King in the middle of the compound. Carol looked up and called, "Come down, Adah, or are you very busy? Do come for coffee!"

"I'll be down right away," she shouted back, happy to escape from her private gloom.

Living in the ditch had its own consolations and advantages. There were always warm and natural friends. Friends who took delight in flouting society's laws. Some women indulged in having more and more children, a way of making the society that forced them into the ditch suffer. Some enjoyed taking it out on the welfare officers of the Ministry of Social Security, others took to drink. Many women in the ditch found consolation in over-eating. Anything goes, fish and chips and very rich creamy, cheap buns—one of the reasons that explained their distorted figures, with waists and hips like over-stuffed pillows.

Adah crossed the compound into Carol's office. All the regulars at Carol's knew of her disappointment, After a few minutes, Adah realized that she was not the first one. Many had had similar experiences. Well, it was consoling to note that many had shared a misfortune like hers.

"Cheer up, Adah," consoled Carol. "I'll phone them right now."

Carol did telephone, and the officer who answered promised to look into it. Yes, the officer would look into it, while the likes of Adah—separated mums, old-age pensioners, and the very poor—waited in the ditch biting their nails.

# Earl Lovelace

Called "an original voice" in Caribbean literature, Earl Lovelace has remained at home to do his writing. This sets him apart from most of the other
internationally known Caribbean authors such as Derek Walcott, V.S.
Naipaul, Wilson Harris, Roy Heath, and Sam Selvon, who chose to live in
England, the United States, or Canada, even as they drew much of their subject matter from their native region. Of African descent, Lovelace was born in
Toco, Trinidad, in 1935, and grew up in Tobago and Port of Spain. In order to
continue writing, he has supported himself through the years as a proofreader,
journalist, forest ranger, and agricultural worker. He now writes full time. He
attended Howard University, and has served as a visiting professor at Johns
Hopkins University and Wellesley College, as well as lecturing at the University of the West Indies.

His first novel, *While Gods Are Falling* (1965), received the BP Independence Literary Award. Like his third book, *The Dragon Can't Dance* (1979),
the action takes place in Port of Spain, the capital city of Trinidad and Tobago. Both books address disillusionment with the island's postcolonial condition, and their protagonists long for a sense of community that has been lost
in the urban setting. They seek a time when once again " 'All o' we is one' "—
as a character describes their quest. *The Dragon Can't Dance* takes as a
metaphor for this search the yearly carnival celebrations, which the text
evokes lovingly and richly. *The Schoolmaster* (1979) reveals a village's loss
of innocence when a corrupt schoolmaster deceives them; at the end, though,
the community restores itself through a decisive action that destroys the
spoiler in their midst and reunites them. The fourth novel, *The Wine of Astonishment* (1982), returns to the rural Trinidad of the 1930s and 1940s, and tells
about the struggles of an actual group from the period, the Spiritual Baptists
whose mixture of African religious tradition with Christianity led the colonial

government to outlaw their supposedly heathen practices. Dispersed by the wartime boom in Trinidad, the members manage to restore their sense of community, not through religion but through the discovery of a "Spirit" that the descendants of slaves share and that transcends colonial influence and restrictions. Lovelace has also published a volume of drama, *Jestina's Calypso and Other Plays* (1984), which explores themes similar to those in the fiction.

In 1997 Lovelace received the prestigious Commonwealth Writers Prize for his fifth novel, *Salt* (1996). Through several voices, Lovelace examines the old captivities by looking at Trinidad's past, then confronts the present, and finally imagines the future. In a congratulatory editorial in the *Trinidad Guardian* when Lovelace received the Commonwealth Prize, the commentator notes: "The major theme Lovelace explores is that of a nation of disparate peoples coming to terms with their history, struggling to understand their liberty and independence in the post (or neo) colonial context of modern Trinidad."

"Joebell and America" comes from Lovelace's 1988 collection of short stories, *A Brief Conversion and Other Stories.* Sad and comic, this tale of the would-be immigrant exposes the insidious effect of a new, more subtle kind of colonialism: that is, American popular culture. Unfortunately, the cultural mix of Trinidad defeats Joebell when he recites the alphabet and trips up by using the British zed instead of the American z. While Joebell fails in his immigration try, he appears satisfied that he carried out the attempt with "class" and seems happy to be back on the island. Lovelace has written in both standard English and in what is sometimes called "new english"—the lower case *e* signifying the move away from accepted forms into the way English has been transformed around the world. "Joebell and America" offers an excellent example of one variation of "new english."

# Joebell and America

## ONE

Joebell find that he seeing too much hell in Trinidad so he make up his mind to leave and go away. The place he find he should go is America, where everybody have a motor car and you could ski on snow and where it have seventy-five channels of color television that never sign off and you could sit down and watch for days, all the boxing and wrestling and basketball, right there as it happening. Money is the one problem that keeping him in Cunaripo; but that year as Christmas was coming, luck hit Joebell in the gamble, and for three days straight he win out the wappie. After he give two good pardners a stake and hand his mother a raise and buy a watch for his girl, he still have nineteen hundred and seventy-five Trinidad and Tobago dollars that is his own. That was the time. If Joebell don't go to America now, he will never go again.

But, a couple years earlier, Joebell make prison for a wounding, and before that they had him up for resisting arrest and using obscene language. Joebell have a record; and for him to get a passport he must first get a letter from the police to say that he is of good character. All the bribe Joebell try to bribe, he can't get this letter from the police. He prepare to pay a thousand dollars for the letter; but the police pardner who he had working on the matter keep telling him to come back and come back and come back. But another pardner tell him that with the same thousand dollars he could get a whole new American passport, with new name and everything. The only thing a little ticklish is Joebell will have to talk Yankee.

Joebell smile, because if is one gift he have it is to talk languages, not Spanish and French and Italian and such, but he could talk English and American and Grenadian and Jamaican; and of all of them the one he love best is American. If that is the only problem, well, Joebell in America already.

But it have another problem. The fellar who fixing up the passport business for him tell him straight, if he try to go direct from Trinidad to America with the US passport, he could get arrest at the Trinidad airport, so the pardner advise that the best thing to do is for Joebell to try to get in through Puerto Rico where they have all those Spanish people and where the immigration don't be so fussy. Matter fix. Joebell write another pardner who he went to school with and who in the States seven years, and tell him he coming over, to look out for him, he will ring him from Puerto Rico.

Up in Independence Recreation Club where we gamble, since Joebell win this big money, he is a hero. All the fellars is suddenly his friend, everybody calling out, "Joebell! Joebell!" some asking his opinion and some giving him advice on how to gamble his money. But Joebell not in no hurry. He know just as how you could win fast playing wappie, so you could lose fast too; and, although he want to stay in the wappie room and hear how we talk up his gambling ability, he decide that the safer thing to do is to go and play poker where if he have to lose he could lose more slow and where if he lucky he could win a good raise too. Joebell don't really have to be in the gambling club at all. His money is his own; but Joebell have himself down as a hero, and to win and run away is not classy. Joebell have himself down as classy.

Fellars' eyes open big big that night when they see Joebell heading for the poker room, because in there it have Japan and Fisherman from Mayaro and Captain and Papoye and a fellar named Morgan who every Thursday does come up from Tunapuna with a paper bag full with money and a knife in his shoe. Every man in there could real play poker.

In wappie, luck is the master; but in poker skill is what make luck work for you. When day break that Friday morning, Joebell stagger out the poker room with his whole body wash down with perspiration, out five hundred of his good dollars. Friday night he come back with the money he had give his girl to keep. By eleven he was down three. Fellars get silent and all of us vex to see how money he wait so long to get he giving away so easy. But, Joebell was really to go America in truth. In the middle of the poker, he leave the game to pee. On his way back, he walk into the wappie room. If you see Joebell: the whole front of his shirt open and wiping sweat from all behind his head. "Heat!" somebody laugh and say. On the table that time is two card: Jack and Trey. Albon and Ram was winning everybody. The both of them like Trey. They gobbling up all bets. Was a Friday night. Waterworks get pay, County Council get pay. It had men from Forestry. It had fellars from the Housing Project. Money high high on the table. Joebell favorite card is Jack.

Ram was a loser the night Joebell win big; now, Ram on top.

"Who against trey?" Ram say. He don't look at Joebell, but everybody know is Joebell he talking to. Out of all Joebell money, one thousand gone to pay for the false passport, and, already in the poker he lose eight. Joebell have himself down as a hero. A hero can't turn away. Everybody waiting to see. They talking, but, they waiting to see what Joebell will do. Joebell wipe his face, then wipe his chest, then he wring out the perspiration from the hand-kerchief, fold the kerchief and put it round his neck, and bam, just like that, like how you see in pictures when the star boy, quiet all the time, begin to make his move, Joebell crawl right up the wappie table, fellars clearing the way for him, and, everything, he empty out everything he had in his two pocket, and, lazy lazy, like he really is that star boy, he say, "Jack for this money!"

Ram was waiting, "Count it, Casa," Ram say.

When they count the money was two hundred and thirteen dollars and some change. Joebell throw the change for a broken hustler, Ram match him. Bam! Bam! Bam! In three card, Jack play.

"Double!" Joebell say. "For all," which mean that Joebell betting that an-other Jack play before any Trey.

Ram put some, and Albon put the rest, they sure is robbery.

Whap! Whap! Whap! Jack play. "Devine!" Joebell say. That night Joe-bell leave the club with fifteen hundred dollars. Fellars calling him The Gam-bler of Natchez.

When we see Joebell next, his beard shave off, his head cut in a GI trim, and he walking with a fast kinda shuffle, his body leaned forward and his hands in his pockets and he talking Yankee: "How ya doin, Main! Hi-ya, Baby!" And then we don't see Joebell in Cunaripo.

"Joebell gone away," his mother, Miss Myrtle say, "Praise God!"

If they have to give a medal for patience in Cunaripo, Miss Myrtle be-lieve that the medal is hers just from the trials and tribulations she undergo with Joebell. Since he leave school his best friend is Trouble and wherever Trouble is, right there is Joebell.

"I shoulda mind my child myself," she complain. "His grandmother spoil him too much, make him feel he is too much of a star, make him believe that the world too easy."

"The world don't owe you anything, boy," she tell him. "Try to be decent, son," she say. Is like a stick break in Joebell two ears, he don't hear a word she have to say. She talk to him. She ask his uncle Floyd to talk to him. She go by the priest in Mount St. Benedict to say a novena for him. She say the ninety-first psalm for him. She go by a *obeah* woman in Moruga to see what really happening to him. The *obeah* woman tell her to bring him quick so she could give him a bath and a guard to keep off the evil spirit that somebody have lighting on him. Joebell fly up in one big vexation with his mother for entic-ing him to go to the *obeah* woman: "Ma, what stupidness you trying to get me in? You know I don't believe in the negromancy business. What blight you want to fall on me now? That is why it so hard for me to win in gamble, you crossing up my luck."

But Miss Myrtle pray and she pray and at last, praise God, the answer come, not as how she did want it—you can't get everything the way you want it—but, praise God, Joebell gone away. And to those that close to her, she whisper, "America!" for that is the destination Joebell give her.

But Joebell aint reach America yet. His girl Alicia, who working at Last Chance snackette on the Cunaripo road is the only one he tell that Puerto Rico is the place he trying to get to. Since she take up with Joebell, her mother quarreling with her every day, "How a nice girl like you could get in with such a vagabond fellar? You don't have eyes in your head to see that the boy is only trouble?" They talk to her, they tell her how he stab a man in the gambling club and went to jail. They tell her how he have this ugly beard on his face and this ugly look in his face. They tell her how he don't work nowhere regular, "Child, why you bringing this cross into your life?" they ask her. They get her Uncle Matthew to talk to her. They carry her to Mount St. Benedict for the priest to say a novena for her. They give her the ninety-first psalm to say. They carry her to Moruga to a *obeah* woman who bathe her in a tub with bush, and smoke incense all over her to untangle her mind from Joebell.

But there is a style about Joebell that she like. Is a dream in him that she see. And a sad craziness that make her sad too but in a happy kinda way. The first time she see him in the snackette, she watch him and don't say nothing but, she think, Hey! who he think he is? He come in the snackette with this foolish grin on his face and this strolling walk and this kinda commanding way about him and sit down at the table with his legs wide open, taking up a big space as if he spending a hundred dollars, and all he ask for is a coconut roll and a juice. And then he call her again, this time he want a napkin and a toothpick. Napkins and toothpicks is for people who eating food; but she give them to him. And still he sit down there with some blight, some trouble hanging over him, looking for somebody to quarrel with or for something to get him vex so he could parade. She just do her work, and not a word she tell him. And just like that, just so by himself he cool down and start talking to her though they didn't introduce.

Everything he talk about is big: big mountains and big cars and race horses and heavyweight boxing champions and people in America—everything big. And she look at him from behind the counter and she see his sad craziness and she hear him talk about all this bigness far away, that make her feel too that she would like to go somewhere and be somebody, and just like that, without any words, or touching it begin.

Sometimes he'd come in the snackette, walking big and singing, and those times he'd be so broke all he could afford to call for'd be a glass of cold water. He wanted to be a calypsonian, he say; but he didn't have no great tune and his compositions wasn't so great either and everything he sing had a kinda sadness about it, no matter how he sing it. Before they start talking direct to one another he'd sing, closing his eyes and hunching his shoulders, and people in the snackette'd think he was just making joke; but, she know the song was for her and she'd feel pretty and sad and think about places far away. He used to sing in a country and western style, this song: his own composition:

Gonna take ma baby
Away on a trip
Gonna take ma baby
Yip yip yip
We gonna travel far
To New Orleans
Me and ma baby
Be digging the scene

If somebody came in and had to be served, he'd stop singing while she served them, then he'd start up again. And just so, without saying anything or touching or anything, she was his girl.

She never tell him about the trouble she was getting at home because of him. In fact she hardly talk at all. She'd just sit there behind the counter and listen to him. He had another calypso that he thought would be a hit.

Look at Mahatma Ghandi
Look at Hitler and Mussolini
Look at Uriah Butler
Look at Kwame Nkrumah
Great as they was
Everyone of them had to stand the pressure

He used to take up the paper that was on one side of the counter and sit down and read it, "Derby day," he would say. "Look at the horses running," and he would read out the horses' names. Or it would be boxing, and he would say Muhammed boxing today, or Sugar. He talked about these people as if they were personal friends of his. One day he brought her five pounds of deer wrapped in a big brown paper bag. She was sure he pay a lot of money for it. "Put this in the fridge until you going home." Chenette, mangoes, oranges, sapodillas, he was always bringing things for her. When her mother ask her where she was getting these things, she tell her that the owner of the place give them to her. For her birthday Joebell bring her a big box wrapped in fancy paper and went away, so proud and shy, he couldn't stand to see her open it, and when she open it it was a vase with a whole bunch of flowers made from colored feathers and a big birthday card with an inscription: From guess who?

"Now, who give you this? The owner?" her mother asked.

She had to make up another story.

When he was broke she would slip him a dollar or two of her own money and if he win in the gamble he would give her some of the money to keep for him, but she didn't keep it long, he mostly always came back for it next day. And they didn't have to say anything to understand each other. He would just watch her and she would know from his face if he was broke and want a dollar or if he just drop in to see her, and he could tell from her face if she want him to stay away altogether that day or if he should make a turn and come again or what. He didn't get to go no place with her, cause in the night when the snackette close her big brother would be waiting to take her home.

"Thank God!" her mother say when she hear Joebell gone away. "Thank you, Master Jesus, for helping to deliver this child from the clutches of that vagabond." She was so happy she hold a thanksgiving feast, buy sweet drinks and make cake and invite all the neighbor's little children; and she was surprise that Alicia was smiling. But Alicia was thinking, Lord, just please let him get to America, they will see who is vagabond. Lord, just let him get through that immigration they will see happiness when he send for me.

The fellars go round by the snackette where Alicia working and they ask for Joebell.

"Joebell gone away," she tell them.

"Gone away and leave a nice girl like you? If was me I would never leave you."

And she just smile that smile that make her look like she crying and she mumble something that don't mean nothing, but if you listen good is, "Well, is not you."

"Why you don't let me take you to the dance in the Centre Saturday? Joey Lewis playing. Why you don't come and forget that crazy fellar?"

But Alicia smile no, all the time thinking, wait until he send for me, you will see who crazy. And she sell the cake and the coconut roll and sweet drink and mauby that they ask for and take their money and give them their change and move off with that soft, bright, drowsy sadness that stir fellars, that make them sit down and drink their sweet drink and eat their coconut roll and look at her face with the spread of her nose and the lips stretch across her mouth in a full round soft curve and her far away eyes and think how lucky Joebell is.

When Joebell get the passport he look at the picture in it and he say, "Wait! This fellar aint look like me. A blind man could see this is not me."

"I know you woulda say that," the pardner with the passport say, "You could see you don't know nothing about the American immigration. Listen, in America, every black face is the same to white people. They don't see no difference. And this fellar here is the same height as you, roughly the same age.

That is what you have to think about, those little details, not how his face looking." That was his pardner talking.

"You saying this is me, this fellar here is me?" Joebell ask again. "You want them to lock me up or what, man? This is what I pay a thousand dollars for? A lock up?"

"Look, you have no worry. I went America one time on a passport where the fellar had a beard and I was shave clean and they aint question me. If you was white you mighta have a problem, but black, man, you easy."

And in truth when he think of it, Joebell could see the point, cause he aint sure he could tell the difference between two Chinese.

"But, wait!" Joebell say, "Suppose I meet up a black immigration?"

"Ah!" the fellar say, "You thinking. Anyhow, it aint have that many, but, if you see one stay far from him."

So Joebell, with his passport in his pocket, get a fellar who running contraband to carry him to Venezuela where his brother was living. He decide to spend a couple days by his brother and from there take a plane to Puerto Rico, in transit to America.

His brother had a job as a motor car mechanic.

"Why you don't stay here?" his brother tell him, "It have work here you could get. And TV does be on whole day."

"The TV in Spanish," Joebell tell him.

"You could learn Spanish."

"By the time I finish learn Spanish I is a old man," Joebell say, "*Caramba! Caramba! Habla! Habla!* No. And besides I done pay my thousand dollars. I have my American passport. I is an American citizen. And," he whisper, softening just at the thought of her, "I have a girl who coming to meet me in America."

Joebell leave Venezuela in a brown suit that he get from his brother, a strong-looking pair of brown leather boots that he buy, with buckles instead of laces, a cowboy hat on his head and an old camera from his brother over his shoulder and in his mouth is a cigar, and now he is James Armstrong Brady of the one hundred and twenty-fifth infantry regiment from Alabama, Vietnam Veteran, twenty-six years old. And when he reach the airport in Puerto Rico he walk with a stagger and he puff his cigar like he already home in the United States of America. And not for one moment it don't strike Joebell that he doing any wrong.

No. Joebell believe the whole world is a hustle. He believe everybody running some game, putting on some show and the only thing that separate people is that some have power and others don't have none, that who in in and who out out, and that is exactly what Joebell kick against, because Joebell have himself down as a hero too and he not prepare to sit down timid timid as if he stupid and see a set of bluffers take over the world, and he stay wasting away in Cunaripo; and that is Joebell's trouble. That is what people call his craziness, is that that mark him out. That is the "light" that the *obeah* woman in Moruga see burning on him, is that that frighten his mother and charm Alicia and make her mother want to pry her loose from him. Is that that fellars see when they see him throw down his last hundred dollars on a single card, as if he know it going to play. The thing is that Joebell really don't be betting on the card, Joebell does be betting on himself. He don't be trying to guess about which card is the right one, he is trying to find that power in himself that will make him call correct. And that power is what Joebell searching for as he queue up in the line leading to the immigration entering Puerto Rico. Is that power that he calling up in himself as he stand there, because if he can feel that power, if that power come inside him, then, nothing could stop him. And now this was it.

"Mr. Brady?" The immigration man look up from Joebell passport and say, same time turning the leaves of the passport. And he glance at Joebell and he look at the picture. And he take up another book and look in it, and look again at Joebell; and maybe it is that power Joebell reaching for, that thing inside him, his craziness that look like arrogance, that put a kinda sneer on his face that make the immigration fellar take another look.

"Vietnam Veteran? Mr. Brady, where you coming from?"

"Venezuela."

The fellar ask a few more questions. He is asking Joebell more questions than he ask anybody.

"Whatsamatta? Watsa problem?" Joebell ask, "Man, I aint never seen such incompetency as you got here. This is boring. Hey, I've got a plane to catch. I aint got all day."

All in the airport people looking at Joebell 'cause Joebell not talking easy, and he biting his cigar so that his words coming to the immigration through his teeth. Why Joebell get on so is because Joebell believe that one of the main marks of a real American is that he don't stand no nonsense. Any time you get a real American in an aggravating situation, the first thing he do is let his voice be heard in objection: in other words, he does get on. In fact that is one of the things Joebell admire most about Americans: they like to get on. They don't care who hear them, they going to open their mouth and talk for their rights. So that is why Joebell get on so about incompetency and missing his plane and so on. Most fellars who didn't know what it was to be a real American woulda take it cool. Joebell know what he doing.

"Sir, please step into the first room on your right and take a seat until your name is called." Now is the immigration talking, and the fellar firm and he not frighten, 'cause he is American too. I don't know if Joebell didn't realize that before he get on. That is the kind of miscalculation Joebell does make sometimes in gambling and in life.

"Maan, just you remember I gotta plane to catch," and Joebell step off, with that slow, tall insolence like Jack Palance getting off his horse in *Shane,* but he take off his hat and go and sit down where the fellar tell him to sit down.

It had seven other people in the room but Joebell go and sit down alone by himself because with all the talk he talking big, Joebell is just playing for time, just trying to put them off; and now he start figuring serious how he going to get through this one. And he feeling for that power, that craziness that sometimes take him over when he in a wappie game, when every bet he call he call right; and he telling himself they can't trap him with any question because he grow up in America right there in Trinidad. In his grandmother days was the British; but he know from Al Jolson to James Brown. He know Tallahashie bridge and Rocktow mountain. He know Doris Day and Frank Sinatra. He know America. And Joebell settle himself down not bothering to remember anything, just calling up his power. And then he see this tall black fellar over six foot five enter the room. At a glance Joebell could tell he's a crook, and next thing he know is this fellar coming to sit down side of him.

## TWO

I sit down there by myself alone and I know they watching me. Everybody else in the room white. This black fellar come in the room, with beads of perspiration running down his face and his eyes wild and he looking round like he escape. As soon as I see him I say "Oh God!" because I know with all the empty seats all about the place is me he coming to. He don't know my troubles. He believe I want friends. I want to tell him "Listen, man, I love you. I really dig my people, but now is not the time to come and talk to me. Go and be friendly by those other people, they could afford to be friends with you." But I can't tell him that 'cause I don't want to offend him and I have to watch how I talking in case in my situation I slip from American to Trinidadian. He shake my hand in the Black Power sign. And we sit down there side by side, two crooks, he and me, unless he's a spy they send to spy on me.

I letting him do all the talking, I just nodding and saying yeah, yeah.

He's an American who just come out of jail in Puerto Rico for dope or something. He was in Vietnam too. He talking, but I really aint listening to him. I thinking how my plane going. I thinking about Alicia and how sad her face will get when she don't get the letter that I suppose to send for her to come to America. I thinking about my mother and about the fellars up in Independence Recreation Club and around the wappie table when the betting slow, how they will talk about me, "Natchez," who win in the wappie and go to America—nobody ever do that before—and I thinking how nice it will be for me and Alicia after we spend some time in America to go back home to Trinidad for a holiday and stay in the Hilton and hire a big car and go to see her mother. I think about the Spanish I woulda have to learn if I did stay in Venezuela.

At last they call me inside another room. This time I go cool. It have two fellars in this room, a big tough one with a stone face and a jaw like a steel trap, and a small brisk one with eyes like a squirrel. The small one is smoking a cigarette. The tough one is the one asking questions. The small one just sit down there with his squirrel eyes watching me, and smoking his cigarette.

"What's your name?"

And I watching his jaw how they clamping down on the words. "Ma name is James Armstrong Brady."

"Age?"

And he go through a whole long set of questions.

"You're a Vietnam Veteran, you say? Where did you train?"

And I smile 'cause I see enough war pictures to know, "Nor' Carolina," I say.

"Went to school there?"

I tell him where I went to school. He ask questions until I dizzy.

The both of them know I lying, and maybe they coulda just throw me in jail just so without no big interrogation; but, America. That is why I love America. They love a challenge. Something in my style is a challenge to them, and they just don't want to lock me up because they have the power, they want to trap me plain for even me to see. So now is me, Joebell, and these two Yankees. And I waiting, 'cause I grow up on John Wayne and Gary Cooper and Audie Murphy and James Stewart and Jeff Chandler. I know the Dodgers and Phillies, the Redskins and the Dallas Cowboys, Green Bay Packers and the Vikings. I know Walt Frazier and Doctor J, and Bill Russell and Wilt Chamberlain. Really, in truth, I know America so much, I feel American. Is just that I aint born there.

As fast as the squirrel-eye one finish smoke one cigarette, he light another one. He aint saying nothing, only listening. At last he put out his cigarette, he say, "Recite the alphabet."

"Say what?"

"The alphabet. Recite it."

And just so I know I get catch. The question too easy. Too easy like a calm blue sea. And, pardner, I look at that sea and I think about Alicia and the warm soft curving sadness of her lips and her eyes full with crying, make me feel to cry for me and Alicia and Trinidad and America and I know like when you make a bet you see a certain card play that it will be a miracle if the card you bet on play. I lose, I know. But I is still a hero. I can't bluff forever. I have myself down as classy. And, really, I wasn't frighten for nothing, not for nothing, wasn't afraid of jail or of poverty or of Puerto Rico or America and I wasn't vex with the fellar who sell me the passport for the thousand dollars, nor with Iron Jaw and Squirrel Eyes. In fact, I kinda respect them. "A . . . B . . . C . . ." And Squirrel Eyes take out another cigarette and don't light it, just keep knocking it against the pack, Tock! Tock! Tock! K . . . L . . . M . . . And I feel I love Alicia . . . V . . . W . . . and I hear Paul Robeson sing "Old Man River" and I see Sammy Davis Junior dance Mr. Bojangle's dance and I hear Nina Simone humming humming "Suzanne," and I love Alicia; and I hear Harry Belafonte's rasping call, "Daay-o, Daaay-o! Daylight come and me want to go home," and Aretha Franklyn screaming screaming, ". . . Y . . . Zed."

"Bastard!" the squirrel eyes cry out, "Got you!"

And straightaway from another door two police weighed down with all their keys and their handcuffs and their pistols and their night stick and torch light enter and clink their handcuffs on my hands. They catch me. God! And now, how to go? I think about getting on like an American, but I never see an American lose. I think about making a performance like the British, steady, stiff upper lip like Alec Guinness in *The Bridge over the River Kwai,* but with my hat and my boots and my piece of cigar, that didn't match, so I say I might as well take my losses like a West Indian, like a Trinidadian. I decide to sing. It was the classiest thing that ever pass through Puerto Rico airport, me with these handcuffs on, walking between these two police and singing,

> Gonna take ma baby
> Away on a trip
> Gonna take ma baby
> Yip yip yip
> We gonna travel far
> To New Orleans
> Me and ma Baby
> Be digging the scene

# Hanif Kureishi

Although Hanif Kureishi's fiction and drama focus on the immigrant experience, he is not an immigrant. He was born in a London suburb around 1954, his father Pakistani, his mother English. He recalls in his autobiographical essay "The Rainbow Sign" that when he was growing up he faced the prejudice directed toward immigrants, and admits that "from the start I tried to deny my Pakistani self . . . it was a curse and I wanted to be rid of it." These early confrontations with discrimination and consequent denials of his background remained with him and have motivated much of his writing. The particularity of his encounter allows him to speak in a distinctive vein about the pain of immigration through recounting the tension experienced by the sons and daughters of immigrants.

Kureishi received a degree in philosophy from King's College, London. Afterward, in an effort to fulfill his ambition to become a writer, he supported himself by publishing pornography under the pseudonym Antonia French. At first he directed his serious efforts toward the stage and television, and in 1976 his first play, *Soaking Up the Heat*, was produced, followed in 1980 by *The Mother Country*, which received the Thames Television Playwright Award. A series of theatrical, television, and film successes followed. In 1983 a collection, *Outskirts and Other Plays*, appeared, and in 1991 another collection of screenplays and essays, *London Kills Me*. When *My Beautiful Laundrette* was produced on British television in 1985, it received such favorable notice that a year later it was released as a film and received international acclaim, gaining an Academy Award nomination for best original screenplay and the New York Film Critics Circle Award. While telling the central story of a young Pakistani man who opens a laundromat with his white male lover, it also offers a vivid picture of Pakistani immigrant culture in London. The screenplay, along with Kureishi's autobiographical essay, was published as *My Beautiful Laundrette and The Rainbow Sign* in 1986.

Kureishi's first novel, *The Buddha of Suburbia* (1990), is autobiographical to a degree as it relates through a first-person narrator the perils of a young man who calls himself "an Englishman born and bred, almost." His English mother and Indian father enjoy a typical life in London suburbs until the father turns into the "Buddha of Suburbia" and attracts a motley following of aspiring mystics. This venture and its bizarre consequences are treated with a comic inventiveness that unveils all sides of the immigrant community and its relationship to the British. Although Kureishi's next novel, *The Black Album* (1995), takes a serious look at the growth of Islamic fundamentalism among young British-born Asians, it also displays his comic flair and talent for satire.

The freshness with which Kureishi treats the recurrent theme of dislocation among immigrants has drawn praise from critics and general readers, but has been condemned by many Pakistani groups. They find offensive that Kureishi portrays some Pakistanis as gay, drug dealing, greedy, dishonest, and promiscuous. To this complaint, Kureishi replied in the magazine *Interview*: "It would destroy you as a writer if every time you wrote something you thought, is this a positive role model?"

"My Son the Fanatic" comes from Kureishi's collection *Love in a Blue Time* (1997), whose ten stories provide a far-reaching look at contemporary life in London. This narrative takes an ironic stance by reversing the predictable conflict between father and son. And it offers no solution to their dilemma.

# My Son the Fanatic

Surreptitiously the father began going into his son's bedroom. He would sit there for hours, rousing himself only to seek clues. What bewildered him was that Ali was getting tidier. Instead of the usual tangle of clothes, books, cricket bats, video games, the room was becoming neat and ordered; spaces began appearing where before there had been only mess.

Initially Parvez had been pleased; his son was outgrowing his teenage attitudes. But one day, beside the dustbin, Parvez found a torn bag which contained not only old toys, but computer discs, video tapes, new books and fashionable clothes the boy had bought just a few months before. Also without explanation, Ali had parted from the English girlfriend who used to come often to the house. His old friends had stopped ringing.

For reasons he didn't himself understand, Parvez wasn't able to bring up the subject of Ali's unusual behavior. He was aware that he had become slightly afraid of his son, who, alongside his silences, was developing a sharp tongue. One remark Parvez did make, "You don't play your guitar any more," elicited the mysterious but conclusive reply, "There are more important things to be done."

Yet Parvez felt his son's eccentricity as an injustice. He had always been aware of the pitfalls which other men's sons had fallen into in England. And so, for Ali, he had worked long hours and spent a lot of money paying for his education as an accountant. He had bought him good suits, all the books he required and a computer. And now the boy was throwing his possessions out!

The TV, video and sound system followed the guitar. Soon the room was practically bare. Even the unhappy walls bore marks where Ali's pictures had been removed.

Parvez couldn't sleep; he went more to the whisky bottle, even when he was at work. He realized it was imperative to discuss the matter with someone sympathetic.

Parvez had been a taxi driver for twenty years. Half that time he'd worked for the same firm. Like him, most of the other drivers were Punjabis. They preferred to work at night, the roads were clearer and the money better. They slept during the day, avoiding their wives. Together they led almost a boy's life in the cabbies' office, playing cards and practical jokes, exchanging lewd stories, eating together and discussing politics and their problems.

But Parvez had been unable to bring this subject up with his friends. He was too ashamed. And he was afraid, too, that they would blame him for the wrong turning his boy had taken, just as he had blamed other fathers whose sons had taken to running around with bad girls, truanting from school and joining gangs.

For years Parvez had boasted to the other men about how Ali excelled at cricket, swimming and football, and how attentive a scholar he was, getting straight "A's" in most subjects. Was it asking too much for Ali to get a good job now, marry the right girl and start a family? Once this happened, Parvez would be happy. His dreams of doing well in England would have come true. Where had he gone wrong?

But one night, sitting in the taxi office on busted chairs with his two closest friends watching a Sylvester Stallone film, he broke his silence.

"I can't understand it!" he burst out. "Everything is going from his room. And I can't talk to him any more. We were not father and son—we were brothers! Where has he gone? Why is he torturing me!"

And Parvez put his head in his hands.

Even as he poured out his account the men shook their heads and gave one another knowing glances. From their grave looks Parvez realized they understood the situation.

"Tell me what is happening!" he demanded.

The reply was almost triumphant. They had guessed something was going wrong. Now it was clear. Ali was taking drugs and selling his possessions to pay for them. That was why his bedroom was emptying.

"What must I do then?"

Parvez's friends instructed him to watch Ali scrupulously and then be severe with him, before the boy went mad, overdosed or murdered someone.

Parvez staggered out into the early morning air, terrified they were right. His boy—the drug addict killer!

To his relief he found Bettina sitting in his car.

Usually the last customers of the night were local "brasses" or prostitutes. The taxi drivers knew them well, often driving them to liaisons. At the end of the girls' shifts, the men would ferry them home, though sometimes the women would join them for a drinking session in the office. Occasionally the drivers would go with the girls. "A ride in exchange for a ride," it was called.

Bettina had known Parvez for three years. She lived outside the town and on the long drive home, where she sat not in the passenger seat but beside him, Parvez had talked to her about his life and hopes, just as she talked about hers. They saw each other most nights.

He could talk to her about things he'd never be able to discuss with his own wife. Bettina, in turn, always reported on her night's activities. He liked to know where she was and with whom. Once he had rescued her from a violent client, and since then they had come to care for one another.

Though Bettina had never met the boy, she heard about Ali continually. That late night, when he told Bettina that he suspected Ali was on drugs, she judged neither the boy nor his father, but became businesslike and told him what to watch for.

"It's all in the eyes," she said. They might be bloodshot; the pupils might be dilated; he might look tired. He could be liable to sweats, or sudden mood changes. "Okay?"

Parvez began his vigil gratefully. Now he knew what the problem might be, he felt better. And surely, he figured, things couldn't have gone too far? With Bettina's help he would soon sort it out.

He watched each mouthful the boy took. He sat beside him at every opportunity and looked into his eyes. When he could he took the boy's hand, checking his temperature. If the boy wasn't at home Parvez was active, looking under the carpet, in his drawers, behind the empty wardrobe, sniffing, inspecting, probing. He knew what to look for: Bettina had drawn pictures of capsules, syringes, pills, powders, rocks.

Every night she waited to hear news of what he'd witnessed.

After a few days of constant observation, Parvez was able to report that although the boy had given up sports, he seemed healthy, with clear eyes. He didn't, as his father expected, flinch guiltily from his gaze. In fact the boy's mood was alert and steady in this sense: as well as being sullen, he was very watchful. He returned his father's long looks with more than a hint of criticism, of reproach even, so much so that Parvez began to feel that it was he who was in the wrong, and not the boy!

"And there's nothing else physically different?" Bettina asked.

"No!" Parvez thought for a moment. "But he is growing a beard."

One night, after sitting with Bettina in an all-night coffee shop, Parvez came home particularly late. Reluctantly he and Bettina had abandoned their only explanation, the drug theory, for Parvez had found nothing resembling any drug in Ali's room. Besides, Ali wasn't selling his belongings. He threw them out, gave them away or donated them to charity shops.

Standing in the hall, Parvez heard his boy's alarm clock go off. Parvez hurried into his bedroom where his wife was still awake, sewing in bed. He ordered her to sit down and keep quiet, though she had neither stood up nor said a word. From this post, and with her watching him curiously, he observed his son through the crack in the door.

The boy went into the bathroom to wash. When he returned to his room Parvez sprang across the hall and set his ear at Ali's door. A muttering sound came from within. Parvez was puzzled but relieved.

Once this clue had been established, Parvez watched him at other times. The boy was praying. Without fail, when he was at home, he prayed five times a day.

Parvez had grown up in Lahore where all the boys had been taught the Koran. To stop him falling asleep when he studied, the Moulvi had attached a piece of string to the ceiling and tied it to Parvez's hair, so that if his head fell forward, he would instantly awake. After this indignity Parvez had avoided all religions. Not that the other taxi drivers had more respect. In fact they made jokes about the local mullahs walking around with their caps and beards, thinking they could tell people how to live, while their eyes roved over the boys and girls in their care.

Parvez described to Bettina what he had discovered. He informed the men in the taxi office. The friends, who had been so curious before, now became oddly silent. They could hardly condemn the boy for his devotions.

Parvez decided to take a night off and go out with the boy. They could talk things over. He wanted to hear how things were going at college; he wanted to tell him stories about their family in Pakistan. More than anything he yearned to understand how Ali had discovered the "spiritual dimension," as Bettina described it.

To Parvez's surprise, the boy refused to accompany him. He claimed he had an appointment. Parvez had to insist that no appointment could be more important than that of a son with his father.

The next day, Parvez went immediately to the street where Bettina stood in the rain wearing high heels, a short skirt and a long mac on top, which she would open hopefully at passing cars.

"Get in, get in!" he said.

They drove out across the moors and parked at the spot where on better days, with a view unimpeded for many miles by nothing but wild deer and horses, they'd lie back, with their eyes half closed, saying "This is the life." This time Parvez was trembling. Bettina put her arms around him.

"What's happened?"

"I've just had the worst experience of my life."

As Bettina rubbed his head Parvez told her that the previous evening he and Ali had gone to a restaurant. As they studied the menu, the waiter, whom Parvez knew, brought him his usual whisky and water. Parvez had been so nervous he had even prepared a question. He was going to ask Ali if he was worried about his imminent exams. But first, wanting to relax, he loosened his tie, crunched a popadom and took a long drink.

Before Parvez could speak, Ali made a face.

"Don't you know it's wrong to drink alcohol?" he said.

"He spoke to me very harshly," Parvez told Bettina. "I was about to castigate the boy for being insolent, but managed to control myself."

He had explained patiently to Ali that for years he had worked more than ten hours a day, that he had few enjoyments or hobbies and never went on holiday. Surely it wasn't a crime to have a drink when he wanted one?

"But it is forbidden," the boy said.

Parvez shrugged, "I know."

"And so is gambling, isn't it?"

"Yes. But surely we are only human?"

Each time Parvez took a drink, the boy winced, or made a fastidious face as an accompaniment. This made Parvez drink more quickly. The waiter, wanting to please his friend, brought another glass of whisky. Parvez knew he was getting drunk, but he couldn't stop himself. Ali had a horrible look on his face, full of disgust and censure. It was as if he hated his father.

Halfway through the meal Parvez suddenly lost his temper and threw a plate on the floor. He had felt like ripping the cloth from the table, but the waiters and other customers were staring at him. Yet he wouldn't stand for his own son telling him the difference between right and wrong. He knew he wasn't a bad man. He had a conscience. There were a few things of which he was ashamed, but on the whole he had lived a decent life.

"When have I had time to be wicked?" he asked Ali.

In a low monotonous voice the boy explained that Parvez had not, in fact, lived a good life. He had broken countless rules of the Koran.

"For instance?" Parvez demanded.

Ali hadn't needed time to think. As if he had been waiting for this moment, he asked his father if he didn't relish pork pies?

"Well . . ."

Parvez couldn't deny that he loved crispy bacon smothered with mushrooms and mustard and sandwiched between slices of fried bread. In face he ate this for breakfast every morning.

Ali then reminded Parvez that he had ordered his own wife to cook pork sausages, saying to her, "You're not in the village now, this is England. We have to fit in!"

Parvez was so annoyed and perplexed by this attack that he called for more drink.

"The problem is this," the boy said. He leaned across the table. For the first time that night his eyes were alive. "You are too implicated in Western civilization."

Parvez burped; he thought he was going to choke. "Implicated!" he said. "But we live here!"

"The Western materialists hate us," Ali said. "Papa, how can you love something which hates you?"

"What is the answer then?" Parvez said miserably. "According to you."

Ali addressed his father fluently, as if Parvez were a rowdy crowd that had to be quelled and convinced. The Law of Islam would rule the world; the skin of the infidel would burn off again and again; the Jews and Christers would be routed. The West was a sink of hypocrites, adulterers, homosexuals, drug takers and prostitutes.

As Ali talked, Parvez looked out of the window as if to check that they were still in London.

"My people have taken enough. If the persecution doesn't stop there will be *jihad*. I, and millions of others, will gladly give our lives for the cause."

"But why, why?" Parvez said.

"For us the reward will be in paradise."

"Paradise!"

Finally, as Parvez's eyes filled with tears, the boy urged him to mend his ways.

"How is that possible?" Parvez asked.

"Pray," Ali said. "Pray beside me."

Parvez called for the bill and ushered his boy out of the restaurant as soon as he was able. He couldn't take any more. Ali sounded as if he'd swallowed someone else's voice.

On the way home the boy sat in the back of the taxi, as if he were a customer.

"What has made you like this?" Parvez asked him, afraid that somehow he was to blame for all this. "Is there a particular event which has influenced you?"

"Living in this country."

"But I love England," Parvez said, watching his boy in the mirror. "They let you do almost anything here."

"That is the problem," he replied.

For the first time in years Parvez couldn't see straight. He knocked the side of the car against a lorry, ripping off the wing mirror. They were lucky not to have been stopped by the police. Parvez would have lost his license and therefore his job.

Getting out of the car back at the house, Parvez stumbled and fell in the road, scraping his hands and ripping his trousers. he managed to haul himself up. The boy didn't even offer him his hand.

Parvez told Bettina he was now willing to pray, if that was what the boy wanted, if that would dislodge the pitiless look from his eyes.

"But what I object to," he said, "is being told by my own son that I am going to hell!"

What finished Parvez off was that the boy had said he was giving up accountancy. When Parvez had asked why, Ali had said sarcastically that it was obvious.

"Western education cultivates an anti-religious attitude."

And, according to Ali, in the world of accountants it was usual to meet women, drink alcohol and practice usury.

"But it's well-paid work," Parvez argued. "For years you've been preparing!"

Ali said he was going to begin to work in prisons, with poor Muslims who were struggling to maintain their purity in the face of corruption. Finally, at the end of the evening, as Ali was going to bed, he had asked his father why he didn't have a beard, or at least a moustache.

"I feel as if I've lost my son," Parvez told Bettina. "I can't bear to be looked at as if I'm a criminal. I've decided what to do."

"What is it?"

"I'm going to tell him to pick up his prayer mat and get out of my house. It will be the hardest thing I've ever done, but tonight I'm going to do it."

"But you mustn't give up on him," said Bettina. "Many young people fall into cults and superstitious groups. It doesn't mean they'll always feel the same way."

She said Parvez had to stick by his boy, giving him support, until he came through.

Parvez was persuaded that she was right, even though he didn't feel like giving his son more love when he had hardly been thanked for all he had already given.

Nevertheless, Parvez tried to endure his son's looks and reproaches. He attempted to make conversation about his beliefs. But if Parvez ventured any criticism, Ali always had a brusque reply. On one occasion Ali accused Parvez of "groveling" to the whites; in contrast, he explained, he was not "inferior"; there was more to the world than the West, though the West always thought it was best.

"How is it you know that?" Parvez said, "seeing as you've never left England?"

Ali replied with a look of contempt.

One night, having ensured there was no alcohol on his breath, Parvez sat down at the kitchen table with Ali. He hoped Ali would compliment him on the beard he was growing but Ali didn't appear to notice.

The previous day Parvez had been telling Bettina that he thought people in the West sometimes felt inwardly empty and that people needed a philosophy to live by.

"Yes," said Bettina. "That's the answer. You must tell him what your philosophy of life is. Then he will understand that there are other beliefs."

After some fatiguing consideration, Parvez was ready to begin. The boy watched him as if he expected nothing.

Haltingly Parvez said that people had to treat one another with respect, particularly children their parents. This did seem, for a moment, to affect the boy. Heartened, Parvez continued. In his view this life was all there was and when you died you rotted in the earth. "Grass and flowers will grow out of me, but something of me will live on—"

"How?"

"In other people. I will continue—in you." At this the boy appeared a little distressed. And your grandchildren," Parvez added for good measure. "But while I am here on earth I want to make the best of it. And I want you to, as well!"

"What d'you mean by 'make the best of it'?" asked the boy.

"Well," said Parvez. "For a start . . . you should enjoy yourself. Yes. Enjoy yourself without hurting others."

Ali said that enjoyment was a "bottomless pit."

"But I don't mean enjoyment like that!" said Parvez. "I mean the beauty of living!"

"All over the world our people are oppressed," was the boy's reply.

"I know," Parvez replied, not entirely sure who "our people" were, "but still—life is for living!"

Ali said, "Real morality has existed for hundreds of years. Around the world millions and millions of people share my beliefs. Are you saying you are right and they are all wrong?"

Ali looked at his father with such aggressive confidence that Parvez could say no more.

One evening Bettina was sitting in Parvez's car, after visiting a client, when they passed a boy on the street.

"That's my son," Parvez said suddenly. They were on the other side of town, in a poor district, where there were two mosques.

Parvez set his face hard.

Bettina turned to watch him. "Slow down then, slow down!" She said, "He's good-looking. Reminds me of you. But with a more determined face. Please, can't we stop?"

"What for?"

"I'd like to talk to him."

Parvez turned the cab round and stopped beside the boy.

"Coming home?" Parvez asked. "It's quite a way."

The sullen boy shrugged and got into the back seat. Bettina sat in the front. Parvez became aware of Bettina's short skirt, gaudy rings and ice-blue eyeshadow. He became conscious that the smell of her perfume, which he loved, filled the cab. He opened the window.

While Parvez drove as fast as he could, Bettina said gently to Ali, "Where have you been?"

"The mosque," he said.

"And how are you getting on at college? Are you working hard?"

"Who are you to ask me these questions?" he said, looking out of the window. Then they hit bad traffic and the car came to a standstill.

By now Bettina had inadvertently laid her hand on Parvez's shoulder. She said, "Your father, who is a good man, is very worried about you. You know he loves you more than his own life."

"You say he loves me," the boy said.

"Yes!" said Bettina.

"Then why is he letting a woman like you touch him like that?"

If Bettina looked at the boy in anger, he looked back at her with twice as much cold fury.

She said, "What kind of woman am I that deserves to be spoken to like that?"

"You know," he said. "Now let me out."

"Never," Parvez replied.

"Don't worry, I'm getting out," Bettina said.

"No, don't!" said Parvez. But even as the car moved she opened the door, threw herself out and ran away across the road. Parvez shouted after her several times, but she had gone.

Parvez took Ali back to the house, saying nothing more to him. Ali went straight to his room. Parvez was unable to read the paper, watch television or even sit down. He kept pouring himself drinks.

At last he went upstairs and paced up and down outside Ali's room. When, finally, he opened the door, Ali was praying. The boy didn't even glance his way.

Parvez kicked him over. Then he dragged the boy up by his shirt and hit him. The boy fell back. Parvez hit him again. The boy's face was bloody. Parvez was panting. He knew that the boy was unreachable, but he struck him nonetheless. The boy neither covered himself nor retaliated; there was no fear in his eyes. He only said, through his split lip: "So who's the fanatic now?"

# Salman Rushdie

Born in Bombay on 19 June 1947, the eve of India's independence from Great Britain and the division of the subcontinent into India and Pakistan, Salman Rushdie makes use of this happenstance in his most widely praised novel, *Midnight's Children* (1981). Rushdie's father, a Cambridge-educated businessman, and his family remained in Bombay until 1964 when they moved to Karachi, Pakistan. Rushdie recalls that his childhood in an anglicized, Muslim household was spent in "an atmosphere of books," and by age five he had decided to become a writer. In 1961 he was sent to Rugby, one of England's elite schools, and in 1965 entered Cambridge University, where he received in 1968 a master's degree with honors in history. After working as an actor for a year in a London theater, then spending another year as an advertising copywriter, Rushdie started writing full time. He continues to live in London under difficult circumstances. In 1988 Ayatollah Khomeini of Iran, imposed a death sentence on Rushdie as punishment for the perceived blasphemy against Islam in his fourth novel, *The Satanic Verses* (1988). The order has been rescinded, but Rushdie remains under the protection of the British government.

Although his first novel, *Grimus* (1975), received limited attention, Rushdie gained international acclaim when *Midnight's Children* appeared six years later and received the prestigious Booker Prize. It is one of the few colonial-postcolonial novels to make the Modern Library's list of the twentieth century's one hundred great novels. This sprawling, allegorical, sometimes comic, sometimes tragic book chronicles modern history on the subcontinent by tracing the lives of 1,001 children born during the midnight hour of 15 August 1947, the day a truncated India and a newly established Pakistan shed colonialism and emerged as independent nations. The book, translated into numerous languages, established Rushdie's reputation, and has been credited by its admirers for galvanizing Indian fiction in English and dimissed by its detractors as stunting the Indian novel. Rushdie, the creator of the rallying cry "The empire writes back," is a defender of the English language as an appropriate device to tell the colonial and postcolonial story, even though others argue that the language was superimposed on the colonies and should be abolished as a literary form.

*Shame* (1983) addresses the political violence and social turbulence that has afflicted Pakistan since its creation. While *Shame* did not enjoy the wide reception accorded to the previous novel, Rushdie's next work, *The Satanic Verses*, gained extensive attention but not the kind usually reserved for a novel. Its publication provoked riots in Islamic countries, bomb threats against its publishers, and a death sentence for the author. An extended allegory that makes use of Islamic mythology in part, the narrative moves back and forth in time, encompasses numerous themes—the colonial legacy among them, and shifts from India to England to the ancient world to other landscapes. In 1990 *Haroun and the Sea of Stories* appeared. Ostensibly a children's book in fable form, the text could be read as a reply to the controversy created by *The Satanic Verses*. Something of a family history, *The Moor's Last Sigh* was published in 1995. In Rushdie's usual expansive way, the book embellishes India's historic encounter with colonialism, beginning with the spice trade in South India and moving into the present. *The Ground Beneath Her Feet* (1999) develops Rushdie's recurrent themes of dislocation and alienation through the metaphor of popular music. The narrative spans India—Bombay in particular—England, and the United States as it traces the careers of two musicians and a photographer.

"The Angel Azraeel" is taken out of context from *The Satanic Verses*, but this novel about the power of story is no conventional narrative. So the passage can stand alone as an imaginative treatment of the immigrant wandering through London, the former seat of empire. He is bent on destruction and revenge. In the shabby immigrant neighborhood, he discovers among the refuse and debris "derelict kitchen units, deflated bicycle tires, shards of broken doors" alongside "abandoned hopes, lost illusions, . . .vomited fear." It is a nightmarish encounter with the aftermath of colonialism.

# The Angel Azraeel
from *The Satanic Verses*

Gibreel:

Moves as if through a dream, because after days of wandering the city without eating or sleeping, with the trumpet named Azraeel tucked safely in a pocket
of his greatcoat, he no longer recognizes the distinction between the waking and
dreaming states;—he understands now something of what omnipresence must
be like, because he is moving through several stories at once, there is a Gibreel
who mourns his betrayal by Alleluia Cone, and a Gibreel hovering over the
death-bed of a Prophet, and a Gibreel watching in secret over the progress of a
pilgrimage to the sea, waiting for the moment at which he will reveal himself,
and a Gibreel who feels, more powerfully every day, the will of the adversary,
drawing him ever closer, leading him towards their final embrace: the subtle, deceiving adversary, who has taken the face of his friend, of Saladin his truest
friend, in order to lull him into lowering his guard. And there is a Gibreel who
walks down the streets of London, trying to understand the will of God.

Is he to be the agent of God's wrath?

Or of his love?

Is he vengeance or forgiveness? Should the fatal trumpet remain in his
pocket, or should he take it out and blow?

(I'm giving him no instruction. I, too, am interested in his choices—in
the result of his wrestling match. Character *vs* destiny: a free-style bout. Two
falls, two submissions or a knockout will decide.)

Wrestling, through his many stories, he proceeds.

There are times when he aches for her, Alleluia, her very name an exalta-

*355*

tion; but then he remembers the diabolic verses, and turns his thoughts away. The horn in his pocket demands to be blown; but he restrains himself. Now is not the time. Searching for clues—*what is to be done?*—he stalks the city streets.

Somewhere he sees a television set through an evening window. There is a woman's head on the screen, a famous "presenter," being interviewed by an equally famous, twinkling Irish "host."—What would be the worst thing you could imagine?—Oh, I think, I'm sure, it would be, oh, *yes*: to be alone on Christmas Eve. You'd really have to face yourself, wouldn't you, you'd look into a harsh mirror and ask yourself, *is this all there is?*—Gibreel, alone, not knowing the date, walks on. In the mirror, the adversary approaches at the same pace as his own, beckoning, stretching out his arms.

The city sends him messages. Here, it says, is where the Dutch king decided to live when he came over three centuries ago. In those days this was out of town, a village, set in green English fields. But when the King arrived to set up house, London squares sprang up amid the fields, red-brick buildings with Dutch crenellations rising against the sky, so that his courtiers might have places in which to reside. Not all migrants are powerless, the still-standing edifices whisper. They impose their needs on their new earth, bringing their own coherence to the new-found land, imagining it afresh. But look out, the city warns. Incoherence, too, must have its day. Riding in the parkland in which he'd chosen to live—which he'd *civilized*—William III was thrown by his horse, fell hard against the recalcitrant ground, and broke his royal neck.

Some days he finds himself among walking corpses, great crowds of the dead, all of them refusing to admit they're done for, corpses mutinously continuing to behave like living people, shopping, catching buses, flirting, going home to make love, smoking cigarettes. *But you're dead*, he shouts at them. *Zombies, get into your graves.* They ignore him, or laugh, or look embarrassed, or menace him with their fists. He falls silent, and hurries on.

The city becomes vague, amorphous. It is becoming impossible to describe the world. Pilgrimage, prophet, adversary merge, fade into mists, emerge. As does she: Allie, Al-Lat. *She is the exalted bird. Greatly to be desired.* He remembers now: she told him, long ago, about Jumpy's poetry. *He's trying to make a collection. A book.* The thumb-sucking artist with his infernal views. A book is a product of a pact with the Devil that inverts the Faustian contract, he'd told Allie. Dr. Faustus sacrificed eternity in return for two dozen years of power; the writer agrees to the ruination of his life, and gains (but only if he's lucky) maybe not eternity, but posterity, at least. Either way (this was Jumpy's point) it's the Devil who wins.

What does a poet write? Verses. What jingle-jangles in Gibreel's brain? Verses. What broke his heart? Verses and again verses.

The trumpet, Azraeel, calls out from a greatcoat pocket: *Pick me up!*

*Yesyesyes: the Trump. To hell with it all, the whole sorry mess: just puff up your cheeks and rooty-toot-toot. Come on, it's party time.*

How hot it is: steamy, close, intolerable. This is no Proper London: not this improper city. Airstrip One, Mahagonny, Alphaville. He wanders through a confusion of languages. Babel: a contraction of the Assyrian "babilu." "The gate of God." Babylondon.

Where's this?

—Yes.—He meanders, one night, behind the cathedrals of the Industrial Revolution, the railway termini of north London. Anonymous King's Cross, the bat-like menace of the St. Pancras tower, the red-and-black gas-holders inflating and deflating like giant iron lungs. Where once in battle Queen Boudicca fell, Gibreel Farishta wrestles with himself.

The Goodsway: —but O what succulent goods lounge in doorways and under tungsten lamps, what delicacies are on offer in that way!—Swinging handbags, calling out, silver-skirted, wearing fish-net tights: these are not only young goods (average age thirteen to fifteen) but also cheap. They have short, identical histories: all have babies stashed away somewhere, all have been thrown out of their homes by irate, puritanical parents, none of them are white. Pimps with knives take ninety per cent of their earnings. Goods are only goods, after all, especially when they're trash.

—Gibreel Farishta in the Goodsway is hailed from shadows and lamps; and quickens, at first, his pace. *What's this to do with me? Bloody pussies-galore.* But then he slows and stops, hearing something else calling to him from lamps and shadows, some need, some wordless plea, hidden just under the tinny voices of ten-pound tarts. His footsteps slow down, then halt. He is held by their desires. *For what?* They are moving towards him now, drawn to him like fishes on unseen hooks. As they near him their walks change, their hips lose their swagger, their faces start looking their age, in spite of all the make-up. When they reach him, they kneel. *Who do you say that I am?* he asks, and wants to add: *I know your names. I met you once before, elsewhere, behind a curtain. Twelve of you then as now. Ayesha, Hafsah, Ramlah, Sawdah, Zainab, Zainab, Maimunah, Safia, Juwairiyah, Umm Salamah the Makhzumite, Rehana the Jew, and the beautiful Mary the Copt.* Silently, they remain on their knees. Their wishes are made known to him without words. *What is an archangel but a puppet? Kathputli, marionette. The faithful bend us to their will. We are forces of nature and they, our masters. Mistresses, too.* The heaviness in his limbs, the heat, and in his ears a buzzing like bees on summer afternoons. It would be easy to faint.

He does not faint.

He stands among the kneeling children, waiting for the pimps.

And when they come, he at last takes out, and presses to his lips, his unquiet horn: the exterminator, Azraeel.

After the stream of fire has emerged from the mouth of his golden trumpet and consumed the approaching men, wrapping them in a cocoon of flame, unmaking them so completely that not even their shoes remain sizzling on the sidewalk, Gibreel understands.

He is walking again, leaving behind him the gratitude of the whores, heading in the direction of the borough of Brickhall, Azraeel once more in his capacious pocket. Things are becoming clear.

He is the Archangel Gibreel, the angel of the Recitation, with the power of revelation in his hands. He can reach into the breasts of men and women, pick out the desires of their inmost hearts, and make them real. He is the quencher of desires, the slaker of lusts, the fulfiller of dreams. He is the genie of the lamp, and his master is the Roc.

What desires, what imperatives are in the midnight air? He breathes them in.—And nods, so be it, yes.—Let it be fire. This is a city that has cleansed itself in flame, purged itself by burning down to the ground.

Fire, falling fire. "This is the judgment of God in his wrath," Gibreel Farishta proclaims to the riotous night, "that men be granted their heart's desires, and that they be by them consumed."

Low-cost high-rise housing enfolds him. *Nigger eat white man's shit*, suggest the unoriginal walls. The buildings have names: "Isandhlwana," "Rorke's Drift." But a revisionist enterprise is underway, for two of the four towers have been renamed, and bear, now, the names "Mandela" and "Toussaint l'Ouverture."—The towers stand up on stilts, and in the concrete formlessness beneath and between them there is the howling of a perpetual wind, and the eddying of debris: derelict kitchen units, deflated bicycle tires, shards of broken doors, dolls' legs, vegetable refuse extracted from plastic disposal bags by hungry cats and dogs, fast-food packets, rolling cans, shattered job prospects, abandoned hopes, lost illusions, expended angers, accumulated bitterness, vomited fear, and a rusting bath. He stands motionless while small groups of residents rush past in different directions. Some (not all) are carrying weapons. Clubs, bottles, knives. All of the groups contain white youngsters as well as black. He raises his trumpet to his lips and begins to play.

Little buds of flame spring up on the concrete, fueled by the discarded heaps of possessions and dreams. There is a little, rotting pile of envy: it burns greenly in the night. The fires are every color of the rainbow, and not all of them need fuel. He blows the little fire-flowers out of his horn and they dance upon the concrete, needing neither combustible materials nor roots. Here, a pink one! There, what would be nice?, I know: a silver rose.—And now the buds are blossoming into bushes, they are climbing like creepers up the sides of the towers, they reach out towards their neighbors, forming hedges of multicolored flame. It is like watching a luminous garden, its growth accelerated many thousands of times, a garden blossoming, flourishing, becoming overgrown, tangled, becoming impenetrable, a garden of dense intertwined chimeras, rivaling in its own incandescent fashion the thornwood that sprang up around the palace of the sleeping beauty in another fairy-tale, long ago.

But here, there is no beauty, sleeping within. There is Gibreel Farishta, walking in a world of fire. In the High Street he sees houses built of flame, with walls of fire, and flames like gathered curtains hanging at the windows.—And there are men and women with fiery skins strolling, running, milling around him, dressed in coats of fire. The street has become red hot, molten, a river the color of blood.—All, all is ablaze as he toots his merry horn, *giving the people what they want*, the hair and teeth of the citizenry are smoking and red, glass burns, and birds fly overhead on blazing wings.

The adversary is very close. The adversary is a magnet, is a whirlpool's eye, is the irresistible center of a black hole, his gravitational force creating an event horizon from which neither Gibreel, nor light, can escape. *This way*, the adversary calls. *I'm over here.*

Not a palace, but only a café. And in the rooms above, a bed and breakfast joint. No sleeping princess, but a disappointed woman, overpowered by smoke, lies unconscious here; and beside her, on the floor beside their bed, and likewise unconscious, her husband, the Mecca-returned ex-schoolteacher, Sufyan.—While, elsewhere in the burning Shaandaar, faceless persons stand at windows waving piteously for help, being unable (no mouths) to scream.

PART 4

# Personal Encounters

*Knowledge was never a matter of geography.*
*Quite the reverse, it overflows all maps*
*that exist. Perhaps true knowledge only*
*comes of death by torture in the country of*
*the mind.*
—Patrick White, *Voss*

# Patrick White

The first colonial-postcolonial writer to receive the Nobel Prize (1973), Patrick White is considered by many critics as one of the most important novelists of the twentieth century. He was born in London, 28 May 1912, into an Australian family who called England "home" but whose wealth came primarily from Australian sheep. These members of the grazier class were often dubbed "squatocrats" by unimpressed Australians who resented the way some families had "squatted" on unoccupied land, made fortunes from these holdings, then assumed aristocratic airs. This aspect of White's family background regularly receives satiric treatment in his work. At age thirteen he was sent to a British boarding school; he returned to Australia in 1929 to work on a sheep station, supposedly in preparation for the family business. In 1932 he entered King's College, Cambridge, and took a degree in modern languages. He then settled in London, where his hopes for a theatrical career were dashed but where he succeeded as a novelist and published *Happy Valley* in 1939. During the late 1930s he traveled in the United States, but came back to England at the beginning of World War II, joined the Royal Air Force intelligence division, and served in Greece and the Middle East. After the war White returned to Sydney and remained there until his death on 30 September 1990. He placed the Nobel Prize money into a fund to recognize other Australian writers, and each year a substantial financial award is given in his name.

The author of twelve novels, three short-story collections, a memoir, and several plays and screenplays, White established his reputation first in the United States and England, then in Australia where only a few critics recognized early on that his work would alter the face of Australian literature. Treating conventional Australian materials in untried ways, White ignored the realistic tradition of national fiction and moved instead into metaphysical realms. Although most of his work is set in Australia and is altogether Australian in context, he remains an international figure. His novels have been translated into several European languages, and the abundant criticism on them comes from all parts of the world.

The fiction in some ways contains an extended record of spiritual yearning, a condition to which a long line of visionary characters submit. Yet these visionaries never quite reach the understanding they seek, and the open endings of the novels maintain a nervous, restless quality that suggests such a human quest for fulfillment ends in futility. The range of White's characters, settings, and time periods is immense. His first major novel, *The Aunt's Story* (1948), introduces the themes that are to be worked out more fully in subsequent fiction, such as *The Tree of Man* (1955), which depicts an Australian farm couple's ordinary lives while it examines the extraordinary possibilities of their inner being. In *Voss* (1957) White reverses heroic myths of explorers by subverting Voss's desert trek from an actual one into a metaphysical journey. *The Vivisector* (1970) takes up the plight of the artist in a postcolonial society, and *A Fringe of Leaves* (1976) returns to Australia's colonial period to tell of a woman captured by Aborigines and to reveal the partial self-knowledge she gains. White has been criticized for his style, especially the tortured syntax, which actually reinforces the characters' interior struggles, for language can also fail to express personal discovery.

"Down at the Dump" comes from *The Burnt Ones*, a collection published in 1964. Set in Sarsaparilla, the imaginary Sydney suburb that White created for much of his fiction, the story essentially captures a moment of sexual awareness between Lummy Whalley and Meg Hogben, with the sensuality of the dead Aunt Daisy looming in the background. White's fiction consistently radiates a sexual energy that permeates the characters' actions. "Down at the Dump" illustrates as well White's idiosyncratic style, his attention to minute detail, the satirical treatment of social pretensions, and, above all, the way individuals find themselves in unsettling but potentially meaningful circumstances that they do not fully grasp.

# Down at the Dump

"Hi!"

He called from out of the house, and she went on chopping in the yard. Her right arm swung, firm still, muscular, though parts of her were beginning to sag. She swung with her right, and her left arm hung free. She chipped at the log, left right. She was expert with the axe.

Because you had to be. You couldn't expect all that much from a man.

"Hi!" It was Wal Whalley calling again from out of the home.

He came to the door then, in that dirty old baseball cap he had shook off the Yankee disposals. Still a fairly appetizing male, though his belly had begun to push against the belt.

"Puttin' on yer act?" he asked, easing the singlet under his armpits; easy was policy at Whalleys' place.

"Ere !" she protested. "Waddaya make me out ter be? A lump of wood?"

Her eyes were of that blazing blue, her skin that of a brown peach. But whenever she smiled, something would happen, her mouth opening on watery sockets and the jags of brown, rotting stumps.

"A woman likes to be addressed," she said.

No one had ever heard Wal address his wife by her first name. Nobody had ever heard her name, though it was printed in the electoral roll. It was, in fact, Isba.

"Don't know about a dress," said Wal. "I got a idea, though."

His wife stood tossing her hair. It was natural at least; the sun had done it. All the kids had inherited their mother's color, and when they stood together,

---

golden-skinned, tossing back their unmanageable hair, you would have said a mob of taffy brumbies.

"What is the bloody idea?" she asked, because she couldn't go on standing there.

"Pick up a coupla cold bottles, and spend the mornun at the dump."

"But that's the same old idea," she grumbled.

"No, it ain't. Not our own dump. We ain't done Sarsaparilla since Christmas."

She began to grumble her way across the yard and into the house. A smell of sink strayed out of gray, unpainted weatherboard, to oppose the stench of crushed boggabri and cotton pear. Perhaps because Whalleys were in the bits-and-pieces trade their home was threatening to give in to them.

Wal Whalley did the dumps. Of course there were the other lurks besides. But no one had an eye like Wal for the things a person needs: dead batteries and musical bedsteads, a carpet you wouldn't notice was stained, wire, and again wire, clocks only waiting to jump back into the race of time. Objects of commerce and mystery littered Whalleys' back yard. Best of all, a rusty boiler into which the twins would climb to play at cubby.

"Eh? Waddaboutut?" Wal shouted, and pushed against his wife with his side.

She almost put her foot through the hole that had come in the kitchen boards.

"Waddabout what?"

Half-suspecting, she half-sniggered. Because Wal knew how to play on her weakness.

"The fuckun *idea!*"

So that she began again to grumble. As she slopped through the house her clothes irritated her skin. The sunlight fell yellow on the gray masses of the unmade beds, turned the fluff in the corners of the rooms to gold. Something was nagging at her, something heavy continued to weigh her down.

Of course. It was the funeral.

"Why, Wal," she said, the way she would suddenly come round, "you could certainly of thought of a worse idea. It'll keep the kids out of mischief. Wonder if that bloody Lummy's gunna decide to honor us?"

"One day I'll knock 'is block off," said Wal.

"He's only at the awkward age."

She stood at the window, looking as though she might know the hell of a lot. It was the funeral made her feel solemn. Brought the goose-flesh out on her.

"Good job you thought about the dump," she said, outstaring a red-brick propriety the other side of the road. "If there's anythun gets me down, it's havin' ter watch a funeral pass."

"Won't be from 'ere," he consoled. "They took 'er away same evenun. It's gunna start from Jackson's Personal Service."

"Good job she popped off at the beginnun of the week. They're not so personal at the weekend."

She began to prepare for the journey to the dump. Pulled her frock down a bit. Slipped on a pair of shoes.

"Bet *She*'ll be relieved. Wouldn't show it, though. Not about 'er sister. I bet Daise stuck in 'er fuckun guts."

Then Mrs. Whalley was compelled to return to the window. As if her instinct. And sure enough there She was. Looking inside the letter-box, as if she hadn't collected already. Bent above the brick pillar in which the letter-box had been cemented, Mrs. Hogben's face wore all that people expect of the bereaved.

"Daise was all right," said Wal.

"Daise was all right," agreed his wife.

Suddenly she wondered: What if Wal, if Wal had ever. . . . ?

Mrs. Whalley settled her hair. If she hadn't been all that satisfied at home—and she *was* satisfied, her recollective eyes would admit—she too might have done a line like Daise Morrow.

Over the road Mrs. Hogben was calling.

"Meg?" she called. "Marg*ret*?"

Though from pure habit, without direction. Her voice sounded thinner today.

Then Mrs. Hogben went away.

"Once I got took to a funeral," Mrs. Whalley said. "They made me look in the coffin. It was the bloke's wife. He was that cut up."

"Did yer have a squint?"

"Pretended to."

Wal Whalley was breathing hard in the airless room.

"How soon do yer reckon they begin ter smell?"

"Smell? They wouldn't let 'em!" his wife said very definite. "You're the one that smells, Wal. I wonder you don't think of takin' a bath."

But she liked his smell, for all that. It followed her out of the shadow into the strong shaft of light. Looking at each other their two bodies asserted themselves. Their faces were lit by the certainty of life.

Wal tweaked her left nipple.

"We'll slip inter the Bull on the way, and pick up those cold bottles."

He spoke soft for him.

Mrs. Hogben called another once or twice. Inside the brick entrance the cool of the house struck at her. She liked it cool, but not cold, and this was if not exactly cold, anyway, too sudden. So now she whimpered, very faintly, for everything you have to suffer, and death on top of all. Although it was her sister Daise who had died, Mrs. Hogben was crying for the death which was waiting to carry her off in turn. She called: "Me-ehg?" But no one ever came to your rescue. She stopped to loosen the soil round the roots of the aluminium plant. She always had to be doing something. It made her feel better.

Meg did not hear, of course. She was standing amongst the fuchsia bushes, looking out from their greenish shade. She was thin and freckly. She looked awful, because Mum had made her wear her uniform, because it was sort of a formal occasion, to Auntie Daise's funeral. In the circumstances she not only looked, but was thin. That Mrs. Ireland who was all for sport had told her she must turn her toes out, and watch out—she might grow up knock-kneed besides.

So Meg Hogben was, and felt, altogether awful. Her skin was green, except when the war between light and shade worried her face into scraps, and the fuchsia tassels, trembling against her unknowing cheek, infused something of their own blood, brindled her with shifting crimson. Only her eyes resisted. They were not exactly an ordinary gray. Lorrae Jensen, who was blue, said they were the eyes of a mopey cat.

A bunch of six or seven kids from Second-Grade, Lorrae, Edna, Val, Sherry, Sue Smith and Sue Goldstein, stuck together in the holidays, though Meg sometimes wondered why. The others had come around to Hogbens' Tuesday evening.

Lorrae said: "We're going down to Barranugli pool Thursday. There's some boys Sherry knows with a couple of Gs. They've promised to take us for a run after we come out."

Meg did not know whether she was glad or ashamed.

"I can't," she said. "My auntie's died."

"Arrr!" their voices trailed.

They couldn't get away too quick, as if it had been something contagious.

But murmuring.

Meg sensed she had become temporarily important.

So now she was alone with her dead importance, in the fuchsia bushes, on the day of Auntie Daise's funeral. She had turned fourteen. She remembered the ring in plaited gold Auntie Daise had promised her. When I am gone, her aunt had said. And now it had really happened. Without rancor Meg suspected there hadn't been time to think about the ring, and Mum would grab it, to add to all the other things she had.

Then that Lummy Whalley showed up, amongst the camphor laurels opposite, tossing his head of bleached hair. She hated boys with white hair. For that matter she hated boys, or any intrusion on her privacy. She hated Lum most of all. The day he threw the dog poo at her. It made the gristle come in her neck. Ugh! Although the old poo had only skittered over her skin, too dry to really matter, she had gone in and cried because, well, there were times when she cultivated dignity.

Now Meg Hogben and Lummy Whalley did not notice each other even when they looked.

> "Who wants Meg Skinny-leg?
> I'd rather take the clothes-peg . . ."

Lum Whalley vibrated like a comb-and-paper over amongst the camphor laurels they lopped back every so many years for firewood. He slashed with his knife into bark. Once in a hot dusk he had carved I LOVE MEG, because that was something you did, like on lavatory walls, and in the trains, but it didn't mean anything of course. Afterwards he slashed the darkness as if it had been a train seat.

Lum Whalley pretended not to watch Meg Hogben skulking in the fuchsia bushes. Wearing her brown uniform. Stiffer, browner than for school, because it was her auntie's funeral.

"Me-ehg?" called Mrs. Hogben. "Meg!"

"Lummy! Where the devil are yer?" called his mum.

She was calling all around, in the woodshed, behind the dunny. Let her!

"Lum? Lummy, for Chris*sake*!" she called.

He hated that. Like some bloody kid. At school he had got them to call him Bill, halfway between, not so shameful as Lum, nor yet as awful as William.

Mrs. Whalley came round the comer.

"Shoutin' me bloody lungs up!" she said. "When your dad's got a nice idea. We're goin' down to Sarsaparilla dump."

"Arr!" he said.

But didn't spit.

"What gets inter you?" she asked.

Even at their most inaccessible Mrs. Whalley liked to finger her children. Touch often assisted thought. But she liked the feel of them as well. She was glad she hadn't had girls. Boys turned into men, and you couldn't do without men, even when they took you for a mug, or got snickered, or bashed you up.

So she put her hand on Lummy, tried to get through to him. He was dressed, but might not have been. Lummy's was never ever born for clothes. At fourteen he looked more.

"Well," she said, sourer than she felt, "I'm not gunna cry over any sulky boy. Suit yourself."

She moved off.

As Dad had got out the old rattle-bones by now, Lum begun to clamber up. The back of the ute was at least private, though it wasn't no Customline.

The fact that Whalleys ran a Customline as well puzzled more unreasonable minds. Drawn up amongst the paspalum in front of Whalleys' shack, it looked stolen, and almost was—the third payment overdue. But would slither with ease a little longer to Barranugli, and snooze outside the Northern Hotel. Lum could have stood all day to admire their own two-tone car. Or would stretch out inside, his fingers at work on plastic flesh.

Now it was the ute for business. The bones of his buttocks bit into the boards. His father's meaty arm stuck out at the window, disgusting him. And soon the twins were squeezing from the rusty boiler. The taffy Gary—or was it Barry? had fallen down and barked his knee.

"For Chrissake!" Mrs. Whalley shrieked, and tossed her identical taffy hair.

Mrs. Hogben watched those Whalleys leave.

"In a brick area, I wouldn't of thought," she remarked to her husband once again.

"All in good time, Myrtle," Councilor Hogben replied as before.

"Of course," she said, "if there are *reasons*."

Because councilors, she knew, did have reasons.

"But that home! And a Customline!"

The saliva of bitterness came in her mouth.

It was Daise who had said: I'm going to enjoy the good things of life— and died in that pokey little hutch, with only a cotton frock to her back. While Myrtle had the liver-colored brick home—not a single dampmark on the ceilings—she had the washing machine, the septic, the TV, and the cream Holden Special, not to forget her husband. Les Hogben, the councilor. A builder into the bargain.

Now Myrtle stood amongst her things, and would have continued to regret the Ford the Whalleys hadn't paid for, if she hadn't been regretting Daise. It was not so much her sister's death as her life Mrs. Hogben deplored. Still, everybody knew, and there was nothing you could do about it.

"Do you think anybody will come?" Mrs. Hogben asked.

"What do you take me for?" her husband replied. "One of these cleervoyants?"

Mrs. Hogben did not hear.

After giving the matter consideration she had advertised the death in the *Herald*:

> MORROW, Daisy (Mrs.), suddenly, at her residence, Showground
> Road, Sarsaparilla.

There was nothing more you could put. It wasn't fair on Les, a public servant, to rake up relationships. And the Mrs.—well, everyone had got into the habit when Daise started going with Cunningham. It seemed sort of natural as things dragged on and on. Don't work yourself up, Myrt, Daise used to say; Jack will when his wife dies. But it was Jack Cunningham who died first. Daise said: It's the way it happened, that's all.

"Do you think Ossie will come?" Councilor Hogben asked his wife slower than she liked.

"I hadn't thought about it," she said.

Which meant she had. She had, in fact, woken in the night, and lain there cold and stiff, as her mind's eye focused on Ossie's runny nose.

Mrs. Hogben rushed at a drawer which somebody—never herself—had left hanging out. She was a thin woman, but wiry.

"Meg?" she called. "Did you polish your shoes?"

Les Hogben laughed behind his closed mouth. He always did when he thought of Daise's parting folly: to take up with that old scabby deadbeat Ossie from down at the showground. But who cared?

No one, unless her family.

Mrs. Hogben dreaded the possibility of Ossie, a Roman Catholic for extra value, standing beside Daise's grave, even if nobody, even if only Mr. Brickle saw.

Whenever the thought of Ossie Coogan crossed Councilor Hogben's mind he would twist the knife in his sister-in-law. Perhaps, now, he was glad she had died. A small woman, smaller than his wife, Daise Morrow was large by nature. Whenever she dropped in she was all around the place. Yarn her head off if she got the chance. It got so as Les Hogben could not stand hearing her laugh. Pressed against her in the hall once. He had forgotten that, or almost. How Daise laughed then. I'm not so short of men I'd pick me own brother-in-law. Had he pressed? Not all that much, not intentional, anyway. So the incident had been allowed to fade, dim as the brown-linoleum hall, in Councilor Hogben's mind.

"There's the phone, Leslie." It was his wife.

"I'm too upset," she said, "to answer."

And began to cry.

Easing his crutch Councilor Hogben went into the hall.

It was good old Horrie Last.

"Yairs . . . yairs . . ." said Mr. Hogben, speaking into the telephone which his wife kept swabbed with Breath-o'-Pine. "Yairs . . . Eleven, Horrie . . . from Barranugli . . . from Jackson's Personal . . . Yairs, that's decent of you, Horrie."

"Horrie Last," Councilor Hogben reported to his wife, "is gunna put in an appearance."

If no one else, a second councilor for Daise. Myrtle Hogben was consoled.

What could you do? Horrie Last put down the phone. He and Les had stuck together. Teamed up to catch the more progressive vote. Hogben and Last had developed the shire. Les had built Horrie's home, Lasts had sold Hogbens theirs. If certain people were spreading the rumor that Last and Hogben had caused a contraction of the Green Belt, then certain people failed to realize the term itself implied flexibility.

"What did you tell them?" asked Mrs. Last.

"Said I'd go," her husband said, doing things to the change in his pocket.

He was a short man, given to standing with his legs apart.

Georgina Last withheld her reply. Formally of interest, her shape suggested she had been made out of several scones joined together in the baking.

"Daise Morrow," said Horrie Last, "wasn't such a bad sort." Mrs. Last did not answer.

So he stirred the money in his pocket harder, hoping perhaps it would emulsify. He wasn't irritated, mind you, by his wife who had brought him a parcel of property, as well as a flair for real estate—but had often felt he might have done a dash with Daise Morrow on the side. Wouldn't have minded betting old Les Hogben had tinkered a bit with his wife's sister. Helped her buy her home, they said. Always lights on at Daise's place after dark. Postman left her mail on the veranda instead of in the box. In summer, when the men went round to read the meters, she'd ask them in for a glass of beer. Daise knew how to get service.

Georgina Last cleared her threat.

"Funerals are not for women," she declared, and took up a cardigan she was knitting for a cousin.

"You didn't do your shoes!" Mrs. Hogben protested.

"I did," said Meg. "It's the dust. Don't know why we bother to clean shoes at all. They always get dirty again."

She stood there looking awful in the school uniform. Her cheeks were hollow from what she read could only be despair.

"A person must keep to her principles," Mrs. Hogben said, and added: "Dadda is bringing round the car. Where's your hat, dear? We'll be ready to leave in two minutes."

"Arr, Mum! The hat?"

That old school hat. It had shrunk already a year ago, but had to see her through.

"You wear it to church, don't you?"

"But this isn't church!"

"It's as good as. Besides, you owe it to your aunt," Mrs. Hogben said, to win.

Meg went and got her hat. They were going out through the fuchsia bushes, past the plaster pixies, which Mrs. Hogben had trained her child to cover with plastic at the first drops of rain. Meg Hogben hated the sight of those corny old pixies, even after the plastic cones had snuffed them out.

It was sad in the car, dreamier. As she sat looking out through the window, the tight Panama perched on her head lost its power to humiliate. Her always persistent, gray eyes, under the line of dark fringe, had taken up the search again: she had never yet looked enough. Along the road they passed the house in which her aunt, they told her, had died. The small, pink, tilted house, standing amongst the carnation plants, had certainly lost some of its life. Or the glare had drained the color from it. How the mornings used to sparkle in which Aunt Daise went up and down between the rows, her gown dragging heavy with dew, binding with bast the fuzzy flowers by handfuls and handfuls. Auntie's voice clear as morning. No one, she called, could argue they look stiff when they're bunched tight eh Meg what would you say they remind you of? But you never knew the answers to the sort of things people asked. Frozen fireworks, Daise suggested. Meg loved the idea of it, she loved Daise. Not so frozen either, she dared. The sun getting at the wet flowers broke them up and made them spin.

And the clovey scent rose up in the stale-smelling car, and smote Meg Hogben, out of the reeling heads of flowers, their cold stalks dusted with blue. Then she knew she would write a poem about Aunt Daise and the carnations. She wondered she hadn't thought of it before.

At that point the passengers were used most brutally as the car entered on a chain of potholes. For once Mrs. Hogben failed to invoke the Main Roads Board. She was asking herself whether Ossie could be hiding in there behind the blinds. Or whether, whether. She fished for her second handkerchief. Prudence had induced her to bring two—the good one with the lace insertion for use beside the grave.

"The weeds will grow like one thing," her voice blared, "now that they'll have their way."

Then she began to unfold the less important of her handkerchiefs.

Myrtle Morrow had always been the sensitive one. Myrtle had understood the Bible. Her needlework, her crochet doilies had taken prizes at country shows. No one had fiddled such pathos out of the pianola. It was Daise who loved flowers, though. It's a moss-rose, Daise had said, sort of rolling it round on her tongue, while she was still a little thing.

When she had had her cry, Mrs. Hogben remarked: "Girls don't know they're happy until it's too late."

Thus addressed, the other occupants of the car did not answer. They knew they were not expected to.

Councilor Hogben drove in the direction of Barranugli. He had arranged his hat before leaving. He removed a smile the mirror reminded him was there. Although he no longer took any risks in a re-election photograph by venturing out of the past, he often succeeded in the fleshy present. But now, in difficult circumstances, he was exercising his sense of duty. He drove, he drove, past the retinosperas, heavy with their own gold, past the lager-stroemias, their pink sugar running into mildew.

Down at the dump Whalleys were having an argument about whether the beer was to be drunk on arrival or after they had developed a thirst.

"Keep it, then!" Mum Whalley turned her back. "What was the point of buyin' it cold if you gotta wait till it hots up? Anyways," she said, "I thought the beer was an excuse for comin'."

"Arr, stuff it!" says Wal. "A dump's business, ain't it? With or without beer. Ain't it? Any day of the week."

He saw she had begun to sulk. He saw her rather long breasts floating around inside her dress. Silly cow! He laughed. But cracked a bottle.

Barry said he wanted a drink.

You could hear the sound of angry suction as his mum's lips called off a swig.

"I'm not gunna stand by and watch any kid of mine," said the wet lips, "turn 'isself into a bloody dipso!"

Her eyes were at their blazing bluest. Perhaps it was because Wal Whalley admired his wife that he continued to desire her.

But Lummy pushed off on his own. When his mum went crook, and swore, he was too aware of the stumps of teeth, the rotting brown of nastiness. It was different, of course, if you swore yourself. Sometimes it was unavoidable.

Now he avoided by slipping away, between the old mattresses, and boots the sun had buckled up. Pitfalls abounded: the rusty traps of open tins lay in wait for guiltless ankles, the necks of broken bottles might have been prepared to gash a face. So he went thoughtfully, his feet scuffing the leaves of stained asbestos, crunching the torso of a celluloid doll. Here and there it appeared as though trash might win. The onslaught of metal was pushing the scrub into the gully. But in many secret, steamy pockets, a rout was in progress; seeds had been sown in the lumps of gray, disintegrating kapok and the laps of burst chairs, .the coils of springs, locked in the spirals of wirier vines, had surrendered to superior resilience. Somewhere on the edge of the whole shambles a human ally, before retiring, had lit a fire, which by now the green had almost choked, leaving a stench of smoke to compete with the sicklier one of slow corruption.

Lum Whalley walked with a grace of which he himself had never been aware. He had had about enough of this rubbish jazz. He would have liked to know how to live neat. Like Darkie Black. Everything in its place in the cabin of Darkie's trailer. Suddenly his throat yearned for Darkie's company. Darkie's hands, twisting the wheel, appeared to control the whole world.

A couple of strands of barbed wire separated Sarsaparilla dump from

Sarsaparilla cemetery. The denominations were separated too, but there you had to tell by the names, or by the angels and things the RIPs went in for. Over in what must have been the Church of England Alf Herbert was finishing Mrs. Morrow's grave. He had reached the clay, and the going was heavy. The clods fell resentfully.

If what they said about Mrs. Morrow was true, then she had lived it up all right. Lum Whalley wondered what, supposing he had met her walking towards him down a bush track, smiling. His skin tingled. Lummy had never done a girl, although he pretended he had, so as to hold his own with the kids. He wondered if a girl, if that sourpuss Meg Hogben. Would of bitten as likely as not. Lummy felt a bit afraid, and returned to thinking of Darkie Black, who never talked about things like that.

Presently he moved away. Alf Herbert, leaning on his shovel, could have been in need of a yarn. Lummy was not prepared to yarn. He turned back into the speckled bush, into the pretenses of a shade. He lay down under a banksia, and opened his fly to look at himself. But pretty soon got sick of it.

The procession from Barranugli back to Sarsaparilla was hardly what you would have called a procession: the Reverend Brickle, the Hogben's Holden, Horrie's Holden, following the smaller of Jackson's hearses. In the circumstances they were doing things cheap—there was no reason for splashing it around. At Sarsaparilla Mr. Gill joined in, sitting high in that old Chev. It would have been practical, Councilor Hogben sighed, to join the hearse at Sarsaparilla. Old Gill was only there on account of Daise being his customer for years. A grocer lacking in enterprise, Daise had stuck to him, she said, because she liked him. Well, if that was what you put first, but where did it get you?

At the last dip before the cemetery a disemboweled mattress from the dump had begun to writhe across the road. It looked like a kind of monster from out of the depths of somebody's mind, the part a decent person ignored.

"Ah, dear! At the cemetery too!" Mrs. Hogben protested. "I wonder the Council," she added, in spite of her husband.

"All right, Myrtle," he said between his teeth. "I made a mental note."

Councilor Hogben was good at that.

"And the Whalleys on your own doorstep," Mrs. Hogben moaned.

The things she had seen on hot days, in front of their kiddies too.

The hearse had entered the cemetery gate. They had reached the bumpy stage toppling over the paspalum clumps, before the thinner, bush grass. All around, the leaves of the trees presented so many gray blades. Not even a magpie to put heart into a Christian. But Alf Herbert came forward, his hands dusted with yellow clay, to guide the hearse between the Methoes and the Presbyterians, onto Church of England ground.

Jolting had shaken Mrs. Hogben's grief up to the surface again. Mr.

Brickle was impressed. He spoke for a moment of the near and dear. His hands were kind and professional in helping her out.

But Meg jumped. And landed. It was a shock to hear a stick crack so loud. Perhaps it was what Mum would have called irreverent. At the same time her banana-colored panama fell off her head into the tussocks.

It was really a bit confusing at the grave. Some of the men helped with the coffin, and Councilor Last was far too short.

Then Mrs. Hogben saw, she saw, from out of the lace handkerchief, it was that Ossie Coogan she saw, standing the other side of the grave. Had old Gill given him a lift? Ossie, only indifferently buttoned, stood sniveling behind the mound of yellow clay.

Nothing would have stopped his nose. Daise used to say: You don't want to be frightened, Ossie, not when I'm here, see? But she wasn't any longer. So now he was afraid. Excepting Daise, Protestants had always frightened him. Well, I'm nothing, she used to say, nothing that you could pigeonhole, but love what we are given to love.

Myrtle Hogben was ropeable, if only because of what Councilor Last must think. She would have liked to express her feelings in words, if she could have done so without giving offense to God. Then the ants ran up her legs, for she was standing on a nest, and her body cringed before the teeming injustices.

Daise, she had protested the day it all began, whatever has come over you? The sight of her sister had made her run out leaving the white sauce to burn. Wherever will you take him? He's sick, said Daise. *But you can't,* Myrtle Hogben cried. For there was her sister Daise pushing some old deadbeat in a barrow. All along Showground Road people had come out of homes to look. Daise appeared smaller pushing the wheelbarrow down the hollow and up the hill. Her hair was half uncoiled. *You can't!* Myrtle called. But Daise could, and did.

When all the few people were assembled at the graveside in their good clothes, Mr. Brickle opened the book, though his voice soon suggested he needn't have.

*"I am the resurrection and the life,"* he said.

And Ossie cried. Because he didn't believe it, not when it came to the real thing.

He looked down at the coffin, which was what remained of what he knew. He remembered eating a baked apple, very slowly, the toffee on it. And again the dark of the horse-stall swallowed him up, where he lay hopeless amongst the shit, and her coming at him with the barrow. What do you want? he asked straight out. I came down to the showground, she said, for a bit of honest-to-God manure, I've had those fertilizers, she said, and what are you, are you sick? I live 'ere, he said. And began to cry, and rub the snot from his snivelly nose. After a bit Daise said: We're going back to my place, What's-yer-name—Ossie. The way she spoke he knew it was true. All the way up the hill in the barrow the wind was giving his eyes gyp, and blowing his thin hair apart. Over the years he had come across one or two lice in his hair, but thought, or hoped he had got rid of them by the time Daise took him up. As she pushed and struggled with the barrow, sometimes she would lean forward, and he felt her warmth, her firm diddies pressed against his back.

"*Lord, let me know mine end, and the number of my days: that I may be certified how long I have to live,*" Mr. Brickle read.

*Certified* was the word, decided Councilor Hogben looking at that old Ossie.

Who stood there mumbling a few Aspirations, very quiet, on the strength of what they had taught him as a boy.

When all this was under way, all these words of which, she knew, her Auntie Daise would not have approved, Meg Hogben went and got beneath the strands of wire separating the cemetery from the dump. She had never been to the dump before, and her heart was lively in her side. She walked shyly through the bush. She came across an old suspender-belt. She stumbled over a blackened primus.

She saw Lummy Whalley then. He was standing under a banksia, twisting at one of its dead heads.

Suddenly they knew there was something neither of them could continue to avoid.

"I came here to the funeral," she said.

She sounded, well, almost relieved.

"Do you come here often?" she asked.

"Nah," he answered, hoarse. "Not here. To dumps, yes."

But her intrusion had destroyed the predetermined ceremony of his life, and caused a trembling in his hand.

"Is there anything to see? she asked.

"Junk," he said. "Same old junk."

"Have you ever looked at a dead person?"

Because she noticed the trembling of his hand.

"No," he said. "Have you?"

She hadn't. Nor did it seem probable that she would have to now. Not as they began breathing evenly again.

"What do you do with yourself?" he asked.

Then, even though she would have liked to stop herself, she could not. She said: "I write poems. I'm going to write one about my Aunt Daise, like she was, gathering carnations early in the dew."

"What'll you get out of that?"

"Nothing," she said, "I suppose."

But it did not matter.

"What other sorts of pomes do you write?" he asked, twisting at last the dead head of the banksia off.

"I wrote one," she said, "about the things in a cupboard. I wrote about a dream I had. And the smell of rain. That was a bit too short."

He began to look at her then. He had never looked into the eyes of a girl. They were gray and cool, unlike the hot, or burnt-out eyes of a woman.

"What are you going to be?" she asked.

"I dunno."

"You're not a white-collar type."

"Eh?"

"I mean you're not for figures, and books, and banks and offices," she said.

He was too disgusted to agree.

"I'm gunna have me own truck. Like Mr. Black. Darkie's got a trailer."

"What?"

"Well," he said, "a semi-trailer."

"Oh," she said, more diffident.

"Darkie took me on a trip to Maryborough. It was pretty tough goin'. Sometimes we drove right through the night. Sometimes we slept on the road. Or in places where you get rooms. Gee, it was good though, shootin' through the country towns at night."

She saw it. She saw the people standing at their doors, frozen in the blocks of yellow light. The rushing of the night made the figures for ever still. All around she could feel the furry darkness, as the semi-trailer roared and bucked, its skeleton of colored lights. While in the cabin, in which they sat, all was stability and order. If she glanced sideways she could see how his taffy hair shone when raked by the bursts of electric light. They had brought cases with tooth-brushes, combs, one or two things—the pad on which she would write the poem somewhere when they stopped in the smell of sunlight dust ants. But his hands had acquired such mastery over the wheel, it appeared this might never happen. Nor did she care.

"This Mr. Black" she said, her mouth getting thinner, "does he take you with him often?"

"Only once interstate," said Lummy, pitching the banksia head away. "Once in a while short trips."

As they drove they rocked together. He had never been closer to anyone than when bumping against Darkie's ribs. He waited to experience again the little spasm of gratitude and pleasure. He would have liked to wear, and would in time, a striped sweatshirt like Darkie wore.

"I'd like to go in with Darkie," he said, "when I get a trailer of me own. Darkie's the best friend I got."

With a drawnout shiver of distrust she saw the darker hands, the little black hairs on the backs of the fingers.

"Oh, well," she said, withdrawn, "praps you will in the end," she said.

On the surrounding graves the brown flowers stood in their jars of browner water. The more top-heavy, plastic bunches had been slapped down by a westerly, but had not come to worse grief than to lie strewn in pale disorder on the uncharitable granite chips.

The heat made Councilor Last yawn. He began to read the carved names, those within sight at least, some of which he had just about forgot. He almost laughed once. If the dead could have sat up in their graves there would have been an argument or two.

"*In the midst of life we are in death*," said the parson bloke.

JACK CUNNINGHAM
BELOVED HUSBAND OF FLORENCE MARY,

Read Horrie Last.

Who would have thought Cunningham, straight as a silky-oak, would fall going up the path to Daise Morrow's place. Horrie used to watch them together, sitting a while on the veranda before going in to their tea. They made no bones about it, because everybody knew. Good teeth Cunningham had. Always a white, well-ironed shirt. Wonder which of the ladies did the laundry. Florence Mary was an invalid, they said. Daise Morrow liked to laugh with men, but for Jack Cunningham she had a silence, promising intimacies at which Horrie Last could only guess, whose own private life had been lived in almost total darkness.

Good Christ, and then there was Ossie. The woman could only have been at heart a perv of a kind you hadn't heard about.

"*Forasmuch as it hath pleased Almighty God of his great mercy to take unto himself the soul . . .*" read Mr. Brickle.

As it was doubtful who should cast the earth, Mr. Gill the grocer did. They heard the handful rattle on the coffin.

Then the tears truly ran out of Ossie's scaly eyes. Out of darkness. Out of darkness Daise had called: What's up, Ossie, you don't wanta cry. I got the cramps, he answered. They were twisting him. The cramps? she said drowsily. Or do you imagine? If it isn't the cramps it's something else. Could have been. He'd take Daise's word for it. He was never all that bright since he had the meningitis. Tell you what, Daise said, you come in here, into my bed, I'll warm you, Os, in a jiffy. He listened in the dark to his own snivelling. Arr, Daise, I couldn't, he said, I couldn't get a stand, not if you was to give me the jackpot, he said. She sounded very still then. He lay and counted the throbbing of the darkness. Not like that, she said—she didn't laugh at him as he had half expected—besides, she said, it only ever really comes to you once. That way. And at once he was parting the darkness, bumping and shambling, to get to her. He had never known it so gentle. Because Daise wasn't afraid. She ran her hands through his hair, on and on like water flowing. She soothed the cramps out of his legs. Until in the end they were breathing in time. Dozing. Then the lad Ossie Coogan rode again down from the mountain, the sound of the snaffle in the blue air, the smell of sweat from under the saddlecloth, towards the great, flowing river. He rocked and flowed with the motion of the strong, never-ending river, burying his mouth in brown cool water, to drown would have been worth it.

Once during the night Ossie had woken, afraid the distance might have come between them. But Daise was still holding him against her breast. If he had been different, say. Ossie's throat had begun to wobble. Only then, Daise, Daise might have turned different. So he nuzzled against the warm darkness, and was again received.

"If you want to enough, you can do what you want," Meg Hogben insisted.

She had read it in a book, and wasn't altogether convinced, but theories sometimes come to the rescue.

"If you want," she said, kicking a hole in the stony ground.

"Not everything you can't."

"You can!" she said. "But you can!"

She who had never looked at a boy, not right into one, was looking at him as never before.

"That's a lot of crap," he said.

"Well," she admitted, "there are limits."

It made him frown. He was again suspicious. She was acting clever. All those pomes.

But to reach understanding she would have surrendered her cleverness. She was no longer proud of it.

"And what'll happen if you get married? Riding around the country in a truck. How'll your wife like it? Stuck at home with a lot of kids."

"Some of 'em take the wife along. Darkie takes his missus and kids. Not always, like. But now and again. On short runs."

"You didn't tell me Mr. Black was married."

"Can't tell you everything, can I? Not at once."

The women who sat in the drivers' cabins of the semi-trailers he saw as predominantly thin and dark. They seldom returned glances, but wiped their hands on Kleenex, and peered into little mirrors, waiting for their men to show up again. Which in time they had to. So he walked across from the service station, to take possession of his property. Sauntering, frowning slightly, touching the yellow stubble on his chin, he did not bother to look. Glanced sideways perhaps. She was the thinnest, the darkest he knew, the coolest of all the women who sat looking out from the cabin windows of the semi-trailers.

In the meantime they strolled a bit, amongst the rusty tins at Sarsaparilla dump. He broke a few sticks and threw away the pieces. She tore off a narrow leaf and smelled it. She would have liked to smell Lummy's hair.

"Gee, you're fair," she had to say.

"Some are born fair," he admitted.

He began pelting a rock with stones. He was strong, she saw. So many discoveries in a short while were making her tremble at the knees.

And as they rushed through the brilliant light, roaring and lurching, the cabin filled with fair-skinned, taffy children, the youngest of whom she was protecting by holding the palm of her hand behind his neck, as she had noticed women do. Occupied in this way, she almost forgot Lum at times, who would pull up, and she would climb down, to rinse the nappies in tepid water, and hang them on a bush to dry.

"All these pomes and things," he said, "I never knew a clever person before."

"But clever isn't any different," she begged, afraid he might not accept her peculiarity and power.

She would go with a desperate wariness from now. She sensed that, if not in years, she was older than Lum, but this was the secret he must never guess: that for all his strength, all his beauty, she was, and must remain the stronger.

"What's that?" he asked, and touched.

But drew back his hand in self-protection.

"A scar," she said. "I cut my wrist opening a tin of condensed milk."

For once she was glad of the paler seam in her freckled skin, hoping that it might heal a breach.

And he looked at her out of his hard blue Whalley eyes. He liked her. Although she was ugly, and clever, and a girl.

"Condensed milk on bread," he said, "that's something I could eat till I bust."

"Oh, yes!" she agreed.

She did honestly believe, although she had never thought of it before.

Flies clustered in irregular jet embroideries on the backs of best suits. Nobody bothered any longer to shrug them off. As Alf Herbert grunted against the shovelfuls, dust clogged increasingly, promises settled thicker. Although they had been told they might expect Christ to redeem, it would have been no less incongruous if He had appeared out of the scrub to perform on altars of burning sandstone a sacrifice for which nobody had prepared them. In any case, the mourners waited—they had been taught to accept whatever might be imposed—while the heat stupefied the remnants of their minds, and inflated their Australian fingers into foreign-looking sausages.

Myrtle Hogben was the first to protest. She broke down—into the wrong handkerchief. *Who shall change our vile body?* The words were more than her decency could bear.

"Easy on it," her husband whispered, putting a finger under her elbow.

She submitted to his sympathy, just as in their life together she had submitted to his darker wishes. Never wanting more than peace, and one or two perquisites.

A thin woman, Mrs. Hogben continued to cry for all the wrongs that had been done her. For Daise had only made things viler. While understanding, yes, at moments. It was girls who really understood, not even women—sisters, sisters. Before events whirled them apart. So Myrtle Morrow was again walking through the orchard, and Daise Morrow twined her arm around her sister; confession filled the air, together with a scent of crushed, fermenting apples. Myrtle said: Daise, there's something I'd like to do, I'd like to chuck a lemon into a Salvation Army tuba. Daise giggled. You're a nut, Myrt, she said. But never *vile*. So Myrtle Hogben cried. Once, only once she had thought how she'd like to push someone off a cliff, and watch their expression as it happened. But Myrtle had not confessed that.

So Mrs. Hogben cried, for those things she was unable to confess, for anything she might not be able to control.

As the blander words had begun falling, *Our Father*, that she knew by heart, *our daily bread*, she should have felt comforted. She should of. Should of.

Where was Meg, though?

Mrs. Hogben separated herself from the others. Walking stiffly. If any of the men noticed, they took it for granted she had been overcome, or wanted to relieve herself.

She would have liked to relieve herself by calling: "Margaret Meg wherever don't you hear me Me-ehg?" drawing it out thin in anger. But could not cut across a clergyman's words. So she stalked. She was not unlike a guinea-hen, its spotted silk catching on a strand of barbed-wire.

When they had walked a little farther, round and about, anywhere, they overheard voices.

"What's that?" asked Meg.

"Me mum and dad," Lummy said. "Rousin' about somethun or other."

Mum Whalley had just found two bottles of unopened beer. Down at the dump. Waddayaknow. Must be something screwy somewhere.

"Could of put poison in it," her husband warned.

"Poison? My arse!" she shouted. "That's because *I* found it!"

"Whoever found it," he said, "who's gunna drink a coupla bottlesa hot beer?"

"I am!" she said.

"When what we brought was good an' cold?"

He too was shouting a bit. She behaved unreasonable at times. "Who wanted ter keep what we brought? Till it got good an' hot!" she shrieked.

Sweat was running down both the Whalleys.

Suddenly Lum felt he wanted to lead this girl out of earshot. He had just about had the drunken sods. He would have liked to find himself walking with his girl over mown lawn, like at the Botanical Gardens, a green turf giving beneath their leisured feet. Statues pointed a way through the glare, to where they finally sat, under enormous shiny leaves, looking out at boats on water. They unpacked their cut lunch from its layers of fresh tissue-paper.

"They're rough as bags," Lummy explained.

"I don't care," Meg Hogben assured.

Nothing on earth could make her care—was it more, or was it less?

She walked giddily behind him, past a rusted fuel-stove, over a field of deathly feltex. Or ran, or slid, to keep up. Flowers would have wilted in her hands, if she hadn't crushed them brutally, to keep her balance. Somewhere in their private labyrinth Meg Hogben had lost her hat.

When they were farther from the scene of anger, and a silence of heat had descended again, he took her little finger, because it seemed natural to do so, after all they had experienced. They swung hands for a while, according to some special law of motion.

Till Lum Whalley frowned, and threw the girl's hand away.

If she accepted his behavior it was because she no longer believed in what he did, only in what she knew he felt. That might have been the trouble. She was so horribly sure, he would have to resist to the last moment of all. As a bird, singing in the prickly tree under which they found themselves standing, seemed to cling to the air. Then his fingers took control. She was amazed at the hardness of his boy's body. The tremors of her flinty skin, the membrane of the white sky appalled him. Before fright and expectation melted their mouths. And they took little grateful sips of each other. Holding up their throats in between. Like birds drinking.

Ossie could no longer see Alf Herbert's shovel working at the earth.

"Never knew a man cry at a funeral," Councilor Hogben complained, very low, although he was ripe enough to burst.

If you could count Ossie as a man, Councilor Last suggested in a couple of noises.

But Ossie could not see or hear, only Daise, still lying on that upheaval of a bed. Seemed she must have burst a button, for her breasts stood out from her. He would never forget how they labored against the heavy yellow morning light. In the early light, the flesh turned yellow, sluggish. What's gunna happen to me, Daisy? It'll be decided, Os, she said, like it is for any of us. I ought to know, she said, to tell you, but give me time to rest a bit, to get me breath. Then he got down on his painful knees. He put his mouth to Daise's

neck. Her skin tasted terrible bitter. The great glistening river, to which the
lad Ossie Coogan had ridden jingling down from the mountain, was slowing
into thick, yellow mud. Himself an old, scabby man attempting to refresh his
forehead in the last pothole.

Mr. Brickle said: "*We give thee hearty thanks for that it hath pleased thee
to deliver this our sister out of the miseries of this sinful world.*"

"No! No!" Ossie protested, so choked nobody heard, though it was vehe-
ment enough in its intention.

As far as he could understand, nobody wanted to be delivered. Not him,
not Daise, anyways. When you could sit together by the fire on winter nights
baking potatoes under the ashes.

It took Mrs. Hogben some little while to free her *crêpe de Chine* from the
wire. It was her nerves, not to mention Meg on her mind. In the circumstances
she tore herself worse, and looked up to see her child, just over there, without
shame, in a rubbish tip, kissing with the Whalley boy. What if Meg was another of Daise? It was in the blood, you couldn't deny.

Mrs. Hogben did not exactly call, but released some kind of noise from
her extended throat. Her mouth was too full of tongue to find room for words
as well.

Then Meg looked. She was smiling.

She said: "Yes, Mother."

She came and got through the wire, tearing herself also a little.

Mrs. Hogben said, and her teeth clicked: "You chose the likeliest time.
Your aunt hardly in her grave. Though, of course, it is only your aunt, if anyone, to blame."

The accusations were falling fast. Meg could not answer. Since joy had
laid her open, she had forgotten how to defend herself.

"If you were a little bit younger"—Mrs. Hogben lowered her voice because they had begun to approach the parson—"I'd break a stick on you, my
girl."

Meg tried to close her face, so that nobody would see inside.

"What will they say?" Mrs. Hogben moaned. "What ever will happen to
us?"

"What, Mother?" Meg asked.

"You're the only one can answer that. And someone else."

Then Meg looked over her shoulder and recognized the hate which, for a
while she had forgotten existed. And at once her face closed up tight, like a
fist. She was ready to protect whatever justly needed her protection.

Even if their rage, grief, contempt, boredom, apathy, and sense of injustice had not occupied the mourners, it is doubtful whether they would have
realized the dead woman was standing amongst them. The risen dead—that

was something which happened, or didn't happen, in the Bible. Fanfares of light did not blare for a loose woman in floral cotton. Those who had known her remembered her by now only fitfully in some of the wooden attitudes of life. How could they have heard, let alone believed in, her affirmation? Yet Daise Morrow continued to proclaim.

*Listen, all of you, I'm not leaving, except those who want to be left, and even those aren't so sure—they might be parting with a bit of themselves. Listen to me, all you successful no-hopers, all you who wake in the night, jittery because something may be escaping you, or terrified to think there may never have been anything to find. Come to me, you sour women, public servants, anxious children, and old scabby, desperate men. . . .*

Physically small, words had seemed too big for her. She would push back her hair in exasperation. And take refuge in acts. Because her feet had been planted in the earth, she would have been the last to resent its pressure now, while her always rather hoarse voice continued to exhort in borrowed syllables of dust.

*Truly, we needn't experience tortures, unless we build chambers in our minds to house instruments of hatred in. Don't you know, my darling creatures, that death isn't death, unless it's the death of love? Love should be the greatest explosion it is reasonable to expect. Which sends us whirling, spinning, creating millions of other worlds. Never destroying.*

From the fresh mound which they had formed unimaginatively in the shape of her earthly body, she persisted in appealing to them.

*I will comfort you. If you will let me. Do you understand?*

But nobody did, as they were only human.

*For ever and ever. And ever.*

Leaves quivered lifted in the first suggestion of a breeze.

So the aspirations of Daise Morrow were laid alongside her small-boned wrists, smooth thighs and pretty ankles. She surrendered at last to the formal crumbling which, it was hoped, would make an honest woman of her.

But had not altogether died.

Meg Hogben had never exactly succeeded in interpreting her aunt's messages, nor could she have witnessed the last moments of the burial, because the sun was dazzling her. She did experience, however, along with a shiver of recollected joy, the down laid against her cheek, a little breeze trickling through the moist roots of her hair, as she got inside the car, and waited for whatever next.

Well, they had dumped Daise.

Somewhere the other side of the wire there was the sound of smashed glass and discussion.

Councilor Hogben went across to the parson and said the right kind of things. Half-turning his back he took a note or two from his wallet, and immediately felt disengaged. If Horrie Last had been there Les Hogben would have gone back at this point and put an arm around his mate's shoulder, to feel whether he was forgiven for unorthodox behavior in a certain individual—no relation, mind you, but. In any case Horrie had driven away.

Horrie drove, or flew, across the dip in which the dump joined the cemetery. For a second Ossie Coogan's back flickered inside a spiral of dust.

Ought to give the coot a lift, Councilor Last suspected, and wondered, as he drove on, whether a man's better intentions were worth, say, half a mark in the event of their remaining unfulfilled. For by now it was far too late to stop, and there was that Ossie, in the mirror, turning off the road towards the dump, where, after all, the bugger belonged.

All along the road, stones, dust, and leaves, were settling back into normally unemotional focus. Seated in his high Chev, Gill the grocer, a slow man, who carried his change in a little, soiled canvas bag, looked ahead through thick lenses. He was relieved to realize he would reach home almost on the dot of three-thirty, and his wife pour him his cup of tea. Whatever he understood was punctual, decent, docketed.

As he drove, prudently, he avoided the mattress the dump had spewed, from under the wire, half across the road. Strange things had happened at the dump on and off, the grocer recollected. Screaming girls, their long tight pants ripped to tatters. An arm in a sugar-bag, and not a sign of the body that went with it. Yet some found peace amongst the refuse: elderly derelict men, whose pale, dead, fish eyes never divulged anything of what they had lived, and women with blue, metho skins, hanging around the doors of shacks put together from sheets of bark and rusty iron. Once an old downandout had crawled amongst the rubbish apparently to rot, and did, before they sent for the constable, to examine what seemed at first a bundle of stinking rags.

Mr. Gill accelerated judiciously.

They were driving. They were driving.

Alone in the back of the ute, Lum Whalley sat forward on the empty crate, locking his hands between his knees, as he forgot having seen Darkie do. He was completely independent now. His face had been reshaped by the wind. He liked that. It felt good. He no longer resented the junk they were dragging home, the rust flaking off at his feet, the roll of mouldy feltex trying to fur his nostrils up. Nor his family—discussing, or quarrelling, you could never tell—behind him in the cabin.

The Whalleys were in fact singing. One of their own versions. They always sang their own versions, the two little boys joining in.

> *"Show me the way to go home,*
> *I'm not too tired for bed.*
> *I had a little drink about an hour ago,*

*And it put ideas in me head..."*

Suddenly Mum Whalley began belting into young Gary—or was it Barry?

"Wadda *you* know, eh? Wadda *you?"*

"What's bitten yer?" her husband shouted. "Can't touch a drop without yer turn nasty!"

She didn't answer. He could tell a grouse was coming, though. The little boy had started to cry, but only as a formality.

"It's that bloody Lummy," Mrs. Whalley complained.

"Why pick on Lum?"

"Give a kid all the love and affection, and waddayaget?"

Wal grunted. Abstractions always embarrassed him. Mum Whalley spat out of the window, and the spit came back at her.

"Arrrr!" she protested.

And fell silenter. It was not strictly Lum, not if you was honest. It was nothing. Or everything. The grog. You was never ever gunna touch it no more. Until you did. And that bloody Lummy, what with the caesar and all, you was never ever going again with a man.

"That's somethink a man don't understand."

"What?" asked Wal.

"A caesar."

"Eh?"

You just couldn't discuss with a man. So you had to get into bed with him. Grogged up half the time. That was how she copped the twins, after she had said never ever.

"Stop cryun, for Chrissake!" Mum Whalley coaxed, touching the little boy's blowing hair.

Everything was sad.

"Wonder how often they bury someone alive," she said.

Taking a corner in his cream Holden Councilor Hogben felt quite rakish, but would restrain himself at the critical moment from skidding the wrong side of the law.

They were driving and driving, in long, lovely bursts, and at the corners, in semi-circular swirls.

On those occasions in her life when she tried to pray, begging for an experience, Meg Hogben would fail, but return to the attempt with clenched teeth. Now she did so want to think of her dead aunt with love, and the image blurred repeatedly. She was superficial, that was it. Yet, each time she failed, the landscape leaped lovingly. They were driving under the telephone wires. She could have translated any message into the language of peace. The wind burning, whenever it did not cut cold, left the stable things alone: the wooden houses stuck beside the road, the trunks of willows standing round the brown saucer of a dam. Her too candid, gray eyes seemed to have deepened, as though to accommodate all she still had to see, feel.

It was lovely curled on the back seat, even with Mum and Dad in front.

"I haven't forgotten, Margret," Mum called over her shoulder.

Fortunately Dadda wasn't interested enough to inquire.

"Did Daise owe anything on the home?" Mrs. Hogben asked. "She was never at all practical."

Councilor Hogben cleared his throat.

"Give us time to find out," he said.

Mrs. Hogben respected her husband for the things which she, secretly, did not understand: Time the mysterious, for instance, Business, and worst of all, the Valuer General.

"I wonder Jack Cunningham," she said, "took up with Daise. He was a fine man. Though Daise had a way with her."

They were driving. They were driving.

When Mrs. Hogben remembered the little ring in plaited gold.

"Do you think those undertakers are honest?"

"Honest?" her husband repeated.

A dubious word.

"Yes," she said. "That ring that Daise."

You couldn't very well accuse. When she had plucked up the courage she would go down to the closed house. The thought of it made her chest tighten. She would go inside, and feel her way into the back corners of drawers, where perhaps a twist of tissue-paper. But the closed houses of the dead frightened Mrs. Hogben, she had to admit. The stuffiness, the light strained through brown holland. It was as if you were stealing, though you weren't.

And then those Whalleys creeping up.

They were driving and driving, the ute and the sedan almost rubbing on each other.

"No one who hasn't had a migraine," cried Mrs. Hogben, averting her face, "can guess what it feels like."

Her husband had heard that before.

"It's a wonder it don't leave you," he said. "They say it does when you've passed a certain age."

Though they weren't passing the Whalleys he would make every effort to throw the situation off. Wal Whalley leaning forward, though not so far you couldn't see the hair bursting out of the front of his shirt. His wife thumping his shoulder. They were singing one of their own versions. Her gums all watery.

So they drove and drove.

"I could sick up, Leslie," Mrs. Hogben gulped, and fished for her lesser handkerchief.

The Whalley twins were laughing through their taffy forelocks.

At the back of the ute that sulky Lum turned towards the opposite direction. Meg Hogben was looking her farthest off. Any sign of acknowledgment had been so faint the wind had immediately blown it off their faces. As Meg and Lummy sat, they held their sharp, but comforting knees. They sank their chins as low as they would go. They lowered their eyes, as if they had seen enough for the present, and wished to cherish what they knew.

The warm core of certainty settled stiller as driving faster the wind payed out the telephone wires the fences the flattened heads of gray grass always raising themselves again again again

# David Malouf

Although he grew up in the tropical Australian city of Brisbane, where he was born on 20 March 1934, David Malouf has long identified with both Australia and Europe. His mother of British descent and his father Lebanese, Malouf early on saw beyond the provincial boundaries of Brisbane, and this clash between two continents manifests itself in his work. He graduated from the University of Queensland in 1954, then worked at odd jobs for five years until he moved to England, where he taught until he returned to Australia in 1968. For the next ten years he lectured in literature at the University of Sydney. After publishing several poetry collections and two novels, he moved to a Tuscan village and devoted himself to writing. Malouf has since 1985 divided his time between Italy and Australia.

Malouf is an accomplished poet, but he has established his international reputation as a novelist. His work is preoccupied with the way oppositional forces within individuals function and the manner in which these forces determine human behavior. The role language plays in the absorption of personal experience and the cognizance of the larger world also dominates the fiction. His first novel, *Johnno* (1975), takes place in World War II Brisbane when it was threatened by Japanese invasion. Autobiographical in nature, this bildungsroman captures the atmosphere of the sleepy city transformed into a center for Allied troops. Yet it focuses mainly on how the two main characters, Johnno and Dante, behave as opposites. The novel many critics consider Malouf's finest work, *An Imaginary Life* (1978), moves to a time and place distant from Australia by recounting Ovid's exile from Rome. Living a rudimentary life along the Black Sea in what is now Romania, the poet regards his greatest trial to be severance from his language, a circumstance that prevents him from grasping experience. This short, poetic novel also develops a contrasting relationship between Ovid and a wild boy reared by wolves, which is reminiscent of the alliance between Johnno and Dante.

In *Harland's Half Acre* (1984), Malouf returns to Brisbane and contemplates another set of opposites: the contrast between the artist and the ordinary person. This richly textured narrative about a painter explores as well the predicament of the artist in a postcolonial society, which suggests that such a culture cannot nurture "real artists" who come only from Europe. *Remembering Babylon* (1993) re-creates colonial Australia to negotiate the conflicts between civilization and primitivism, past and present, understanding and ignorance. This novel, which relates the story of a young Englishman who has lived for years with Aboriginals, then joins a pioneer settlement, received the inaugural IMPAC Dublin Literary Award and was short-listed for the Booker Prize. Returning again to the colonial period, *The Conversations at Curlow Creek* (1996) records the conversations between two contrasting types: a man sentenced to death and the police officer dispatched to supervise the hanging. As they talk through the night in the desolate Australian bush, their past lives unfold to reveal the conflicting circumstances that led them to this pivotal moment.

Malouf said in an interview that the habits he developed as a poet he has applied "in making the fictions," which he considers "are in their structures very poetic." That description certainly applies to all of Malouf's fiction, including "The Sun in Winter," which comes from his 1985 collection of short stories, *Antipodes*. As the young Australian and the Flemish woman tour the ancient city of Bruges in Belgium, Malouf improvises on a recurring theme in postcolonial literature: the disparity between the New World and the Old. Their encounter concludes with a glimpse into the greatest of all oppositions, life and death.

# The Sun in Winter

It was dark in the church, even at noon. Diagonals of chill sunlight were stacked between the piers, sifting down luminous dust, and so thick with it that they seemed more substantial almost than stone. He had a sense of two churches, one raised vertically on gothic arches and a thousand years old, the other compounded of light and dust, at an angle to the first and newly created in the moment of his looking. At the end of the nave, set far back on a platform, like a miraculous vision that the arctic air had immediately snap-frozen, was a Virgin with a child at her knee. The Michelangelo. So this church he was in must be the Onze Vrouw.

"Excuse me."

The voice came from a pew two rows away, behind him: a plain woman of maybe forty, with the stolid look and close-pored waxy skin of those wives of donors he had been looking at earlier in the side panels of local altars. She was buttoned to the neck in a square-shouldered raincoat and wore a scarf rather than a wimple, but behind her as she knelt might have been two or three miniatures of herself—infant daughters with their hands strictly clasped—and if he peeped under her shoes, he thought, there would be a monster of the deep, a sad-eyed amorphous creature with a hump to its back, gloomily committed to evil but sick with love for the world it glimpsed, all angels, beyond the hem of her skirt.

"You're not Flemish, are you," she was saying, half in question (that was her politeness) and half as fact.

"No," he admitted. "Australian."

They were whispering—this was after all a church—but her "Ah, the *New* World" was no more than a breath. She made it sound so romantic, so

From *Antipodes* by David Malouf. Copyright © 1986. Used by permission of Chatto and Windus, Random House UK.

much more of a venture than he had ever seen it, that he laughed outright, then checked himself; but not before his laughter came back to him, oddly transformed, from the hollow vault. No Australian in those days thought of himself as coming under so grand a term. Things are different now.

"You see," she told him in a delighted whisper, "I guessed! I knew you were not Flemish—that, if you don't mind, is obvious—so I thought, I'll speak to him in English, or maybe on this occasion I'll try Esperanto. Do you by any chance know Esperanto?" He shook his head. "Well, never mind," she said, "there's plenty of time." She did not say for what. "But you *are* Catholic."

Wrong again. Well, not exactly, but his "No" was emphatic, she was taken aback. She refrained from putting the further question and looked for a moment as if she did not know how to proceed. Then following the turn of his head she found the Madonna. "Ah," she said, "you are interested in art. You have come for the Madonna." Relieved at last to have comprehended him she regarded the figure with a proprietary air. Silently, and with a certain old world grandeur and largesse, she presented it to him.

He should, to be honest, have informed her then that he had been a Catholic once (he was just twenty) and still wasn't so far gone as to be lapsed—though too far to claim communion; and that for today he had rather exhausted his interest in art at the little hospital full of Memlings and over their splendid van Eycks. Which left no reason for his being here but the crude one: his need to find sanctuary for a time from their killing cold.

Out there, blades of ice slicing in off the North Sea had found no obstacle, it seemed, in more than twenty miles of flat lands crawling with fog, till they found *him*, the one vertical (given a belltower or two) on the whole ring of the horizon. He had been, for long minutes out there, the assembly-point for forty-seven demons. His bones scraped like glaciers. Huge ice-plates ground in his skull. He had been afraid his eyeballs might freeze, contract, drop out, and go rolling away over the ancient flags. It seemed foolish after all that to say simply, "I was cold."

"Well, in that case," she told him, "you must allow me to make an appointment. I am an official guide of this town. I am working all day in a government office, motor-vehicle licenses, but precisely at four we can meet and I will show you our dear sad Bruges—that is, of course, if you are agreeable. No, no—please—it is for my own pleasure, no fee is involved. Because I see that you are interested, I glimpsed it right off." She turned up the collar of her coat and gave him an engaging smile. "It is OK?" She produced the Americanism with a cluck of clear self-satisfaction, as proof that she was, though a guide of this old and impressively dead city, very much of his own century and not at all hoity-toity about the usages of the New World. It was a brief kick of the heels that promised fun as well as instruction in the splendors and miseries of the place.

"Well then," she said when he made no protest, "it is decided—till four. You will see that our Bruges is very beautiful, very *triste,* you understand French? *Bruges la Morte.* And German too maybe, a little? *Die tote Stadt."* She pronounced this with a small shiver in her voice, a kind of silvery chill that made him think of the backs of mirrors. At the same time she gave him just the tips of her gloved fingers. "So—I must be off now. We meet at four."

Which is how, without especially wanting it, he came to know the whole history of the town. On a cold afternoon in the Fifties, with fog swirling thick white in the polled avenues and lying in ghostly drifts above the canals, and the red-brick façades of palaces, convents, museums laid bare under the claws of ivy, he tramped with his guide over little humpbacked bridges, across sodden lawns, to see a window the size of a hand-mirror with a bloody history, a group of torture instruments (themselves twisted now and flaking rust), the site, almost too ordinary, of a minor miracle, a courtyard where five old ladies were making lace with fingers as knobbled and misshapen as twigs, and the statue of a man in a frock coat who had given birth to the decimal system.

The woman's story he caught in the gaps between centuries and he got the two histories, her own and the city's, rather mixed, so that he could not recall later whether it was his lady or the daughter of a local duke who had suffered a fall in the woods, and her young man or some earlier one who had been shut up and tortured in one of the many towers. The building she pointed to as being the former Gestapo headquarters looked much like all the rest, though it might of course have been a late imitation.

She made light of things, including her own life, which had not, he gathered, been happy; but she could be serious as well as ironic. To see what all this really was, she insisted—beyond the relics and the old-fashioned horrors and shows—you needed a passion for the everyday. That was how she put it. And for that, mere looking got you nowhere. "All you see then," she told him, "is what catches the eye, the odd thing, the unusual. But to see what is common, that is the difficult thing, don't you think? For that we need imagination, and there is never enough of it—never, never enough."

She had spoken with feeling, and now that it was over, her own small show, there was an awkwardness. It had grown dark. The night, a block of solid ice with herrings in it, deep blue, was being cranked down over the plain; you could hear it creaking. He stamped a little, puffing clouds of white, and shyly, sheepishly grinned. "Cold," he sang, shuffling his feet, and when she laughed at the little dance he was doing he continued it, waving his arms about as well. Then they came, rather too quickly, to the end of his small show. She pulled at her gloves and stood waiting.

Something more was expected of him, he knew that. But what? Was he to name it? Should he perhaps, in spite of her earlier disclaimer, offer a tip? Was that it? Surely not. But money was just one of the things, here in Europe, that he hadn't got the hang of, the weight, the place, the meaning; one of the many—along with tones, looks, little movements of the hands and eyebrows, unspoken demands and the easy meeting of them—that more than galleries or torture chambers made up what he had come here to see, and to absorb too if he could manage it. He felt hopelessly young and raw. He ought to have known—he had known—from that invisible kick of the heels, that she had more to show him than this crumblingly haunted and picturesque corner of the past, where sadness, a mood of silvery reflection, had been turned into the high worship of death—a glory perhaps, but one that was too full of shadows to bear the sun. He felt suddenly a great wish for the sun in its full power as at home, and it burned up in him. He *was* the sun. It belonged to the world he had come from and to his youth.

The woman had taken his hand. "My dear friend," she was saying, with that soft tremor in her voice, "—I *can* call you that, can't I? I feel that we *are* friends. In such a short time we have grown close. I would like to show you one thing more—very beautiful but not of the past. Something personal."

She led him along the edge of the canal and out into a street broader than the rest, its cobbles gleaming in the mist. Stone steps led up to classical porticoes, and in long, brightly-lit windows there were Christmas decorations, holly with red ribbons, and bells powdered with frost. They came to a halt in front of one of the largest and brightest of these displays, and he wondered why. Still at the antipodes, deep in his dream of sunlight and youth, he did not see at first that they had arrived.

"There," the woman was saying. She put her nose to the glass and there was a ring of fog.

The window was full of funerary objects: ornamental wreaths in iridescent enamel, candles of all sizes like organ-pipes in carved and colored wax, angels large and small, some in glass, some in plaster, some in honey-colored wood in which you saw all the decades of growth; one of them was playing a lute; others had viols, pan pipes, primitive sidedrums; others again pointed a slender index finger as at a naughty child and were smiling in an ambiguous, un-otherworldly way. It was all so lively and colorful that he might have missed its meaning altogether without the coffin, which held a central place in the foreground and was tilted so that you saw the richness of the buttoned interior. Very comfortable it looked too—luxuriously inviting. Though the scene did not suggest repose. The heavy lid had been pushed strongly aside, as if what lay there just a moment ago had got up, shaken itself after long sleep, and gone striding off down the quay. The whole thing puzzled him. He wondered for a moment if she hadn't led him to the site of another and more recent miracle. But no.

"Such a coffin," she was telling him softly, "I have ordered for myself.— Oh, don't look surprised!—I am not planning to die so soon, not at all! I am paying it off. The same. Exactly."

He swallowed, nodded, smiled, but was dismayed; he couldn't have been more so, or felt more exposed and naked, if she had climbed up into the window, among the plump and knowing angels, and got into the thing—lain right down on the buttoned blue satin, and with her skirt rocked up to show stockings rolled tight over snowy thighs, had crooked a finger and beckoned him with a leer to join her. He blushed for the grossness of the vision, which was all his own.

But his moment of incomprehension passed. His shock, he saw, was for an impropriety she took quite for granted and for an event that belonged, as she calmly surveyed it, to a world of exuberant and even vulgar life. The window was the brightest thing she had shown him, the brightest thing he had seen all day, the most lively, least doleful.

So he survived the experience. They both did. And he was glad to recall years after, that when she smiled and touched his hand in token of their secret sympathy, a kind of grace had come over him and he did not start as he might have done; he was relieved of awkwardness, and was moved, for all his raw youth, by an emotion he could not have named, not then—for her, but also for himself and which he would catch up with only later, when sufficient time had passed to make them of an age.

As they already were for a second, before she let him go, and in a burst of whitened breath, said "Now my dear, dear friend, I will exact my fee. You may buy me a cup of chocolate at one of our excellent cafés. OK?"

# Margaret Atwood

Margaret Atwood has had a varied career as a writer and activist. In addition to her fiction for which she is internationally known and admired, Atwood has written poetry, criticism, radio and television scripts, libretti, and travel articles. She has participated in feminist and human rights organizations, serving at one time on the Board of Directors of the Canadian Civil Liberties Association. Born in Ottawa, Canada, 18 November 1939, Atwood grew up in Toronto where her father was a professor of entomology at the University of Toronto. In 1961 she received a B.A. in English from Victoria College, University of Toronto. For most of her life Atwood has lived in Toronto, but has traveled widely, giving readings throughout the world and teaching at universities in Canada, the United States, and Australia. She has earned numerous awards for her work and several honorary doctorates. Her writing has received extensive critical attention, especially from feminist critics.

The author of nine novels, four collections of short stories, and numerous volumes of poetry, Atwood published her first novel, *The Edible Woman*, in 1969. One of her most highly regarded novels, *Surfacing*, appeared next, in 1972. The same year she published an inventive book of criticism, *Survival: A Thematic Guide to Canadian Literature*, in which she discusses Canadian writers in a refreshingly informal and practical way. *Lady Oracle* was published in 1976 and *Life Before Man* in 1979. The first four novels are set in Canada and focus on male-female relationships. With a style characterized by tautness and admirable simplicity, Atwood traces the disintegration of marriages, recites the complications of sexual liaisons, satirizes urban life, depicts with compassion and incisiveness the conflicts between the sexes, and constructs characters, most often female, who face everyday dilemmas. Her record of contemporary times transcends Canada, Toronto in particular, and speaks widely to those caught up in the commonplace situations she makes familiar and meaningful.

Her fifth novel, *Bodily Harm* (1981), moves from Canada to the Caribbean, where a young woman journalist confronts not only her own shattered life but also the precarious sphere of postcolonial politics. Like the previous novel, *The Handmaid's Tale* takes an original turn, this time as a fable about women in a futuristic society. At this point in Atwood's career, *Cat's Eye* (1988) stands as her most complex work, especially in its use of myth and allusions to Shakespeare, the Bible, and popular culture. The narrator traces her development through an unhappy childhood and adolescence into a celebrated painter. Typical of the earlier fiction, *Cat's Eye* remains on a realistic level and borders on a comedy of manners, but at the same time explores the inner world of the artist, especially one in a postcolonial society. Once more set in Toronto, *The Robber Bride* (1993) follows the lives of three women haunted by a fourth woman who had damaged each of them in earlier encounters. A female character dominates *Alias Grace* (1996), but this time she comes from nineteenth-century Canadian history; Grace is based on an actual woman convicted of murder and sentenced to life in prison. Atwood handles the colonial period in Toronto with the same deftness she applies to the modern city, and she explores once more through Grace's story the familiar circumstances that shape female consciousness.

Taken from the collection *Bluebeard's Egg and Other Stories* (1983), "Scarlet Ibis" recalls an incident from a family vacation in the Caribbean, a favorite destination for Canadians escaping their cold climate. The understated narrative technique, which helps to insinuate Christine's self-deprecation and lack of personal confidence, is typical of Atwood's work. So is the way irony undercuts the near-metaphysical moment that occurs when the scarlet ibis descend and assume their decorative positions.

# Scarlet Ibis

Some years ago now, Christine went with Don to Trinidad. They took Lilian, their youngest child, who was four then. The others, who were in school, stayed with their grandmother.

Christine and Don sat beside the hotel pool in the damp heat, drinking rum punch and eating strange-tasting hamburgers. Lilian wanted to be in the pool all the time—she could already swim a little—but Christine didn't think it was a good idea, because of the sun. Christine rubbed sun block on her nose, and on the noses of Lilian and Don. She felt that her legs were too white and that people were looking at her and finding her faintly ridiculous, because of her pinky-white skin and the large hat she wore. More than likely, the young black waiters who brought the rum punch and the hamburgers, who walked easily through the sun without paying any attention to it, who joked among themselves but were solemn when they set down the glasses and plates, had put her in a category; one that included fat, although she was not fat exactly. She suggested to Don that perhaps he was tipping too much. Don said he felt tired.

"You felt tired before," Christine said. "That's why we came, remember? So you could get some rest."

Don took afternoon naps, sprawled on his back on one of the twin beds in the room—Lilian had a fold-out cot—his mouth slightly open, the skin of his face pushed by gravity back down towards his ears, so that he looked tauter, thinner, and more aquiline in this position than he did when awake. Deader, thought Christine, taking a closer look. People lying on their backs in coffins usually—in her limited experience—seemed to have lost weight. This image, of Don encoffined, was one that had been drifting through her mind too often for comfort lately.

It was hopeless expecting Lilian to have an afternoon nap too, so Christine took her down to the pool or tried to keep her quiet by drawing with her, using Magic Markers. At that age Lilian drew nothing but women or girls, wearing very fancy dresses, full-skirted, with a lot of decoration. They were always smiling, with red, curvy mouths, and had abnormally long thick eyelashes. They did not stand on any ground—Lilian was not yet putting the ground into her pictures—but floated on the page as if it were a pond they were spread out on, arms outstretched, feet at the opposite sides of their skirts, their elaborate hair billowing around their heads. Sometimes Lilian put in some birds or the sun, which gave these women the appearance of giant airborne balloons, as if the wind had caught them under their skirts and carried them off, light as feathers, away from everything. Yet, if she were asked, Lilian would say these women were walking.

After a few days of all this, when they ought to have adjusted to the heat, Christine felt they should get out of the hotel and do something. She did not want to go shopping by herself, although Don suggested it; she felt that nothing she tried on helped her look any better, or, to be more precise, that it didn't much matter how she looked. She tried to think of some other distraction, mostly for the sake of Don. Don was not noticeably more rested, although he had a sunburn—which, instead of giving him a glow of health, made him seem angry—and he'd started drumming his fingers on tabletops again. He said he was having trouble sleeping: bad dreams, which he could not remember. Also the air-conditioning was clogging up his nose. He had been under a lot of pressure lately, he said.

Christine didn't need to be told. She could feel the pressure he was under, like a clenched mass of something, tissue, congealed blood, at the back of her own head. She thought of Don as being encased in a sort of metal carapace, like the shell of a crab, that was slowly tightening on him, on all parts of him at once, so that something was sure to burst, like a thumb closed slowly in a car door. The metal skin was his entire body, and Christine didn't know how to unlock it for him and let him out. She felt as if all her ministrations—the cold washcloths for his headaches, the trips to the drugstore for this or that bottle of pills, the hours of tiptoeing around, intercepting the phone, keeping Lilian quiet, above all the mere act of witnessing him, which was so draining—were noticed by him hardly at all: moths beating on the outside of a lit window, behind which someone important was thinking about something of major significance that had nothing to do with moths. This vacation, for instance, had been her idea, but Don was only getting redder and redder.

Unfortunately, it was not carnival season. There were restaurants, but, Lilian hated sitting still in them, and one thing Don did not need was more food and especially more drink. Christine wished Don had a sport, but considering the way he was, he would probably overdo it and break something.

"I had an uncle who took up hooking rugs," she'd said to him one evening after dinner. "When he retired. He got them in kits. He said he found it very restful." The aunt that went with that uncle used to say, "I said for better or for worse, but I never said for lunch."

"Oh, for God's sake, Christine," was all Don had to say to that. He'd never thought much of her relatives. His view was that Christine was still on the raw side of being raw material. Christine did not look forward to the time, twenty years away at least, when he would be home all day, pacing, drumming his fingers, wanting whatever it was that she could never identify and never provide.

In the morning, while the other two were beginning breakfast, Christine went bravely to the hotel's reception desk. There was a thin, elegant brown girl behind it, in lime green, Rasta beads, and Vogue make-up, coiled like spaghetti around the phone. Christine, feeling hot and porous, asked if there was any material on things to do. The girl, sliding her eyes over and past Christine as if she were a minor architectural feature, selected and fanned an assortment of brochures, continuing to laugh lightly into the phone.

Christine took the brochures into the ladies' room to preview them. Not the beach, she decided, because of the sun. Not the boutiques, not the night clubs, not the memories of Old Spain.

She examined her face, added lipstick to her lips, which were getting thin and pinched together. She really needed to do something about herself, before it was too late. She made her way back to the breakfast table. Lilian was saying that the pancakes weren't the same as the ones at home. Don said she had to eat them because she had ordered them, and if she was old enough to order for herself she was old enough to know that they cost money and couldn't be wasted like that. Christine wondered silently if it was a bad pattern, making a child eat everything on her plate, whether she liked the food or not: perhaps Lilian would become fat, later on.

Don was having bacon and eggs. Christine had asked Don to order yogurt and fresh fruit for her, but there was nothing at her place.

"They didn't have it," Don said.

"Did you order anything else?" said Christine, who was now hungry.

"How was I supposed to know what you want?" said Don.

"We're going to see the Scarlet Ibis," Christine announced brightly to Lilian. She would ask them to bring back the menu, so she could order.

"What? " said Don. Christine handed him the brochure, which showed some red birds with long curved bills sitting in a tree; there was another picture of one close up, in profile, one demented-looking eye staring out from its red feathers like a target.

"They're very rare," said Christine, looking around for a waiter. "It's a preservation."

"You mean a preserve," said Don, reading the brochure. "In a swamp? Probably crawling with mosquitoes."

"I don't want to go," said Lilian, pushing scraps of a pancake around in a pool of watery syrup. This was her other complaint, that it wasn't the right kind of syrup.

"Imitation maple flavoring," Don said, reading the label.

"You don't even know what it is," said Christine. "We'll take some fly dope. Anyway, they wouldn't let tourists go there if there were that many mosquitoes. It's a *mangrove* swamp; that isn't the same as our kind."

"I'm going to get a paper," said Don. He stood up and walked away. His legs, coming out of the bottoms of his Bermuda shorts, were still very white, with an overglaze of pink down the backs. His body, once muscular, was losing tone, sliding down towards his waist and buttocks. He was beginning to slope. From the back, he had the lax, demoralized look of a man who has been confined in an institution, though from the front he was brisk enough.

Watching him go, Christine felt the sickness in the pit of her stomach that was becoming familiar to her these days. Maybe the pressure he was under was her. Maybe she was a weight. Maybe he wanted her to lift up, blow away somewhere, like a kite, the children hanging on behind her in a long string. She didn't know when she had first noticed this feeling; probably after it had been there some time, like a knocking on the front door when you're asleep. There had been a shifting of forces, unseen, unheard, underground, the sliding against each other of giant stones; some tremendous damage had occurred between them, but who could tell when?

"Eat your pancakes," she said to Lilian, "or your father will be annoyed." He would be annoyed anyway: she annoyed him. Even when they made love, which was not frequently any more, it was perfunctory, as if he were listening for something else, a phone call, a footfall. He was like a man scratching himself. She was like his hand. Christine had a scenario she ran through often, the way she used to run through scenarios of courtship, back in high school: flirtation, pursuit, joyful acquiescence. This was an adult scenario, however. One evening she would say to Don as he was getting up from the table after dinner, "Stay there." He would be so surprised by the tone of voice that he would stay.

"I just want you to sit there and look at me," she would say.

He would not say, "For God's sake, Christine." He would know this was serious.

"I'm not asking much from you," she would say, lying.

"What's going on?" he would say.

"I want you to see what I really look like," she would say. "I'm tired of being invisible." Maybe he would, maybe he wouldn't. Maybe he would say he was coming on with a headache. Maybe she would find herself walking on nothing, because maybe there was nothing there. So far she hadn't even come close to beginning, to giving the initial command: "Stay," as if he were a trained dog. But that was what she wanted him to do, wasn't it? "Come back" was more like it. He hadn't always been under pressure.

Once Lilian was old enough, Christine thought, she could go back to work full time. She could brush up her typing and shorthand, find something. That would be good for her; she wouldn't concentrate so much on Don, she would have a reason to look better, she would either find new scenarios or act out the one that was preoccuppying her. Maybe she was making things up, about Don. It might be a form of laziness.

Christine's preparations for the afternoon were careful. She bought some mosquito repellent at a drugstore, and a chocolate bar. She took two scarves, one for herself, one for Lilian, in case it was sunny. The big hat would blow off, she thought, as they were going to be in a boat. After a short argument with one of the waiters, who said she could only have drinks by the glass, she succeeded in buying three cans of Pepsi, not chilled. All these things she packed into her bag; Lilian's bag, actually, which was striped in orange and yellow and blue and had a picture of Mickey Mouse on it. They'd used it for the toys Lilian brought with her on the plane.

After lunch they took a taxi, first through the hot streets of the town, where the sidewalks were too narrow or nonexistent and the people crowded onto the road and there was a lot of honking, then out through the cane fields, the road becoming bumpier, the driver increasing speed. He drove with the car radio on, the left-hand window open, and his elbow out, a pink jockey cap tipped back on his head. Christine had shown him the brochure and asked him if he knew where the swamp was; he'd grinned at her and said everybody knew. He said he could take them, but it was too far to go out and back so he would wait there for them. Christine knew it meant extra money, but did not argue.

They passed a man riding a donkey, and two cows wandering around by the roadside, anchored by ropes around their necks which were tied to dragging stones. Christine pointed these out to Lilian. The little houses among the tall cane were made of cement blocks, painted light green or pink or light blue; they were built up on open-work foundations, almost as if they were on stilts. The women who sat on the steps turned their heads, unsmiling, to watch their taxi as it went by.

Lilian asked Christine if she had any gum. Christine didn't. Lilian began chewing on her nails, which she'd taken up since Don had been under pressure. Christine told her to stop. Then Lilian said she wanted to go for a swim. Don looked out the window. "How long did you say?" he asked. It was a reproach, not a question.

Christine hadn't said how long because she didn't know; she didn't know because she'd forgotten to ask. Finally they turned off the main road onto a smaller, muddier one, and parked beside some other cars in a rutted space that had once been part of a field.

"I meet you here," said the driver. He got out of the car, stretched, turned up the car radio. There were other drivers hanging around, some of them in cars, others sitting on the ground drinking from a bottle they were passing around, one asleep.

Christine took Lilian's hand. She didn't want to appear stupid by having to ask where they were supposed to go next. She didn't see anything that looked like a ticket office.

"It must be that shack," Don said, so they walked towards it, a long shed with a tin roof; on the other side of it was a steep bank and the beginning of the water. There were wooden steps leading down to a wharf, which was the same brown as the water itself. Several boats were tied up to it, all of similar design: long and thin, almost like barges, with rows of bench-like seats. Each boat had a small outboard motor at the back. The names painted on the boats looked East Indian.

Christine took the scarves out of her bag and tied one on her own head and one on Lilian's. Although it was beginning to cloud over, the sun was still very bright, and she knew about rays coming through overcast, especially in the tropics. She put sun block on their noses, and thought that the chocolate bar had been a silly idea. Soon it would be a brown puddle at the bottom of her bag, which luckily was waterproof. Don paced behind them as Christine knelt.

An odd smell was coming up from the water: a swamp smell, but with something else mixed in. Christine wondered about sewage disposal. She was glad she'd made Lilian go to the bathroom before they'd left.

There didn't seem to be anyone in charge, anyone to buy the tickets from, although there were several people beside the shed, waiting, probably: two plumpish, middle-aged men in T-shirts and baseball caps turned around back-wards, an athletic couple in shorts with outside pockets, who were loaded down with cameras and binoculars, a trim gray-haired woman in a tailored pink summer suit that must have been far too hot. There was another woman off to the side, a somewhat large woman in a floral print dress. She'd spread a Mexican-looking shawl on the weedy grass near the shed and was sitting down on it, drinking a pint carton of orange juice through a straw. The others looked wilted and dispirited, but not this woman. For her, waiting seemed to be an activity, not something imposed: she gazed around her, at the bank, the brown water, the line of sullen mangrove trees beyond, as if she were enjoying every minute.

This woman seemed the easiest to approach, so Christine went over to her. "Are we in the right place?" she said. "For the birds."

The woman smiled at her and said they were. She had a broad face, with high, almost Slavic cheekbones and round red cheeks like those of an old-fashioned wooden doll, except that they were not painted on. Her taffy-colored hair was done in waves and rolls, and reminded Christine of the pictures on the Toni home-permanent boxes of several decades before.

"We will leave soon," said the woman. "Have you seen these birds before? They come back only at sunset. The rest of the time they are away, fishing." She smiled again and Christine thought to herself that it was a pity she hadn't had bands put on to even out her teeth when she was young.

This was the woman's second visit to the Scarlet Ibis preserve, she told Christine. The first was three years ago when she stopped over here on her way to South America with her husband and children. This time her husband and children had stayed back at the hotel: they hadn't seen a swimming pool for such a long time. She and her husband were Mennonite missionaries, she said. She herself didn't seem embarrassed by this, but Christine blushed a little. She had been raised Anglican, but the only vestige of that was the kind of Christmas cards she favored: prints of mediaeval or Renaissance old masters. Religious people of any serious kind made her nervous: they were like men in raincoats who might or might not be flashers. You would be going along with them in the ordinary way and then there could be a swift movement and you would look down to find the coat wide open and nothing on under it but some pant legs held up by rubber bands. This had happened to Christine in a train station once.

"How many children do you have?" she said, to change the subject. Mennonite would explain the wide hips: they liked women who could have a lot of children.

The woman's crooked-toothed smile did not falter. "Four," she said, "but one of them is dead."

"Oh," said Christine. It wasn't clear whether the four included the one dead, or whether that was extra. She knew better than to say, "That's too bad." Such a comment was sure to produce something about the will of God, and she didn't want to deal with that. She looked to make sure Lilian was still there, over by Don. Much of the time Lilian was a given, but there were moments at which she was threatened, unknown to herself, with sudden disappearance. "That's my little girl, over there," Christine said, feeling immediately that this was a callous comment; but the woman continued to smile, in a way that Christine now found eerie.

A small brown man in a Hawaiian-patterned shirt came around from behind the shed and went quickly down the steps to the wharf. He climbed into one of the boats and lowered the outboard motor into the water.

"Now maybe we'll get some action," Don said. He had come up behind her, but he was talking more to himself than to her. Christine sometimes wondered whether he talked in the same way when she wasn't there at all.

A second man, East Indian, like the first, and also in hula-dancer shirt, was standing at the top of the steps, and they understood they were to go over. He took their money and gave each of them a business card in return; on one side of it was a colored picture of an ibis, on the other a name and a phone number. They went single file down the steps and the first man handed them into the boat. When they were all seated—Don, Christine, Lilian, and the pink-suited woman in a crowded row, the two baseball-cap men in front of them, the Mennonite woman and the couple with the cameras at the very front—the second man cast off and hopped lightly into the bow. After a few tries the first man got the motor started, and they putt-putted slowly towards an opening in the trees, leaving a wispy trail of smoke behind them.

It was cloudier now, and not so hot. Christine talked with the pink-suited woman, who had blonde hair elegantly done up in a French roll. She was from Vienna, she said; her husband was here on business. This was the first time she had been on this side of the Atlantic Ocean. The beaches were beautiful, much finer than those of the Mediterranean. Christine complimented her on her good English, and the woman smiled and told her what a beautiful little girl she had, and Christine said Lilian would get conceited, a word that the woman had not yet added to her vocabulary. Lilian was quiet; she had caught sight of the woman's bracelet, which was silver and lavishly engraved. The woman showed it to her. Christine began to enjoy herself, despite the fact that the two men in front of her were talking too loudly. They were drinking beer, from cans they'd brought with them in a paper bag. She opened a Pepsi and shared some with Lilian. Don didn't want any.

They were in a channel now; she looked at the trees on either side, which were all the same, dark-leaved, rising up out of the water, on masses of spindly roots. She didn't know how long they'd been going.

It began to rain, not a downpour but heavily enough, large cold drops. The Viennese woman said, "It's raining," her eyes open in a parody of surprise, holding out her hand and looking up at the sky like someone in a child's picture book. This was for the benefit of Lilian. "We will get wet," she said. She took a white embroidered handkerchief out of her purse and spread it on the top of her head. Lilian was enchanted with the handkerchief and asked Christine if she could have one, too. Don said they should have known, since it always rained in the afternoons here.

The men in baseball caps hunched their shoulders, and one of them said to the Indian in the bow, "Hey, we're getting wet!"

The Indian's timid but closed expression did not change; with apparent reluctance he pulled a rolled-up sheet of plastic out from somewhere under the front seat and handed it to the men. They spent some time unrolling it and getting it straightened out, and then everyone helped to hold the plastic overhead like a roof, while the boat glided on at its unvarying pace, through the mangroves and the steam or mist that was now rising around them.

"Isn't this an adventure?" Christine said, aiming it at Lilian. Lilian was biting her nails. The rain pattered down. Don said he wished he'd brought a paper. The men in baseball caps began to sing, sounding oddly like boys at a summer camp who had gone to sleep one day and awakened thirty years later, unaware of the sinister changes that had taken place in them, the growth and recession of hair and flesh, the exchange of their once-clear voices for the murky ones that were now singing off-key, out of time:

"They say that in the army,
the girls are rather fine,
They promise Betty Grable,
        they give you Frankenstein . . ."

They had not yet run out beer. One of them finished a can and tossed it overboard, and it bobbed beside the boat for a moment before falling behind, a bright red dot in the borderless expanse of dull green and dull gray. Christine felt virtuous: she'd put her Pepsi can carefully into her bag, for disposal later.

Then the rain stopped, and after some debate about whether it was going to start again or not, the two baseball-cap men began to roll up the plastic sheet. While they were doing this there was a jarring thud. The boat rocked violently, and the one man who was standing up almost pitched overboard, then sat down with a jerk.

"What the hell?" he said.

The Indian at the back reversed the motor.

"We hit something," said the Viennese woman. She clasped her hands, another classic gesture.

"Obviously," Don said in an undertone. Christine smiled at Lilian, who was looking anxious. The boat started forward again.

"Probably a mangrove root," said the man with the cameras, turning half round. "They grow out under the water." He was the kind who would know.

"Or an alligator," said one of the men in baseball caps. The other man laughed.

"He's joking, darling," Christine said to Lilian.

"But we are sinking," said the Viennese woman, pointing with one outstretched hand, one dramatic finger.

Then they all saw what they had not noticed before. There was a hole in the boat, near the front, right above the platform of loose boards that served as a floor. It was the size of a small fist. Whatever they'd hit had punched right through the wood, as if it were cardboard. Water was pouring through.

"This tub must be completely rotten," Don muttered directly to Christine this time. This was a role she was sometimes given when they were among people Don didn't know: the listener. "They get like that in the tropics."

"Hey," said one of the men in baseball caps. "You up front. There's a hole in the goddamned boat."

The Indian glanced over his shoulder at the hole. He shrugged, looked away, began fishing in the breast pocket of his sports shirt for a cigarette.

"Hey. Turn this thing around," said the man with the camera.

"Couldn't we get it fixed, and then start again?" said Christine, intending to conciliate. She glanced at the Mennonite woman, hoping for support, but the woman's broad flowered back was towards her.

"If we go back," the Indian said patiently—he could understand English after all—"you miss the birds. It will be too dark."

"Yeah, but if we go forward we sink."

"You will not sink," said the Indian. He had found a cigarette, already half-smoked, and was lighting it.

"He's done it before," said the largest baseball cap. "Every week he gets a hole in the goddamned boat. Nothing to it."

The brown water continued to come in. The boat went forward.

"Right," Don said, loudly, to everyone this time. "He thinks if we don't see the birds, we won't pay him."

That made sense to Christine. For the Indians, it was a lot of money. They probably couldn't afford the gas if they lost the fares. "If you go back, we'll pay you anyway," she called to the Indian. Ordinarily she would have made this suggestion to Don, but she was getting frightened.

Either the Indian didn't hear her or he didn't trust them, or it wasn't his idea of a fair bargain. He didn't smile or reply.

For a few minutes they all sat there, waiting for the problem to be solved. The trees went past. Finally Don said, "We'd better bail. At this rate we'll be in serious trouble in about half an hour."

"I should not have come," said the Viennese woman, in a tone of tragic despair.

"What with!" said the man with the cameras. The men in baseball caps had turned to look at Don, as if he were worthy of attention.

"Mummy, are we going to sink?" said Lilian.

"Of course not, darling," said Christine. "Daddy won't let us."

"Anything there is," said the largest baseball-cap man. He poured the rest of his beer over the side. "You got a jack-knife?" he said.

Don didn't, but the man with the cameras did. They watched while he cut the top out of the can, knelt down, moved a loose platform board so he could get at the water, scooped, dumped brown water over the side. Then the other men started taking the tops off their own beer cans, including the full ones, which they emptied out. Christine produced the Pepsi can from her bag. The Mennonite woman had her pint juice carton.

"No mosquitoes, at any rate," Don said, almost cheerfully.

They'd lost a lot of time, and the water was almost up to the floor platform. It seemed to Christine that the boat was becoming heavier, moving more slowly through the water, that the water itself was thicker. They could not empty much water at a time with such small containers, but maybe, with so many of them doing it, it would work.

"This really is an adventure," she said to Lilian, who was white-faced and forlorn. "Isn't this fun?"

The Viennese woman was not bailing; she had no container. She was making visible efforts to calm herself. She had taken out a tangerine, which she was peeling, over the embroidered handkerchief which she'd spread out on her lap. Now she produced a beautiful little pen-knife with a mother-of-pearl handle. To Lilian she said, "You are hungry? Look, I will cut in pieces, one piece for you, then one for me, *ja*." The knife was not really needed of course. It was to distract Lilian, and Christine was grateful.

There was an audible rhythm in the boat: scrape, dump; scrape, dump. The men in baseball caps, rowdy earlier were not at all drunk now. Don appeared to be enjoying himself, for the first time on the trip.

But despite their efforts, the level of the water was rising.

"This is ridiculous," Christine said to Don. She stopped bailing with her Pepsi can. She was discouraged and also frightened. She told herself that the Indians wouldn't keep going if they thought there was any real danger, but she wasn't convinced. Maybe they didn't care if everybody drowned; maybe they thought it was Karma. Through the hole the brown water poured, with a steady flow, like a cut vein. It was up to the level of the loose floor boards now.

Then the Mennonite woman stood up. Balancing herself, she removed her shoes, placing them carefully side by side under the seat. Christine had once watched a man do this in a subway station; he'd put the shoes under the bench where she was sitting, and a few minutes later had thrown himself in front of the oncoming train. The two shoes had remained on the neat yellow-tiled floor, like bones on a plate after a meal. It flashed through Christine's head that maybe the woman had become unhinged and was going to leap overboard; this was plausible, because of the dead child. The woman's perpetual smile was a fraud then, as Christine's would have been in her place.

But the woman did not jump over the side of the boat. Instead she bent over and moved the platform boards. Then she turned around and lowered her large flowered rump onto the hole. Her face was towards Christine now; she continued to smile, gazing over the side of the boat at the mangroves and their monotonous roots and leaves as if they were the most interesting scenery she had seen in a long time. The water was above her ankles; her skirt was wet. Did she look a little smug, a little clever or self-consciously heroic? Possibly, thought Christine, though from that round face it was hard to tell.

"Hey," said one of the men in baseball caps, "now you're cooking with gas!" The Indian in the bow looked at the woman; his white teeth appeared briefly.

The others continued to bail, and after a moment Christine began to scoop and pour with the Pepsi can again. Despite herself, the woman impressed her.

The water probably wasn't that cold but it was certainly filthy, and who could tell what might be on the other side of the hole? Were they far enough south for piranhas? Yet there was the Mennonite woman plugging the hole with her bottom, serene as a brooding hen, and no doubt unaware of the fact that she was more than a little ridiculous. Christine could imagine the kinds of remarks the men in baseball caps would make about the woman afterwards. "Saved by a big butt." "Hey, never knew it had more than one use." "Finger in the dike had nothing on her." That was the part that would have stopped Christine from doing such a thing, even if she'd managed to think of it.

Now they reached the long aisle of mangroves and emerged into the open; they were in a central space, like a lake, with the dark mangroves walling it around. There was a chicken-wire fence strung across it, to keep any boats from going too close to the Scarlet Ibis' roosting area: that was what the sign said, nailed to a post that was sticking at an angle out of the water. The Indian cut the motor and they drifted towards the fence; the other Indian caught hold of the fence, held on, and the boat stopped, rocking a little. Apart from the ripples they'd caused, the water was dead flat calm; the trees doubled in it appeared black, and the sun, which was just above the western rim of the real trees, was a red disk in the hazy gray sky. The light coming from it was orangy-red and tinted the water. For a few minutes nothing happened. The man with the cameras looked at his watch. Lilian was restless, squirming on the seat. She wanted to draw; she wanted to swim in the pool. If Christine had known the whole thing would take so long she wouldn't have brought her.

"They coming," said the Indian in the bow.

"Birds ahoy," said one of the men in baseball caps, and pointed, and then there were the birds all right, flying through the reddish light, right on cue, first singly, then in flocks of four or five, so bright, so fluorescent that they were like painted flames. They settled into the trees, screaming hoarsely. It was only the screams that revealed them as real birds.

The others had their binoculars up. Even the Viennese woman had a little pair of opera glasses. "Would you look at that," said one of the men. "Wish I'd brought my movie camera."

Don and Christine were without technology. So was the Mennonite woman. "You could watch them forever," she said, to nobody in particular. Christine, afraid that she would go on to say something embarrassing pretended not to hear her. *Forever* was loaded.

She took Lilian's hand. "See those red birds?" she said. "You might never see one of those again in your entire life." But she knew that for Lilian these birds were no more special than anything else. She was too young for them. She said, "Oh," which was what she would have said if they had been pterodactyls or angels with wings as red as blood. Magicians, Christine knew from Lilian's last birthday party, were a failure with small children, who didn't see any reason why rabbits shouldn't come out of hats.

Don took hold of Christine's hand, a thing he had not done for some time; but Christine, watching the birds, noticed this only afterwards. She felt she was looking at a picture, of exotic flowers or of red fruit growing on trees, evenly spaced, like the fruit in the gardens of medieval paintings, solid, clear-edged, in primary colors. On the other side of the fence was another world, not real but at the same time more real than the one on this side, the men and women in their flimsy clothes and aging bodies, the decrepit boat. Her own body seemed fragile and empty, like blown glass.

The Mennonite woman had her face turned up to the sunset; her body was cut off at the neck by shadow, so that her head appeared to be floating in the air. For the first time she looked sad; but when she felt Christine watching her she smiled again, as if to reassure her, her face luminous and pink and round as a plum. Christine felt the two hands holding her own, mooring her, one on either side.

Weight returned to her body. The light was fading, the air chillier. Soon they would have to return in the increasing darkness, in a boat so rotten a misplaced foot would go through it. The water would be black, not brown; it would be full of roots.

"Shouldn't we go back?" she said to Don.

Lilian said, "Mummy, I'm hungry," and Christine remembered the chocolate bar and rummaged in her bag. It was down at the bottom, limp as a slab of bacon but not liquid. She brought it out and peeled off the silver paper, and gave a square to Lilian and one to Don, and ate one herself. The light was pink and dark at the same time, and it was difficult to see what she was doing.

When she told about this later, after they were safely home, Christine put in the swamp and the awful boat, and the men singing and the suspicious smell of the water. She put in Don's irritability, but only on days when he wasn't particularly irritable. (By then, there was less pressure; these things went in phases, Christine decided. She was glad she had never said anything, forced any issues.) She put in how good Lilian had been even though she hadn't wanted to go. She put in the hole in the boat, her own panic, which she made amusing and the ridiculous bailing with the cans, and the Indians' indifference to their fate. She put in the Mennonite woman sitting on the hole like a big fat hen, making this funny, but admiring also, since the woman's solution to the problem had been so simple and obvious that no one else had thought of it. She left out the dead child.

She put in the rather hilarious trip back to the wharf, with the Indian standing up in the bow, beaming his heavy-duty flashlight at the endless, boring mangrove and the two men in the baseball caps getting into a mickey and singing dirty songs.

She ended with the birds, which were worth every minute of it, she said. She presented them as a form of entertainment, like the Grand Canyon: something that really ought to be seen, if you liked birds, and if you should happen to be in that part of the world.

# Anita Desai

Unlike many Indian writers in English, Anita Desai pays little attention to political and social issues but focuses instead on character. Born of mixed parentage, her mother German and her father Indian, on 24 June 1937 in Northern India, Desai recalls that she spoke English at school, German at home, and Hindi with her friends. At age seven she began writing in English and publishing work in children's magazines. She attended Queen Mary's School in Delhi and received a B.A. in English at the University of Delhi in 1957. Six years later her first novel, *Cry the Peacock*, was published. Desai has lived in various parts of India, including Calcutta, which figures in her second novel, *Voices in the City* (1965). She now divides her time between Delhi and Boston.

Her nine novels, a collection of short fiction, and three children's books create a varied picture of India, but it is for the most part a miniature drawing that depicts the individual's battle with personal isolation and an inability to communicate. Some critics have called her "the pioneer of the psychological novel" in India's English-language fiction; others have described her as the Chekhov of India. At the same time, the texture of the Indian city or countryside and the vibrance of traditional Indian life are fully realized. Many of her early novels trace the struggle of Indian women to establish identity. A prime example is *Clear Light of Day* (1980), one of Desai's most admired novels, which looks into the tradition-motivated conflicts of a middle-class family in Delhi. The narrative traces the discord between two sisters: one a traditional woman maintaining the family home and caring for their retarded brother; the other, a sophisticated diplomat's wife who has left India and returns for an obligatory visit.

The first novel to move away from the closed narrative that dwells on personal disharmony is *Bye-Bye Blackbird* (1985), which examines the plight of Indian immigrants—the "blackbirds"—in London, a theme that has not been amply treated in the literature. In 1988 Desai took another radical turn from her previous work and published one of her most engaging novels, *Baumgartner's Bombay*. The central character is a Jewish immigrant named Baumgartner who fled Nazi Germany and remained in India for forty years. Through an economy of narrative but one with resonance, Desai unfolds the likable character's full story, from his pampered childhood in prewar Germany to his successful ventures and high life in Calcutta to his wartime internment in an Allied camp, then finally to his last years in Bombay as a derelict old man scrounging scraps for his cats. This reversal of the immigrant story opens up the larger world, Bombay in particular—its crowded streets, smells, sounds, all its chaotic reality. In the 1995 novel, *Journey to Ithaca*, Desai directs her attention to another broader theme by tracing the pilgrimage of two Europeans seeking an elusive spirituality in India. The narrative incorporates as well the intriguing history of the Holy Mother under whose influence they fall. Through this fictional account, Desai recalls the actual migration during the 1970s of privileged young men and women from the West who went to India searching for fulfillment, and most often failed. Whatever her subject—the inner life of Indian women or the immigrant experience in England or the Western encounter with the East, Desai has never faltered in her prose style, one of the most exquisite in the English-language literature of India.

"Pigeons at Daybreak," which was published in *Games at Twilight and Other Stories* (1978), captures in its few pages the essence of an India far removed from political strife, Western influence, and social upheaval. At the conclusion, a moment of inexplicable beauty compels the cranky old man to affirm life. It is a very "Indian" encounter.

# Pigeons at Daybreak

One of his worst afflictions, Mr. Basu thought, was not to be able to read the newspaper himself. To have them read to him by his wife. He watched with fiercely controlled irritation that made the corners of his mouth jerk suddenly upwards and outwards, as she searched for her spectacles through the flat. By the time she found them—on the ledge above the bathing place in the bathroom, of all places: what did she want with her spectacles in *there*?—she had lost the newspaper. When she found it, it was spotted all over with grease for she had left it beside the stove on which the fish was frying. This reminded her to see to the fish before it was overdone. "You don't want charred fish for your lunch, do you?" she shouted back when he called. He sat back then, in his tall-backed cane chair, folded his hands over his stomach and knew that if he were to open his mouth now, even a slit, it would be to let out a scream of abuse. So he kept it tightly shut.

When she had finally come to the end of that round of bumbling activity, moving from stove to bucket, shelf to table, cupboard to kitchen, she came out on the balcony again, triumphantly carrying with her the newspaper as well as the spectacles. "So," she said, "are you ready to listen to the news now?"

"Now," he said, parting his lips with the sound of tearing paper, "I'm ready."

But Otima Basu never heard such sounds, such ironies or distresses. Quite pleased with all she had accomplished, and at having half an hour in which to sit down comfortably, she settled herself on top of a cane stool like a large soft cushion of white cotton, oiled hair and gold bangles. Humming a little air from the last Hindi film she had seen, she opened out the newspaper on her soft, doughy lap and began to hum out the headlines. In spite of himself, Amul Basu leaned forward, strained his eyes to catch an interesting headline for he simply couldn't believe this was all the papers had to offer.

"'Rice smugglers caught'" she read out, but immediately ran along a train of thought of her own. "What can they expect? Everyone knows there is enough rice in the land, it's the hoarders and black-marketeers who keep it from us, naturally people will break the law and take to smuggling . . ."

"What else? What else?" Mr. Basu snapped at her. "Nothing else in the papers?"

"Ah—ah—hmm," she muttered as her eyes roved up and down the columns, looking very round and glassy behind the steel-rimmed spectacles. "'Blue bull menace in Delhi airport can be solved by narcotic drug—'"

"Blue bulls? Blue bulls?" snorted Mr. Basu, almost tipping out of his chair. "How do you mean, 'blue bulls'? What's a blue bull? You can't be reading right."

"I am reading right," she protested. "Think I can't read? Did my B.A., helped two children through school and college, and you think I can't read? Blue bulls it says here, blue bulls it is."

"Can't be," he grumbled, but retreated into his chair from her unexpectedly spirited defense. "Must be a printing mistake. There are bulls, buffaloes, bullocks, and *bul-buls,* but whoever heard of a blue bull? Nilgai, do they mean? But that creature is nearly extinct. How can there be any at the airport? It's all rot, somebody's fantasy—"

"All right, I'll stop reading, if you'd rather. I have enough to do in the kitchen, you know," she threatened him, but he pressed his lips together and, with a little stab of his hand, beckoned her to pick up the papers and continue.

"Ah—ah—hmm. What pictures are on this week, I wonder?" she continued, partly because that was a subject of consuming interest to her, and partly because she thought it a safe subject to move onto. "*Teri Meri Kismet*—'the heartwarming saga of an unhappy wife.' No, no, no. *Do Dost*—winner of three Filmfare awards—ahh . . ."

"Please, please, Otima, the news," Mr. Basu reminded her.

"Nothing to interest you," she said but tore herself away from the entertainments column for his sake. "'Anti-arthritis drug'—not your problem. 'Betel leaves cause cancer.' Hmph. I know at least a hundred people who chew betel leaves and are as fit—"

"All right. All right. What else?"

"What news are you interested in then?" she flared up, but immediately subsided and browsed on, comfortably scratching the sole of her foot as she did so. "'Floods in Assam.' 'Drought in Maharashtra.' When is there not? 'Two hundred cholera deaths.' 'A woman and child have a miraculous escape when their house collapses.' 'Husband held for murder of wife.' See?" she cried excitedly. "Once more. How often does this happen? 'Husband and mother-in-law have been arrested on charge of pouring kerosene on Kantibai's clothes and setting her on fire while she slept.' Yes, that is how they always do it. Why? Probably the dowry didn't satisfy them, they must have hoped to get one more . . .'"

He groaned and sank back in his chair. He knew there was no stopping her now. Except for stories of grotesque births like those of two-headed children or five-legged calves, there was nothing she loved as dearly as tales of murder and atrocity, and short of his having a stroke or the fish-seller arriving at the door, nothing could distract her now. He even heaved himself out of his chair and shuffled off to the other end of the balcony to feed the parrot in its cage a green chilli or two without her so much as noticing his departure. But when she had read to the end of that fascinating item, she ran into another that she read out in a voice like a law-maker's, and he heard it without wishing to: "'Electricity will be switched off as urgent repairs to power lines must be made, in Darya Ganj and Kashmere Gate area, from 8 p.m. to 6 a.m. on the twenty-first of May.' My God, that is today."

"Today? Tonight? No electricity?" he echoed, letting the green chilli fall to the floor of the cage where other offered and refused chillies lay in a rotting heap. "How will I sleep then?" he gasped fearfully, "without a fan? In this heat?" and already his diaphragm seemed to cave in, his chest to rise and fall as he panted for breath. Clutching his throat, he groped his way back to the cane chair. "Otima, Otima, I can't breathe," he moaned.

She put the papers away and rose with a sigh of irritation and anxiety, the kind a sickly child arouses in its tired mother. She herself, at fifty-six, had not a wrinkle on her oiled face, scarcely a gray hair on her head. As smooth as butter, as round as a cake, life might still have been delectable to her if it had not been for the asthma that afflicted her husband and made him seem, at sixty-one, almost decrepit.

"I'll bring you your inhaler. Don't get worried, just don't get worried," she told him and bustled off to find his inhaler and cortisone. When she held them out to him, he lowered his head into the inhaler like a dying man at the one straw left. He grasped it with frantic hands, almost clawing her. She shook her head, watching him. "Why do you let yourself get so upset?" she asked, cursing herself for having read out that particular piece of news to him. "It won't be so bad. Many people in the city sleep without electric fans— most do. We'll manage—"

"*You'll* manage," he spat at her, "but I?"

There was no soothing him now. She knew how rapidly he would advance from imagined breathlessness into the first frightening stage of a full-blown attack of asthma. His chest was already heaving, he imagined there was no oxygen left for him to breathe, that his lungs had collapsed and could not take in any air. He stared up at the strings of washing that hung from end to end of the balcony, the overflow of furniture that cluttered it, the listless parrot in its cage, the view of all the other crowded, washing-hung balconies up and down the length of the road, and felt there was no oxygen left in the air.

"Stay out here on the balcony, it's a little cooler than inside," his wife said calmly and left him to go about her work. But she did it absently. Normally she would have relished bargaining with the fish-seller who came to the door with a *beckti,* some whiskered black river fish and a little squirming hill of pale pink prawns in his flat basket. But today she made her purchases and paid him off rather quickly—she was in a hurry to return to the balcony. "All right?" she asked, looking down at her husband sunk into a heap on his chair, shaking with the effort to suck in air. His lips tightened and whitened in silent reply. She sighed and went away to sort out spices in the kitchen, to pour them out of large containers into small containers, to fill those that were empty and empty those that were full, giving everything that came her way a little loving polish with the end of her sari for it was something she loved to do, but she did not stay very long. She worried about her husband. Foolish and unreasonable as he seemed to her in his sickness, she could not quite leave him to his agony, whether real or imagined. When the postman brought them a letter from their son in Bhilai, she read out to him the boy's report on his work in the steel mills. The father said nothing but seemed calmer and she was able, after that, to make him eat a little rice and fish *jhol,* very lightly prepared, just as the doctor prescribed. "Lie down now," she said, sucking at a fish bone as she removed the dishes from the table. "It's too hot out on the balcony. Take some rest."

"Rest?" he snapped at her, but shuffled off into the bedroom and allowed her to make up his bed with all the pillows and bolsters that kept him in an almost sitting position on the flat wooden bed. He shifted and groaned as she heaped up a bolster here, flattened a cushion there, and said he could not possibly sleep, but she thought he did for she kept an eye on him while she leafed through a heap of film and women's magazines on her side of the bed, and thought his eyes were closed genuinely in sleep and that his breathing was almost as regular as the slow circling of the electric fan above them. The fan needed oiling, it made a disturbing clicking sound with every revolution, but who was there to climb up to it and do the oiling and cleaning? Not so easy to get these things done when one's husband is old and ill, she thought. She yawned. She rolled over.

When she brought him his afternoon tea, she asked "Had a good sleep?" which annoyed him. "Never slept at all," he snapped, taking the cup from her hands and spilling some tea. "How can one sleep if one can't breathe?" he growled, and she turned away with a little smile at his stubbornness. But later that evening he was genuinely ill, choked, in a panic at his inability to breathe as well as at the prospect of a hot night without a fan. "What will I do?" he kept moaning in between violent struggles for air that shook his body and left it limp. "What will I do?"

"I'll tell you," she suddenly answered, and wiped the perspiration from her face in relief. "I'll have your bed taken up on the terrace. I can call Bulu from next door to do it—you can sleep out in the open air tonight, eh? That'll be nice, won't it? That will do you good." She brightened both at the thought of a night spent in the open air on the terrace, just as they had done when they were younger and climbing up and down stairs was nothing to them, and at the thought of having an excuse to visit the neighbors and having a little chat while getting them to come and carry up a string bed for them. Of course old Basu made a protest and a great fuss and coughed and spat and shook and said he could not possibly move in this condition, or be moved by anyone, but she insisted and, ignoring him, went out to make the arrangements.

Basu had not been on the terrace for years. While his wife and Bulu led him up the stairs, hauling him up and propping him upright by their shoulders as though he were some lifeless bag containing something fragile and valuable, he tried to think when he had last attempted or achieved what now seemed a tortuous struggle up the steep concrete steps to the warped green door at the top.

They had given up sleeping there on summer nights long ago, not so much on account of old age or weak knees, really, but because of their perpetual quarrels with the neighbors on the next terrace, separated from theirs by only a broken wooden trellis. Noisy, inconsiderate people, addicted to the radio turned on full blast. At times the man had been drunk and troubled and abused his wife who gave as good as she got. It had been intolerable. Otima had urged her husband, night after night, to protest. When he did, they had almost killed him. At least they would have had they managed to cross over to the Basus' terrace which they were physically prevented from doing by their sons and daughters. The next night they had been even more offensive. Finally the Basus had been forced to give in and retreat down the stairs to sleep in their closed, airless room under the relentlessly ticking ceiling fan. At least it was private there. After the first few restless nights they wondered how they had ever put up with the public sleeping outdoors and its disturbances—its "nuisance," as Otima called it in English, thinking it an effective word.

That had not—he groaned aloud as they led him up over the last step to the green door—been the last visit he had paid to the rooftop. As Bulu kicked open the door—half-witted he may be, but he was burly too, and good-natured, like so many half-wits—and the city sky revealed itself, in its dirt-swept grays and mauves, on the same level with them, Basu recalled how, not so many years ago, he had taken his daughter Charu's son by the hand to show him the pigeon roosts on so many of the Darya Ganj rooftops, and pointed out to him a flock of collector's pigeons like so many silk and ivory fans flirting in the sky. The boy had watched in silence, holding onto his grandfather's thumb with tense delight. The memory of it silenced his groans as they lowered him onto the bed they had earlier carried up and spread with his many pillows and bolsters. He sat there, getting back his breath, and thinking of Nikhil. When would he see Nikhil again? What would he not give to have that child hold his thumb again and go for a walk with him!

Punctually at eight o'clock the electricity was switched off, immediately sucking up Darya Ganj into a box of shadows, so that the distant glow of Connaught Place, still lit up, was emphasized. The horizon was illuminated as by a fire, roasted red. The traffic made long stripes of light up and down the streets below them. Lying back, Basu saw the dome of the sky as absolutely impenetrable, shrouded with summer dust, and it seemed to him as airless as the room below. Nikhil, Nikhil, he wept, as though the child might have helped.

Nor could he find any ease, any comfort on that unaccustomed string bed (the wooden pallet in their room was of course too heavy to carry up, even for Bulu). He complained that his heavy body sank into it as into a hammock, that the strings cut into him, that he could not turn on that wobbling net in which he was caught like some dying fish, gasping for air. It was no cooler than it had been indoors, he complained—there was not the slightest breeze, and the dust was stifling.

Otima soon lost the lightheartedness that had come to her with this unaccustomed change of scene. She tired of dragging around the pillows and piling up the bolsters, helping him into a sitting position and then lowering him into a horizontal one, bringing him his medicines, fanning him with a palm leaf and eventually of his groans and sobs as well. Finally she gave up and collapsed onto her own string bed, lying there exhausted and sleepless, too distracted by the sound of traffic to sleep. All through the night her husband moaned and gasped for air. Towards dawn it was so bad that she had to get up and massage his chest. When done long and patiently enough, it seemed to relieve him.

"Now lie down for a while. I'll go and get some iced water for your head," she said, lowering him onto the bed, and went tiredly down the stairs like some bundle of damp washing slowly falling. Her eyes drooped, heavy bags held the tiredness under them.

To her surprise, there was a light on in their flat. Then she heard the ticking of the fan. She had forgotten to turn it off when they went up to the terrace and it seemed the electricity had been switched on again, earlier than they had expected. The relief of it brought her energy back in a bound. She bustled up the stairs. I'll bring him down—he'll get some hours of sleep after all, she told herself.

"It's all right," she called out as she went up to the terrace again. "The electricity is on again. Come, I'll help you down—you'll get some sleep in your own bed after all."

"Leave me alone," he replied, quite gently.

"Why? Why?" she cried. "I'll help you. You can get into your own bed, you'll be quite comfortable—"

"Leave me alone," he said again in that still voice. "It is cool now."

It was. Morning had stirred up some breeze off the sluggish river Jumna beneath the city walls, and it was carried over the rooftops of the stifled city, pale and fresh and delicate. It brought with it the morning light, as delicate and sweet as the breeze itself, a pure pallor unlike the livid glow of artificial lights. This lifted higher and higher into the dome of the sky, diluting the darkness there till it, too, grew pale and gradually shades of blue and mauve tinted it lightly.

The old man lay flat and still, gazing up, his mouth hanging open as if to let it pour into him, as cool and fresh as water.

Then, with a swirl and flutter of feathers, a flock of pigeons hurtled upwards and spread out against the dome of the sky—opalescent, sunlit, like small pearls. They caught the light as they rose, turned brighter till they turned at last into crystals, into prisms of light. Then they disappeared into the soft, deep blue of the morning.

# Janet Frame

While setting most of her work in New Zealand and helping to place the country on the world literary map, Janet Frame has created a fiction that is neither New Zealand in sensibility nor traditional in form. A reclusive woman, she has made rare public appearances and given few interviews. In 1982 *To the Is-land*, the first volume of her autobiography, was published, followed by *An Angel at My Table* in 1984 and *The Envoy from Mirror City* in 1985. Distinctive in the way Frame reconstructs the customary autobiographical form, the books offer insight into her life, consider the reading that influenced her writing, and offer observations on her own work and technique—especially on the role language plays in human experience and, correspondingly, in fiction.

Born in Dunedin, New Zealand, in 1924, she was one of five children, their father an itinerant railway worker, the mother a dreamer who longed to be a writer. Frame grew up in poverty and in a home haunted by misfortunes, including drowning accidents that claimed her two sisters and the epilepsy that afflicted her brother. A brilliant student, Frame received a scholarship to the University of Otago and prepared for a teaching career, which was soon interrupted by a nervous disorder. She spent eight years in mental hospitals, where she endured electric shock treatments and barely avoided a lobotomy. Frame's second novel, *Faces in the Water* (1961), recounts in fictional terms her experiences in the back ward of what she calls Seacliff Hospital for "loonies." Years later a London psychiatrist confirmed that the original diagnosis of schizophrenia had been mistaken. After she left the hospital, the New Zealand writer Frank Sargeson befriended her, gave her a place to live, and encouraged her to write. Frame's fortunes soon improved, and in 1957 she published a novel based on her childhood, *Owls Do Cry*, the first of eleven novels. *The Lagoon*, a book of short stories that showed great promise, had appeared in 1951 while she was still in the hospital. Frame has traveled extensively and resided for periods in Europe and the United States, but she always returns to New Zealand, where she now lives.

Although Frame's books are called novels, they are not "novelistic" in tenor, and they challenge the very genre she is employing. The narrator, plot, character, setting, and theme are subordinated to their determiner, language. Godfrey, who returns from the dead in *Yellow Flowers in the Antipodean Room* (1969, published as *The Rainbirds* in England), wonders why he had "ever trusted so obvious a deceiver as language." The title of the 1962 novel, *The Edge of the Alphabet*, is suggestive in itself, and its main character observes: "The edge of the alphabet where words crumble and all forms of communication between the living are useless." One of Frame's most inventive fictions is *Living in the Maniototo* (1979), whose first-person narrator shifts from one identity to another as she moves from city to city, each starting with the letter b: Blenheim, New Zealand; Baltimore, Maryland; Berkeley, California. But she travels only figuratively to the place in the book's title, Maniototo—a desolate, cold plain in the middle of New Zealand's South Island. Once more a narrative in which language poses as the central character, it also represents the way Frame links New Zealand to the larger world in much of her work. And the questionable narrator in *Living in the Maniototo* sums up Frame's approach to the novel: "I decided to break the rules, not because I felt my writing would even approach the shadow of perfection, but because nothing in art is forbidden."

That Alan in "The Triumph of Poetry," taken from *The Reservoir* (1963), refuses to give himself over to language brings about his defeat, so at the end he is simply writing nonsense. The detached narrative, the luxuriance of the language, the satiric thrusts at academia, provincialism and literary criticism, and the castigation of the would-be artist are all typical of Frame's work.

# The Triumph of Poetry

When he was born they named him Alan, meaning that in future the area of himself would be known as Alan. The area of oneself is like a drop of ink absorbed by blotting paper, gradually spreading, blurring at the edges, receiving upon it other blots in different shapes and colors until finally the original is dim, indistinguishable, while the saturated sheet of humanity upon which it lies is cast as worthless into the wastebasket, and another sheet, a clean sheet provided by the advertisers, is placed upon the desk.

Alan was a bright boy at school. He was Junior, Intermediate, and Senior Chess Champion. He could play tennis and swim well. He was liked by his classmates. He enjoyed school.

"What do you want to be?" they asked him.

He was not sure. In the holidays when he was fourteen he began to write verse, prospecting a trampled earth with a seam of gold shining through it. The gold was his cousin Lorna's hair, fluffed like wattle, rubbing gold dust on his fingers when he touched it, but only in his dreams. During the day he swam in an ice-cold mountain pool with a knife between his teeth.

In his final year at school they repeated their question because they preferred to watch their pupils heading, like runners emerging into the sun, each to his separate lane with his number in bold letters printed on his body. They preferred the course to remain clear in order that, should they have occasion to cheer their pupils in times of darkness or dim light, they should not discover to their humiliation, when the course was again visible, that they had been giving encouragement to pupils running in strange lanes, wearing strange colors, or even to those who were refusing to run at all, those who lagged, content with musing on the scenery, even breaking away from their course, running cross-country where no tracks had ever been marked, and no flags were flying, and there was no one, no official, to greet them at the end!

"What do you want to be?" they asked him again.

He told them that he had decided to be a poet.

"That's not exactly a career," they said.

"We mean what do you want to spend your life doing? Teaching, medicine . . .?"

"I will get my degree," he said (he had won a scholarship to a university), "and then write poetry as my life's work."

"But how will you earn your living?" they asked him. "You can always be a poet as a side line, in your spare time—but how will you keep yourself?"

One needs to be kept, swept, turned inside out, shaken free of insects, polished, pleated, trimmed, preserved in brine which is collected in opaque green bottles from the sea or from tears which fall in the intervals between each death.

They said good-by to him at school. They smiled kindly as he went out into the sun.

"You go ahead, get your degree, perhaps take up teaching; then you might decide what you really want to do."

He did not cower in the sun's blaze. He turned and spoke angrily. There was also a note of puzzlement in his voice. Why did they not understand?

"But I already know what I want to do. I am going to be a poet!"

The First Assistant, standing at the door, walked a little way toward him; there was a smell about him as if he had emerged from a stable where he had been fed on chalk; his gown lay like a bridle over his shoulders, and his eyes were trained not to stare distracted at the revelations in their corner mirrors.

"I used to write poems myself once, Wakefield. Who doesn't? I had a few published, in little magazines here and there. Of course I'm ashamed of them now. I had enough sense to leave that stage behind, get a safe job, regular income, marry, have a family, occupy my time in normal ways. I've seen boys like yourself go off to the University with bright ambitions. The important thing is to have something to fall back on."

The First Assistant glanced a moment at the door behind them, then he frowned; a gust of wind had banged the door shut. He stepped a few paces back toward the door, hitched his gown where it had fallen from his left shoulder.

"It's a phase, a phase, Alan," he said. He looked apprehensively behind him at the closed door. He seemed to be listening, as if his statement, "It's a phase, a phase," had assumed animal shape and was waiting inside to challenge him.

Then he opened the door and boldly walked in, out of the light.

Alan began his studies at the University. He wrote poems which were published and praised in the University Reviews and in a number of little magazines which kept bursting, pop, on the literary scene, and then folding, like delicate flowers, their petals leaning solicitously over their own broken hearts. It troubled Alan that there was so little time for writing. He wanted to write, of course he wanted to write, was he not bursting with ideas for poems, for stories and novels, yet where could he find the time between attending lectures, studying, flirting, making love, holidaying at the beach? Almost before he realized it, the University year had ended, and although he gained First Class Honors in his examinations, the amount of his literary work was very small.

"Why don't you take a job on the wharves in the holidays?" asked one of his friends. "I know someone who is writing a novel that way. He has chucked University and is working as a wharfie during the day and writing at night."

The proposal sounded interesting. Another friend told Alan of a poet who was working as a postman and writing in his spare time. In fact, the friend said, it was the fashion for poets to work as postman; indeed, housewives were beginning to look suspiciously at the uniformed civil servants who flung their letters through the regulation letter boxes; for poets were questionable characters whom you could not see working, as you could see other people, in whirling activity like washing in a washing machine.

Poets no longer brushed the passion from their souls like dust from a plum, by writing about kowhai trees and the felling of the bush; no, they retired to their own houses, pulled down the blinds, disconnected the telephone, cut off the electricity, and in the darkness and isolation they were sitting down like Little Jack Horner to try to crack the stone of the plum, and everybody knew that fruit stones contained arsenic which was of course a safeguard against the self-congratulatory phrases of Little Jack Horner, What a Good Boy Am I. . . . But the secretive way of writing was inclined (Alan's friend told him) to rouse envy in people, to make them wish that they too could work in secret instead of being exposed like washing in a washing machine; and this (Alan's friend told him) made them inclined to sabotage washing machines—and poets!

"I'm a novelist myself," Alan's friend said. "But a poet working as a postman is a risk, and housewives know it. Can poets be trusted to carry and deliver private communications? Ever, even in their own writings?"

And Alan's friend pointed out the dangers to poets and to the public (multiple dangers if the identity of the two coincided) of sorting mail in small caged rooms; of franking with strange marks invitations accepted or rejected, summonses to appear in court, eviction orders, declarations of love and hate, notifications of death, and the dead letters themselves, address not known, addressee departed leaving no trace, deceased. . . .

For the holidays, then, Alan did not work as a postman. He found a job as porter in a hospital morgue, attaching tickets and tying toes together, and looking for vacant spaces on the shelves of the refrigerator in order to keep a state of efficiency. He found that the atmosphere stimulated his thinking, but only while he was among the corpses, for as soon as he went to his digs to carry out his plan of writing at night, his thoughts seemed to vanish. It's the revenge of the dead, he complained, being at that time inclined to generalizations and simplifications, chiefly because he was tired and felt in need of a milestone to rest against, or if not a milestone as they were now historical treasures and no longer legitimate resting-places, a road signal, ROAD UP, DANGEROUS CORNER.

But he knew it was not the revenge of the dead. Their toes were tied with pink tape, in bows, as for a festive occasion. Their faces were in unsealed envelopes, forwarded at half-rates with five conventional words of greeting. All was in order. The dead did not need revenge.

Before the beginning of the next University year Alan found it hard to decide between continuing his studies and finding a job as a wharfie, farm roustabout, shearing hand, freezing-work hand, sharemilker, milk-bar attendant, or waiter in a tourist hotel. Or postman. Then he met Sylvia and instead of being afflicted with the recklessness of a lover, climbing hazardous mountains, plunging into milling torrents, he put on his oldest clothes and sat all night on the beach, threading and tightening possibilities, like a poor fisherman mending a hole in his net.

He decided to be cautious, to continue his studies, for he realized that the net and the mended hole in it would be needed to keep out the rain when rain had the impertinence to fall upon Sylvia.

Do nets keep out the rain?

Alan decided Yes, after he had spent all night on the beach.

Such decisions are not taken lightly which does not prove that they are correct because their birth has caused inconvenience, only that they are defended with more passion than reason, as statesmen know, who carry tight-lipped umbrellas and receive blows to their pride.

Alan loved Sylvia. He courted her on the beaches and the riverbanks and over the desk of the University library where she worked. They married and rented a washhouse which they converted into a tiny flat. They had a folding bed, an electric cooker, two chairs, a table, a bookcase which held books instead of ornaments, and they shared a bathroom and lavatory with the young couple, Tony and Leila, living in the adjacent washhouse. Tony had been a stock hand in Australia and was now working on the wharves and writing short stories in his spare time.

"As soon as I see my way clear," he told Alan, "I'll be writing a novel. How's your poetry coming along?"

"If conditions are favorable . . ." Alan began. "We might be talking about prize flowers or a proposed truce in a long drawn-out civil war. . . ."

"Perhaps a harvest of opportunities; reaped and bound, stacked by machine, but with no mechanical device for grinding; only two stones, grave-stones. . . ."

Alan and Sylvia, Tony and Leila were enjoying their married life although making love gave little time for study and less time for writing the poems and novels which it inspired. Then the long summer evenings were so pleasant! How lucky they were to be living so close to the beach where they could have picnic meals, dig down to Spain if they were so inclined, romp in the water, surfing, swimming, fishing from the rocks, or wandering hand in hand by starlight and moonlight, plodging their toes in the wet sand, their ankles entangled with seaweed, the stink of salt in their throats. Summer was wonderful and warm, no one could stay inside chewing at books, the sky in the daytime was pure blue, now solid, like rock so that you might have hammered it and been showered with lethal stones and pieces of blue cliff, now like bright blue glass that endured the sun until it shattered in a storm with lightning and thunder, and silver-wet outer space seeped through crackling like cellophane, sheeting the hills with rain and mist.

Who could study and pore over novels in the summer?

Yet when the two young couples wandered along the beach in the evenings they liked to recite poems, but they were not poems which Alan had written.

"You have to get your voice right for mine," he said, laughing. "The salt air pickles my language, shrivels the skin of it; the roots lose their grip; my words are not endowed with prehensile characteristics."

They skimmed stones on the sea, stones cold as a turned-aside human cheek, if death can be defined as the lure of a new direction where eyes and face target the unseen.

They set crabs on one another, laughing when the pincers closed on the loved skin. They stamped and shouted; dived in the water and made floating love, merman to mermaid above the crusted wrecks of nothing and the discarded bicycle wheels and car bodies.

Life was idyllic.

At one time Sylvia discovered that she was pregnant. Her heart flurried with alarm. How could she rear a child in a washhouse? Besides, Alan was still studying, she would have to give up her job. . . .

Alan wanted her to have the child. He began (when he found time) to write poems about it, "Lines to my son, Aged Three"; "To My Daughter Lying in Her Pram"—

My wild-west daughter in your covered wagon somber
    waterproofed against the sky and the tears of your mother. . . .

One afternoon, however, Alan and Sylvia kept an appointment in a house in Freeman's Bay where both were blindfolded, and Sylvia underwent an operation. That evening Sylvia lay seriously ill in the local hospital, but after a few days she recovered, no questions were asked, and she and Alan resumed their idyllic life, less forty pounds of their savings, and with an unidentified fear which greeted them each evening in their tiny washhouse flat as if it were lord of their mansion. They chose not to identify their fear. Names, they realized, bestow space, keys, power on the nameless which encircle human lives, waiting their chance.

"How fortunate we are to be so intelligent," they said to each other when one night they came home to find their fear standing waiting for the double bed to be unfolded for love and sleep.

Soon it was Alan's fourth year at the University. He had gained a brilliant degree and was sitting his Honors Examination. He found little time for writing poetry.

Leila and Tony had sailed overseas where Tony was to seek his fortune and where he would find time for writing his novel.

There was a prevalent idea that Time overseas was different from Time in one's own country; it could be juggled, coaxed, extended in a most extraordinary and satisfying manner. Leila and Tony were already installed in a tiny flat in London and their first letter (they had written no more since their arrival) had been enthusiastic and full of plans for the future. It did seem, Alan thought wistfully, that Time overseas was more abundant, looped and lazy like spaghetti, dangling everywhere, one only needed to twirl a fork of thought and hook an endless length of Time.

Occasionally, however, Alan would set to work and produce a poem which he sent to one of the literary magazines. He was beginning to gain a reputation. One or two people spoke of him as "that promising young poet Alan Wakefield" Another had remarked, in rather sinister fashion, Alan thought, "Alan Wakefield is a poet who should be watched"; while yet another critic noted that it was "impossible to judge Alan Wakefield until he has given us a small but representative volume of his work."

I wonder, Alan thought, reading the critics' words, if I have enough poems to make a book, to submit to a publisher? Oh, if only I had more time! What would I not do with more time!

How excited he became when he thought of the prospect of more time! It's like the old days, he would think, feeling a quickening in his blood and an acceleration of thoughts in his mind.

The old days, and he was only twenty-four!

Still, life was good, life was satisfying. He was studying hard for his examination. He was very much in love with his wife. He had many friends. There were parties, picnics, expeditions to the bush, to the mountains. People called at all hours to their tiny flat, "Hey Alan, anyone home? Hey Sylvie!"

Sometimes at night when all the visitors had gone and Sylvia, exhausted, had already fallen asleep, Alan would go to the tiny window of the washhouse flat, draw aside the skimpy lace curtain, and look down at the sea crouched moaning and restless at their back door. He would time his breathing to the sighing rise and fall of the water, and find himself sighing also, or moaning.

The patience of the sea depressed him. Why should it go on waiting and waiting, moaning and beating its forehead, shedding a fury of tears or, placid, swallowing them and shining with pretended peace, yet always waiting and waiting as if it were so sure of the outcome and the end?

Often Alan would watch the sea until far into the night. Then he would start from his dream and think guiltily, I could have been writing a poem. Then he would try to console himself. "Still," he would say, "it's worth it to be able to observe all that beach in all tides and seasons."

"Worth what?" his muse and his conscience asked together.

Yes, he would think, I could have been writing a poem. He was beginning to think more often of writing poems than of the poems themselves. People talked to him of poetry. He began to feel hemmed in, as if people were trying to decide his life for him. "I don't have to write poems just because they ask me to," he would say. It seemed as if people were invading him, his private territory and putting up their own signposts. He resented this. There were times now when he stayed silent for days, and one or two of his acquaintances began to whisper amongst themselves and tap their foreheads, which was a means of charming themselves against their fate, or of waking up their thoughts which had overslept, or of trying to enter the perpetually closed mountain skull. Who knows?

Alan gained his Honors degree and was appointed to the post of lecturer at the University. Life was gay once more, social, controversial. Lectures took a long time to prepare. The weather that summer was again very warm. There were swimming parties to the beach, morning, noon, and night, moonlight bonfires and barbecues. In a quarterly review of literature one of the critics asked, "What has happened to our promising younger poets?"

That means Alan, of course, Sylvia thought as she read it, but she did not say so directly to Alan. Besides, he could no longer be called "one of our promising younger poets." His hair was thinning at the temples and a bald patch had appeared at the back of his head. It was early for Alan to be losing his hair, many kept theirs well into middle age or did not lose it at all, but Alan seemed to be subject to the pressures of a personal age which took its toll not by years but by a secret ringing, as of trees, of the life of his heart. The thinning of his hair was merely a concession to recognized Time, to allay the suspicions of those who, tiring of the marks of chronological age, might seek to explore the more secret areas of a man's life where Time is personal with its own rules and measurements.

The fact remains, Sylvia thought, that Alan can no longer be regarded as "one of our promising younger poets." Sylvia had an increasing desire to care for his poetry, to dress it to appear in public, to attend to the toileting of its language.

Also, a number of new poets were emerging from the schools and universities, and these were now appearing regularly in the literary magazines. Sometimes entire issues were devoted to "the new young poets." Once, when Alan was flipping through the pages of one of these magazines, he was touched to read a tribute to himself as "one of the country's established poets, Alan Wakefield, who pursues his own quiet line of thought."

Yes, Alan thought bitterly, a quiet line all right, a branch line about to be closed because nobody travels there any more and weeds are growing over the track; and everybody dizzies back and forth on the Main Trunk Line with stops for organized refreshment at fixed prices—yes, a branch line with no train and no timetable, no flags, no signals.

Yet the reference to his work inspired Alan to write a poem for the next issue of the magazine which was called *Trend III*, following upon *Trend I* and *Trend II* which had ceased through lack of financial support because poetry was not yet as popular as the T.A.B. and there was no legitimate reason why it should be unless it flashes winners and numbers in orderly and accurate gold lights that peck and stab like a surgeon's knife where one keeps one's heart wrapped snug against the fivers. . . .

Alan's poem, which was not printed by the magazine, began:

> For drowning in rock-pools the face-downward men
> find cupful of tide enough to evict from their human home
> the put-you-up and put-upon generations of breath. . . .

His poem was confused and chaotic. It dealt with the stifling effects of teacups, teaspoons, phials, eggcups, eyebaths. . . .

Then came verses which Alan would have been ashamed of writing five or six years before.

> With the hairs of my head I trap
> the night-flying thoughts.
> My hair, like grass, covers the mountain
> where insects, knocking in the dark, are bruised upon the stone.
>
> Nude statues overgrown with glances,
> silent temples biding their time in the forenoon of civilization,
> weapon-crammed outposts of the guiding touch,
> aphasic cities unable to extricate the knives and bullets of
> past utterance . . .

Justice like an oilstove must burn
with the correct blue flame
or the inhabitant of the room will die,
and the maker shed all responsibility. . . .

Green moss in the hollows between person to person calls.
drifts of snow, the telephone wires blown down;
beasts of prey encircling the stranded town . . .
Nothing has changed since I stood
in the Hangman's Wood.
Between thefts of death, night, and the arson of love
sounds the automatic alarm of light.
Still waits the noose on the hanging-tree,
still creeps the hooded assembly
of the declared honest brave and good,
still the sun carries its golden opinions and witnesses in the sky,
No, nothing has changed since I stood
in the Hangman's Wood.

Neptune, loyal to his nature, drives three white precepts home.
They are
Rest, Punctuality in meeting whirlpools and lagoons,
Patience in retaining more than a fair share of death.
These, say Neptune, are the trident of success
to sustain, to lean upon,
to thrust in three places through the hearts of enemies,
But *I* say, only jocularity and age
would burden *my* loneliness with three white precepts.
Salt grinds in the great wound everywhere,
more than two-thirds the surface of life.

Alan's poem rambled on thus. When it was returned to him he tore it to pieces and flushed it down the lavatory. He rarely wrote another poem, but now from time to time he reviewed books of poetry, and his reviews were printed in the back pages of the small literary magazines.

"Mr. Walters," he wrote in one review, "has twenty-two wombs, seven bloods, eight, six, nine, fires, ices, bones, respectively, three thighs, one cornucopia. Mr. Walters is indeed a composite wonder with immense physical, geological, decorative, but few poetic possibilities."

The reply came from Mr. Walters in "Letters to the Editor."

"There is nothing left but sour grapes to quench the dry mouths of a certain academic coterie."

Mr. Walters (Ted) was a promising young student who had abandoned his university career for poetry and who earned his living working as a shearing hand, a rabbiter, sharemilker, and, at Christmas, a postman, furthering the exchange of robin-stained holly-festooned blood-robed platitudes.

Two, three, four years passed. Alan was now a Ph.D. Sylvia still worked in the University library. With an increase in Alan's salary they bought an old colonial house in the fashionable suburb of Tuapere. They had enough money now to buy books, records, to attend concerts and plays, to give parties. Although Alan worked hard preparing his lectures, and although they were witty, insightful his manner of delivery had grown increasingly hesitant. Where he had once been noted for his forthright delivery, his clarity of speech, now he was often inaudible; he had picked up irritating gestures, such as waving his hand vigorously before his face as if he were trying to remove not a massive obstacle but a congregation of small ones which clustered in more formidable solidity, threatening his line of perspective; sometimes he would draw his head briskly back as if in bending it forward he had thrust his face into invisible prongs. He would gaze toward the far wall of the old-fashioned tiered lecture room, at the students sitting in the distance, close to the roof, staring down at him like planets. A feeling of irritation and dismay would come over him as he wondered what exactly they were writing in their lecture books, and what they scribbled on the notes which they passed endlessly to and fro during the lecture. Perhaps one of them had ideas of being a poet? Perhaps he was writing poetry? If this thought occurred, Alan would be seized with a sense of responsibility, as if it were his duty to perform a particular act, to give a certain piece of advice, but always the urgency faded and he was left standing there, slightly dazed, with his notes propped on his lectern and the students waiting, some politely, others restlessly, for him to conclude his lesson. In appearance he seemed now far more than thirty. He was stooped. He was almost bald. The blue veins of his head intertwined like lines on a map of the world.

Sylvia had grown more beautiful over the past years. She was plump and matronly. She had the appearance of being a mother though she had borne no children, a fact which was outwardly accepted and faced by herself and Alan, but which was the cause of friction with relatives, for their respective parents grew more impatient as year by year they failed to achieve the status of grandparents (both Alan and Sylvia had been their only children). There were from both the Wakefields and the Simpsons, visits, whispers, suggestions, remedies, hints; clothes were knitted, toys were bought; even lists of names were drawn up.

"We are happy, aren't we?" Sylvia said to Alan. "We have almost everything. And we love each other."

Yes, they loved each other, and every night when they went to bed, the fear which they were intelligent enough not to endow with a name and power, crept between the sheets with them and lay next to each of them, warming it-self at their skin and picking at the leftovers of their day's thoughts, lifting the flaps of their dreams to read their secret desires, trying with all its tiny power to find an identity.

But Alan and Sylvia were wise. Don't you think they were wise?

How happy they were!

"Fancy," Alan said, "Can you imagine that I wanted to be a poet?"

Suddenly he yearned for Sylvia to say quickly and fiercely, "Yes, Yes." But she laughed and looked at him fondly and said, "No, I'm afraid not."

They were very devoted.

She kept the home neat and employed a gardener to attend to the shrubs, for their section was nearly two acres, while she often worked in the garden with the flowers. She bought packets of seed and planted them in borders, and was so disappointed if the blooms did not match the illustrations in the cata-logue.

"I should learn from experience, shouldn't I?" she said to Alan one day when one of the dahlia blooms was attacked by disease and died.

He smiled affectionately at her. He knew that she was particularly clever with dahlias. He was sitting in the corner by the bookshelf, opening the packet containing the latest edition of *Seascape*, the literary quarterly, and wishing that the dispatch department had not made such a complicated parcel with so much useless string. There were none of his poems in this edition. He rarely wrote poems now. Sometimes, in a panic, in the night when Sylvia was asleep and the house was quiet, he tried to discover his excuse for not writing any more. It was not lack of time; it had long ago ceased to be lack of time. What was the excuse now? He tried desperately to find it. Age? Glands? Con-tentment? But who was contented?

He would have been happier if he had written a book of poems—just one book, a slim volume between hard covers—with the title on the outside and the dedication on the appropriate page. "To Sylvia, my wife." Or "To Sylvia."

He loved Sylvia more than ever. He loved the way her body had acquired a plump stored look, like a well-filled larder. He had the feeling that in some way she would provide for him. He was alarmed one evening when he was considering his dream of a book of poems with a dedication to her, "To Sylvia, my wife," and he found himself murmuring instead, "For self-service stores everywhere, for the brave, for the watered-down dreamer, for dried-up ponds full of dead frogs, caked with mud. . . ."

No, no. For Sylvia. Her dahlias are more wonderful this year than ever before; she has green fingers in the garden; she has been born to it.

Then from his seat in the corner by the bookshelf he had smiled fondly at her. He told himself how intelligent she was. Two intelligent people. They kept up with the trends in modern art and literature. When the National Or-chestra played at the city festival each year they always bought tickets. They

visited the Art Galleries. He subscribed to overseas journals, to poetry magazines from America, to one in particular called *The Triumph of Poetry* where
in his student days he had been given a commendation in an annual award.
"Just imagine. Alan Wakefield, a commendation in America," people had
said. Now, each year when the award was made Alan would eagerly turn the
pages of *The Triumph of Poetry* (Has my *Triumph of Poetry* arrived? he would
ask Sylvia as soon as he came home on the twenty-fifth of each month) and
study the winning and commended poems and compare them with his own of
so long ago. How absurd, he would think. But people in literary circles still
spoke of his poem. It had gained him a kind of national distinction. After all,
America . . .

He sometimes felt ludicrous when he had been asked to take part in a
radio book panel and the chairman's introduction referred to him as "the poet
who was commended in *The Triumph of Poetry* award for promising young
poets," while the other members of the panel, waiting impatiently for their
own credits, would gaze incredulously at his thinning stooped figure and his
bald head. Alan was a valued member of the book panel. He was an astute
critic. His wit was sharp. Only his voice lacked the sense of urgency which
made it compelling to listen to in the days when he had not enough time to
write. He talked ramblingly as if all urgency had lost itself within him, or as if
in traveling from him it had suddenly disappeared, like something wading out
of its depths in unknown seas.

Alan Wakefield. One of the trees of lost poets who contribute to the
shade, magnificence, density of the forest, who give concealment, food and
space to tiny hibernating metaphors, the parasitic clichés, the feathered no-
tions, the furred images that are so often slain and their coats transformed into
collars to protect the necks of human beings from strangulation, and into
muffs to warm in the winter season the pickpocket pickheart fingers.

A lost poet. A man with a little talent and not enough time; the promising
poet who never fulfilled his promise; thwarted by sociology, circumstance,
self.

But is not his life happy? He has a loving wife, a home, a secure job, an
academic reputation. He interests himself in current affairs, oppressed peoples, decimal coinage, imports and exports, swimming (they own a beach
house in the subtropical north where they spend every Christmas); and he is
passionately devoted to literature, painting, music, the theater. He and his
wife know how to cook continental food. . . . Some day they will travel overseas, perhaps visit Tony and Leila who have a luxury flat in Kensington, since
Tony saw his opportunity and joined a literary agency of which he is now a
director, marketing the works of scores of well-known and flourishing authors. . . . Tony and Leila go for holidays on the Continent; once they visited
the United States. . . .

Yes, Alan is surely happy. He and his wife are intelligent, they enjoy good conversation, they have interesting tolerant friends who prefer to send ideas rather than people to the scaffold for murder, to lash intolerance and bigotry rather than the flesh of human beings. Every day brings so much to do, so much to discuss, plans to be made, letters to write, invitations to answer, lectures to prepare. And for Sylvia there is always the garden. How enthusiastically she prepares for each season!

It was late summer, merging into autumn with the lack of drama which disappointed Sylvia when in her gardening diary she checked the outlines of the seasons and their characteristic flowers. Summer each year took up so much room, leaving so little time for autumn. But summer was wonderful, so carefree and warm, and you walked with next-to-nothing on when you went shopping, and you swam day and night in the warm Pacific or, across the other side of the island, in the Tasman surf, riding in on the crests of the waves, picnicking by moonlight, wandering here and there, restless, turbulent as the sea. . . .

It was late summer.

Alan was on his way home from the University. He had not taken his car, and was traveling by tram. It was the last tram running in the city, the others having been replaced by trolley-buses. Alan enjoyed riding in the tram, sitting on the worn brown seats barred like washing-boards, rocking back and forth along the rails, strap-hanging when he got up to give his seat to a woman and her two children. It had been so long since he had traveled this way; it was so much easier to take the car. A feeling of exhilaration surged through him as he alighted at the stop and watched the tram rollicking by, noisy, exuberant.

"And it's not even spring," Alan said to himself, trying to explain his joy as he turned the corner into the quiet street where he lived. But as he walked by the gate and into the garden of his home he was surprised to notice the beauty of the flowers; he had not realized, he thought, what patience and time Sylvia was putting into the garden. The dahlias lined the path right up to the house. There was one dahlia which was particularly beautiful hacked with fire, its ragged petals chopped with fire, lined with red silk, overskirt upon overskirt of burning silk; alone it would abolish night.

He picked the dahlia.

"I'll write a poem," he thought, excitement surging through him.

"I'll write a poem. 'To my wife Sylvia upon plucking the first dahlia.'"

He hurried up to the house. Sylvia was out. He remembered that she had a meeting—a meeting where? He did not know, could not remember. He noticed when he changed from his dark suit that she must have been wearing her new dress, the one she bought for the Silverstone's party.

He did not stop to find anything to eat but went quickly to the room which he used as a study, and placing the dahlia upon the desk in front of him, he took a sheet of paper and wrote

"To my wife Sylvia upon plucking the first dahlia."

What a pity, he thought, that the seasons are not dramatic in the north, that first flowers do not burst upon us with shock. How she must have cared for them, he thought, stroking the petals which drooped a little and had stains on their tips, like inward bruises.

"To My Wife Sylvia upon plucking the first dahlia."

"True to tradition," he said. "A dedication at last. And we used to sleep like two mice in a matchbox, in a bed that dropped obligingly from the wall, in a washhouse fronting the sea!"

"A dedication," he repeated.

It did not seem to matter any more that he had not published his slim volume of verse. He was writing a poem to Sylvia.

He began to write.

The quick brown fox noses the earth,
the dog is lazy,
and where are all the good men of the world who will come to our aid?
For now is the time, now is the time,
while the quick brown fox noses the earth

Impatiently he scribbled over the nonsense he had written, drawing a face, a childhood face with deep eyes deep inside spectacles.

"To my wife Sylvia," he wrote once more.

### THE PRISONER

In a dialogue with Time he said,
You handcuff me to humankind,
You sentence me who am the sentence.
When will you learn that I am nothing,
that giant mirrors are propped against your heart?
You sleep alone in your cell.
The twin delusional cell whose prisoner receives your sympathy and rage
is empty, thick with dust,
its lock eaten by worms and rust.

Alan considered what he had written. "It's poor," he said, "But if I start writing again something may come, I may yet write a complete book of poems. This is only a flexing of the muscles, so to speak. What is there now to hinder me from writing? Nothing, nothing at all."

His hand trembled. He could feel his heart pounding; he knew a slight anxiety in noting his heartbeats. Too much sedentary work? he questioned.

"But I swim. The sea is my second home."

Then Sylvia came in the door. She looked radiant. Yes, she was wearing the dress bought for the Silverstone's party.

"Writing?" she asked fondly. "Don't stay at it too long, darling." As a mother might talk to her child. "Playing trains, mud pies? Don't get your nice clean hands all dirty will you?"

Sylvia was quick to see that her approach had been wrong.

"Take no notice," she said, giving him a quick kiss. "Go on writing as long as you like—it's the dinner that won't let you. It'll be ready in two shakes of a lamb's tail."

Then she glanced at the desk and noticed the dahlia, and a change came over her. Her voice was shrill.

"My dahlia!" she cried. "It's the prize one, the one I'm showing at the Society at the end of the week, I've been waiting and waiting for it to bloom. And you've picked it, you've picked it!"

She was almost in tears.

Alan was bewildered.

"I didn't realize," he began. He was staring at her in a dazed way. Out of all the flowers in the garden, did she recognize each one in this way? And the society, which society?

"Which society?" he asked. "What's the name of it, dear? "

"The name of the dahlia?" she said quickly. He could almost see her checking the list of names. How strange, she knew each one personally!

"The Dahlia Society, of course. Oh Alan!"

He stared. So she called them by names, she belonged to a society where they sat in a small room talking all evening about dahlias. . . .

"It's the loveliest one I've ever had, Alan! And you picked it. And look, you've bruised one of the petals! And is that ink on it, ink!"

Then she leaned forward suddenly and snatching the paper where he had been writing his verses she tore it to pieces. Then she seized the drooping dahlia and held it close to her breast. Then she began to cry.

"I'm sorry," she said. "Do forgive me, Alan!"

She picked up the pieces of paper and without looking at them she replaced them on his desk. He took a vase from the window sill and filling it with water from the tap in the adjacent bathroom, he tenderly took the dahlia from her and put it in the vase. He noticed a brown stain spreading in the water. Then he and Sylvia embraced. Everything was all right. They were intelligent, they understood each other.

They went then to their dining room overlooking the garden. They had dinner, talking brightly to each other, making jokes. Alan told her about his journey home in the tram. How they laughed over it! How they yearned for the old days!

"Do you know," Sylvia said, "I passed our flat the other day, you know, the washhouse, and I couldn't resist knocking on the door. Do you know who lives there? You'll never guess!"

Of course he guessed, but he said "Who?"

"A young student and his wife, one of your students, too. He's going to be a novelist when he has time . . . I'm sorry. . . ."

"Don't pity me. You know that I was never much of a poet."

He hoped that she would say, "Yes you were, you were!" but she looked vague and sad and murmured, "Oh well!"

She brightened.

"Well anyway this young couple spend nearly all their time on the beach, the sea is so tempting, oh isn't it marvelous, quick as a wink the summer will be around and we'll be off up north; there's the garden though. . . ."

"You don't like leaving it do you?"

She was defensive.

"There's no harm in that is there? No harm in being fond of something. It was my best dahlia, Alan."

"I'm sorry, I've told you I'm sorry. I didn't know. . . ."

Her voice became sharp.

"You should have known. Oh Alan! We were so close! What has come over us?"

They went early to bed. He told her he had meant to write a poem to her, and she wept, and all was forgiven. They were very tender toward each other. They slept. Alan dreamed that writing a poem became so easy, all that was necessary was to take a packet of dahlia seed and spill it upon the paper. He took a packet of seed; it fell like fly-dirt, full-stops, pinpricks but Sylvia began to cry, it was her best seed, she said, the packet she had saved specially. Then she looked closer at the packet. She grinned. Her mouth was wide like a lake, and dark. No, she said, the best seed is at the Silverstone's; this is the cheap variety which never blooms, I can't think how I came by it. She took the seed and tossed it out of the window and a huge bird flew down and swallowed it, stabbing his beak upon each grain.

"An indemnity," Alan said, and woke up. Sylvia was smiling in her sleep.

Soon the house was quiet. No one was awake, that is no one who had not his own right, like mice, traveling beetles, moths, beams of light; and the named fear who had at last been given power, space, keys, and lay supreme between Sylvia and Alan, waiting to devour their lives.

# Nadine Gordimer

A substantial body of fiction written over a span of forty or so years earned Nadine Gordimer the Nobel Prize in literature in 1991. Her work reflects the social and political milieu of South Africa, where she was born on 20 November 1923 to immigrant Jewish parents in a mining town near Johannesburg. Removed by her mother from school at age eleven until she was sixteen as protection against what turned out to be a nonexistent heart condition, Gordimer read extensively and started to write. At age thirteen her first story appeared in a South African newspaper, and in 1949 *Face to Face*, a collection of short stories, was published in Johannesburg. Gordimer attended the University of Witwatersrand in Johannesburg but left without completing a degree. In 1953 a volume of short fiction, *The Soft Voice of the Serpent*, was published in London and New York. Well received, the book launched her as an international figure whose reputation has grown steadily over the years. She has traveled extensively in Africa, Europe, and North America, but has always made her home in Johannesburg.

Gordimer has been criticized for her narrative detachment, which has been described as exhibiting a "frozen sensibility." Yet this aloofness in narrative technique is what makes her writing distinctive. The author of twelve novels, eleven volumes of short stories, and three collections of essays, as well as numerous magazine articles, she has long been identified as an outspoken opponent of the South African political order known as apartheid. When this system officially ended and a new South Africa emerged, some were ready to dismiss her work, arguing that it so closely represented a particular era that it was no longer relevant. Granted, the most widely known novels, such as *The Conservationist* (1974), which received the Booker Prize, *The Burger's Daughter* (1979), and the apocalyptic *July's People* (1981), center on race and the tragic consequences of partitioning individuals by color. These novels, as well as many of the other books, effectively depict the social and cultural context of a country at war with itself. At first pessimistic and static, the fiction gradually moved away from the intractability of racial division, and assumed a more hopeful stance. Finally, in *A Sport of Nature* (1987) Gordimer imagines in a utopian moment "the proclamation of the new African state that used to be South Africa."

At the same time, though, there emerges far more in the work than polemics or politics or social history. For Gordimer's characters battle the outer world, which constantly intrudes on the personal realm. As the title of the 1984 novella suggests, "Something Out There" always threatens. And it is that ever present force that dominates the narratives and the characters' responses, whether the force be political, racial, social, or personal in nature. Such is the case with Gordimer's second postapartheid novel, *The House Gun*, published in 1998. The text opens with the simple sentence: "Something terrible happened." The son of a middle-class white couple has committed murder, then is arrested, tried, and sentenced to prison. Something out there—in this instance the violence of the city that the insulated couple once thought affected only blacks—irrevocably alters their lives. The novel reflects current conditions in South Africa, but as always it reflects as well the fragility of the human condition in the midst of a chaotic world.

In "Some Are Born to Sweet Delight," which appeared in *Jump and Other Stories* (1991), Gordimer reveals how the mysterious pull of sexuality, then the malignant forces of a larger world intrude on the limited sphere of naïve Vera and her commonplace parents—products of a colonial society. And the detached manner of the third-person narrator makes more terrible the encounter that brings about the corruption of Vera by something out there, something she does not fully comprehend. Although the instrument of Vera's destruction, Rad is not a villain but another victim caught up in a web of circumstances.

# Some Are Born to Sweet Delight

*Some are Born to sweet delight,*
*Some are Born to Endless Night.*
        —William Blake, *"Auguries of Innocence"*

They took him in. Since their son had got himself signed up at sea for eighteen months on an oil rig, the boy's cubbyhole of a room was vacant; and the rent money was a help. There had rubbed off on the braid of the commissionaire father's uniform, through the contact of club members' coats and briefcases he relieved them of, loyal consciousness of the danger of bombs affixed under the cars of members of parliament and financiers. The father said "I've no quarrel with that" when the owners of the house whose basement flat the family occupied stipulated "No Irish." But to discriminate against any other foreigners from the old Empire was against the principles of the house owners, who were also the mother's employers—cleaning three times a week and baby-sitting through the childhood of three boys she thought of as her own. So it was a way of pleasing Upstairs to let the room to this young man, a foreigner who likely had been turned away from other vacancies posted on a board at the supermarket. He was clean and tidy enough; and he didn't hang around the kitchen, hoping to be asked to eat with the family, the way one of their own kind would. He didn't eye Vera.

Vera was seventeen, and a filing clerk with prospects of advancement; her father had got her started in an important firm through the kindness of one of his gentlemen at the club. A word in the right place; and now it was up to her to become a secretary, maybe one day even a private secretary to someone like the members of the club, and travel to the Continent, America—any-where.

—You have to dress decently for a firm like that. Let others show their backsides.—

—Dad!— The flat was small, the walls thin—suppose the lodger heard him. Her pupils dilated with a blush, half shyness, half annoyance. On Friday and Saturday nights she wore T-shirts with spangled graffiti across her breasts and went with girl-friends to the discothèque, although she'd had to let the pink side of her hair grow out. On Sundays they sat on wooden benches out-side the pub with teasing local boys, drinking beer shandies. Once it was straight beer laced with something and they made her drunk, but her father had been engaged as doorman for a private party and her mother had taken the Upstairs children to the zoo, so nobody heard her vomiting in the bath-room.

So she thought.

*He* was in the kitchen when she went, wiping the slime from her panting mouth, to drink water. He always addressed her as "miss"—Good afternoon, miss.— He was himself filling a glass.

She stopped where she was; sourness was in her mouth and nose, oozing towards the foreign stranger, she mustn't go a step nearer. Shame tingled over nausea and tears. Shame heaved in her stomach, her throat opened, and she just reached the sink in time to disgorge the final remains of a pizza minced by her teeth and digestive juices, floating in beer.—Go away. Go away!—her hand flung in rejection behind her. She opened both taps to blast her shame down the drain.—Get out!—

He was there beside her, in the disgusting stink of her, and he had wetted a dish-towel and was wiping her face, her dirty mouth, her tears. He was steadying her by the arm and sitting her down at the kitchen table. And she knew that his kind didn't even drink, he probably never had smelled alcohol before. If it had been one of her own crowd it would have been different.

She began to cry again. Very quietly, slowly, he put his hand on hers, tak-ing charge of the wrist like a doctor preparing to follow the measure of a heart in a pulse-beat. Slowly—the pace was his—she quietened; she looked down, without moving her head, at the hand. Slowly, she drew her own hand from underneath, in parting.

As she left the kitchen a few meaningless echoes of what had happened to her went back and forth—are you all right yes I'm all right are you sure yes I'm all right.

She slept through her parents' return and next morning said she'd had flu.

He could no longer be an unnoticed presence in the house, outside her occupation with her work and the friends she made among the other junior employees, and her preoccupation, in her leisure, with the discothèque and cinema where the hand-holding and sex-tussels with local boys took place.

He said, Good afternoon, as they saw each other approaching in the passage between the family's quarters and his room, or couldn't avoid coinciding at the gate of the tiny area garden where her mother's geraniums bloomed and the empty milk bottles were set out. He didn't say "miss"; it was as if the omission were assuring, Don't worry, I won't tell anyone, *although I know all about what you do,* everything, I won't talk about you among my friends— did he even have any friends? Her mother told her he worked in the kitchens of a smart restaurant—her mother had to be sure a lodger had steady pay before he could be let into the house. Vera saw other foreigners like him about, gathered loosely as if they didn't know where to go; of course, they didn't come to the disco and they were not part of the crowd of familiars at the cinema. They were together but looked alone. It was something noticed the way she might notice, without expecting to fathom, the strange expression of a caged animal, far from wherever it belonged.

She owed him a signal in return for his trustworthiness. Next time they happened to meet in the house she said —I'm Vera.—

As if he didn't know, hadn't heard her mother and father call her. Again he did the right thing, merely nodded politely.

—I've never really caught your name.—

—Our names are hard for you, here. Just call me Rad.—His English was stiff, pronounced syllable by syllable in a soft voice.

—So it's short for something?—

—What is that?—

—A nickname. Bob for Robert.—

—Something like that.—

She ended this first meeting on a new footing the only way she knew how:—Well, see you later, then—the vague dismissal used casually among her friends when no such commitment existed. But on a Sunday when she was leaving the house to wander down to see who was gathered at the pub she went up the basement steps and saw that he was in the area garden. He was reading newspapers—three or four of them stacked on the mud-plastered grass at his side. She picked up his name and used it for the first time, easily as a key turning in a greased lock.—Hullo, Rad.—

He rose from the chair he had brought out from his room.—I hope your mother won't mind? I wanted to ask, but she's not at home.—

—Oh no, not Ma, we've had that old chair for ages, a bit of fresh air won't crack it up more than it is already—

She stood on the short path, he stood beside the old rattan chair; then sat down again so that she could walk off without giving offense—she left to her friends, he left to his reading.

She said—I won't tell.—

And so it was out, what was between them alone, in the family house.

And they laughed, smiled, both of them. She walked over to where he sat.— Got the day off? You work in some restaurant, don't you, what's it like?—

—I'm on the evening shift today.— He stayed himself a moment, head on one side, with aloof boredom. —It's something. Just a job. What you can get.—

—I know. But I suppose working in a restaurant at least the food's thrown in, as well.—

He looked out over the railings a moment, away from her. —I don't eat that food.—

She began to be overcome by a strong reluctance to go through the gate, round the corner, down the road to The Mitre and the whistles and appreciative pinches which would greet her in her new flowered Bermudas, his black eyes following her all the way, although he'd be reading his papers with her forgotten. To gain time she looked at the papers. The one in his hand was English. On the others, lying there, she was confronted with a flowing script of tails and gliding flourishes, the secret of somebody else's language. She could not go to the pub; she could not let him know that was where she was going. The deceptions that did for parents were not for him. But the fact was there was no deception: she *wasn't* going to the pub, she suddenly wasn't going.

She sat down on the motoring section of the English newspaper he'd discarded and crossed her legs in an X from the bare round knees. —Good news from home?—

He gestured with his foot towards the papers in his secret language; his naked foot was an intimate object, another secret.

—From my home, no good news.—

She understood this must be some business about politics, over there— she was in awe and ignorance of politics, nothing to do with her. —So that's why you went away—

He didn't need to answer.

—You know, I can't imagine going away.—

—You don't want to leave your friends.—

She caught the allusion, pulled a childish face, dismissing them. —Mum and Dad . . . everything.—

He nodded, as if in sympathy for her imagined loss, but made no admission of what must be his own.

—Though I'm mad keen to travel. I mean, that's my idea, taking this job. Seeing other places—just visiting, you know. If I make myself capable and that, I might get the chance. There's one secretary in our offices who goes everywhere with her boss, she brings us all back souvenirs, she's very generous.—

—You want to see the world. But now your friends are waiting for you—

She shook off the insistence with a laugh. —And you want to go home!—

—No.— He looked at her with the distant expression of an adult before the innocence of a child. —Not yet—

The authority of his mood over hers, that had been established in the kitchen that time, was there. She was hesitant and humble rather than flirtatious when she changed the subject. —Shall we have—will you have some tea if I make it? Is it all right?— He'd never eaten in the house; perhaps the family's food and drink were taboo for him in his religion, like the stuff he could have eaten free in the restaurant.

He smiled. —Yes it's all right.— And he got up and padded along behind her on his slim feet to the kitchen. As with a wipe over the clean surfaces of her mother's sink and table, the other time in the kitchen was cleared by ordinary business about brewing tea, putting out cups. She set him to cut the gingerbread: —Go on, try it, it's my mother's homemade.— She watched with an anxious smile, curiosity, while his beautiful teeth broke into its crumbling softness. He nodded, granting grave approval with a full mouth. She mimicked him, nodding and smiling; and, like a doe approaching a leaf, she took from his hand the fragrant slice with the semicircle marked by his teeth, and took a bite out of it.

Vera didn't go to the pub any more. At first they came to look for her— her chums, her mates—and nobody believed her excuses when she wouldn't come along with them. She hung about the house on Sundays, helping her mother. —Have you had a tiff or something?—

As she always told her bosom friends, she was lucky with her kind of mother, not strict and suspicious like some. —No, Ma. They're okay, but it's always the same thing, same things to say, every weekend.—

—Well . . . shows you're growing up, moving on—it's natural. You'll find new friends, more interesting, more your type.—

Vera listened to hear if he was in his room or had to go to work—his shifts at the restaurant, she had learnt from timing his presence and absences, were irregular. He was very quiet, didn't play a radio or cassettes but she always could feel if he was there, in his room. That summer was a real summer for once; if he was off shift he would bring the old rattan chair into the garden and read, or stretch out his legs and lie back with his face lifted to the humid sun. He must be thinking of where he came from; very hot, she imagined it, desert and thickly-white cubes of houses with palm trees. She went out with a rug—nothing unusual about wanting to sunbathe in your own area garden— and chatted to him as if just because he happened to be there. She watched his eyes traveling from right to left along the scrolling print of his newspapers, and when he paused, yawned, rested his head and closed his lids against the light, could ask him about home—his home. He described streets and cities

and cafés and bazaars—it wasn't at all like her idea of desert and oases. —
But there are palm trees?—

—Yes, nightclubs, rich people's palaces to show tourists, but there are
also factories and prison camps and poor people living on a handful of beans
a day.—

She picked at the grass: I see. —Were you—were your family—do you
like beans?—

He was not to be drawn; he was never to be drawn.

—If you know how to make them, they are good.—

—If we get some, will you tell us how they're cooked?—

—I'll make them for you.—

So one Sunday Vera told her mother Rad, the lodger, wanted to prepare a
meal for the family. Her parents were rather touched; nice, here was a delicate
mark of gratitude, such a glum character, he'd never shown any sign before.
Her father was prepared to put up with something that probably wouldn't
agree with him. —Different people, different ways. Maybe it's a custom with
them, when they're taken in, like bringing a bunch of flowers.— The meal
went off well. The dish was delicious and not too spicy; after all, gingerbread
was spiced, too. When her father opened a bottle of beer and put it down at
Rad's place, Vera quickly lifted it away. —He doesn't drink, Dad.—

Graciousness called forth graciousness; Vera's mother issued a recipro-
cal invitation.—You must come and have our Sunday dinner one day—my
chicken with apple pie to follow.—

But the invitation was in the same code as "See you later." It was not
mentioned again. One Sunday Vera shook the grass from her rug. —I'm
going for a walk.— And the lodger slowly got up from his chair, put his newspaper aside, and they went through the gate. The neighbors must have seen
her with him. The pair went where she led, although they were side by side,
loosely, the way she'd seen young men of his kind together. They went on
walking a long way, down streets and then into a park. She loved to watch
people flying kites; now he was the one who watched her as she watched. It
seemed to be his way of getting to know her; to know anything. It wasn't the
way of other boys—her kind—but then he was a foreigner here, there must be
so much he needed to find out. Another weekend she had the idea to take a
picnic. That meant an outing for the whole day. She packed apples and bread
and cheese—remembering no ham—under the eyes of her mother. There was
a silence between them. In it was her mother's recognition of the accusation
she, Vera, knew she ought to bring against herself: Vera was "chasing" a man;
this man. All her mother said was—Are you joining other friends?— She did-
n't lie. —No. He's never been up the river. I thought we'd take a boat trip.—

In time she began to miss the cinema. Without guile she asked him if he
had seen this film or that; she presumed that when he was heard going out for
the evening the cinema would be where he went, with friends of his—his

kind—she never saw. What did they do if they didn't go to a movie? It wouldn't be bars, and she knew instinctively he wouldn't be found in a disco, she couldn't see him shaking and stomping under twitching colored lights.

He hadn't seen any film she mentioned. —Won't you come?— It happened like the first walk. He looked at her again as he had then. —D'you think so?—

—Why ever not. Everybody goes to movies.—

But she knew why not. She sat beside him in the theater with solemnity. It was unlike any other time, in that familiar place of pleasure. He did not hold her hand; only that time, that time in the kitchen. They went together to the cinema regularly. The silence between her and her parents grew; her mother was like a cheerful bird whose cage had been covered. Whatever her mother and father thought, whatever they feared—nothing had happened, nothing happened until one public holiday when Vera and the lodger were both off work and they went on one of their long walks into the country (that was all they could do, he didn't play sport, there wasn't any activity with other young people he knew how to enjoy). On that day celebrated for a royal birthday or religious anniversary that couldn't mean anything to him, in deep grass under profound trees he made love to Vera for the first time. He had never so much as kissed her, before, not on any evening walking home from the cinema, not when they were alone in the house and the opportunity was obvious as the discretion of the kitchen clock sounding through the empty passage, and the blind eye of the television set in the sitting-room. All that he had never done with her was begun and accomplished with unstoppable passion, summoned up as if at a mere command to himself; between this and the placing of his hand on hers in the kitchen, months before, there was nothing. Now she had the lips from which, like a doe, she had taken a morsel touched with his saliva, she had the naked body promised by the first glimpse of the naked feet. She had lost her virginity, like all her sister schoolgirls, at fourteen or fifteen, she had been fucked, half-struggling, by some awkward local in a car or a back room, once or twice. But now she was overcome, amazed, engulfed by a sensuality she had no idea was inside her, a bounty of talent unexpected and unknown as a burst of song would have been welling from one who knew she had no voice. She wept with love for this man who might never, never have come to her, never have found her from so far away. She wept because she was so afraid it might so nearly never have happened. He wiped her tears, he dressed her with the comforting resignation to her emotion a mother shows with an over-excited child.

She didn't hope to conceal from her mother what they were doing; she knew her mother knew. Her mother felt her gliding silently from her room down the passage to the lodger's room, the room that still smelt of her brother, late at night, and returning very early in the morning. In the dark Vera knew every floorboard that creaked, how to avoid the swish of her pajamas touching past a wall; at dawn saw the squinting beam of the rising sun sloped through a window that she had never known was so placed it could let in any phase of the sun's passage across the sky. Everything was changed.

What could her mother have said? Maybe he had different words in his language; the only ones she and her mother had wouldn't do, weren't meant for a situation not provided for in their lives. *Do you know what you're doing? Do you know what he is? We don't have any objection to them, but all the same. What about your life? What about the good firm your father's got you into? What'll it look like, there?*

The innocent release of sensuality in the girl gave her an authority that prevailed in the house. She brought him to the table for meals, now; he ate what he could. Her parents knew this presence, in the code of their kind, only as the signal by which an "engaged" daughter would bring home her intended. But outwardly between Vera and her father and mother the form was kept up that his position was still that of a lodger, a lodger who had somehow become part of the household in that capacity. There was no need for him to pretend or assume any role; he never showed any kind of presumption towards their daughter, spoke to her with the same reserve that he, a stranger, showed to them. When he and the girl rose from the table to go out together it was always as if he accompanied her, without interest, at her volition.

Because her father was a man, even if an old one and her father, he recognized the power of sensuality in a female and was defeated, intimidated by its obstinacy. *He* couldn't take the whole business up with her; her mother must do that. He quarreled with his wife over it. So she confronted their daughter. *Where will it end?* Both she and the girl understood: he'll go back where he comes from, and where'll you be? He'll drop you when he's had enough of what he wanted from you.

Where would it end? Rad occasionally acknowledged her among his friends, now—it turned out he did have some friends, yes, young men like him, from his home. He and she encountered them on the street and instead of excusing himself and leaving her waiting obediently like one of those pet dogs tied up outside the supermarket, as he usually had done when he went over to speak to his friends, he took her with him and, as if remembering her presence after a minute or two of talk, interrupted himself: She's Vera. Their greetings, the way they looked at her, made her feel that he had told them about her, after all, and she was happy. They made remarks in their own language she was sure referred to her. If she had moved on, from the pub, the disco, the parents, she was accepted, belonged somewhere else.

And then she found she was pregnant. She had no girlfriend to turn to who could be trusted not to say those things: he'll go back where he comes from he'll drop you when he's had enough of what he wanted from you. After the second month she bought a kit from the pharmacy and tested her urine.

Then she went to a doctor because that do-it-yourself thing might be mistaken.

—I thought you said you would be all right.—

That was all he said, after thinking for a moment, when she told him.

—Don't worry, I'll find something. I'll do something about it. I'm sorry, Rad. Just forget it.— She was afraid he would stop loving her—her term for lovemaking.

When she went to him tentatively that night he caressed her more beautifully and earnestly than ever while possessing her.

She remembered reading in some women's magazine that it was dangerous to do anything to get rid of "it" (she gave her pregnancy no other identity) after three months. Through roundabout inquiries she found a doctor who did abortions, and booked an appointment, taking an advance on her holiday bonus to meet the fee asked.

—By the way, it'll be all over next Saturday. I've found someone.— Timidly, that week, she brought up the subject she had avoided between them.

He looked at her as if thinking very carefully before he spoke, thinking apart from her, in his own language, as she was often sure he was doing. Perhaps he had forgotten it was really her business, her fault, she knew. Then he pronounced what neither had: —The baby?—

—Well . . .— She waited, granting this.

He did not take her in his arms, he did not touch her. —You will have the baby. We will marry.—

It flew from her awkward, unbelieving, aghast with joy: —You want to marry me!—

—Yes, you're going to be my wife.—

—Because of this?—a baby?—

He was gazing at her intensely, wandering over the sight of her. —Because I've chosen you.—

Of course, being a foreigner, he didn't come out with things the way an English speaker would express them.

And I love *you*, she said, I love you, I love you—babbling through vows and tears. He put a hand on one of hers, as he had done in the kitchen of her mother's house; once, and never since.

She saw a couple in a miniseries standing hand-in–hand, telling them; "We're getting married"—hugs and laughter.

But she told her parents alone, without him there. It was safer that way, she thought, for him. And she phrased it in proof of his good intentions as a triumphant answer to her mother's warnings, spoken and unspoken. —Rad's going to marry me.—

—He wants to marry you?— Her mother corrected. The burst of a high-pitched cry. The father twitched an angry look at his wife.

Now it was time for the scene to conform to the TV family announcement. —We're going to get married.—

Her father's head flew up and sank slowly, he turned away.

—You want to be married to him?— Her mother's palm spread on her breast to cover the blow.

The girl was brimming feeling, reaching for them.

Her father was shaking his head like a sick dog.

—And I'm pregnant and he's glad.—

Her mother turned to her father but there was no help coming from him. She spoke impatiently flatly. —So that's it.—

—No, that's not it. It's not it at all.— She would not say to them "I love him," she would not let them spoil that by trying to make her feel ashamed. — It's what I want.—

—It's what she wants.— Her mother was addressing her father.

He had to speak. He gestured towards his daughter's body, where there was no sign yet to show life growing there.—Nothing to be done then.—

When the girl had left the room he glared at his wife. —Bloody bastard.—

—Hush. Hush.— There was a baby to be born, poor innocent.

And it was, indeed, the new life the father had gestured at in Vera's belly that changed everything. The foreigner, the lodger—had to think of him now as the future son-in-law, Vera's intended—told Vera and her parents he was sending her to his home for his parents to meet her.—To your country?—

He answered with the gravity with which, they realized, marriage was regarded where he came from. —The bride must meet the parents. They must know her as I know hers.—

If anyone had doubted the seriousness of his intentions—well, they could be ashamed of those doubts, now; he was sending her home, openly and proudly, his foreigner, to be accepted by his parents. —But have you told them about the baby, Rad?— She didn't express this embarrassment in front of her mother and father. —What do you think? That is why you are going.— He slowed, then spoke again. —It's a child of our family.—

So she was going to travel at last! In addition to every other joy! In a state of continual excitement between desire for Rad—now openly sharing her room with her—and the pride of telling her work-mates why she was taking her annual leave just then, she went out of her way to encounter former friends whom she had avoided. To say she was traveling to meet her fiancé's family; she was getting married in a few months, she was having a baby— yes—proof of this now in the rounding under the flowered jumpsuit she wore to show it off. For her mother, too, a son-in-law who was not one of their kind became a distinction rather than a shame. —Our Vera's a girl who's always known her own mind. It's a changing world, she's not one just to go on repeating the same life as we've had.— The only thing that hadn't changed in the world was joy over a little one coming. Vera was thrilled, they were all thrilled at the idea of a baby, a first grandchild. Oh that one was going to be spoilt all right! The prospective grandmother was knitting, although Vera laughed and said babies weren't dressed in that sort of thing any more, hers was going to wear those little unisex frog suits in bright colors. There was a deposit down on a pram fit for an infant prince or princess.

It was understood that if the intended could afford to send his girl all the way home just to meet his parents before the wedding, he had advanced himself in the restaurant business, despite the disadvantages young men like him had in an unwelcoming country. Upstairs was pleased with the news; Upstairs came down one evening and brought a bottle of champagne as a gift to toast Vera, whom they'd known since she was a child, and her boy—much pleasant laughter when the prospective husband filled everyone's glass and then served himself with orange juice. Even the commissionaire felt confident enough to tell one of his gentlemen at the club that his daughter was getting married, but first about to go abroad to meet the young man's parents. His gentlemen's children were always traveling; in his ears every day were overheard snatches of destinations—"by bicycle in China, can you believe it" . . . "two months in Peru, rather nice . . ." ". . . snorkeling on the Barrier Reef, last I heard." *Visiting her future parents–in–law where there is desert and palm trees;* not bad!

The parents wanted to have a little party, before she left, a combined engagement party and farewell. Vera had in mind a few of her old friends brought together with those friends of his she'd been introduced to and with whom she knew he still spent some time—she didn't expect to go along with him, it wasn't their custom for women, and she couldn't understand their language, anyway. But he didn't seem to think a party would work. She had her holiday bonus (to remember what she had drawn it for, originally, was something that, feeling the baby tapping its presence softly inside her, she couldn't believe of herself) and she kept asking him what she could buy as presents for his family—his parents, his sisters and brothers, she had learnt all their names. He said he would buy things, he knew what to get. As the day for her departure approached, he still had not done so. —But I want to pack! I want to know how much room to leave, Rad!— He brought some men's clothing she couldn't judge and some dresses and scarves she didn't like but didn't dare say so—she supposed the clothes his sisters liked were quite different from what she enjoyed wearing—a good thing she hadn't done the choosing.

She didn't want her mother to come to the airport; they'd both be too emotional. Leaving Rad was strangely different; it was not leaving Rad but going, carrying his baby, to the mystery that was Rad, that was in Rad's silences, his blind love-making, the way he watched her, thinking in his own language so that she could not follow anything in his eyes. It would all be revealed when she arrived where he came from.

He had to work, the day she left, until it was time to take her to the airport. Two of his friends, whom she could scarcely recognize from the others in the group she had met occasionally, came with him to fetch her in the taxi one of them drove. She held Rad's hand, making a tight double fist on his thigh, while the men talked in their language. At the airport the others left him to go in alone with her. He gave her another, last-minute gift for home. —Oh Rad where'm I going to put it? The ticket says one hand-baggage!— But she squeezed his arm in happy recognition of his thoughts for his family. —It can go in—easy, easy. He unzipped her carryall as they stood in the queue at the check-in counter. She knelt with her knees spread to accommodate her belly, and helped him. —What is it, anyway—I hope not something that's going to break?— He was making a bed for the package. —Just toys for my sister's kid. Plastic.— —I could have put them in the suitcase—oh Rad . . . what room'll I have for duty-free!— In her excitement, she was addressing the queue for the American airline's flight which would take her on the first leg of her journey. These fellow passengers were another kind of foreigner, Americans, but she felt she knew them all; they were going to be traveling in her happiness, she was taking them with her.

She held him with all her strength and he kept her pressed against his body; she could not see his face. He stood and watched her as she went through passport control and she stopped again and again to wave but she saw Rad could not wave, could not wave. Only watch her until he could not see her any longer. And she saw him in her mind, still looking at her, as she had done at the beginning when she had imagined herself as still under his eyes if she had gone to the pub on a Sunday morning.

Over the sea, the airliner blew up in midair. Everyone on board died. The black box was recovered from the bed of the sea and revealed that there had been an explosion in the tourist-class cabin followed by a fire; and there the messages ended; silence, the disintegration of the plane. No one knows if all were killed outright or if some survived to drown. An inquiry into the disaster continued for a year. The background of every passenger was traced, and the circumstances that led to the journey of each. There were some arrests; people detained for questioning and then released. They were innocent—but they were foreigners, of course. Then there was another disaster of the same nature, and a statement from a group with an apocalyptic name representing a faction of the world's wronged, claiming the destruction of both planes in some complication of vengeance for holy wars, land annexation, invasions, imprisonments, cross-border raids, territorial disputes, bombings, sinkings, kidnappings no one outside the initiated could understand. A member of the group, a young man known as Rad among many other aliases, had placed in the hand-baggage of the daughter of the family with whom he lodged, and who was pregnant by him, an explosive device. Plastic. A bomb of a plastic type undetectable by the usual procedures of airport security.

Vera was chosen.

Vera had taken them all, taken the baby inside her; down, along with her happiness.